Zhigeng Pan   Adrian David Cheok
Wolfgang Müller   Maiga Chang
Mingmin Zhang (Eds.)

Transactions on Edutainment VII

Springer

Editors-in-Chief

Zhigeng Pan
Hangzhou Normal University, Hangzhou, China
E-mail: zhigengpan@gmail.com

Adrian David Cheok
National University of Singapore, Singapore
E-mail: adriancheok@mixedrealitylab.org

Wolfgang Müller
University of Education, Weingarten, Germany
E-mail: mueller@md-phw.de

Guest Editors

Maiga Chang
Athabasca University, AB, Canada
E-mail: maigac@athabascau.ca

Mingmin Zhang
Zhejiang University, Hangzhou, China
E-mail: zmm@cad.zju.edu.cn

ISSN 0302-9743 (LNCS) e-ISSN 1611-3349 (LNCS)
ISSN 1867-7207 (TEDUTAIN) e-ISSN 1867-7754 (TEDUTAIN)
ISBN 978-3-642-29049-7 ISBN 978-3-642-29050-3 (eBook)
DOI 10.1007/978-3-642-29050-3
Springer Heidelberg Dordrecht London New York

CR Subject Classification (1998): K.3.1-2, I.2.1, H.5, H.3, I.3-5

Typesetting: Camera-ready by author, data conversion by Scientific Publishing Services, Chennai, India

Printed on acid-free paper

Springer is part of Springer Science+Business Media (www.springer.com)

Preface

In this issue, the papers are from two main sources. The first set of articles comprises 16 selected papers from the CASA 2011 conference, which was held during May 25–28, 2011. The second set of 11 papers are from DMDCM 2010, which was held during December 19–20, 2010.

In the first set, the first five papers are on virtual humans. In the paper by Stephane Bonneaud et al., the authors introduce a study of small crowds walking toward a common goal and propose to make the link between individual behavior and crowd dynamics. Experimental data show that participants, even though not instructed to behave collectively, do form a cohesive group and do not merely treat one another as obstacles. They also present qualitative and quantitative measurements of this collective behavior. In the second paper, Julien Valentin et al. present their work on simulating fire evacuation, whose aim is to analyze how easily a building can be evacuated in different fire scenarios, at the early stages of building design. In the third paper, Lin Zhang et al. discuss the application of virtual reality and physical system simulation technology to physical education and athletic training as well as interactive methodological advances. In the fourth paper, Wei Hua et al. propose a novel depth-varying human video sprite synthesis method, which significantly increases the degrees of freedom of human video sprites. A novel image distance function encoding scale variation is proposed, which can effectively measure human snapshots with different depths/scales and poses. In the fifth paper, the authors introduce a system for expressive locomotion generation that takes as input a set of sample locomotion clips and a motion path.

The following six papers are on graphics rendering and 3D animation. In the first paper, by Wenshan Fan et al., the authors present a new approach for constructing normal maps that capture high-frequency geometric detail from dense models of arbitrary topology and applies to the simplified version of the same models generated by any simplification method to mimic the same level of detail. In the paper by Jianxin Luo et al., a novel framework for terrain visualization is proposed. The main ideal of the framework is to lay the height field textures and the color textures of all visible terrain tiles in a big texture, then use the single big height field texture and the single big color texture to perform ray casting to get the final image. In the next paper, Shao-Shin Hung proposes a new object-oriented hypergraph-based clustering approach based on a behavioral walkthrough system that uses traversal patterns to model relationships between users and exploits semantic-based clustering techniques, such as association, intra-relationships, and inter-relationships, to explore additional links throughout the behavioral walkthrough system. In the fourth paper, Yujian Gao et al. introduce a method for interactive deformation of large-detail meshes. Their method allows the users to manipulate the mesh directly using freely selected handles on the mesh. To best preserve surface details, the authors introduce a new surface representation, the skin-detached surface. In the fifth paper, Shiguang Liu et al. present a novel method for realistic simulation of solid objects burning. The temperature field is first constructed based on combustion theories. Then, a temperature field–motivated interaction model is proposed to simulate the interactions between the fire and the objects during burning. In the sixth paper, by Chao Wang et al., the authors simulate tunneling blasting by combining blasting animation of computer graphics with mining empirical formulas. A connected voxel model is used to represent rocks and their failure mechanism. This simulation helps engineers test and adjust blasting schemes before real operations.

The following five papers in the first set are on games and 2D animation. In the paper by Gustavo Aranda et al., the model and method behind this architecture are presented, paying special attention to the definition and design of the "Game Zones," the representation of the virtual environment. Also, the authors detail the components and steps to follow in the design of MMOGs based on organizations. In the paper by Zhiying He et al., a novel skeleton-extracting and animation approach for point models is put forward, which explores the differential properties of point models without triangulating the discrete points. In the next paper, Xin Zhang et al. present a novel density control algorithm to achieve interactive line drawing of 3D scenes. The kernel of their approach is a line selection method that considers both the geometric property of lines and the view-dependent line density in the image space. Nicolas Szilas et al. take a look at narrative forms as of yet unexplored in the field of digital interactive storytelling, and describe methods of how they can be used in engaging ways for the user. The paper by Shengnan Chen et al. presents a virtual informal learning system for the famous ancient painting "Qing-ming Festival by the Riverside." Innovative multi-screen projection and interaction techniques are also presented.

The second set of papers focuses on digital media and its applications. In the paper by Xingquan Cai et al., an efficient multi-samples texture synthesis method is provided for dynamic terrains based on constraint conditions. In the next paper Zhicheng Liu et al. prove that principal component analysis and linear discriminant analysis can be directly implemented in the wavelet cosine transform domain and the results are exactly the same as those obtained from the spatial domain. In the paper by Shidu Dong et al., an area measurement method of paint bubble based on computer vision is introduced. In the paper by Xifan Shi et al., a high-precision fresco scanner is presented and the authors discuss the way to improve image sharpness from the perspective of both theory and practice. In the paper by Zhijun Fang et al., a multiwavelet video coding scheme based on DCT time-domain filtering is proposed. Xingquan Cai et al. then present an efficient simulation method for realistic ocean scenes on GPU. Lili Zhai et al. compare the use of 2D wire-framed images and 3D wire-framed animations as stimuli for the judgment of female physical attractiveness and estimation of body weight and waist-to-hip ratio. In the next paper, Jianxun Zhang et al. propose a new method of medical image registration based on wavelet transform using Hausdorff distance. In the paper by Jiali Feng et al., the key technology of HPSIN-based distributed vector geo-data online services is studied, and a pattern of vector geo-data organization based on linking mechanisms, segmentation and lossless reconstruction is proposed. The paper by Jingrong Zhang et al. introduces a method based on ant colony optimization to enhance the plate quality of cold rolted strip steel, a method based on ant colony optimization with quantumaction. In the last paper, by He Yan et al., a new shift-invariant non-aliasing ridgelet transform is presented to avoid aliasing and shift-variant in the old ridgelet transform.

We believe that this issue contains a nice selection of the current research in edutainment and its applications, and we hope these papers will contribute to and attract more research interest in this area.

Mingmin Zhang

Transactions on Edutainment

This journal subline serves as a forum for stimulating and disseminating innovative research ideas, theories, emerging technologies, empirical investigations, state-of-the-art methods, and tools in all different genres of edutainment, such as game-based learning and serious games, interactive storytelling, virtual learning environments, VR-based education, and related fields. It covers aspects from educational and game theories, human-computer interaction, computer graphics, artificial intelligence, and systems design.

Editorial Office

Address: Ninghai Road 122, Edu-Game Research Center, School of Education Science, Nanjing Normal University, Nanjing, 210097, China
E-mail: njnu.edutainment@gmail.com; edutainment@njnu.edu.cn
Tel/Fax: 86-25-83598921

Table of Contents

Papers from CASA 2011

Papers from DMDCM 2010

Accounting for Patterns of Collective Behavior in Crowd Locomotor Dynamics for Realistic Simulations

Stéphane Bonneaud[1], Kevin Rio[1], Pierre Chevaillier[2], and William H. Warren[1]

[1] Dept. of Cognitive, Linguistic and Psychological Sciences, Brown University, USA
[2] ENIB–UEB, LISYC: Laboratory of Computer Science for Complex Systems, France

Abstract. Do people in a crowd behave like a set of isolated individuals or like a cohesive group? Studies of crowd modeling usually consider pedestrian behavior either from the point of view of an isolated individual or from that of large swarms. We introduce here a study of small crowds walking towards a common goal and propose to make the link between individual behavior and crowd dynamics. Data show that participants, even though not instructed to behave collectively, do form a cohesive group and do not merely treat one another as obstacles. We present qualitative and quantitative measurements of this collective behavior, and propose a first set of patterns characterizing such behavior. This work is part of a wider effort to test crowd models against observed data.

Keywords: locomotion dynamics, collective behavior, crowd simulation.

1 Introduction

Crowd models for virtual worlds need to be persuasive, which can be achieved by developing (1) more plausible behavioral animation models, (2) richer models of the environment or (3) more efficient crowd rendering techniques [16,8,22]. Our interest here lies in building more reliable behavioral animation models of locomotor behavior for pedestrians that aggregate into crowds.

We advocate that, before developing new crowd simulation models, there is a need to better understand how collective behavior can emerge from the individual locomotion behaviors of pedestrians aggregating in a crowd. This necessary first step requires the identification of reproducible behavioral patterns from observations and systematic measures of individual behavior. By rigorously identifying the patterns that simulations should account for, psychologists can help computer animation go beyond the limitations of existing crowd simulations.

Most crowd simulation studies focus either on isolated pedestrians and their behaviors in virtual cities [9] or on large swarms and large-scale self-organisation phenomena [10,8]. However, how collective behavior emerges from interactions among individual pedestrians is still not fully understood [15]. Very few studies

Z. Pan et al. (Eds.): Transactions on Edutainment VII, LNCS 7145, pp. 1–11, 2012.

have focused on the modelling of local interactions of pedestrians building up small groups and most agent-based models of crowd dynamics [11,18] have not been tested against field observations of human behavior [12]. [14] has studied the behavior of a pedestrian walking in a corridor and interacting with a stationary pedestrian and with another pedestrian walking in the opposite direction, but these are not common situations in crowd simulation and do not explain self-organisation phenomena. More recently, [15] emphasized the need to empirically study pedestrian groups, showing that social groups are very common in crowds and that crowd density impacts these groups' spatial patterns.

This paper presents the analysis of the results obtained from a cognitive psychology experiment on small crowds aimed at understanding whether and how individuals form a cohesive group when walking towards a common goal. These results allow us to identify patterns that could be explained by general laws and that could be later implemented into crowd simulation models for computer animation. The main objective here is to identify invariants in pedestrian behavior, namely locomotion behaviors, and not to introduce individual variability in crowd simulation, which is another issue [21]. We investigate the impact of density on a small crowd of participants, in order to make the link between individual locomotion and crowd dynamics. If individuals exhibit collective behavior in these conditions, then the phenomenon might help explain larger crowd dynamics. While identifying collective behavior at this level and in a controlled environment is a result in itself, it also allows us to develop measures of such behavior and to extract patterns that characterize human crowds.

In this article, we first contextualize the need for empirical data in the computer animation field. Second, we describe the behavioral experiment that was conducted and the resulting observations. Finally, we identify patterns characterizing collective behavior and the control variables that might yield coherent crowds. We argue that this knowledge is crucial for the computer animation field and could be used to develop and validate computational models of crowd dynamics.

2 Crowd Simulation

The best way to produce realistic simulations of crowds is to develop behavioral models that account for what real pedestrians do, and validate these models against observations of real pedestrians. Many studies have tried to understand how nearly all species can locomote and navigate in space with no apparent effort [6,20,3]. More specifically, humans walk in groups, avoid moving or stationary obstacles, and steer to common goals, while being involved at the same time in other cognitive activities, like social interactions with other members of the group. According to this theoretical framework [6,24], it should be possible to identify typical patterns resulting from these fundamental behavioral rules.

Surely, from a computer animation perspective, it is necessary to obtain agent-based simulations that (1) account for complex scenarios, e.g. interacting with a street artist while in a crowd, and (2) avoid forbidden behaviors, e.g. walking through walls or colliding with other pedestrians. Agent architectures and complex technological solutions have been proposed for generating such behaviors. Several models of locomotion are thus based on cognitive maps and internal models of the environment that enable the agent to calculate an optimal route and avoid collisions in a given local environment [23,17]. [19] have proposed a solution inspired from social psychology, but advocated obtaining unnatural motions at the micro level. Generally speaking, one of the main issues with such approaches is that these models have many parameters and thus are difficult to calibrate. Others try to use videos and learning algorithms to either automatically extract behavioral rules of locomotion in crowds [13] or to calibrate their models [14]. But this research, though very promising, has yet to come up with definitive solutions. Unfortunately, research in psychology or sociology cannot yet solve these problems because we don't know the control laws that actually govern human locomotion.

More reactive approaches have been proposed, based on the assumption that the agent's trajectories in space emerge from the interactions between the agent and its local environment without any internal representation of it [1]. Following such an approach, [24,4,5] have produced a model of individual locomotion that precisely accounts for individual trajectories in space in various scenarios. This model has a number of advantages, namely: (1) it is grounded in a clear theoretical framework; (2) it explains what control variables and strategies are used by humans when they locomote in space and interact with moving or stationary targets and obstacles; (3) it is low parameterized, as the same few processes and parameters are used for each of the scenarios the model accounts for. Although the model of [4,5] only accounts for simple scenarios thus far, making its use in computer animation not straightforward, we argue that this approach is currently the most relevant one to obtain validated simulations that can account for general laws of collective behaviors in crowds and thus allows us to identify typical behavioral patterns.

3 Experiment

3.1 Objective

The experiment aims at understanding the formation and structure of small groups of pedestrians walking towards a common goal; more specifically, we want to determine whether participants behave as a set of individuals or a coherent group, and how to characterize such collective behavior. We further wish to understand the control variables that govern local interactions among participants, and may underlie group formation. The independent variables were (1) the initial density of the group, characterized by the initial distance between participants, and (2) the initial bearing angle between the goal and the participants.

3.2 Apparatus

The experiment was built upon the approach and method of [4,5]. The experiment setup (Fig. 1) was based on experiment 1A of [4] that was designed to study how a single pedestrian steers towards a stationary target. The only difference in the setup is that we now consider four individuals walking together, instead of one.

Participants walked freely in a $12m \times 12m$ room. Their task was to walk to one of three goals (Fig. 1) specified out loud to all participants after the beginning of each trial. The goals were represented by poles of ~2m high and ~30cm wide. Participants were initially positioned in a "square" shape, whose side length characterized the initial density. As shown in the figure, there were four conditions for the initial density (x-small, .5m; small, 1m; wide, 1.5m; and x-wide, 2.5m) and three possible goals.

For each trial, participants were first arranged in a randomly chosen configuration (density). Experimenters told each participant to stand on top of a number on the floor, announcing them out loud. Note that experimenters never spoke directly about density or the global "square" shape, but only spoke to participants as individuals, giving them information specific to each of them individually. Then, participants were told to start walking at a self-selected "comfortable pace" in a straight line. Once the last participant had crossed an invisible line 1m from the front of the group (the dashed line in Fig. 1), an experimenter directed the participants to one randomly selected goal. Participants were instructed to walk to the goal and remain in contact with it (e.g. by keeping a hand on it). When all four participants were in contact with it, an experimenter asked them to walk back to other randomly chosen starting locations.

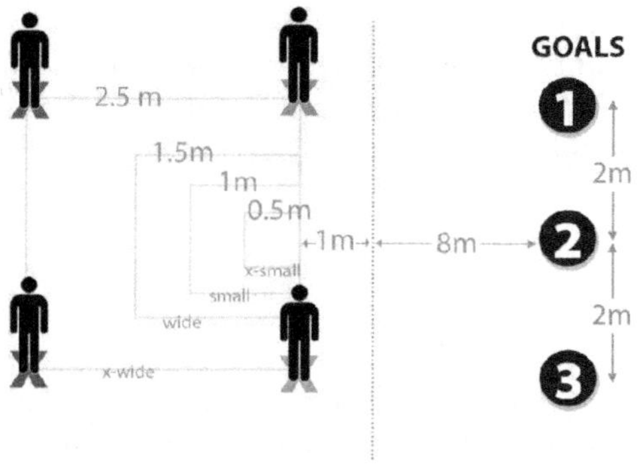

Fig. 1. Experimental setup: initial spatial setup of participants and goals

There were 12 conditions: 4 densities × 3 goals. Five groups of four participants were studied, with each group receiving 8 trials per condition (total: 96 trials). For each of those 8 trials, the initial locations of the participants were randomized, so that each density condition was tested with participants at different positions in the "square" shape. There were 20 participants (12 female), with a mean age of 23.35 years old (SD = 5.2). Participants did not know each other and groups were always mixed. Participants' head positions (4 mm root-mean-square error) were measured by a hybrid inertial-ultrasonic tracking system (IS-900, Intersense, Burlington, MA) with six degrees of freedom, at a sampling rate of 60 Hz.

3.3 Definitions

Position in group – The initial "square" shape had four relative *positions* defined with respect to the walking direction of the group: front-left, front-right, back-left and back-right. The goal can be characterized in the same way. The same reference system is used to characterize the direction of the group and the direction of the goal. With such reference system, participants walking towards the goal see the back of it.
Heading – A participant's *heading* or direction of travel was computed from the walking trajectory (rather than from head orientation data). The heading at time t is calculated using the participant's positions at time t and $t+1$.
Alone vs group speed – Participants were asked to walk on their own, one at a time, to goal 2 before starting the experiment. In this way, we obtained a baseline measure of each participant's self-selected "comfortable pace". These speeds are designated here as the *alone speeds* as opposed to *speeds in group.*
Interpersonal distance – The density of the group is characterized by the distances between participants. The *interpersonal distance* of the group (or average individual interpersonal distance) is here the mean of all six distances between each participant. We also computed the average anterior-posterior ($\sim$ back to front) distance and the average lateral ($\sim$ shoulder to shoulder) distance.
Collective behavior – This term is used here to contrast with more individualistic behavior: where isolated pedestrians may simply avoid other pedestrians as if they were obstacles, pedestrians exhibiting collective behavior show evidence of synchronizing their behaviors and the system at the group level exhibits stable patterns.

3.4 Results

Individual Behaviors. First, participants were consistent throughout the trials and they tended to maintain the initial group structure throughout trials. That is, participants' positions in the group were stable as shown in Fig. 2 and, overall, the group's geometry was stable as well: e.g. an individual starting at the front-right in the group had the tendency to have its ending position on the front-right side of the goal.

Second, while alone speeds were significantly different across participants, individuals adjusted their speed when walking in a group: specifically, they tended to walk slower when in a group ($M = 1.02$ m/s) than when alone ($M = 1.09$ m/s), $t(15) = 2.36$, $p < .05$. These adjustments are more pronounced for faster individuals, as shown in Fig. 3. There is a negative correlation ($r(14) = -.842$, $p < .001$) between an individual's preferred speed and their adjustment when in a group (i.e. the difference between their group and alone speeds).

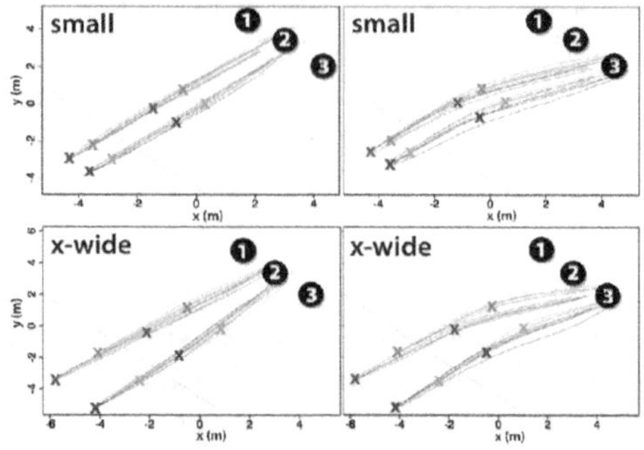

Fig. 2. Each line is an average of 8 individual trajectories of one group for a given "position" in the group (e.g. top left); for each "position" (each color), there are 5 lines for the 5 groups. Initial positions and positions at half time of the trial are designated by the crosses.

Third, individual heading trajectories were consistent across participants as shown in Fig. 4. The figure shows that the variability of the average heading for each condition is low, which is strong evidence that participants had a tendency to steer towards the goal consistently with the group. Note that the heading's dynamics seem to be alike whatever the initial density of the group.

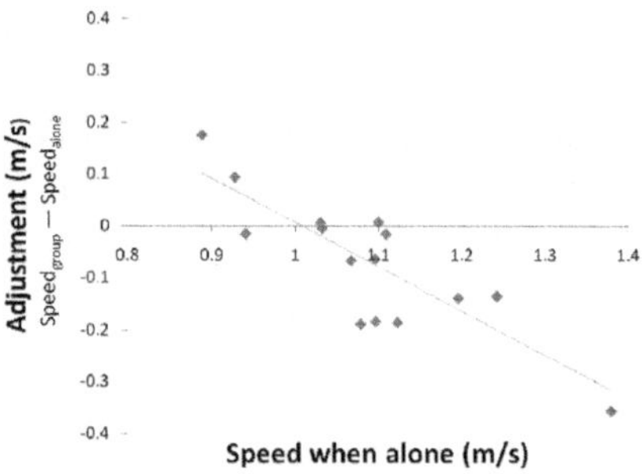

Fig. 3. Difference between the *group speeds* and *alone speeds* against the *alone speeds* for each participant

Group Dynamics. In Fig. 5, the graph on the left shows the evolution in time of the mean *interpersonal distance* per condition. The x-small, small and wide configurations exhibit a convergence towards distances in between 1.3 and 1.6 meters. This could represent a preferred or stable density of the group. In the wide configuration, the mean interpersonal distance seems stable during most of the trial before dropping when participants reach the goal. In the x-small configuration, the distance first increases very quickly as participants, in order not to collide with each other, spread out and double the initial $.5m$ that separates them. After this quick expansion, the distance continues to increase more slowly,

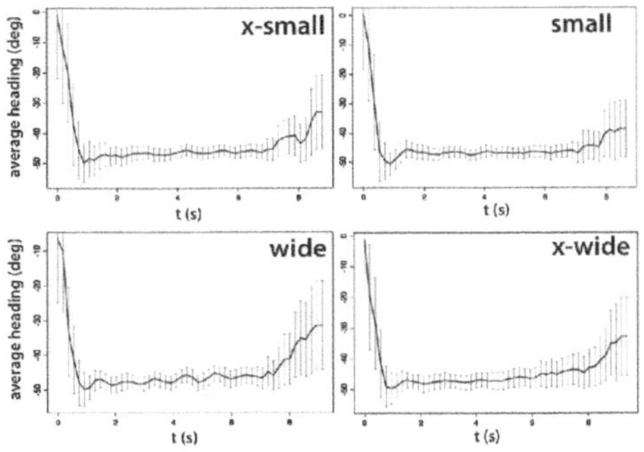

Fig. 4. Average heading dynamic in time for goal 2 and per density. The vertical lines show the standard error.

and the distance's dynamic seems to be closer to that observed in small configuration. In the small configuration, the distance appears to increase slightly to reach a more stable density close to that observed in the wide configuration. In the x-wide configuration, the distance never stabilizes, but continues to contract to the goal. It is not clear whether the distance would stabilize itself around 1.5m if the goal was further away.

Finally, Fig. 5 shows that the dynamics of the anterior-posterior and lateral distances are quite similar, implying that the same processes could control them. The anterior-posterior distance tends towards a larger preferred value than the lateral distance. Presumably, the anterior-posterior distance is controlled by the participant in back, whereas the lateral distance is controlled by both members of a pair. Nevertheless, the anterior-posterior variability is no greater than the lateral variability.

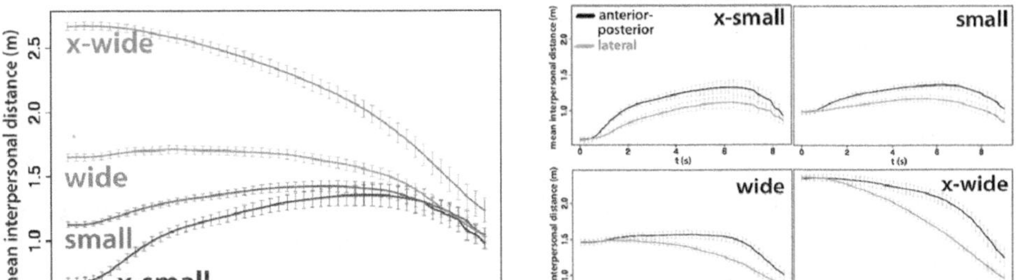

Fig. 5. Interpersonal distance per condition through time. The vertical lines show the standard error.

4 Patterns of Collective Behavior

4.1 Analysis

A first remark for crowd simulation is that the group's consistency in structure and dynamic, of the heading and speeds, is a strong sign that the modeling of the phenomenon is accessible and that the patterns are reliably identifiable.

Second, the most important result of this study is that participants do not seem to behave like isolated pedestrians, but exhibit *collective behavior*. This is a clear result that has not yet been shown in a small crowd, with participants who do not know each other and with no explicit instruction to exhibit such behavior.

Strong evidence of *collective behavior* appears in the results on speed and on interpersonal distances. Consistency of the group's dynamic is suggestive of *collective behavior*, although it might be explained by the physical constraints of the task itself. Seen through the stability of the geometry of the group, the consistency also reveals how the group self-organizes upon arrival at the goal. The first paragraph of section 3.4 shows how individuals tend to keep their positions in the group and organize themselves around the goal as they were organized in the group. Findings of [4] show that a single individual goes directly on the goal. Here, the task does partly explain their distribution around the goal, and one could argue that it is easier for participants to reach the goal in such a manner. However, participants' trajectories are very direct towards these pre-selected positions (or sub-goals) around the goal.

4.2 Patterns

Group structure: the group exhibits consistency and little variability (visible in the dynamics of the heading and structure or geometry of the group);

Speed synchronization: individuals adopt a common speed; this speed is closer to the slower individuals so that faster individuals change their speed more;

Preferred density: individuals adjust their interpersonal distances in order to approach a stable density between 1.3 and 1.6 m;

Anisotropy of interpersonal distances: individuals tend to keep a greater distance from others that are in front or behind, than from those that are next to them.

5 Discussion

This study shows that pedestrians, when surrounded by other pedestrians going to the same goal, tend to modify their behaviors according to others and exhibit collective behavior. They tend to adjust their speed to coordinate with others, adopting a common speed that is closer to the speeds of the slowest individuals. The structure of the group tends to maintain a stable "rectangular" shape, with a smaller shoulder-to-shoulder distance, leaving a bigger front-to-back distance. More strikingly, the density of the group tends to converge towards a preferred stable value, which is very clear for the x-small, small and wide configurations. Low variabilities of the standard errors for the interpersonal distances show that those results are consistent across trials and groups, and confirm the structure of the group. Even though the task itself constrains the behavior of the individuals, such clear self-organization with only four people was not implied by the instructions or the simple nature of the task. Finally, the similar dynamics and comparably low variability of the front-and-back and shoulder-to-shoulder distances may imply that the same control variables are being used to organize both distances.

As with many psychological experiments, the experimental setup constrained the participants to a task in order to make systematic observations in a controlled environment. To a certain extent, these constraints might force individual trajectories into dynamics that could, after analysis, be mistakenly interpreted as collective behavior. The initial positioning of participants in a "square" shape and the initial distance to the goal (less than 10m) are two strong constraints. Concerning the initial positioning, observational studies [2] show that, when in groups, pedestrians tend to walk two by two, so the configuration is reasonable in this context. Concerning the distance to the goal, one limitation of the setup is that a longer distance would emphasize the stability of the observed dynamics. Yet, steering to a goal is a very general and common activity in crowd locomotion. Observing collective behavior and behavioral synchronization in such a short time and distance show the rapid and pronounced impact of other pedestrians on individual behavior. Also, in a few trials, participants switched positions (e.g. some participants passed those in front) showing that the task was not so constrained. And longer paths alone would not guarantee that participants would be less socially constrained. As such, the experimental setup does enable us to isolate patterns of collective locomotion and to answer the question of this article.

From the computer animation point of view, this bridging between data and models, cognitive science and computer animation, can lead to better models, based on or inspired by the patterns of collective behavior shown here. We argue that such work is a necessary step towards a full understanding of collective behavior in large crowds. Crowd simulations dramatically need validation and testing against empirical observations. Patterns are the best way to do this [7]. But, such patterns also give evidence of the control variables humans might use, therefore helping make modeling assumptions. Much work remains to be done to clearly and fully identify the behavioral strategies used by humans that give rise to such collective behavior.

6 Conclusion

Our focus here was to address whether individuals act as isolated pedestrians or as a cohesive group when locomoting with others towards a common goal. We presented an experiment on small crowds of four pedestrians, not instructed to act collectively, in order to bridge between individual locomotion and crowd dynamics. The experiment was built based on [4,5] who studied individual locomotion. This approach enabled us to show that individuals self-organize into groups, maintaining a consistent group structure, while adopting a common speed and a preferred interpersonal density. We have identified patterns that can be used to build and validate models of crowd dynamics and help identify the control variables that govern the emergence of such collective behavior.

The next step is threefold. First, it is necessary to analyse to what extent existing computational models of pedestrian locomotion could account for the patterns we have identified, determine their sensitivity and robustness for a given set of parameter values, and consider how they could be extended to better fit the experimental data. Second, additional experiments need to be performed in order to improve our list of patterns. Third, laboratory data has to be compared to ecological data. Laboratory conditions offer controlled and regular trajectories, a systemic study of behavior, and clear patterns. And, most likely, individuals use the same environmental information and behavioral strategies to interact with others whatever the conditions. If anything is different, we believe that it might be the level of activation of each behavioral strategy, i.e. their parametrization, making the patterns still valid, but necessitating comparison with ecological data.

Acknowledgments. This work was supported by the NIH grant R01 EY010923.

References

1. Brooks, R.A.: Intelligence without representation. Artificial Intelligence 47, 139–159 (1991)
2. Costa, M.: Interpersonal distances in group walking. J. Nonverbal Behav. 34, 15–26 (2010)
3. Duchon, A.P., Warren, W.H.: A visual equalization strategy for locomotor control: of honeybees, robots, and humans. Psychological Science 21, 183–202 (2002)
4. Fajen, B.R., Warren, W.H.: Behavioral dynamics of steering, obstacle avoidance, and route selection. Journal of Experimental Psychology: Human Perception and Performance 29, 343–362 (2003)
5. Fajen, B.R., Warren, W.H.: Behavioral dynamics of intercepting a moving target. Exp. Brain Res. 180, 303–319 (2007)
6. Gibson, J.J.: Visually controlled locomotion and visual orientation in animals. Ecological Psychology 10, 161–176 (1998); (Reprinted from British Journal of Psychology 49, 182–194 (1958))
7. Grimm, V., Revilla, E., Berger, U., Jeltsch, F., Mooij, W.M., Railsback, S.F., Thulke, H.-H., Weiner, J., Wiegand, T., DeAngelis, D.L.: Pattern-oriented modeling of agent-based complex systems: lessons from ecology. Science 310, 987–991 (2005)
8. Heigeas, L., Luciani, A., Thollot, J., Castagné, N.: A physically-based particle model of emergent crowd behaviors. In: Graphicon (2003), `http://artis.imag.fr/Publications/2003/HLTC03`
9. Helbing, D.: A mathematical model for the behavior of pedestrians. Behavioral Science 36, 298–310 (1991)
10. Helbing, D.: Modelling the evolution of human trail systems. Nature 388, 47–50 (1997)
11. Helbing, D., Molnár, P.: Social force model for pedestrian dynamics. Physical Review E 51, 4282–4286 (1995)

12. Lakoba, T.I., Kaup, D.J., Finkelstein, N.M.: Modifications of the Helbing-Molnár-Farkas-Vicsek social force model for pedestrian evolution. Simulation 81, 339–352 (2005)
13. Lee, K.H., Choi, M.G., Hong, Q., Lee, J.: Group behavior from video: a data-driven approach to crowd simulation. In: ACM SIGGRAPH/Eurographics Symposium on Computer Animation (2007), `http://portal.acm.org/citation.cfm?id=1272706`
14. Moussaid, M., Helbing, D., Garnier, S., Johansson, A., Combe, M., Theraulaz, G.: Experimental study of the behavioural mechanisms underlying self-organization in human crowds. Proceedings of the Royal Society B (2009)
15. Moussaïd, M., Perozo, N., Garnier, S., Helbing, D., Theraulaz, G.: The walking behaviour of pedestrian social groups and its impact on crowd dynamics. PloS ONE 5(4), e10047 (2010)
16. Musse, S.R., Thalmann, D.: Hierarchical model for real time simulation of virtual human crowds. IEEE Transactions on Visualization and Computer Graphics 7, 152–164 (2001)
17. Paris, S., Pettré, J., Donikian, S.: Pedestrian reactive navigation for crowd simulation: a predictive approach. EUROGRAPHICS, Computer Graphics Forum 26, 665–674 (2007)
18. Reynolds, C.W.: Steering behaviors for autonomous characters. In: Game Developers Conference (1999)
19. Sakuma, T., Mukai, T., Kuriyama, S.: Psychological model for animating crowded pedestrians. Computer Animation & Virtual Worlds 16(3-4), 343–351 (2005), `http://doi.wiley.com/10.1002/cav.105`
20. Schoner, G., Dose, M.: A dynamical systems approach to task-level system integration used to plan and control autonomous vehicle motion. Robotics and Autonomous Systems 10, 253–267 (1992)
21. Thalmann, D., Grillon, H., Maim, J., Yersin, B.: Challenges in crowd simulation. In: Proceedings of the 2009 International Conference on Cyber Worlds, Washington, DC, USA, pp. 1–12 (2009), `http://dx.doi.org/10.1109/CW.2009.23`
22. Thalmann, D., Musse, S.R.: Crowd simulation. Springer, Heidelburg (2007), `http://books.google.com/books?id=-aY5V-ykawcC`
23. Thomas, R., Donikian, S.: A Spatial Cognitive Map and a Human-Like Memory Model Dedicated to Pedestrian Navigation in Virtual Urban Environments. In: Barkowsky, T., Knauff, M., Ligozat, G., Montello, D.R. (eds.) Spatial Cognition 2007. LNCS (LNAI), vol. 4387, pp. 421–438. Springer, Heidelberg (2007)
24. Warren, W.H., Fajen, B.R.: Behavioral Dynamics of Visually Guided Locomotion. In: Understanding Complex Systems, pp. 45–75. Springer, Heidelberg (2007)

Human Behaviour Modelling for Simulating Evacuation of Buildings on Fire

Julien Valentin[1], Florent Coudret[2], Eric Gouardères[1], and Wilfrid Lefer[1]

[1] Université de Pau et des Pays de l'Adour, Pau, France
{Julien.Valentin,Eric.Gouarderes,Wilfrid.Lefer}@univ-pau.fr
[2] Centre Scientifique et Technique du Bâtiment, Sophia-Antipolis, France
florent.coudret@cstb.fr

Abstract. Many simulators currently attempt to take account of the human factor in peoples use of infrastructure. The aim of simulating fire evacuation is to analyse how easily a building can be evacuated in different fire scenarios, at the early stages of building design. Such simulations may be used to inform decision-making in implementing various aids to evacuation (signage, smoke extraction systems, ...), in reviewing building design, or in the development of building-specific evacuation procedures. In this article we describe a software architecture and a set of concepts for controlling how human behaviour adapts in a fire evacuation scenario.

Keywords: Behavioural animation, Crowd simulation, Microscopic modelling, Emergency situations, Security, Building on fire.

1 Introduction

Simulation tools for various natural phenomena (fires, hurricanes, earthquakes) applied to digital models of man-made structures are increasingly used nowadays to detect design faults before these structures are actually built. Visual display of these simulation results is used as the basis of visual communication between Project Management and design professionals. This enables a diagnosis to be produced to improve site safety. Building fire evacuation simulation is one of these tools, but significantly, relies on a very poorly understood mechanism, namely the behaviour of the buildings occupants.

Most simulation models assume that people are completely rational, and simulate the diversity of individuals by giving them different physical and physiological characteristics and different tasks to perform. This set of properties is referred to as a behavioural archetype. However, as H. Simon [8] claims in his theory of bounded rationality, human behaviour cannot be explained solely by these properties but is also related to the limitations of human rationality in terms of the cognitive resources and information available to an individual.

This paper presents work carried out on the development of a microscopic simulation architecture implemented for building fire evacuation scenarios. First, a review of the current state of the art in behavioural simulation is presented

Z. Pan et al. (Eds.): Transactions on Edutainment VII, LNCS 7145, pp. 12–23, 2012.

and the main evacuation simulators evaluated. Next, a new architecture for behavioural adaptation is outlined. The next part of the document seeks to set out our decision model, based on the concept of bounded rationality. A GPU implementation is then presented and we conclude by summarising the properties of our architecture.

Since the aim of this study was to evaluate building safety, the result of the observed behaviour is more important than the quality of rendering. We will therefore focus our study on the behavioural aspect. The reader may, in parallel, refer to [13] for a complete review of the state of the art in real-time rendering of crowds.

2 Behavioural Simulation

Behavioural simulation attempts to reproduce the action-oriented decision-making processes of virtual entities, based on an objective and the constraints imposed by their environment. Numerous crowd simulation systems differentiate between two main types of behaviour: navigational behaviour, which takes account of immediate or short-term movement constraints, and planned behaviour, which achieves the objective, taking movement constraints into account. This distinction is commonly used with the aim of decoupling the concept of behaviour from the rendering engine: the evaluation of navigational behaviour tracks the rendering frequency, while planned behaviour is re-evaluated with a lower frequency, which enables a smooth simulation. Instead, we have used it as a design guide for building a hybrid architecture aimed at customizing behaviour according to the bounded rationality theory.

2.1 Navigational Behaviour

Navigational behaviour enables an agents behaviour to be adapted in line with local movement constraints. In the continuous domain, they are expressed in terms of forces applied to an agent, which force it to move. They form a category of reactive behaviours in multi-agent terminology. They are used solely for resolving local constraints, without including any concept of goal.

A typical example of navigational behaviour is contained in Helbings panic behaviour [5]. Reynolds [10] made the physical description of pedestrian behaviours more proactive by describing them in the velocity domain (Steering). *Velocity Obstacles* and related work [15] also belongs to this class and defines the set of velocities with no intersection with a geometric obstacle. They include an awareness of agent dynamics in behavioural expression. Reynoldss work has been revisited, giving rise to *Inverse steering* [1]. This principle is based on associating a performance evaluation function with every behaviour. Thus, the various possible changes to the agents state sequences of atomic behaviours can be evaluated to select the best, according to a given cost criterion. These behaviours enable better adaptation to the environment than do previous classes.

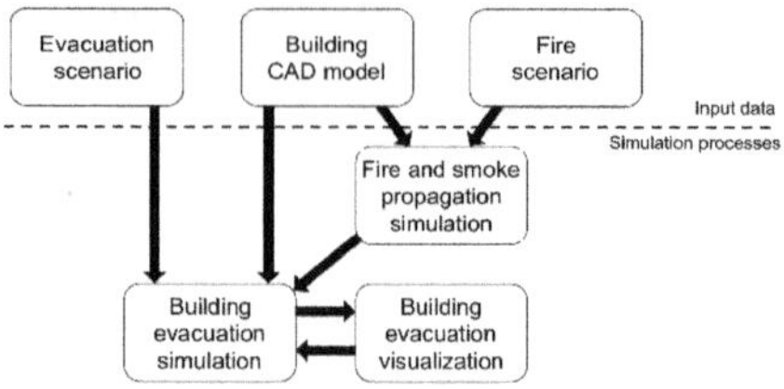

Fig. 1. General pipeline for building fire evacuation simulation

2.2 Planned Behaviour

Planned behaviours, also referred to as cognitive behaviours, seek to reproduce action-oriented deductive reasoning. In the movement domain, they typically consist of seeking a path leading to a goal.

Discrete path planning was initiated by the work of Dijkstra. The subsequent A^* algorithm is distinguished by the use of a heuristic evaluation which directs the search. Later the D^* and LPA^* [7] introduced local repairing of the path.

In the continuous domain, [14] describes a technique for solving the problem for groups of agents with a shared goal and view of the environment, based on the Fast Marching Method [11]. [12] proposes a GPU-based implementation of a variant of this technique the Fast Iterative Method [6] which is better suited to parallel processing architectures. [9] proposes the E^* algorithm, which incorporates local repair, as introduced by D^*, into the Fast Marching Method. To reduce the cost of these algorithms when the number of cells is very large, [4] suggests prioritising these grids into several levels of abstraction by merging adjacent cells where possible.

3 Simulation Architecture

We are working on simulating evacuation of buildings on fire as part of a collaboration with CSTB [1] of Sophia Antipolis. The digital models developed by the CSTB are IFC-format (Industry Foundation Classes) models designed using Archicad software [2] or geometric-only models produced by modellers such as Blender. The buildings are displayed in real time using the OpenSceneGraph library [3]. The fire scenarios are simulated using the fire and smoke propagation software FDS [4](Fire Dynamics Simulator) provided by NIST (National Institute of Standards and Technology). These two tools represent the technological constraints of the implementation produced. The overral architecture of our simulator is described on Fig. 1.

---

[1] Centre Scientifique et Technique du Btiment

[2] http://www.abvent.com/softwares/archicad

[3] http://www.openscenegraph.org

[4] http://www.fire.nist.gov/fds

3.1 Overview

The scenarios simulated using FDS serve as a base for building evacuation simulations carried out downstream. The particularity of this type of simulation is the highly dynamic environment, including fire, smoke, other people. Our evacuation simulation environment consists of geometric models of future buildings. The processing needed is based on this type of representation and not on IFC models. The design and implementation of a simulation consists of four stages:

1. Produce a fire scenario and an evacuation scenario.
2. Simulate the fire with third party software (FDS).
3. Simulate the evacuation based on the fire simulation results.
4. Visualize the results of the building evacuation simulation.

The fire simulation is computationaly highly demanding (commonly several days of computation) and hence is run in batch mode before the evacuation simulation.

3.2 Individual Behaviour Model

Our contribution concerns the uppest layer of the extended computer graphics pyramid presented by [3], which is implemented by the cognitive model described on Fig. 2 right. Analysis of different evacuation systems as well as the review of current practice have identified several distinctive aspects of fire evacuation simulation :

- The environment is highly dynamic (fire, smoke, people in motion).
- Individuals adopt different strategies during the evacuation.
- Site knowledge and cognitive resources available to individuals differ (postulate of bounded rationality [8]).
- Physical interactions are the main sources of injury during crowd movements [2].

Geometry and Kinematics Layer. This layer handles the rendering and animation of avatars. Since realism of animation is not the main objective of this work, we use direct kinematics, using the Cal3D [5] animation library for virtual characters . This allows different gaits to be combined depending on characters speeds to ensure fluid movement, including when changing speed.

This layer receives a movement vector from the layer above (physical layer) at each time step of the simulation. Knowing the time step, one can deduce the average speed during this time period.

[5] https://gna.org/projects/cal3d

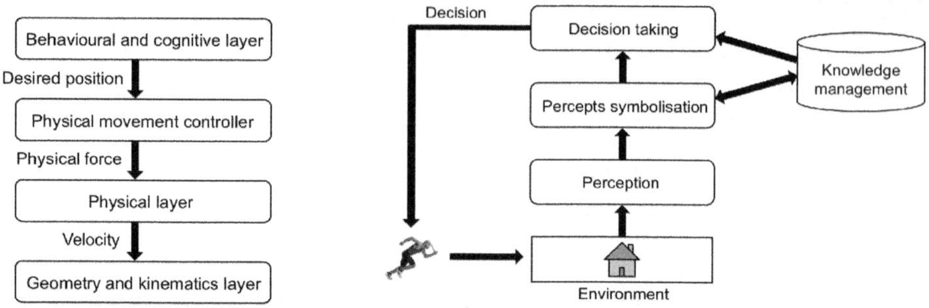

Fig. 2. Left: Virtual agent model. Right: Simulated cognitive model.

Physical Layer. The physical layer is an important component of the architecture because it is through this layer that the physical interactions are controlled, which are very important in crowd movement [2]. Since handling collisions in continuous environments is a rather complex problem, the Bullet [6] physics engine is used. This layer includes a physiological crush-resistance model and also a toxicological model based on the FED model.

This layer receives two forces applied to the individual from the physical motion controller: directional force and rotational force (torque).

The Physical Movement Controller. This is responsible for transforming the actual decision to move (desired position) into physical forces which need to be applied to the agent to make it reach this position. For this we use reverse integration of the Newtonian dynamics, based on the desired position, which provides directional force and torque, if the desired position and orientation are known. These two forces are calculated independently (and may then be adjusted), as well as speed, to meet the motor constraints of the individual (V_{max}, $MaxForce$ et $MaxTorque$).

This layer receives a position in space from the behavioural and cognitive layer.

4 Cognitive Behaviour Model

The behavioural and cognitive layer involves four cognitive modules (Fig. 2 left) whose goal is to make the decision to move based on the agents subjective perception of its environment.

4.1 The Perception Model

This is responsible for collecting data from the environment. The percepts which agents can capture are: fire, building walls, other agents, communications signals

[6] http://www.bulletphysics.com

(logical), temperature, smoke (toxicity index), and evacuation panels. Toxicity information is not perceived since the human olfactory system cannot perceive it.

Of the five human senses, two are used and simulated:

- Touch is simulated by probing the cell where the agent is located.
- Hearing is simulated by detecting the presence of the agent in a circle centred around each other agent, representing the reach of his voice.
- Vision is simulated by ray casting, rays being stopped when the accumulated opacity reaches a certain threshold.

4.2 The Memory Management Model

This module is responsible for maintaining the consistency of stored information and is based on the concept of temporal reliability of constraints, using the principle of removing information where it has not been confirmed by actual observation. The advantage of this method in a dynamic environment is obvious: if someone sees a fire starting, leaves that location for any reason then plans to return later, they will consider the information that was previously acquired as unreliable, as the fire may have been extinguished or have significantly increased. The validity of information acquired in a dynamic environment, if it has not been updated in the meantime, decreases over time. We implement this concept by attaching a time stamp to each dynamic constraint symbol (C_{Tox}, C_{Temp} et C_{Vital}). Reliability is then defined over the interval [0,1] by the following formula:

$$rel = 1 - \frac{(T_{cur} - T_{obs})}{T_{max}} \tag{1}$$

with rel the reliability index of a dynamic stress symbol, T_{obs} the time stamp of the last observation, T_{cur} the current time and T_{max} the maximum time of belief in a dynamic observation (the agent's own). When rel reaches 0, the symbol is considered unreliable and is removed from memory.

The memory has been modelled based on two levels of abstraction:

- Short-term memory (STM), dedicated to the satisfaction of constraints: the stored information is very local in that information expiry is defined on a very short time horizon ($T_{max}^{CourtTerme} \approx 1s$) and applies to all information, whether dynamic or static.
- Long-term memory (LTM) used for the satisfaction of goals: all short-term memory information is re-transcribed into the LTM by symbolisation.

4.3 Constraint Symbolisation Module

This module is responsible for transforming percepts into higher level abstractions (symbols representing constraints) and storing them in memory. Short term memory (STM) stores constraints associated with navigational behaviours, in other words not associated with goal resolution (repulsive force associated with

Table 1. Percepts, sense which detects each percept, associated navigational constraints and resulting behaviour. The sign indicates the nature of the force exerted (+ for an attractive force, for a repulsive force).

Sense	Percept	Constraint	Behaviour
Sight	*Fire*	*Spatial*	$-\nabla CDist(CDist_{cur})$
Sight	*Obstructions*	*Spatial*	$-\nabla CDist(CDist_{cur})$
Sight	*Walkablespace*	*Spatial*	$-\nabla CDist(CDist_{cur})$
Sight	*Smoke*	*Toxicity*	$-\nabla CTox(CTox_{cur})$
Touch	*Temperature*	*Heat*	$-\nabla CTemp(CTemp_{cur})$
Sight	*Otherindividuals*	*Crowddensity*	$-\frac{k}{d}\overrightarrow{n}$
Sight	*Signage*	*Assistance*	$+\frac{k}{d}\overrightarrow{n}$

fire, for example). Long-term memory (LTM) is used for symbols associated with the constraints related to goal resolution (crowd density, for example). The two memories (STM and LTM) constitute two levels of abstraction of constraint symbols. However, the two memories are not isolated from each other, and symbols in short-term memory are transferred into long-term memory (for example, the presence of fire immediately generates a repulsive force but this information will also be used for planning).

This brings us to the computer representation of symbols, which is different depending on the type of memory:

- Vector representation for the STM because this representation is suited to the handling of reactive navigation behaviours.
- Raster representation (regular grids) for LTM enabling a unified representation and hence definition of arithmetic operators to combine behaviours. In fact some constraints are in this form from the outset (smoke density for example) and the others can be sampled in order to put them into raster form.

4.4 The Decision Module

This module is responsible for selecting the most appropriate behaviour for the situation, based on agent archetypes. As the behaviour architecture developed is a hybrid of planned and navigational, both types of behaviour are represented.

Navigational Behaviours. The navigational behaviours used are simple rules of repulsion/ attraction associated with the constraint of movement that they represent (see Table 1). The force is evaluated by calculating:

- The gradient for the raster type symbols ($\nabla C_i \times C_i$).
- Normal, weighted by a distance function ($\frac{i}{d^k}$) for vector type symbols.

Planned Behaviours. Unlike the previous behaviours, these behaviours imply the existence of a goal, and the aim of the resulting decision will be to get closer to this goal. Faced with several possible goals, the agent will have to make a choice. This choice will depend essentially on two parameters: the quality of the goal and the effort necessary to achieve it.

We begin by qualitatively characterising the goals, then we explain how we measure the effort required to move and finally the decision mechanism leading to the choice made by the agent.

Characterisation of Goals. We distinguish three categories of goal:

1. Going to a known, reachable exit: the goal is then the exit and is assigned the value 0 because reaching it fully satisfies the requirement (the agent having left the building).
2. Following a person claiming to know a way out: the goal is then to get to the place where is this person is situated.
3. Exploring the building, looking for an exit: the aim here is to get to an unknown cell which is closer in terms of cost than the agents current cell.

The numbering implies a hierarchy which should lead the agent to prioritise category 1 goals, then category 2 and lastly category 3. However, unlike a rule-based system, we are working in a continuous environment, we will therefore assign a numerical value to each category based on the relative importance of goals in this category versus other categories: 0 for category 1, strictly positive values for others. These values will be fed into a mathematical formula which will also include the cost of travel to reach the goal. Thus the agent may choose a category 2 goal even a category 1 goal is available. An individual could, for example, despite knowing of an emergency exit, prefer to follow another individual who said they knew a shortcut.

Movement Costs. There cannot be an evacuation strategy and therefore a choice unless there is a cost associated with achieving a goal. This is what makes a person choose a nearby exit rather than a more distant one. Each constraint will, following the process of symbolisation, be represented by a grid in the long-term memory. The various grids will then be combined in each agents long-term memory to obtain a single grid that represents the set of movement constraints applied to the agent. The coefficients of this formula may be different from one agent to another, introducing the possibility of behaviour individualisation (this is not the only one).

The general expression of our cost function is:

$$C = \frac{Discomfort}{1 + Comfort} \tag{2}$$

with C the cost function, $Discomfort$ a negative influence (local repulsion) and $Comfort$ a positive influence (local attraction).

This formula implies that anything that hinders movement increases the cost while anything that makes it easier reduces cost.

For the evacuation problem, we define discomfort as follows:

$$Discomfort_i = C_{dist} + \sum_i rel_i \times \alpha_{C_i} \times C_i \quad (3)$$

with C_{dist} a constant constraint symbolising the cost of moving in an unconstrained space, rel_i the reliability attributed to the observation of cell i by this agent (see 1), C_i the value associated with constraint C_i in the cell, normalised over interval [0,1], and α_{C_i} the coefficient of importance associated with constraint C_i for this agent.

In the absence of any constraint only C_{dist} persists, and distance becomes the only relevant criterion.

Comfort is mainly made up of evacuation aids and is defined as:

$$Comfort_i = \sum_i \beta_{A_i} \times A_i \quad (4)$$

with A_i the value associated with aid A_i in the cell, normalised over interval [0,1], and α_{A_i} the coefficient of importance associated with aid A_i for this agent. The coefficients of importance α_{C_i} and α_{A_i} are part of the behaviour archetype and characterise each individual.

Planned decision-making. Once goals are identified and characterised and the cost function for an agent has been determined for all cells in the grid, the decision boils down to finding the shortest path which will take the agent to the nearest goal in terms of cost and characterisation of this goal.

Instantiation of Agents. Now that we have described the various individual cognitive mechanisms, we will see how agents are instantiated through three levels of instantiation: the global agent model, the behavioural archetype, and the individual.

Global Agent Model. The instantiation of the global behaviour model is described following the specifications of the simulation set out in the previous section. The latter involves three steps:

1. Classification of movement constraints and associations with the appropriate percept type (see Table 1).
2. Association of navigational behaviour with constraints. Note that the goal-oriented level is not affected by this design process as the behaviour of goal satisfaction is unique and predetermined.
3. Definition of constraint symbolisation processes.

Behaviour Archetypes. These are a parameterisation of the global model by attaching it to various agent prototypes. A behavioural archetype consists of:

- Physical properties: mass, size, template.
- Pseudo-physical properties: V_{max}, $MaxTorque$, $MaxForce$ (see 3.2).

- Coefficients of importance of each of the constraints: α_{C_i} and β_{C_i} (see 4.4).
- Properties of bounded rationality: the maximum levels of symbolisation of each movement constraint.
- Estimated costs (heuristics) associated with each goal category (see 4.4).

The maximum level of symbolisation of each constraint represents the level of abstraction that each constraints symbolisation process cannot exceed. This offers a way to control the amount of an agents cognitive resources in accordance with the bounded rationality theory [8]. Each archetype thus defined can then be assigned to different agents.

Execution Model of an Agent Instance. The microscopic selection model of triggered behaviour is effected through two complementary phases:

- The rising phase raises the percepts to the maximum level of abstraction via symbolic transformations (symbolisation).
- The descending phase executes the planification by taking the parameter symbols of active constraints into account.

The maximum level of abstraction of each constraint enables some of the symbolic transformations to be inhibited (limited information available) but also to allows the decision-making process to be prevented from selecting the most appropriate behaviours for the situation. So we create a decision context in accordance with the hypotheses of bounded rationality [8]. It is this mechanism that facilitates panic modelling in particular.

5 GPU Implementation

Although real time rendering is not the purpose of our work, we tried to make the simulation as efficient as possible. Thus the various computations involved by the process of goal satisfaction for each agent have been distributed on the computation resources, namely the CPU and the GPU (we only considered a simple harware configuration, i.e. a basic work station). The four steps of the process of goal satisfaction and their assignment to the processing units are:

- Updating of goal cells G (perception process, see 4.1): CPU,
- Updating of the cost grid C (see 4.4): CPU,
- Computing the distance map (FIM): GPU,
- Determining the gradient then the agents speed of movement: GPU.

As stated in 4.4, after the symbolisation process has been run, all the movement constraints for a given agent are represented by a single grid C. The planned decision-making process being the most computationaly expensive part of the simulation, we decided to implement it on the GPU. Rather than a Fast Marching Method, we use a Fast Iterative Method (FIM) [6] to solve this problem because this method is well adapted to a GPU implementation. Actually a modified version of the FIM is used, in order to avoid recomputing the whole distance map at each time step, by a path repairing approach.

OpenSceneGraph and GLSL shaders have been used for this purpose. Agents' grids C (see Equ. 2) are stored in the GPU texture memory and texture rendering mecanism are used to compute the distance maps. Then speed is determined as a function of the constraints affecting it:

$$V(x) = \prod_i (1 - \beta_{C_i} C_i(x)) \tag{5}$$

with $V(x)$ the speed to adopt in cell x, $C_i(x)$ the value associated with constraint i in cell x, normalised over the interval [0,1] and β_{C_i} the impact of constraint C_i on speed of movement. The resultant force $\overrightarrow{F^{plan}}$ can then be determined as follows:

$$\overrightarrow{F^{plan}} = -\frac{\overrightarrow{\nabla\Phi(x)}}{||\overrightarrow{\nabla\Phi(x)}||} V_x \tag{6}$$

This force is useful to us because it will be sent to the Bullet [7] physics engine which will determine the actual movements of individuals in order to avoid collisions.

6 Conclusion

An architecture dedicated to the microscopic simulation of human behaviour in a building fire evacuation situation was presented. It is based on the two main axioms of bounded rationality proposed by H. Simon:

- Limited information available: dynamic management of an individual memory at two levels: short and long term.
- Limited cognitive resources: the level of symbolisation of each constraint is controlled.

The architecture enables human decision-making mechanics to be described at several levels of abstraction, thus providing a means of monitoring the adaptation of the reasoning of an individual faced with a spatial reasoning problem, subject to various movement constraints. In the context of emergency situations, such as a building fire evacuation, it allows us to simulate panic among the occupants, which is a key component in understanding behaviour and in providing appropriate responses.

The individual planning system has been implemented on the GPU and we have obtained real-time performance (16 fps for 100 agents on GPU Nvidia GTX275). However, it does not compare well with the crowd simulators tuned for video games because our individual behaviour model, which is the basement of our approach, obviously does not scale well with the crowd size.

A potential avenue for development of this model lies in adding an enhanced software layer and subsequently a layer of collaboration between individuals to model people helping each other.

[7] http://www.bulletphysics.com

Acknowledgments. This work was supported by the CSTB (Centre Scientifique et Technique du Batiment) in Sophia Antipolis and the ANRT (Agence Nationale Recherche Technologie).

References

1. Amor, H.B., Obst, O., Murray, J.: Fast, neat and under control: Inverse steering behaviors for physical autonomous agents (2003)
2. Fruin, J.J.: The causes and prevention of crowd disasters. Engineering for Crowd Safety, 99–108 (1993)
3. Funge, J., Tu, X., Terzopoulos, D.: Cognitive modeling: knowledge, reasoning and planning for intelligent characters. In: SIGGRAPH 1999: Proceedings of the 26th Annual Conference on Computer Graphics and Interactive Techniques, pp. 29–38. ACM Press/Addison-Wesley Publishing Co., New York, NY (1999)
4. Harabor, D., Botea, A.: Hierarchical path planning for multi-size agents in heterogeneous environments. In: IEEE Symposium on Computational Intelligence and Games, Perth, WA, pp. 258–265 (December 2008)
5. Helbing, D., Molnár, P., Farkas, I., Bolay, K.: Self-organizing pedestrian movement. Environment and Planning B: Planning and Design 28(3), 361–383 (2000), `http://www.envplan.com/abstract.cgi?id=b2697`
6. Jeong, W.K., Whitaker, R.T.: A fast iterative method for a class of hamilton-jacobi equations on parallel systems. Tech. rep., CiteSeerX - Scientific Literature Digital Library and Search Engine, United States (2007), `http://citeseerx.ist.psu.edu/oai2`, `http://citeseerx.ist.psu.edu/viewdoc/summary?doi=?doi=10.1.1.115.8742`
7. Lite, D., Koenig, S., Likhachev, M.: D* lite (2002)
8. Parthenay, C.: Herbert simon: rationalit limite, thorie des organisations et sciences de l'artificiel (2005)
9. Philippsen, R., Jensen, B., Siegwart, R.: Towards Real-Time Sensor-Based Path Planning in Highly Dynamic Environments. In: Autonomous Navigation in Dynamic Environments. Springer Tracts on Advanced Robotics (2006)
10. Reynolds, C.: Big fast crowds on ps3. In: Sandbox 2006: Proceedings of the 2006 ACM SIGGRAPH Symposium on Videogames, pp. 113–121. ACM, New York (2006)
11. Sethian, J.A.: Level Set Methods and Fast Marching Methods Evolving Interfaces in Computational Geometry, Fluid Mechanics, Computer Vision, and Materials Science. Cambridge University Press (1999), `http://math.berkeley.edu/~sethian/2006/Publications/Book/2006/book_1999.html`
12. Shopf, J., Oat, C., Barczak, J.: GPU crowd simulation. AMD, Inc. (2008)
13. Thalmann, D.: Crowd Simulation. Springer-Verlag London Limited (2008), `http://ebooks.ulb.tu-darmstadt.de/11444/`
14. Treuille, A., Cooper, S., Popović, Z.: Continuum crowds. ACM Trans. Graph. 25(3), 1160–1168 (2006)
15. Wilkie, D., van den Berg, J., Manocha, D.: Generalized velocity obstacles. In: IROS 2009: Proceedings of the 2009 IEEE/RSJ International Conference on Intelligent Robots and Systems, pp. 5573–5578. IEEE Press, Piscataway (2009)

Application of Simulation and Virtual Reality to Physical Education and Athletic Training

Lin Zhang[1] and Qing Liu[2]

[1] Department of Physical Education, College of Education, Zhejiang University, Hangzhou, Zhejiang, 310028, China
[2] Department of Physical Education, Zhejiang Forestry College, Linan

Abstract. This paper discusses the application of Virtual Reality and Physical System Simulation technology to Physical Education and Athletic Training as well as interactive methodological advances. In the paper, the simulation technology is applied into the directional movement, which simulate the directional movement in the virtual environment, making it come true for the player to display the scientific, rational, standardized basic technology, and for us to watch and demonstrate their display of the directional movement continuously and dynamically at multi-angle or any angle. Through direct and vivid audio-visual images, the athletes can establish clear imaginable thinking, and form standard, rational concept of directional movement training methods. In addition, in traditional teaching and training, knowledge and skills are only demonstrated statically. In our research work, the defect is overcome and the coach could know the actual situation of his training by using virtual reality.

Keywords: Physical System Simulation (PSS), Virtual Reality (VR), Physical Education (PE), Athletic Training (AT), Interactive Programming (IP).

1 Introduction

Physical System Simulation (PSS) is an experimental tool which simulates PE and AT teaching experiences by modeling coaching goals - on an individual basis and as a team [1,2]. As modern competitive sports reach a development peak in a challenging and precise way it is necessary to measure and tap human potential to its maximum. We can further take advantage of modern technology, integrating disciplines related to Athletic Sciences, such as kinetics, with an exploration of the inherent laws of sport-rule formulation using the PSS approach to raise competition levels [3]. PSS is a technological discipline, which requires the support of computer images and VR technology. As the refinement of images and VR technology advances, it may be logically foreseen that PSS will be extensively applied.

VR, also known as Virtual Environment, is computer-generated, real-time representation of a world that simulates the human senses. It can be both a true

Z. Pan et al. (Eds.): Transactions on Edutainment VII, LNCS 7145, pp. 24–33, 2012.

reproduction of the real world, and a manifestation of an imaginary world. By manipulating the laws of physical kinetics [4], VR technology is providing a new tool for envisioning theoretical athletic performance levels using parameters such as Rigid Collision Detection(RCD), Artificial Intelligence(AI), Real-Time Variations, Viewpoint Control and more. Currently, VR is being used in a early-state in such applications as military simulation, entertainment, games, education, medicine, remote control robotics, virtual design, virtual manufacturing, and other area [5,6,7]. The study of VR technology possesses an interdisciplinary character. Through the continuous advance of interfacing technologies, VR will eventually become widely popular, changing our lifestyle by making our work easier [8].

PSS and VR, as brand-new techno-tools, facilitate the development of novel ideas and act as instruction platforms for modern PE and AT. Not only are the limitations of time and space transcendedallowing us to demonstrate and control canonical athletic motions from arbitrary angles, in scientific and rational ways, but also to exhibit dynamic sports strategies in a continuous manner [9,10]. In traditional PE and AT, athletic techniques and key skills can be analyzed only in the static state, excluding detailed examination in the dynamic condition. These shortcomings can be avoided with PSS and VR, which allow clear moving imagery of athletic strategies accompanied by control of the fourth dimension. This allows the sports analyst and teacher to set the pace. Using these tools, technical key points & skills can be intuited by players, rather than taught.

2 Sports Scenes and Athletic Modeling for VR

The process of modeling for VR Technology involves the construction of three-dimensional images which are used in a Virtual Environment [11]. There are two methods which are currently popular - one employs the use of a Holographic Scanner, which scans the exterior surface of a potential model, yielding a 3D-image which may be manipulated using VR programs; the second uses modeling system. Obviously, the first approach is more suitable for virtual objects which have concrete references of an appropriate size, while the second method is applicable to models which can be visualized by program.

Construction of scenarios with training facilities, equipment and athletic models involves the initial building of a single complex model, and then overlayering with textures and materials, i.e. outputting texture followed by perspective texture mapping [12,13]. A simple numerical model is then established, the scenario is encrypted and UV is used to re-combine textures and materials to reduce file size, which ensures the smooth running of the virtual program.

3 Movement Data Editing

3.1 Technical Movement Data Acquisition

At present, the Motion Capture Systems(MCS) are of two kinds: the Optical MCS, and the Moven Inertial MCS [14].As the Optical MCS is limited by venue

Fig. 1. The volleyball scene and the player models

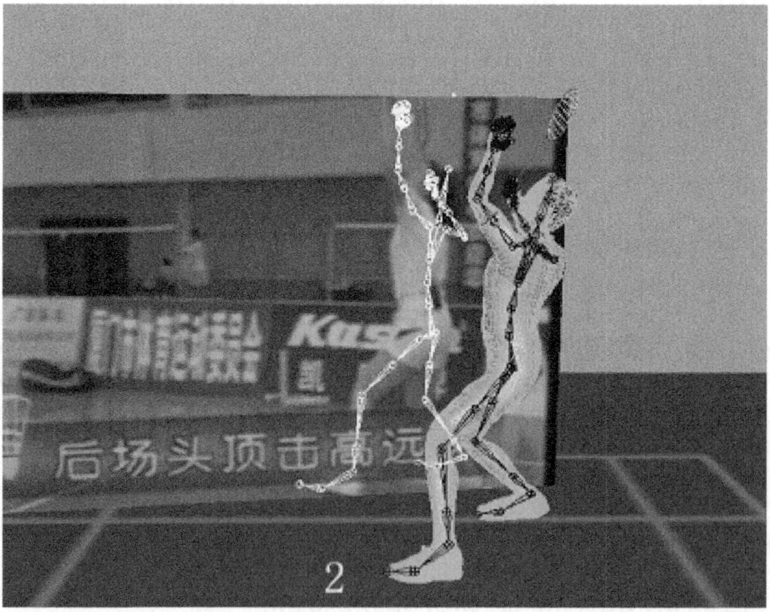

Fig. 2. Comparison of badminton playing movements

and space, many skilled motions can not be captured coherently and completely. While the Moven Inertial MCS is free from space constraints, the user must wear a suit provided by the system, which makes many sports motion captures limited.Currently, the SIMI Kinematic Analysis System is often used for sports movement data capture and research. Through camera shooting and marking the critical point of each frame buffer, trajectory and line animation can be acquired. This method results in a heavy data workload, and data is not universally applicable.

Renting motion capture equipment and athletes is usually of great expense, so we have sought alternatives in order to achieve the greatest cost reduction. In this study, using our 3D software, we build skeletal images; compare the serial maps of technical motions with the outline models; and select key frames via controller. The desired motion data is then simulated. We know that each technical movement has several key elements of action. With analysis of video-time frames, key point comparison and key frame selection, modification of the key-frame transitional motion is achieved. In this way, we can get better motion effects with less workload.

3.2 Combination of Sports Technical Motion

Many skilled sport techniques are comprised not only of single technical movements, but also of complex movement combinations - such as straight-dribbling followed by a reverse-pivot, a behind-the-back-dribble and a cross-legged dribble; the swerving-dribble goes with a stop-jump shot, a turnaround and so on. After comparing and producing a single movement, we can integrate and edit the data to complete the technical combination.

3.3 Synchronization of Technical Action in Basketball

In contrast to the repetitive cyclic movements of computer games, a step-by-step analysis is required to illustrate technical movements in sports. Even if the VR program is set-up to coordinate athlete and ball motions simultaneously, when the program is run on a computer with different settings, two parameters may be unsynchronized.

Setting the ball as a sub-program related to the VR figure can be a better way to solve synchronization problems. This also simplifies the editing of the VR program. However, the ball sub-program will be affected by the motion of the virtual figure. By planning ball-path trajectory and setting key-frames along the path to illustrate ball-control, the impact of the athlete's inertia relative to the ball can negated.

4 Virtual Interactive Program Design

4.1 The Main Interface and the Program Design

The main interface functions in sorting and guiding capacity. According to convention, user navigation is designed so as to be complementary to Microsoft

Fig. 3. Basketball dribbling go with reverse pivot and swerving

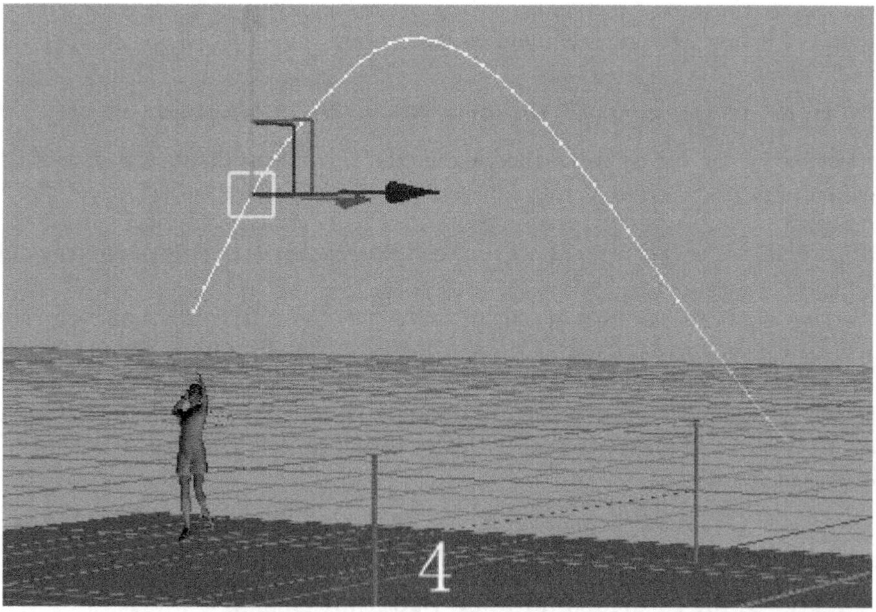

Fig. 4. Setting of synchronization between badminton and technical motion animation

Windows while dealing with PE and AT. There are four sub-program branches which may be navigated from the Start Menu: (i) Technical movements, (ii) Tactical coordination, (iii) Referee methods, and (iv) Help.

Fig. 5. Main program interface and the Start menu

The program flow chart is described as follows (See Figure 7): (1) Click on the logo to enter the main interface and wait for the Start Menu command; (2) Obtain location data & activate the Start Menu; (3) Display the branch-oriented menu; (4) Wait for select; (5) Activate the branch process button on taskbar; (6) Restore.

4.2 Taskbar and Design of Techniques Classification Process

In the technical motion navigation module, the taskbar button is set according to program categorization, each button activating a corresponding control button which allows access to the technical motion contents. The process is composed of the following steps (See Figure 8): (1)Activate the task bar button and wait for the technical category button command; (2) Obtain location data, activate the technical content menu; (3) Wait for select; (4) Activate player motion; (5) Restore. When activating the task bar, technical classification and virtual athletes, the corresponding text is also activated, click the Text button to show or hide the text.

Fig. 6. Task bar activated for volleyball motion

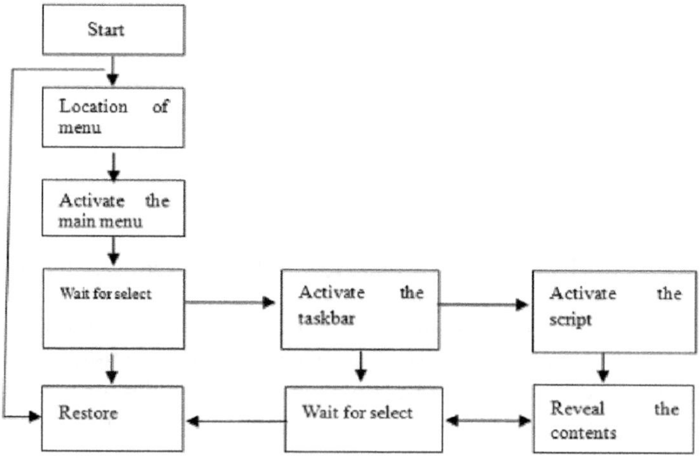

Fig. 7. The complete program design process

4.3 Interactive Program Design of Slow Motion and Frame-by-Frame Analysis

Frame-by-frame analyses, and slow motion replays, are possible through the selection of the appropriate technical motion. The process is composed of the following steps (See Figure 9): (1) Click "move forward frame by frame"; (2) Send message; (3) Frame number forward; (4) Detect current frame of animation; (5) Cycle.

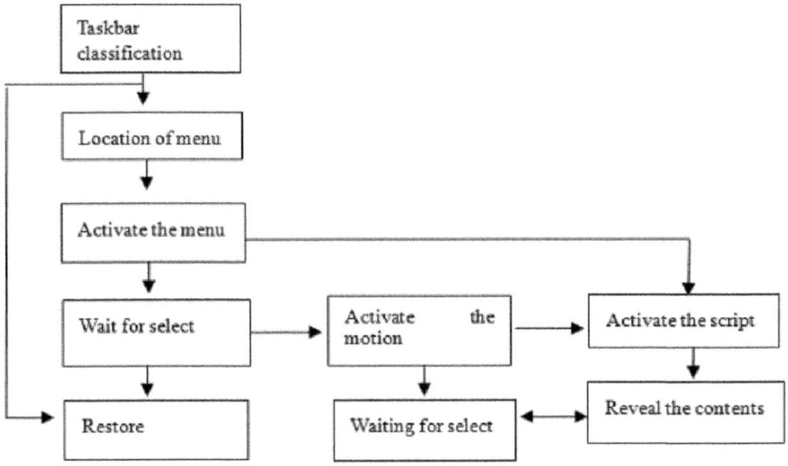

Fig. 8. The flow chart of taskbar and design of techniques classification process

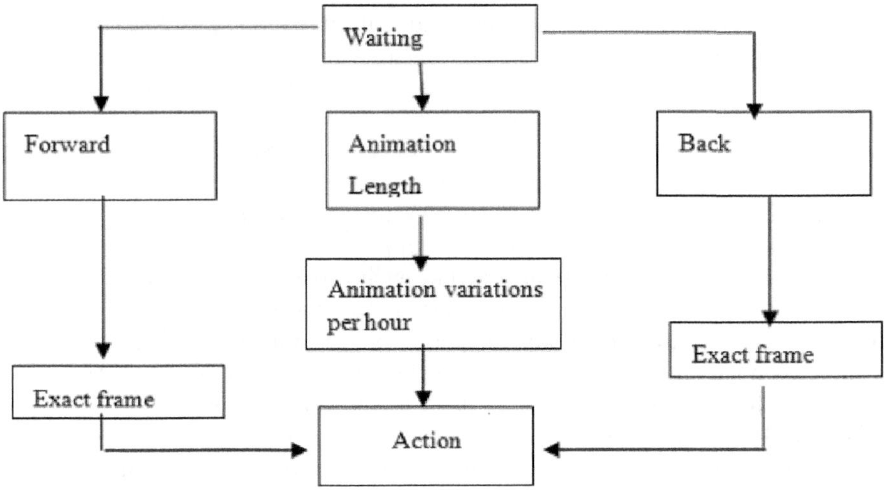

Fig. 9. The flow chart of slow motion and frame-by-frame analysis

4.4 Free Viewpoint Camera Control and Tracking Program Design

Set the 3D-frame of the camera target, binding the 3D-frame with soft shadows of the player. Camera-jitter, which often occurs while following player action, can be avoided. The video speed should also be selected appropriately for a smooth tracking motion. For the program design process see Figure 10.

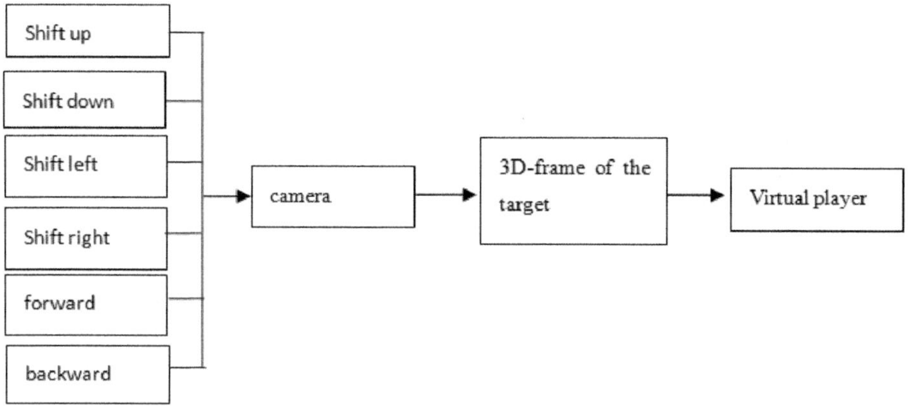

Fig. 10. The flow chart for free viewpoint camera control and tracking

5 Conclusion and Discussion

In this paper, two methods of modeling are discussed - (1) Holographic Scanning & (2) Computer Modeling. Traditional teaching methods, being essentially static, do not facilitate easy demonstration of technical skills. All of these shortcomings are overcome using VR. In a Virtual Environment, individual technical moves, team strategies and referee protocol may be examined from any angle using frame-by-frame analysis and slow-motion replays.

In the design of interactive program, the motion of virtual player cannot be manipulated. As a result, frame-by-frame analysis is used to do with the freeze frame of action. As to the virtual players with more animation data, the only way is to mask others when they are acting. In this case, when the animation is in action, if a sudden command is received, the player won't feel confused, and there won't be mutual interference in the data. And the manipulation of the process of animation data implementation is still under study.

The coach could simulate the environment changes and characteristics, demonstrate them with intuitive, realistic 3D animated VR technology. As a result, players can vividly observe the features of directional movement, and the coach, according to the characteristics of environment, can pointedly develop a teaching and training program.

Acknowledgments. This research is co-funded by NSF Project (Grant NO: 61170318) and 863 project (Grant NO: 2006AA01Z335).

References

1. Pan, Z.G., Xu, W.W., Huang, J.: EasyBowling: Small Bowling Machine Based on Virtual Simulation. Computers & Graphics, 231–238 (2003)
2. Amusitronix, VR Sports (2000)
3. Barzel, R.: Physically-Based Modeling for Computer Graphics, vol. 2. Academic Press (1992)
4. Molet, T., Aubel, A., Capin, T.: Anyone for Tennis. Presence, 140–156 (1999)
5. Wu, C.G.: Technique of simulation, vol. 7. Chemical Industry Press, Beijing (2005)
6. Wu, Q.D.: System simulation And Virtual reality. Chemical Industry Press, Beijing (2002)
7. Li, X.C., Sun, J.H.: Physical System Simulation. People's Sports Press, Beijing (2001)
8. Zhao, M.Q., Yu, S.Q.: Enter Virtual Reality. Academic Press (2003)
9. Pan, Z.G., Chen, W.Z., Zhang, M.M., Liu, J.F., Wu, G.S.: Virtual Reality in the Digital Olympic Museum. IEEE Computer Graphics and Applications, 84–88
10. Corp, L.M.: Research on Domestic and Foreign Virtual Reality Technology (2002)
11. Pan, Z.G., Jiang, X.H., Zhang, M.M., Shi, J.Y.: Overview on distributed Virtual Environment. Journal of Software, 461–467 (2000)
12. Tu, R.S.: System Simulation Methodologies Facing towards Information Era. Journal of System Simulation, 312–315 (1999)
13. He, X.C., Zhao, Y.: Application of VRML-based VR in World Expo Venues mould. Modem Educational Technology, 114–116 (2005)
14. Xu, L.M., Jiang, Y.M.: Modeling and Realization of Roaming Virtual Scene. Journal of System Simulation, 120-10 (2006)

Depth-Varying Human Video Sprite Synthesis*

Wei Hua, Wenzhuo Yang, Zilong Dong**, and Guofeng Zhang

State Key Lab of CAD&CG, Zhejiang University, P.R. China
zldong@cad.zju.edu.cn

Abstract. Video texture is an appealing method to extract and replay natural human motion from video shots. There have been much research on video texture analysis, generation and interactive control. However, the video sprites created by existing methods are typically restricted to constant depths, so that the motion diversity is strongly limited. In this paper, we propose a novel depth-varying human video sprite synthesis method, which significantly increases the degrees of freedom of human video sprite. A novel image distance function encoding scale variation is proposed, which can effectively measure the human snapshots with different depths/scales and poses, so that aligning similar poses with different depths is possible. The transitions among non-consecutive frames are modeled as a 2D transformation matrix, which can effectively avoid drifting without leveraging markers or user intervention. The synthesized depth-varying human video sprites can be seamlessly inserted into new scenes for realistic video composition. A variety of challenging examples demonstrate the effectiveness of our method.

Keywords: human video sprite, video texture, depth-varying, motion graph.

1 Introduction

Realistic human characters are common and important in film and game productions, which are traditionally captured by one or more cameras and stored as videos. However, how to effectively utilize the captured video data for creating realistic human characters is still an issue. Directly extracting a captured human character and inserting it into the desired scene may be inefficient and even intractable for extreme cases. To obtain a long time character motion in this way, the video capture and foreground extraction would be very time-consuming and labor intensive. In particular, creating infinite character motion in this way is obviously intractable.

To address this problem, some researchers proposed to use video textures [16,15] to create a continuous, infinitely varying stream of character motion,

* This work was supported by the 973 program of China (No. 2009CB320802), NSF of China (Nos. 60633070 and 60903135), China Postdoctoral Science Foundation funded project(No. 20100470092).

** Corresponding author.

Z. Pan et al. (Eds.): Transactions on Edutainment VII, LNCS 7145, pp. 34–47, 2012.

which can greatly facilitate the use of captured motion data. Flagg et al. [7] proposed human video textures which can synthesize new motions by rearranging the frame sequence and interpolating the human snapshots during frame transitions. However, for all these methods, the movements of characters are restricted to nearly constant depths and there is no significant scale variation. Therefore, the diversity of the synthesized character motion is rather limited.

In this paper, we propose a novel method which can synthesize infinite depth-varying human video sprites, so that the supply source of motion data can be significantly increased. Our contributions are summarized as follows. First, we introduce a new image distance function encoding shape, color and scale measures, so that the human snapshots with different depths/scales and poses can be reliably measured and aligned. Second, we introduce a robust transition graph inference method which can effectively eliminate transition ambiguities by utilizing temporal information, action cycle recognition and transition interval control. Especially, the transitions among non-consecutive frames are modeled as a 2D translation with scaling, which can effectively eliminate drifting without leveraging markers or user intervention. Our system also allows the user to interactively guide the transition for creating the desired human actions. Finally, we seamlessly insert several synthesized human video sprites into new scenes for realistic video composition, which demonstrates the effectiveness of the proposed method.

2 Related Work

There are two categories of previous related work, i.e. video textures based motion synthesis and video synthesis from motion capture data. Our method is quite related to video textures [16,15]. We will review them respectively in this section.

2.1 Video Textures Based Motion Synthesis

Video textures can be used to model the repetitive natural phenomenon from captured videos, by finding some places in the original video where smooth transitions can be made to some other places in the video clip. It was firstly proposed by Schödl et al. [16], then extended by Schödl et al.[14,15] with the video sprites extracted from original videos, allowing flexible control of transitions by the user for creating controllable animations. Their method can tolerate small depth change, but the frame distance metric was based on linear classifier, and the user had to label a lot of training examples manually (i.e. 1000 pairs of sprite images in [15]). In contrast, our frame distance metric is computed automatically.

Although video textures can handle well simple repetitive motions (e.g., waterfall, fire), it is found to be inadequate for creating complex human actions. Several methods [12,6] have been proposed to extend video textures to synthesize videos of human motion. Mori et al. [12] used motion and shape features [5] to determine the transition between two frames. To perform the kinematically correct morphing for smooth transitions, they greedily selected a set of exemplar frames (e.g. 100 frames), on which the user should label the human body joints, and the joints on all other frames were copied from the nearest exemplar. Celly and Zordan [6] adopted a similar framework, but used the bounding box of human figure to estimate the scale, and interpolated the transitions by feature based morphing [3]. In our work, the transitions between frames are interpolated by optical flow technique [11].

Flagg et al. [7] proposed to utilize Motion Capture (MoCap) data to generate photorealistic animations of human motion. With the help of auxiliary MoCap markers, candidate transition points in video clips can be reliably identified and a video-based motion graph is constructed for infinite replaying. In contrast, our method can create the transitions without leveraging the MoCap markers. In addition, they do not consider the depth variation, so that the synthesized human motions are restricted to constant depth range.

Xu et al. [17] proposed a motion synthesis method which can infer motion graph of animals from still images. Given still pictures of animal groups, they first build a snapshot graph, where the weight of the edge connecting two nodes represents the similarity between the corresponding snapshots. The similarity between two snapshots is measured using shape features [4]. Then the similar snapshots are aligned and the optimal ordering of snapshots is determined for reconstructing the motion cycle. Although the scale factor is estimated for shape normalization, the synthesized motions do not allow scale or depth variation.

In summary, traditional video textures do not allow the depth variation of the synthesized sprites. However, solving this problem is not trivial, especially while dealing with the transitions between non-consecutive frames. Without accurate transformation estimation and alignment, jittering or drift problems will be notable, which is unacceptable in practice.

2.2 Video Synthesis from Motion Capture Data

Many works generate new motions by piecing together example motions from MoCap database [1,8,9,10]. They usually constructed a hierarchical graph called motion graph that encapsulated connections among the database. Motion can be generated simply by building walks on the graph, and the motion can be applied to 3D human models to generate realistic human motion in 3D environment. However, the typical MoCap system needs several synchronized video streams and special cloths attached with markers, and this complex hardware system may prohibit its use for small productions.

3 Framework Overview

The system overview is shown in Figure 1. Given one or multiple input sequences that capture the same dynamic foreground with a stationary camera, our objective is to synthesize an infinite playing video sprite for video composition. To achieve this, we first interactively extract the dynamic foreground using Video

SnapCut [2]. Each sequence is assumed to just contain one kind of human action, such as walking, running, or kicking. If a sequence contains multiple kinds of human actions, we can separate it into multiple subsequences manually beforehand. This strategy can significantly accelerate the computation, and reduce the transition ambiguity.

Then, for each sequence, we compute a distance map using the distance metric defined in Section 4. The estimated distance map is further filtered to reduce transition ambiguities by utilizing temporal information, detecting action cycle and enforcing minimal transition interval. Based on the estimated distance map, the transition graph of each sequence can be constructed. We also match the snapshots from different sequences for finding sequence transitions, and finally construct a complete transition graph for all snapshots. The synthesized human video sprites can be inserted into a new scene for video composition.

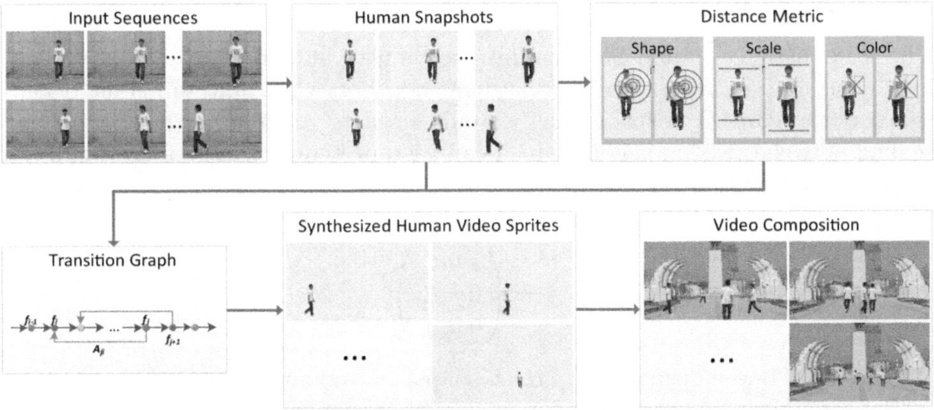

Fig. 1. Framework overview

4 Distance Map Estimation

To allow for constructing transition graph, we first need to estimate the similarity among the extracted foreground objects (namely snapshots) from the input videos. So given an input snapshot sequence $F = \{f_0, f_1, f_2, \ldots\}$, we define the following distance metric between two arbitrary snapshots f_i and f_j:

$$D_{ij} = D_{sc}(f_i, f_j) + \lambda_0 D_s(f_i, f_j) + \lambda_1 D_c(f_i, f_j), \tag{1}$$

where D_{sc}, D_s, D_c are shape, scale and appearance distance terms respectively. λ_0 and λ_1 are the corresponding weights. In our experiments, $\lambda_0 = 0.1$ and $\lambda_1 = 0.1$.

4.1 Shape Distance

Contour shape is an important hint for measuring the snapshot similarity. Here, we use the shape context descriptor proposed in [17]. The *contour points* are uniformly sampled on the shape contour of the segmented object, then the shape context descriptor is created at each point. We consider two snapshots f_i and f_j and suppose that P_i is the set of the contour points of f_i and P_j is f_j's. Let $M = |P_i|$, $N = |P_j|$, then the shape difference can be defined as

$$D_{sc}(f_i, f_j) = \frac{1}{M} \sum_{p \in P_i} C(p, \Pi(P_j, p)) + \frac{1}{N} \sum_{p \in P_j} C(p, \Pi(P_i, p)), \tag{2}$$

where $\Pi(Q, p) = \arg\min_{q \in Q} C(p, q)$. Q denotes P_i or P_j. $C(p, q)$ denotes the descriptor distance between contour points p and q, which is defined as in [4].

4.2 Scale Distance

The scale distance should be taken into account to handle scale/pose alignment and avoid motion transition between two snapshots with quite different resolutions. If the camera is stationary, we only need to model the translation and scaling between two snapshots, which can be represented by the following 3×3 affine transformation matrix,

$$A = \begin{pmatrix} s & 0 & t_x \\ 0 & s & t_y \\ 0 & 0 & 1 \end{pmatrix}$$

We can select one snapshot as *reference* snapshot, and align all other snapshots to it. Because there are so many different poses in the video that it is intractable to align all the contour points. Therefore, we evenly sample some *key* points Q_r on the reference snapshot's contour, as shown in Figure 2(c). For eliminating some unreliable points, we track the key points among adjacent snapshots, and discard those points with large movement (highlighted as green points in Figure 2(c)). Suppose Q_i is the corresponding point set in snapshot f_i, which is matched with Q_r by the shape context descriptor. Then A_{ir} can be computed by

$$A_{ir} = \arg\min_A \sum_k \|AQ_i^k - Q_r^k\|^2, \tag{3}$$

where Q_r^k and Q_i^k are the k-th matched key contour points. It is a quadratic energy function, and can be efficiently solved. The scale distance is defined as follows

$$D_s(f_i, f_j) = \|s_i - s_j\|^2,$$

where s_i and s_j are the scale factors of f_i and f_j relative to the reference snapshot. The estimated D_s is normalized with the maximum value. Figure 2(b) shows the alignment result of "Walking" sequence, where the scale of man becomes larger while he is walking towards the camera.

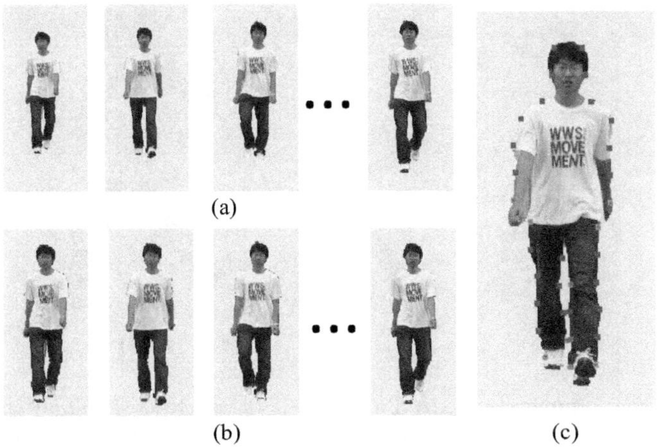

Fig. 2. Alignment result of "Walking" sequence. (a) The extracted snapshots with different depths/scales. (b) The snapshots after alignment. (c) The reference snapshot with selected key contour points (highlighted as red points). The green points are not stable and discarded.

4.3 Color Distance

To avoid visual discontinuities, the transitions between snapshots with large illumination change should be discarded. It can be measured by comparing the color difference in a local window around the matched contour points. Since the snapshots are probably in different scales, we first need to scale them to the smallest one, and then compute the color distance by

$$D_c(f_i, f_j) = \frac{1}{M} \sum_{p \in P_i} \mathcal{D}(I_i(p), I_j(\Pi(P_j, p))) + \frac{1}{N} \sum_{p \in P_j} \mathcal{D}(I_j(p), I_i(\Pi(P_i, p))), \quad (4)$$

where M, N, and $\Pi()$ are defined in the same way as Equation (2). $I_i(p)$ denotes the image patch centered at the contour point p in image i. $\mathcal{D}(,)$ is the Gaussian weighted sum of squared distance between two image patches. The weighting scheme can alleviate the affection of image noise and small misalignments, making the computation more robust. The estimated D_c is normalized with the maximum value.

5 Transition Graph Construction

For each snapshot pair, their distance can be computed by Equation (1). Figure 4(a) shows the computed distance map. However, we find that although the computed distance map can reflect the similarity among different snapshots well, it is still not accurate enough for inferring good transitions. Figure 3 gives a failure example, where it is hard to determine whether the right foot of person is in front of the left one or otherwise by the computed distance map. Therefore,

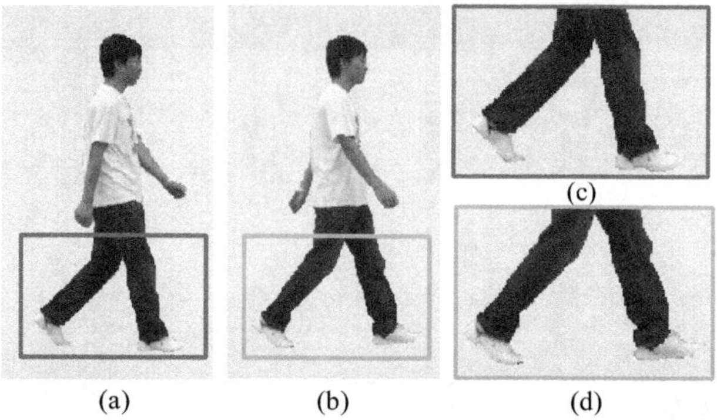

Fig. 3. Transition ambiguity. (a-b) Two snapshots which have similar shapes and appearance but different motions. (c-d) The magnified regions of (a) and (b), respectively.

more information should be considered to solve the ambiguity. Xu et al. [17] require the user to draw auxiliary shape contours to remove ambiguity. Here, we introduce an automatic method to effectively address this problem.

5.1 Preserving Dynamics

To utilize the temporal motion dynamics of human, we use the method as in [16] to filter D with a diagonal kernel with weights $[\omega_{-m}, ..., \omega_m]$,

$$D_{ij}^{(0)} = \sum_{k=-m}^{m} \omega_k D_{i+k,j+k}, \tag{5}$$

where ω_k is binomial weighting, i.e. $\omega_k = C_{2m}^{k+m}/4^m$, and m is set to be 2 in our experiments. The filtered distance map $D^{(0)}$ of an input sequence of "Walking" example is shown in Figure 4(b).

5.2 Action Cycle Recognition

For the periodic action, such as walking or running, it is quite necessary to detect the action cycle and prevent the transitions between the snapshots which have similar appearances but different motions. For example, a walking man mainly has two kinds of poses: one is that the right foot is in front of the left foot, and the other is the left foot is in front of the right foot. These two kinds of poses may have similar shape and color, but quite different motion, as shown in Figure 3. Here, we propose a simple but effective method to address this problem. We first need to detect the motion segments, which are the subsequences of an action cycle divided by the potential transition points (i.e., the beginning and end of each motion segment are two neighboring potential transition points, respectively). We sum up the elements on each diagonal line of the distance map

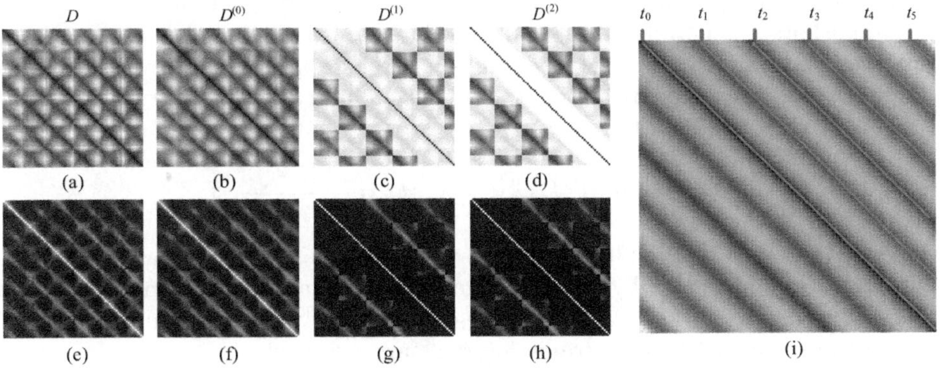

Fig. 4. The estimated distance maps. (a-d) The estimated maps, which are corresponding to D, $D^{(0)}$, $D^{(1)}$, $D^{(2)}$, respectively. (e-f) The corresponding probability maps of (a-d). (i)The computed diagonal lines by summing up the elements on each diagonal line of $D^{(0)}$. $t_0, t_1, ..., t_5$ are the detected points with local minimal values.

as follows,

$$m_i = \frac{1}{N-i}\sum_{k=i}^{N} D^{(0)}_{k,k-i}, i = 0, 1, ...N-1,$$

where N is the number of input snapshots, and m_i denotes the i-th diagonal line. Figure 4(i) shows the computed diagonal lines. Then a set of local minimums $\{m_{t_0}, m_{t_1}, ...m_{t_{K-1}}\}$ can be detected. These local minimal points divide the sequence into K subsequences $\{F_{t_0}, F_{t_1}, ..., F_{t_{K-1}}\}$. F_{t_i} corresponds to a motion segment, which starts from t_i and ends at t_{i+1}.

A complete action cycle may contain more than one motion segments. For example, a walking cycle generally contains two motion segments. For eliminating transition ambiguities, we prohibit the transitions among the snapshots within one action cycle. Thus, if an action cycle contain n motion segments, snapshot pair $(t_i, t_{i+j+n*k})$ should not exist a transition, where $k = 0, 1, \ldots, K-1$, and $j = 1, 2, ..., n-1$. By incorporating this constraint, the distance map $D^{(0)}$ is further modified by

$$D^{(1)}_{ij} = \min\{M, D^{(0)}_{ij} + M(|L(f_i) - L(f_j)| \; mod \; n)\},$$

where M is the penalty parameter, and $L(f_i)$ denotes the segment index that snapshot f_i belongs to. In our experiments, M is set to be the maximum value of $D^{(0)}_{ij}$, and n is set to 2. The computed $D^{(1)}$ is shown in Figure 4(c).

5.3 Transition Interval Control

Generally, good video transitions could be generated based on the computed distance map $D^{(1)}$. However, there may be many transitions among nearby snapshots if the person moves slowly, because the difference among neighboring snapshots is generally quite small. To alleviate this, we involve the transition interval constraint: if two snapshots allow a transition, their interval should be larger than a threshold. By adding the transition interval constraint, the distance map is further modified to

$$D_{ij}^{(2)} = \min\{M, D_{ij}^{(1)} + \lambda_2 M \exp(-\frac{|i-j|^2}{2\delta^2})\},$$

where M is set to the maximum value over $D_{ij}^{(1)}$, λ_2 is the weight, and δ controls the transition interval. Obviously, a larger δ leads to larger transition interval. In our experiments, $\delta = 6.7$, $\lambda_2 = 0.5$. The computed $D^{(2)}$ is shown in Figure 4(d). Some transitions with small frame intervals are removed.

5.4 Transition Graph Inference for Each Sequence

All candidate transitions could be inferred according to the distance map $D^{(2)}$ [16]. If $D_{ij}^{(2)}$ is small, it indicates that there may be a transition from snapshot f_j to f_{i+1}, or from snapshot f_i to f_{j+1}. We define the transition probability matrix P as follows:

$$P_{ij} = \exp(-\frac{D_{ij}^{(2)}}{\sigma}) \ ,$$

where $\sigma = avg(D_{ij}^{(2)})$. Then if P_{ij} is larger than a threshold, the transitions $f_i \to f_{j+1}$ and $f_j \to f_{i+1}$ can be created.

5.5 Transition Graph Construction for All Snapshots

Besides the transitions within the same sequence, we also would like to construct the transitions among different sequences. Without loss of generality, we consider two sequences F^1 and F^2 which contain the same foreground but different actions. Let f_i^1 be the ith snapshot of F^1 and f_j^2 be the jth snapshot of F^2. Then, we use the following metric to measure the snapshot distance,

$$D_{ij}^{12} = D_{sc}(f_i^1, f_j^2) + \lambda_0 D_s(f_i^1, f_j^2) + \lambda_1 D_c(f_i^1, f_j^2). \qquad (6)$$

This metric is almost the same as Equation (1). The minor difference is that, in Equation (1), the scale distance term D_s is computed using the selected key contour points. Here, we simply use all contour points. Then for snapshot f_i^1, we can find the most matchable snapshot $j = \arg\min_j D_{ij}^{12}$ from F^2. Similarly, the transition probability P_{ij}^{12} can be defined by

$$P_{ij}^{12} = \exp(-\frac{D_{ij}^{12}}{\sigma}),$$

where $\sigma = avg(D_{ij}^{12})$. Then, if P_{ij}^{12} is larger than a threshold, two transitions $f_i^1 \to f_{j+1}^2$ and $f_j^2 \to f_{i+1}^1$ can be created.

We match each pair of sequences, and find the transitions among different sequences. Finally, a complete transition graph of all sequences can be constructed.

6 Depth-Varying Human Video Sprite Synthesis

Given multiple input sequences with different motions, we can use the method proposed in Sections 4 and 5 to estimate the distance map and construct the transition graph. Then, we would like to synthesize the complex video textures which contain complex motions with depth variation.

6.1 Sequencing and Aligning Snapshots

For convenient representation, we connect the different snapshot sequences to construct a long snapshot sequence $\hat{F} = \{\hat{f}_i | i = 0, 1, 2, ...\}$. In fact, we just need to rearrange the snapshots. The transition graph is adjusted correspondingly. Then, we can use the represented snapshot sequence $\hat{F}$ to synthesize the target video sprite $S = \{S_t | t = 1, 2, ...\}$.

Because the snapshots may have position and scale variation, just sequencing the snapshots to synthesize a new video sprite may have serious jittering or drifting problems, as demonstrated in our supplementary video [1]. The position and scale of each snapshot should be accurately adjusted to avoid jittering or drifting. We need to estimate the index mapping function Φ and a set of affine transformation matrices $T = \{T_t | t = 1, 2, ...\}$. Then, each target snapshot S_t can be synthesized by

$$S_t = T_t \cdot \hat{f}_{\Phi[t]},$$

where $\Phi[t]$ denotes the corresponding snapshot index in $\hat{F}$, and T_t is a 3×3 affine transformation matrix.

Index function $\Phi[t]$ can be easily determined by sequencing the snapshots based on the constructed transition graph, using the method proposed in [16]. T_t can be estimated iteratively. If T_{t-1} is known, T_t can be computed by

$$T_t = T_{t-1,t} T_{t-1}, \tag{7}$$

where $T_{t-1,t}$ is the transition matrix. It is not difficult to deduce that $T_{t-1,t} = T_{\Phi[t-1],\Phi[t]}$.

Assuming $j = \Phi[t-1]$ and $i = \Phi[t]$, the transition matrix can be denoted as T_{ji}. There are two types of transitions, i.e., consecutive snapshot transitions and non-consecutive snapshot transitions. If snapshot pair (j, i) are consecutive snapshots, T_{ji} is an identity matrix. If snapshot pair (j, i) are non-consecutive snapshots, we need to estimate T_{ij} by snapshot alignment. The transition $\hat{f}_j \to \hat{f}_i$ implies that snapshot pairs $(\hat{f}_j, \hat{f}_{i-1})$ and $(\hat{f}_i, \hat{f}_{j+1})$ should have similar appearance and motion. Therefore, we can align $\hat{f}_j$ to $\hat{f}_{i-1}$ or $\hat{f}_i$ to $\hat{f}_{j+1}$ to estimate T_{ji}. Mathematically, T_{ji} can be estimated by solving the following cost function,

$$T_{ji} = \arg\min_A \left(\sum_k \|AQ_{i-1}^k - Q_j^k\|^2 + \sum_k \|AQ_i^k - Q_{j+1}^k\|^2\right), \tag{8}$$

[1] The video can be downloaded from http://www.cad.zju.edu.cn/home/zldong/

where Q_{i-1}^k, Q_i^k, Q_j^k, Q_{j+1}^k are the matched kth contour points in snapshots $i-1$, i, j, $j+1$, respectively.

While synthesizing the video sprite, we can specify the transformation matrix for the first snapshot, then the transformation of the following snapshots can be automatically estimated by Equation (7).

In practice, we found that the transitions among non-consecutive snapshots may have similar shapes but still not exactly the same, which may result in jittering artifacts during transition. We propose to use interpolation technique to alleviate this problem. For transition $\hat{f}_j \rightarrow \hat{f}_i$, we can estimate the transition matrix T_{ji} by solving Equation (8). For smooth transition, $\hat{f}_i$ is rectified to $\hat{f}_i' = T_{ij}\hat{f}_i$. Then we use the method proposed in [11] to estimate the optical flow of snapshot pair $(\hat{f}_j, \hat{f}_i')$, and interpolate the intermediate snapshots to reduce transition artifacts.

6.2 User Control

After generating the video loop for each action and the transitions between different actions, we can construct an action graph. The graph contains two kinds of action states, i.e. main states and transition states. Figure 5 shows the action graph of "Walking" example. For this example, we capture 12 sequences to synthesize 12 action states, covering kinds of walking and turning around. Then we manually select four states as main states, i.e. walking left/right/close/away. Other eight states are transition states. We need to find two transition states to connect two main states. Without loss of generality, we assume the sequences correspond to the selected two main states are F^1 and F^2. Then for each transition sequence F^k, we can find a set of transition frame pairs $\{(f_{i_1}^1, f_{j_1}^k)|f_{i_1}^1 \in F^1, f_{j_1}^k \in F^k\}$ for $F^1 \rightarrow F^k$ and a set of transition frame pairs $\{(f_{i_2}^k, f_{j_2}^2)|f_{i_2}^k \in F^k, f_{j_2}^2 \in F^2\}$ for $F^k \rightarrow F^2$ by Equation (6). We select the best transition path $F^1 \rightarrow f_{i_1}^1 \rightarrow f_{j_1}^k \rightarrow ... \rightarrow f_{i_2}^k \rightarrow f_{j_2}^2 \rightarrow F^2$ which minimizes $D_{i_1,j_1}^{1k} + D_{i_2,j_2}^{k2}$ with the condition $j_1 < i_2$. Only the best one $k^* = \min_k D_{i_1,j_1}^{1k} + D_{i_2,j_2}^{k2}$ is kept, i.e. selecting sequence F^{k^*} as transition sequence for states 1 and 2. If $D_{i_1,j_1}^{1k^*} + D_{i_2,j_2}^{k^*2}$ is large than a threshold, we do not select any transition sequence for states 1 and 2. The constructed action graph is illustrated in Figure 5.

Each main state in the action graph corresponds to an action button in the system UI. When the user would like to change the action state, he can click the desired button. Then, our system can automatically find a "shortest" path from current state to the desired one. For example, the person is walking close to the camera, and we would like to make him walk away as soon as possible, There are two paths, i.e. *close to right* $\rightarrow$ *walking right* $\rightarrow$ *right to away* $\rightarrow$ *walking away*, and *close to left* $\rightarrow$ *walking left* $\rightarrow$ *left to away* $\rightarrow$ *walking away*. We compare the number of required snapshots for these two paths, and select the shortest one as default. Our user control interface allows realtime response to the user interactions, so that the user can conveniently control the sprite synthesis for desired realtime composition.

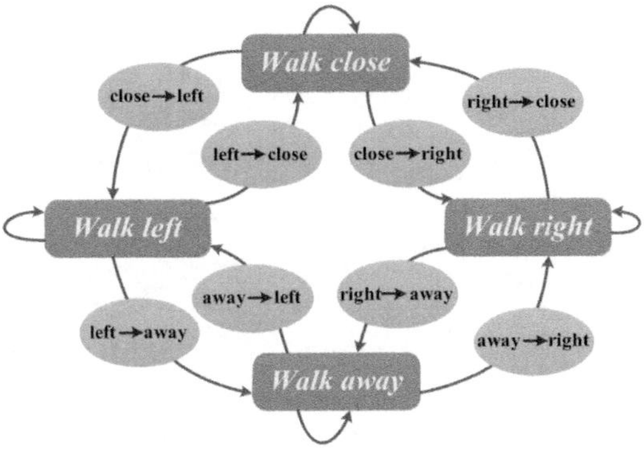

Fig. 5. The action graph of "Walking" example. The square nodes represent the main states, and corresponds to UI buttons in the system, which can be clicked by the user to change the state. The ellipse nodes are the transition states.

Fig. 6. "Walking" example. (a) Input sequences. (b) Three synthesized people walk freely on the ground.

7 Experimental Results

We have experimented with several challenging examples where the sprites undergo complex motions. All our experiments are conducted on a desktop PC with Intel Core2Duo 2.83 GHz CPU. Figure 6 shows the "Walking" example. There are 12 input sequences (about 800 frames in total), covering kinds of actions, including walking, turning left/right, etc. Figure 6 (a) shows several selected frames. We can control the transitions among different actions through a simple user interface (demonstrated in our supplementary video), and synthesize 3 human video sprites and insert them into a new background scene, as shown in Figure 6 (b). While the person is walking close/away the camera, there is significant depth/scale change, which is quite challenging for traditional video texture techniques. In this example, it takes about 5 minutes to estimate the distance maps of all sequences. Then, the transition graph can be quickly constructed, only requiring $80ms$. The texture synthesis can be performed in realtime.

Figure 7 shows another challenging example, which includes 5 input sequences with about 275 frames in total. Several frames of kicking, dodging, holding are

Fig. 7. "Fighting" example. (a) Input sequences. (b) Inserting the synthesized video sprites into a new scene. The person is fighting with himself.

shown in Figure 7 (a). We synthesize two video textures of the same person, and insert them into a new scene, making them fight with each other, as shown in Figure 7(b). Please refer to our supplementary video for the complete frames.

8 Conclusion and Discussion

In this paper, we have proposed an effective method for synthesizing human video sprite which may have significant depth/scale variation. For robustly handling depth variation of human snapshots, we propose a new image distance function, encoding shape, color and scale measures. A robust transition graph inference method is proposed, which can effectively remove transition ambiguities by action cycle recognition and transition interval control. We first construct the transition graph for each sequence independently, and then match the sequences to connect the transition graphs to obtain the whole transition graph for all snapshots. For seamless video sprite synthesis, we also estimate an alignment transformation matrix for each snapshot to avoid jittering or drifting.

Our method still has some limitations. First, we assume that each input sequence only contains one simple kind of action. If one input sequence contains multiple complex actions, the action cycle recognition may fail, which will result in some transition ambiguities. So, one direction of our future work is to relax this limitation by using action/activity recognition techniques [13]. Second, if the input sequences do not contain the snapshots with sufficiently similar appearance and motion, transitions among different actions will fail or contain noticeable artifacts even using interpolation technique. How to resolve this problem remains to be our future work.

References

1. Arikan, O., Forsyth, D.A.: Interactive motion generation from examples. In: SIGGRAPH 2002: Proceedings of the 29th Annual Conference on Computer Graphics and Interactive Techniques, pp. 483–490. ACM, New York (2002)

2. Bai, X., Wang, J., Simons, D., Sapiro, G.: Video snapcut: robust video object cutout using localized classifiers. In: SIGGRAPH 2009: ACM SIGGRAPH 2009 Papers, pp. 1–11. ACM, New York (2009)
3. Beier, T., Neely, S.: Feature-based image metamorphosis. In: Proceedings of the 19th Annual Conference on Computer Graphics and Interactive Techniques, SIGGRAPH 1992, pp. 35–42. ACM, New York (1992), http://doi.acm.org/10.1145/133994.134003
4. Belongie, S., Malik, J., Puzicha, J.: Shape matching and object recognition using shape contexts. IEEE Transactions on Pattern Analysis and Machine Intelligence 24(4), 509–522 (2002)
5. Berg, A.C., Malik, J.: Geometric blur for template matching, vol. 1, p. 607. IEEE Computer Society, Los Alamitos (2001)
6. Celly, B., Zordan, V.B.: Animated people textures. In: Proceedings of 17th International Conference on Computer Animation and Social Agents (CASA), Citeseer (2004)
7. Flagg, M., Nakazawa, A., Zhang, Q., Kang, S.B., Ryu, Y.K., Essa, I., Rehg, J.M.: Human video textures. In: SI3D 2009: Proceedings of the 2009 Symposium on Interactive 3D Graphics and Games (2009)
8. Kovar, L., Gleicher, M., Pighin, F.: Motion graphs. In: Proceedings of the 29th Annual Conference on Computer Graphics and Interactive Techniques, SIGGRAPH 2002, pp. 473–482. ACM, New York (2002), http://doi.acm.org/10.1145/566570.566605
9. Lee, J., Chai, J., Reitsma, P.S.A., Hodgins, J.K., Pollard, N.S.: Interactive control of avatars animated with human motion data. In: Proceedings of the 29th Annual Conference on Computer Graphics and Interactive Techniques, SIGGRAPH 2002, pp. 491–500. ACM, New York (2002), http://doi.acm.org/10.1145/566570.566607
10. Li, Y., Wang, T., Shum, H.Y.: Motion texture: a two-level statistical model for character motion synthesis. In: Proceedings of the 29th Annual Conference on Computer Graphics and Interactive Techniques, SIGGRAPH 2002, pp. 465–472. ACM, New York (2002), http://doi.acm.org/10.1145/566570.566604
11. Liu, C., Freeman, W.T., Adelson, E.H., Weiss, Y.: Human-assisted motion annotation. In: CVPR (2008)
12. Mori, G., Berg, A., Efros, A., Eden, A.: Video based motion synthesis by splicing and morphing. Tech. rep., University of California, Berkeley (2004)
13. Niebles, J.C., Chen, C.-W., Fei-Fei, L.: Modeling Temporal Structure of Decomposable Motion Segments for Activity Classification. In: Daniilidis, K., Maragos, P., Paragios, N. (eds.) ECCV 2010. LNCS, vol. 6312, pp. 392–405. Springer, Heidelberg (2010)
14. Schödl, A., Essa, I.: Machine learning for video-based rendering. In: Advances in Neural Information Processing Systems, pp. 1002–1008. MIT Press (2000)
15. Schödl, A., Essa, I.A.: Controlled animation of video sprites. In: SCA 2002: Proceedings of the 2002 ACM SIGGRAPH/Eurographics Symposium on Computer Animation, pp. 121–127. ACM, New York (2002)
16. Schödl, A., Szeliski, R., Salesin, D.H., Essa, I.: Video textures. In: Proceedings of the 27th Annual Conference on Computer Graphics and Interactive Techniques, SIGGRAPH 2000, pp. 489–498. ACM Press/Addison-Wesley Publishing Co., New York, NY (2000), http://dx.doi.org/10.1145/344779.345012
17. Xu, X., Wan, L., Liu, X., Wong, T.-T., Wang, L., Leung, C.-S.: Animating animal motion from still. ACM Trans. Graph. 27(5), 1–8 (2008)

Automating Expressive Locomotion Generation

Yejin Kim and Michael Neff

University of California, Davis,
Department of Computer Science and Program for Technocultural Studies,
1 Shields Avenue, Davis, CA 95616, U.S.A.
rokkim@ucdavis.edu, neff@cs.ucdavis.edu
http://idav.ucdavis.edu

Abstract. This paper introduces a system for expressive locomotion generation that takes as input a set of sample locomotion clips and a motion path. Significantly, the system only requires a single sample of straight-path locomotion for each style modeled and can produce output locomotion for an arbitrary path with arbitrary motion transition points. For efficient locomotion generation, we represent each sample with a loop sequence which encapsulates its key style and utilize these sequences throughout the synthesis process. Several techniques are applied to automate the synthesis: foot-plant detection from unlabeled samples, estimation of an adaptive blending length for a natural style change, and a post-processing step for enhancing the physical realism of the output animation. Compared to previous approaches, the system requires significantly less data and manual labor, while supporting a large range of styles.

Keywords: character animation, locomotion style, motion transition, motion path, motion capture data.

1 Introduction

The popularity of motion capture technology makes it possible to convert the physical realism of live movements into manageable data. Taking as input a set of recorded motion clips, previous approaches such as *motion blending* and *motion concatenation* have been developed for locomotion synthesis. They all have inherent trade-offs: A large number of sample motions are required to synthesize an output locomotion following an arbitrary motion path. Furthermore, most of them uses a basic locomotion type such as walking or running as their sample set, where a single blending length has been used throughout the synthesis process. With stylistic samples, this can introduce undesirable lag or suddenness during a motion transition [20].

In this paper, we introduce an animation system that generates expressive locomotion from a set of sample clips and a motion path specified by an animator. By using short, straight-path locomotion clips as our sample set, we require only a small amount of data. We focus on automating locomotion synthesis so that

Z. Pan et al. (Eds.): Transactions on Edutainment VII, LNCS 7145, pp. 48–61, 2012.

a virtual character can adapt to the input path without an animator's further intervention. Since the quantitative aspects of various styles such as body speed, number of foot steps, and range of end-effector positions differ, we represent each sample by constructing a *loop sequence* which consists of a minimum number of foot-plants required to capture the key style and loops smoothly with itself. We show how to construct such a loop sequence from an unlabeled sample with minimum manual effort. During the locomotion synthesis, an adaptive blending length is estimated for transition between styles. After the synthesis, we enhance the physical validity of the output animation by enforcing foot constraints and postural adjustments.

Our system contributes an automated method of generating expressive locomotion from unlabeled sample clips. We provide a simple and efficient method of constructing a loop sequence from detected foot-plants that is then used in the synthesis process. An adaptive blend duration is automatically determined to provide natural style changes. Notably, our system only requires a small number of sample clips for a wide range of output. Further, the physical realism is enhanced, especially for turning motions on a curved path. With our system, an animator can quickly generate an output animation through control of a motion path alone, all at interactive speed.

2 Related Work

Motion concatenation is widely used to generate variants of sample motion without destroying the physical details of the original motion. For concatenation of motion segments, a *motion graph* [1,7,9] is typically constructed to represent an output motion sequence as a valid graph path, satisfying edge and node constraints specified by an animator. Coupled with motion blending techniques, this type of approach can provide online locomotion generation [8,12,14], where control parameters such as speed, turning angles, or emotional values can be continuously fed into the system. Kovar and Gleicher [6] investigated the range of motions that can be created automatically using blending. A low-dimensional control model was suggested by Treuille *et al.* [18] to generate continuous locomotion sequences from a reduced number of samples. Oshita [11] proposed an automated system for generating a continuous motion sequences from a set of short motion clips based on the different support phases of the foot between two motions. Recently, Zhao *et al.* [22] introduced an algorithm to reduce the size of motion graph by limiting the transition time between sample motions. Nevertheless, the output quality of graph traversal or multidimensional blending methods is inherently related to the density of input sample motions. Thus, all these approaches require additional sample data, such as various turning motions, for each style modeled, for an arbitrary motion path. Furthermore, they rely on a fixed and user-defined blending length for motion transitions, which is not suitable for generating a natural transition between stylistically different motions. Our system shares a similar goal in terms of generating high-quality locomotion sequences from samples; however, our approach only requires one sample for each style and uses an adaptive blending length for a convincing motion transition.

Some approaches [2,3,10,16,19,21] put more emphasis on editing the locomotion's style by controlling kinematic constraints. Based on the Fourier series approximation of the joint angles, Unuma *et al.* [19] interpolated or extrapolated walking and running with different emotions. Given a set of edited key poses, the displacement mapping technique [2,21] modifies the overall shape of a motion while maintaining the local details; however, its output quality is highly reliant on manual specification of key poses. Gleicher [4] applied a similar mapping technique to edit a sample motion following a different arc-length parameterized path. Although they preserved foot constraints relative to a path, transformed turning motions from a straight-path can be unrealistic due to the physical invalidity. Provided with an arbitrary motion path, Sun and Metaxas [16] presented a gait generation system, where low-level joint rotations are adjusted from the high-level constraint parameters such as step length and height. Glardon *et al.* [3] provided adaptive foot-plant detection and enforcement on noisy data. Recent work has explored style adjustment through interactive control of a set of pose parameters, correlated between different body parts [10]. None of these approaches target expressive locomotion generation from stylistically different samples and an arbitrary motion path directly specified by an animator in a fully automated way.

Maintaining physical realism during the synthesizing process is another key issue for generating a high-quality output animation. Given a kinematically edited motion, several motion filtering techniques [15,17] have employed the ZMP-based balance adjustment which corrects physically implausible postures into balanced ones. Inspired by this, we apply a similar adjustment to create realistic turning motions to match path curvature.

3 Overview

Figure 1 shows an overview of our locomotion generation. For input data, we use a set of unlabeled locomotion clips, capturing from a wide variety of locomotion styles, all on a straight-path, as shown in the accompanying video.

Our locomotion generation starts with constructing a motion path from a series of path points (Section 4). To represent the key style of each sample, a corresponding loop sequence is constructed from detected foot-plants (Section 5) and concatenated repeatedly or blended with another loop sequence until the target path is filled with the sample motions (Section 6). Finally, the physical realism of the initial output animation is enhanced by foot constraint enforcement to remove any foot-skate as well as postural adjustments to generate convincing turning motions on a curved path (Section 7).

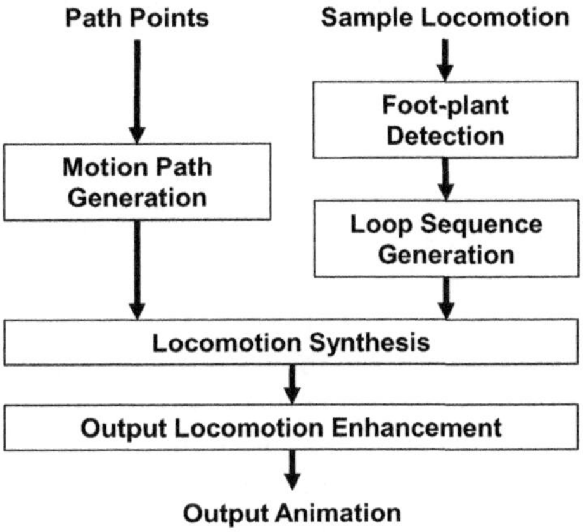

Fig. 1. Overview of the expressive locomotion generation

4 Locomotion Path Generation

In our system, a motion path is defined with a time-varying curve, which specifies the root position and orientation of the character at a given time, t. For intuitive control, it is approximated directly from a series of input path points, sampled from an animator's input device such as a mouse pointer. Thus, given a set of N continuous sample points, each point, p_i, is appended continuously to form a rough path, $\mathbf{p}(t)$. This path undergoes a smoothing operation by applying a 1D Gaussian filter kernel of width one to the last N_p neighborhood points in order to generate $\hat{p_i}$, a weighted average of neighboring points. For the next input point, p_{i+1}, we replace p_i with $\hat{p_i}$ and repeat the operation until all of the remaining points are filtered to form $\hat{\mathbf{p}}(t)$. Here, we set $N_p = 7$, which was sufficient to prevent sudden orientation changes of a character's root following the given path. During locomotion synthesis, $\hat{\mathbf{p}}(t)$ is parameterized by arc length in order to vary the body speed based on the path condition.

5 Loop Sequence Generation

Our sample set includes a wide variety of styles. Since the quantitative aspects of each style differ in speed, foot steps, and the range of body movements, we represent each sample with a processed clip we term a *loop sequence* that is specified from multiple foot-plants detected from unlabeled samples.

5.1 Foot-Plant Detection

A foot-plant is an important physical constraint that must be precisely detected with two boundary points. Manual labeling is a laborious task even for a short locomotion sequence; furthermore, boundary points are difficult to detect precisely with a fixed threshold value as the sample motion contains noise and retargeting errors [3]. For this reason, we initially approximate foot-plants and provide a new ankle trajectory that replaces step transition periods such as heel-strike and toe-off moments (Section 7).

Assuming each sample has been captured with a reasonable noise level, a low-pass filter like the Savitzky-Golay filter [13] can be used to smooth out local peaks of noise from motion curves of ankle joints while maintaining the high peaks which possibly belong to an unconstrained frame. For our sample clips, 12 frames (0.1 frames per second) for the filtering window size with degree 4 of the smoothing polynomial preserve the global shape of significant peaks in target data.

Once ankle joint data are smoothed out, boundary points of each foot-plant can be roughly selected from two geometric thresholds: the height and translational speed of foot. We derived the first threshold at 10 $\sim$ 20% of the vertical range of the extreme high and low ankle positions and the second threshold from the average body speed of the sample locomotion sequence. Due to the lenient smoothing applied by the filter, noisy frames can still exist within a detected foot-plant. Outliers like these tend to last only a few frames; thus, we can include them as a part of a foot-plant by checking their neighboring frames. For each noisy frame, we look at N_f frames on both sides of its position and add $1/(2N_f + 1)$ to the probability of it being a foot-plant frame whenever its neighbor is a foot-plant frame. We include a noisy frame into a foot-plant if its probability is over 0.5. Here, we set N_f with 1/4 of the length of foot-plant.

5.2 Sequential Cycle Construction

Once each sample clip is labeled with foot-plants, the start and end of a loop sequence can be specified as any frame within a foot-plant. We select the middle frame since it is typically a moment during which the foot stands fully on the ground. For the sequence alignment during a motion transition, each loop sequence starts and ends within a foot-plant of the left foot, requiring at least three foot-plants detected from the sample clip as shown in Figure 2.

Loop sequences are constructed so that they can be concatenated repeatedly and will yield smooth motion without further blending. Formally, this requires

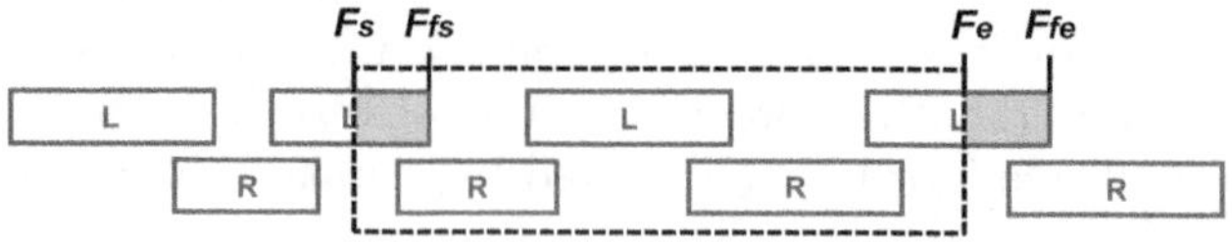

Fig. 2. Specification of a loop sequence: The shaded area is interpolated to create the smooth loop continuity

continuity between the starting frame, F_s, and the ending frame, F_e, of the loop sequence. This is ensured by pre-blending the ends of the loop sequence in order to ensure this continuity; however, the size of blending window, N_b, differs for each loop sequence constructed from samples as follows:

$$N_b = min(F_{fs} - F_s, F_{fe} - F_e),$$

where F_{fs} and F_{fe} are the last frame of the starting foot-plant and of the ending foot-plant respectively. Thus, after blending N_b frames between $F_s + i$ and $F_e + 1 + i$, we append the first $N_b/2$ blended frames to F_e and then replace N_b frames from F_s with the remaining $N_b/2$ blended frames in order to guarantee smooth continuity throughout the sequence. For the ith blending frame, $0 \leq i < N_b$, we linearly interpolate the root position, R_i, and perform spherical linear interpolation on jth joint rotation, q_i^j, as follows:

$$R_i = w(i)R_{a,i} + (1 - w(i))R_{b,i}, \quad (1)$$

$$q_i^j = slerp(q_{R_{a,i}}^j, q_{R_{b,i}}^j, w(i)), \quad (2)$$

where $w(i)$ is a sinusoidal function for blending weights, which should monotonically increase with a range of $[0, 1]$. To ensure the smooth continuity of a loop sequence, we used $w(i) = 1 - \frac{1}{2}cos(\frac{i+0.5}{N_b}\pi) + \frac{1}{2}$. Here, $R_{a,i}$ and $R_{b,i}$ are the ith frame after $F_e + 1$ and after F_s respectively. Since we complete the construction process by replacing the first N_b frames of a loop sequence with second $N_b/2$ frames of the blended frames, the y position of $F_s + i$ is used for $R_{a,i}$ if $i \geq N_b/2$ and of $F_e + 1 + i$ is used for $R_{b,i}$ if $i < N_b/2$. This way, we maintain the original vertical movements of the root for the output synthesis, adjusting to a new root position on an input path.

6 Locomotion Synthesis

An initial output locomotion is generated by concatenating a loop sequence repeatedly or blending with other sequences to transition between styles. Provided with the transition timings specified by an animator as shown in the Figure 3, all loop sequences are fit to an arc-length parameterized motion path.

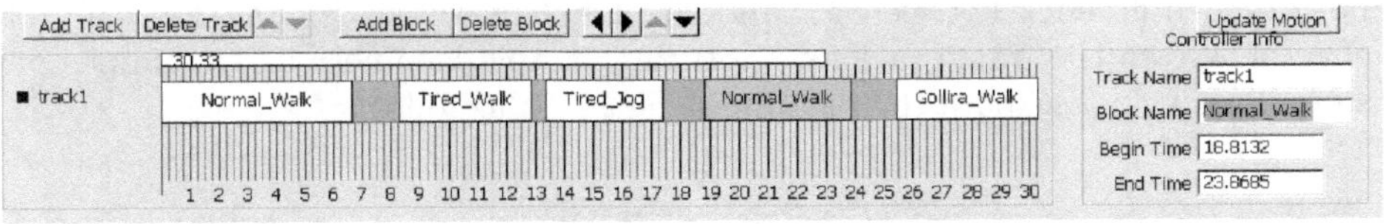

Fig. 3. Temporal placements of loop sequences on a motion path via the timing editor

6.1 Loop Sequence Alignment

Each loop sequence constructed from a sample set differs in the number of foot-plants and the body speed. In order to make a natural transition from one sequence to another, two sequences should be blended with correspondence in time based on their key-times. These key-times can be easily set from the two boundary points of each foot-plant detected in Section 5.1. For loop sequence alignment, we utilized the dynamic time-warping technique suggested by Rose *et al.* [14]. With their method, the normalized key-times are used to map the actual key-times T of each sequence, defined as $\{K_1, \ldots, K_{N_k}\}$, to a generic time $t \in [0, 1]$. Here, $N_k = 2N_{fp}$ and N_{fp} is the number of foot-plants. However, this linear mapping must maintain a consistent number of keys, N_k, for all sample sequences, but this often varies depending on the sampled style. To deal with this problem, we determine the correspondence of each loop sequence to a shorter clip and use this to calculate the correspondence in time of the full loop sequences. For example, if there is a transition between two sequences, S_a and S_b, as shown in Figure 4, we use the shorter clip, S_w, as an intermediary clip such that each cycle (the black vertical lines in Figure 4) of S_a and S_b is aligned with S_w to make the correspondence in key-times from S_a to S_b.

Therefore, for a given t, its corresponding frame F can be calculated for each sequence as follows,

$$F(t) = Fi + \frac{F_{i+1} - F_i}{K_{i+1} - K_i}(t - T_i),$$

where F_i is a key-frame corresponding to K_i, $1 \leq i < N_k$.

6.2 Adaptive Blending Length

Unlike graph-based approaches [1,7,8,9,22], our system allows an animator to start a transition at any point within the loop sequence and uses an adaptive blending length to ensure a natural style change during a motion transition. Since one stylistic locomotion can be distinguished from others with a small number of point configurations [5], we used the end-effectors of the body as such differentiating points: the head, two hands, and two foot positions.

If a motion transition is requested between two poses, P_a within sequence S_a and P_b within sequence S_b, we first find the end-effector that has the largest positional difference between P_a and P_b. Let this value be ΔD_i for ith end-effector. Given the frame rate for capturing sample locomotion, fr (frames per second), we can estimate the blending length, ℓ_b, as follows:

$$\ell_b = (\frac{\Delta D_i}{|T_{i,a} - T_{i,b}|})(\frac{1}{fr}),$$

where $T_{i,a}$ and $T_{i,b}$ is the average distance traveled by ith end-effector in S_a and S_b respectively. This ℓ_b ensures a gradual change of all end-effectors without disturbing the physical coherence of joints.

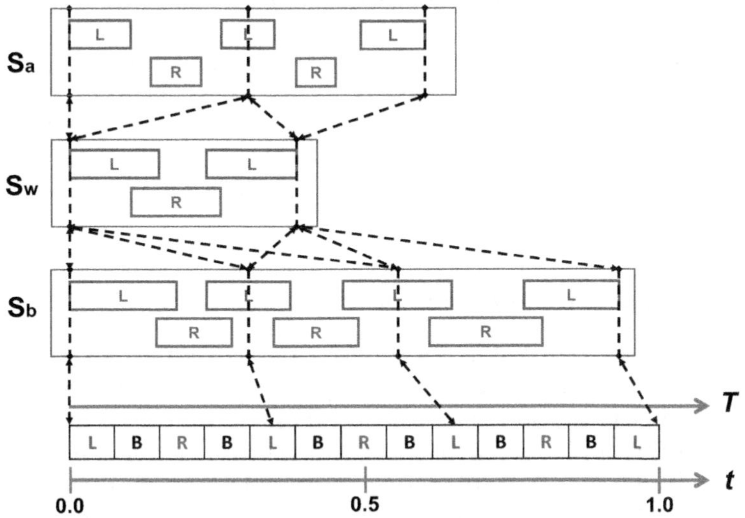

Fig. 4. Loop sequence alignment: L and R represents a left and a right foot on the ground while B represents either both feet on ground or in flight. The dashed lines represent the key-time correspondences of each cycle.

6.3 Displacement Mapping

Once all loop sequences are temporarily specified on an arc-length parameterized motion path, $\hat{\mathbf{p}}(t)$, we now determine the position and orientation of the root for each output frame. To incorporate the varied speed between the sequences into the output generation, the *speed* parameter s_i in the ith sequence is estimated as ℓ_i/N_i, where ℓ_i is an overall length of the reference root line, a linear least squares fit of the root trajectory, and N_i is the total number of frames in a loop sequence. Based on s_i, the current arc length on $\hat{\mathbf{p}}(t)$ determines the root position, $r_m(t)$, and orientation, $q_m(t)$, by interpolating between two sample points on $\hat{\mathbf{p}}(t)$.

For each frame in the sample sequence, we now map the local displacement of the root from its base motion path to the arbitrary output motion path in order to preserve the continuity and global shape of root trajectory from the original sample. Given $r_m(t)$ and $q_m(t)$ from the parametric path at a generic time t, the output root is derived as follows,

$$r_o(t) = r_m(t) + (r_i(t) - \hat{r}_i(t)),$$

$$q_o(t) = q_m(t)\hat{q}_i^{-1}(t)q_i(t),$$

where $r_i(t)$ and $q_i(t)$ are the projected root position and orientation respectively. $\hat{q}_i(t)$ is the orientation aligned to the tangential direction at $\hat{r}_i(t)$ on the reference root trajectory. Notice that the addition of the difference between $r_i(t)$ and $\hat{r}_i(t)$ reflects the side-to-side weight shift of the sample locomotion into the output animation.

7 Output Locomotion Enhancement

An output animation generated so far contains a character following a specified motion path, but lacking two key elements of physical validity. First, foot-skating is significant throughout the output animation, especially during foot-plant transitions. Second, the character does not make any physical reaction to the path curvature. In this section, we enforce such physical validity without using an expensive physics-based simulation.

7.1 Foot Constraint Enforcement

With the foot-plants detected in Section 5.1, we enforce the foot constraints by adopting the low-level IK routine from [10] due to its online performance and simplicity of implementation. However, rooting constrained frames at a single position introduces a motion discontinuity between an unconstrained frame, F_u, and a constrained frame, F_c, after and before each foot-plant. We eliminate such discontinuities by interpolating the frames to produce a new ankle trajectory. As the rate of ankle movements follows an ease-in and out curve between F_u and F_c, we apply the same interpolation function (Equation 1 and 2) with a slightly different weight function, $w(i) = 1 - cos(0.5\frac{i+0.5}{N_b}\pi)$, $0 \leq i < N_b$. Here, N_b is the number of interpolated frames between F_u and F_c and determined based on the Euclidean distance between F_u and F_c divided by the average distance traveled by an ankle joint during each foot-plant. We ensure the smoothness of a new joint trajectory by connecting between F_u and F_c with a Hermite spline. Here, the two tangents at F_u and F_c are determined as $\hat{T}_{F_u} = 0.5\frac{|F_u - F_c|}{|T|}T$ and $\hat{T}_{F_c} = 0.1\frac{|F_u - F_c|}{|T|}T_y$, where T is a tangent obtained from F_u to its closest neighbor frame, and T_y is the y-component of T. The constrained positions of ankle over a new trajectory is shown in Figure 5. We apply a similar constraint enforcement for the leg swivel rotation in order to prevent an undesirable spinning motion of the rooted foot on the ground. For this, an average swivel angle of a foot-plant is used to orient the rooted foot's direction and gradually changes its rotation angle over the new ankle trajectory to prevent any rotation discontinuity.

7.2 Postural Adjustments

Each loop sequence constructed from a straight-path sample set contains a uniform body speed and foot step size. Because of this, an output animation generated from the sequence will lack any physical reaction to the path curvature such as reduced body speed and stride length. Additionally, a character should lean toward the instantaneous center of curvature of the path in order to resist the centripetal force.

For reduced speed and stride length, a set of scaled versions of each loop sequence is generated with progressively shorter strides. This is done by scaling the distance between the foot-plants and the vertical range of the foot and then reconstructing motion comparable to the original using IK techniques based on

Fig. 5. Foot Constraint Enforcement: Original ankle positions (round dots) are enforced to the constrained positions (rectangle dots) on a Hermite spline

[10]. We derive the reduced speed parameter for each scaled loop sequence as described in Section 6.3. The final locomotion is generated by sampling across this family of scaled loop sequences to continuously adjust stride length. Each output frame is selected from one of the scaled sequences based on current curvature of the path.

To automate this adjustment process, the difference of tangential direction between $\hat{p}_i$ and $\hat{p}_{i+1}$ on the arc-length parameterized path is precalculated to determine the degrees of curvature throughout the path. The largest degree is used to determine the number of scaled sequences that need to be constructed in advance. Based on our experiments, we scaled down 1% of the original step size per 0.2 degree difference, to a maximum of 50%, and found no significant motion discontinuity in the output animation. We limit the scaling to 50% since further reduction can impact the physical coherence between foot and torso joints.

The ZMP provides a useful correction guide for maintaining physically plausible postures. Since we only need to adjust ankle joint rotation to mimic body lean during a turning motion, the ZMP-based balance adjustment suggested by [15] is utilized to calculate the rotation value for the ankle joint. For the actual ZMP calculation, we used a $4th$ order central difference with 0.5 seconds as the sampling rate for the acceleration term.

8 Experimental Results

Our experiments were performed on an Intel Core 2 Quad^{TM} 2.4GHz PC with 2GB memory. As a sample set, we used various short locomotion clips as shown in Table 1, where their style differs from each other in a frame duration and number of foot steps. All input clips are sampled at the rate of 120 frames per second and share the same skeletal structure. The skeletal model is defined in a Y-up coordinate frame and includes 6 DOFs for root position and orientation and 42 DOFs for body joint orientations: 12 for the torso and head, 9 for each arm, and 6 for each leg.

Table 1. Number of frames and foot steps for sample locomotion clips and corresponding loop sequences

	Walking	Jogging	Excited	Balancing	Distressed	Energetic	Tired
Sample Frames	296	253	530	1283	558	341	801
Sample Steps	5	6	8	7	7	7	9
Loop Sequence Frames	143	100	365	922	364	226	387
Loop Sequence Steps	2	2	4	6	4	2	4

Our experiments start with constructing loop sequences from various stylistic samples and comparing them with shorter two-step sequences. For the comparison, two versions of a loop sequence are constructed with two steps and multiple steps respectively as shown in the Table 1. The accompanying video shows that the sequences with multiple steps generate physically (balancing) and stylistically (excited) more convincing results than the two step cycle does.

Next, we compare motion transitions using adaptive blending lengths to ones with fixed duration. In this demonstration, two comparisons were made with various samples while the transition point was chosen randomly. For a fixed blending length, we used 0.33s (40 frames) since this value has been widely used in previous approaches [20]. The adaptive blending length takes about $2.22 \sim 3.89s$ for the transition between the walking and balancing sample and about $1.32 \sim 1.78s$ for the transition between energetic and tired sample. In both cases, the blending length varies as the transition can start at any point within each loop sequence. The accompanying video shows that the adaptive blending length achieves gradual motion changes; thus, it generates physically more plausible poses than the fixed blending length does.

To demonstrate the effects of our locomotion enhancement for realistic turning motions, we next compared the constant turning motion with one enhanced by our postural adjustments. In this demonstration, we used walking and jogging samples on a sinusoidal motion path as body speed affects the reaction to centripetal force. For the scaled adjustment, it took less than a minute to generate 50 scaled versions from the samples. The accompanying video shows that applied adjustments generate physically preferable turning motion for both scaled and ZMP-adjusted cases.

Our last result demonstrates an expressive animation generated from a set of stylistic samples and an arbitrary motion path. After the motion path is interactively specified, no user intervention has taken place during the output locomotion synthesis. We used a number of different stylistic samples for output animation as shown in the Figure 6, also in the accompanying video. In this demonstration, it took about $6.8s$ to generate 2401 frames for the first output and about $9.2s$ to generate 2951 frames for the second output, producing over 300 frames per second excluding the rendering time.

Fig. 6. Output Animations: First animation is generated from jogging, walking, and distressed samples. Second animation is generated from walking, distressed, balancing, and excited samples.

9 Conclusions

In this paper, we introduced an animation system for expressive locomotion that generates a continuous output sequence from a set of sample clips and an arbitrary motion path. Conscious of the high cost of preparing motion captured data, our system only requires a single sample of straight-path locomotion for each style modeled, keeping the size of the sample set to a minimum. The system focuses on automating the generation of expressive animation from a wide variety of stylistic locomotion samples. It does this by introducing a concise representation of each style, a loop sequence, which encapsulates its key style in multiple foot steps. Automation is further supported through: foot-plant detection from unlabeled samples, estimation of an adaptive blending length for a natural style change, and post-processing to enhance physical realism for turning motions on a curved path. Our experimental results show that our system is capable of generating output animation at an interactive speed, making our system suitable for both automated and user-controlled virtual characters in various interactive applications.

Currently, our prototype system only supports samples containing cyclic foot steps. To extend the sample set to less cyclic motions like dance and ballet, more sophisticated foot-plant detection is required to anticipate the foot pattern with additional contact points such as toe and heel.

In addition, the system generates a set of scaled versions of loop sequences in order to enhance the turning motions. These redundant samples are linearly generated and controlled for an input path curvature; thus, the result can be physically implausible for certain outlier path conditions, such as radical turns. Directly editing of the kinematic controls of a character might complement our approach without using additional data.

Acknowledgments. Financial support for this research was provided in part by NSF grant 0845529 to University of California, Davis and through a software donation from Autodesk. Thanks to Jonathan Graham for model support and Hilary Bryan for motion capture support.

References

1. Arikan, O., Forsyth, D.A.: Interactive motion generation from examples. ACM Transactions on Graphics 21(3), 483–490 (2002)
2. Bruderlin, A., Williams, L.: Motion signal processing. In: Proceedings of ACM SIGGRAPH 1995, pp. 97–104 (1995)
3. Glardon, P., Boulic, R., Thalmann, D.: Robust on-line adaptive footplant detection and enforcement for locomotion. Visual Comput. 22(3), 194–209 (2006)
4. Gleicher, M.: Motion path editing. In: Proceedings of ACM Symposium on Interactive 3D Graphics, pp. 195–202 (2001)
5. Johansson, G.: Visual perception of biological motion and a model for its analysis. Perception and Psycholophysics 14(38), 201–211 (1973)
6. Kovar, L., Gleicher, M.: Flexible automatic motion blending with registration curves. In: Proceedings of ACM SIGGRAPH/Eurographics Symposium on Computer Animation, pp. 214–224 (2003)
7. Kovar, L., Gleicher, M., Pighin, F.: Motion graphs. ACM Transactions on Graphics 21(3), 473–482 (2002)
8. Kwon, T., Shin, S.Y.: Motion modeling for on-line locomotion synthesis. In: Proceedings of ACM SIGGRAPH/Eurographics Symposium on Computer Animation, pp. 29–38 (2005)
9. Lee, J., Chai, J., Reitsma, P.S.A., Hodgins, J.K., Pollard, N.S.: Interactive control of avatars animated with human motion data. ACM Transactions on Graphics 21(3), 491–500 (2002)
10. Neff, M., Kim, Y.: Interactive editing of motion style using drives and correlations. In: Proceedings of ACM SIGGRAPH/Eurographics Symposium on Computer Animation, pp. 103–112 (2009)

11. Oshita, M.: Smart motion synthesis. Computer Graphics Forum 27(7), 1909–1918 (2008)
12. Park, S.I., Shin, H.J., Kim, T.H., Shin, S.Y.: On-line motion blending for real-time locomotion generation. Computer Animation and Virtual Worlds 15(3-4), 125–138 (2004)
13. Press, W.H., Tukolsky, S.A., Vetterling, W.T., Flannery, B.P.: Numerical Recipes in C++: The Art of Scientific Computing, 2nd edn. Cambridge University Press, New York (2002)
14. Rose, C., Cohen, M.F., Bodenheimer, B.: Verbs and adverbs: Mulidimensional motion interpolation. IEEE Computer Graphics and Applications 18(5), 32–40 (1998)
15. Shin, H.J., Kovar, L., Gleicher, M.: Physical touch-up of human motions. In: Proceedings of Pacific Conference on Computer Graphics and Applications, pp. 194–203 (2003)
16. Sun, H.C., Metaxas, D.N.: Automating gait generation. In: Proceedings of ACM SIGGRAPH, pp. 261–270 (2001)
17. Tak, S., Ko, H.: A physically-based motion retargeting filter. ACM Transactions on Graphics 24(1), 98–117 (2005)
18. Treuille, A., Lee, Y., Popović, Z.: Near-optimal character animation with continuous control. ACM Transactions on Graphics 26(3), article 7 (2007)
19. Unuma, M., Anjyo, K., Tekeuchi, T.: Fourier principles for emotion-based human figure animation. In: Proceedings of ACM SIGGRAPH, pp. 91–96 (1995)
20. Wang, J., Bodenheimer, B.: Computing the duration of motion transitions: An empirical approach. In: Proceedings of ACM SIGGRAPH/Eurographics Symposium on Computer Animation, pp. 335–344 (2004)
21. Witkin, A., Popović, Z.: Motion warping. In: Proceedings of ACM SIGGRAPH, pp. 105–108 (1995)
22. Zhao, L., Normoyle, A., Khanna, S., Safonova, A.: Automatic construction of a minimum size motion graph. In: Proceedings of ACM SIGGRAPH/Eurographics Symposium on Computer Animation, pp. 27–35 (2009)

Recovering Geometric Detail by Octree Normal Maps

Wenshan Fan[1,2,3,4,5], Bin Wang[1], Bin Chan[6], Jean-Claude Paul[7], and Jiaguang Sun[1]

[1] School of Software, Tsinghua University, China
[2] Beijing Aerospace Control Center, China
[3] Department of Computer Science and Technology, Tsinghua University, China
[4] Key Laboratory for Information System Security, Ministry of Education, China
[5] Tsinghua National Laboratory for Information Science and Technology, China
[6] The University of Hong Kong, China
[7] INRIA, France
fws06@mails.tsinghua.edu.cn,
wangbins@tsinghua.edu.cn

Abstract. This paper presents a new approach for constructing normal maps that capture high-frequency geometric detail from dense models of arbitrary topology and are applied to the simplified version of the same models generated by any simplification method to mimic the same level of detail. A variant of loose octree scheme is used to optimally calculate the mesh normals. A B-spline surface fitting based method is employed to solve the issue of thin plate. A memory saving Breadth-First Search (BFS) order construction is designed. Furthermore, a speedup scheme that exploits access coherence is used to accelerate filtering operation. The proposed method can synthesize good quality images of models with extremely high number of polygons while using much less memory and render at much higher frame rate.

Keywords: Large Scale Models, Recovering Geometric Detail, Octree Textures, GPU.

1 Introduction

Despite recent progress, modern graphics hardware is still unable to render in real-time many high-resolution models, which are required in plenty of applications, such as virtual reality, 3D game et al.

Normal maps associated with a surface can sometimes play a more significant role than the surface geometry itself in determining the shading. Inspired by this idea, a lot of methods were proposed to render large scale models by recovering geometric detail on simplified version of meshes with normal maps. However, all these methods either require complex construction or are with poor quality. Recently, Lacoste et al. [1] introduced a GPU-based detail recovering framework with octree textures [2] [3], saving the intricate parameterization [4] from 2D to 3D. However, the quality in their method is not improved substantially, and some issues, such as thin plate, are left to be solved.

Z. Pan et al. (Eds.): Transactions on Edutainment VII, LNCS 7145, pp. 62–73, 2012.

In the proposed approach, a variant of loose octree scheme is employed for the construction of normal maps to optimally capture geometric detail. The classical averaging approach enhanced with a B-spline surface fitting based method is applied to generate normal maps with good quality and remove the issue of thin plate. Due to the lack of flexible memory structure in GPU shader, the octree normal maps generally are encoded into regular 2D textures before rendering. A memory-saving Breadth-First Search (BFS) order construction is employed to combine the octree subdividing and texture encoding into a single pass, saving the unnecessary intermediate storage for entire octree.

The main drawback of using an octree textures is indirect access. In this paper, a speedup scheme that exploits access coherence is used in filtering operation which is essential to improve the rendering quality.

2 Related Work

Geometric Detail Recovering. Krishnamurthy et al. [5] proposed to capture the geometric detail with a displacement map which is applied on the tensor product B-spline surface patch to mimic the dense polygon mesh. However, the patch boundary is placed manually which is not amenable to automation. Cohen et al. [6] used a specific simplification to explicitly construct the map between coarse and dense models. However, the constrained simplification process prevents the use of different simplification methods.

Cignoni et al. [7] [8] introduced a general approach in which the detail recovery step is independent on the simplification scheme. They applied a predefined sampling resolution to sample the detail according to minimal Euclidean distance. However, a proper sampling resolution is hard to be determined. Sander et al. [9] used a ray-casting based method to calculate the correspondence between dense and coarse meshes. But there is a risk of a ray failing to hit the dense mesh in their approach. Tarini et al. [10] presented a visibility based construction method. They compared the rendering quality among the existing construction methods. According to their results, the ray-casting based method and their visibility based method are with good quality, while the minimal Euclidean distance method is robust although with poor rendering quality.

Lacoste et al. [1] introduced a GPU based detail recovering framework by encoding the hierarchy octree textures into plain 2D representation. However, their rendering quality is limited. And similar to the previous methods, there exists the issue of thin plate in their method.

Octree Textures. Benson et al. [2] and DeBry et al. [3] independently developed a texture mapping approach using octree, which they called as octree textures. In their approach, the representative color for each octree node is sampled with an averaging method. The 3D position is used to index the octree textures to retrieve the appropriate value without any global parameterization.

Lefohn et al. [11] and Lefebvre et al. [12] ported octree textures onto graphics hardware to speed up traversal by utilizing the high parallelism of GPU. To improve the representative ability, Lefebvre et al. [13] used a tile and Boubekeur et al. [14] stored a height field in each leaf node of octree. However, the switch from octree subdivision to construction of complex leaf nodes must be designed carefully to avoid the increase of storage of the entire octree textures.

3 Constructing Octree Normal Maps

The whole process of constructing octree normal maps consists of three steps that are combined into one pass in BFS order: octree subdividing, representative normal calculating and texture encoding.

3.1 Octree Subdividing

The 1-to-8 octree subdividing scheme is applied on coarse model M_l generated by any simplification method from dense model M_h. Both sets of triangles of M_l and M_h test intersection with the volume of the processing node and are recorded into T_l and T_h respectively, by which the correspondence between coarse and dense version of the models is defined.

Three terminating criteria for the subdivision are defined:

- The processing node contains empty T_l.
- The predefined maximum octree depth *maxD* is reached.
- The variance of normals in T_h is less than a specified tolerance ε in the processing node. A revised $L^{2,1}$ metric [15] is defined to estimate the variance:

$$L_r^{2,1} = \sum \left\| \hat{n}_i - \hat{n}_{avg} \right\|^2, \tag{1}$$

where $\hat{n}_{avg} = \left\| \dfrac{\sum \hat{n}_i * a_i}{\sum a_i} \right\|$, $\hat{n}_i$ and a_i are the normal and area of each triangle in T_h.

However, due to the differences between M_l and M_h, it is inevitable that the subdivision process will come across situations where part or even all of the desired T_h lies outside the bounding box of the processing node in general octree scheme, which destroys the correspondence between M_l and M_h and hence harms the quality of the captured geometric detail.

In our approach, a variant of loose octree scheme [16] is applied when testing intersection with M_h to optimize the selection of T_h. Considering the approximate spatial distributions between M_l and M_h, a small relaxing coefficient α is employed instead of that in ordinary loose octree where the nodes are extended by half the side width in all six directions. Generally we set α to 0.1 in our tests. For the nodes with non-empty T_l and empty T_h, they are iteratively enlarged with α until T_h is no longer empty, which is assured since the T_h of their parents contains at least a triangle.

For those triangles that span multiple nodes, we assigned them to all nodes they intersect. By doing so, the continuity of representative normals between adjacent nodes is enhanced.

The employment of the variant of loose octree scheme improves the quality of the resultant normal maps, see Figure 1.

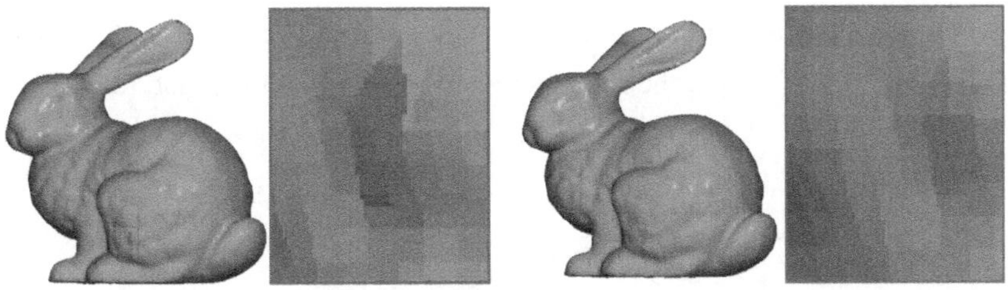

(a) With general octree scheme (b) With loose octree scheme

Fig. 1. The enlarged area in the left image highlights the flaw resulted from the non-optimized T_h selected by general octree scheme, while the employment of loose octree scheme improves the quality. No filtering is applied on both images.

3.2 Representative Normal Calculating

When the processing node meets the terminating criteria, the subdividing on it is halted. For those nodes containing non-empty T_l, the classical calculation by averaging the normals of all primitives in T_h of the node can be applied to calculate a representative normal.

Theoretically the octree subdivision can continue until the leaf nodes contain arbitrarily smooth surface patch. In practice, however, due to the limited depth of the tree, the smoothness within the leaf nodes cannot always be guaranteed, resulting in the issue of thin plate [1] [2] [3], where the classical averaging method will fail.

Therefore, we present a B-spline surface fitting based approach to calculate representative normals for this kind of nodes. The idea (Figure 2) of the proposed method is to construct a proxy of B-spline patch that best represents all the vertices and normals in T_h. The optimized representative normal is then calculated using this proxy.

Due to the importance both in computer graphics and CAD communities, a lot of works [17] [18] [19] [20] have been done on the construction of B-spline surface from scattered points. Considering the performance, we choose the multilevel B-spline algorithm (MBA) [18] for our work.

In MBA, a rectangular domain Ω that can be in any one of the planes xy, xz and yz is first chosen. A coarse lattice of B-spline control points on Ω is defined to approximate the scattered points in the least squares sense and a dyadic lattice is used continuously to refine the coarse one to reduce the deviation between the surface and the points set until the resultant surface fits within an error tolerance.

Following the algorithm, our surface fitting begins with the determination of a proper plane on which Ω lies. The major direction method based on Equation 2 is used to achieve this.

$$\hat{n}_{abs} = \frac{\sum fabs(\hat{n}_i) * a_i}{\sum a_i}, \tag{2}$$

where $\hat{n}_i$ and a_i are the same as those in Equation 1.

The component with the largest absolute value in the vector $\hat{n}_{abs}$ is chosen as the major axis $axis_{major}$ of T_h and the remaining two axes define the plane for Ω.

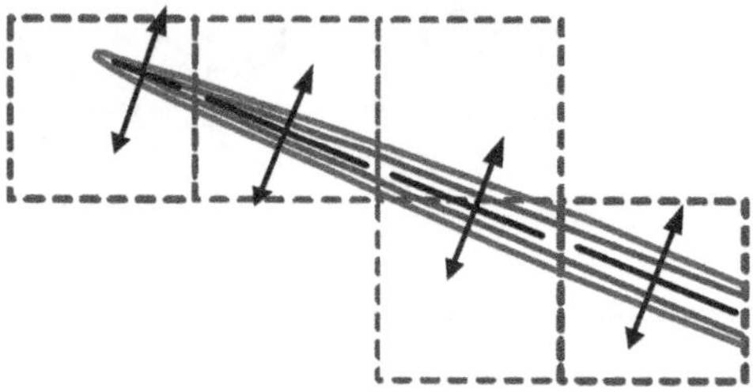

Fig. 2. The red and green lines represent the dense and coarse mesh respectively. The thin plate problem occurs when opposing normals cancel each other out, which causes the averaging method incorrect. In the proposed method, a proxy (in black) is constructed from the scattered vertexes set of T_h, and then sampled to calculate an optimized representative normal.

The next step is to determine the parameter settings for MBA. The dimensions of U and V that define the control lattice and L that tells how many levels are required to approximate the scattered points need to be determined. We define the U and V as the same as that in [19]. For L, we found that 3 levels are enough to assure a fitting good enough for normal estimation.

With the generated surface, a reasonable sample position is selected then to evaluate the representative normal. The selecting process is based on the observation that the triangle with the largest area usually is with the most significant influence among the triangle set.

Once the largest primitive P is found by iterating T_h, its barycenter p is used as the sample position. A parallel projection method [13] is used to project p onto Ω to calculate the parameters (u_p, v_p), which are used to evaluate the corresponding normal on the B-spline surface as the representative normal.

However, both normal vectors pointing at opposite directions of the surface are needed to recover detail for the case of thin plate, while the generated representative normal always assumes the positive direction of $axis_{major}$ as default. To solve the problem, instead of defining an accurate normal direction during construction, a render-time heuristics is employed to calculate adaptively a proper version of representative normal by applying a dot product test on the GPU during rendering phase:

$$\hat{n}_{proper} = \begin{cases} \hat{n}_d \text{ if } \hat{n}_d \cdot \hat{n}_l > 0 \\ -\hat{n}_d, \text{ otherwise}, \end{cases} \tag{3}$$

where $\hat{n}_l$, which can be retrieved easily from the vertex shader during rendering, is the normal from M_l, $\hat{n}_d$ is the default normal stored in the texture. This efficient dot product test is applied to all the nodes, for it does not affect the correctness of recovering detail and makes the code more unified.

Figure 3 shows our synthesized result for a scene mesh containing a plate by the proposed sampling method enhanced with a B-spline surface filtering.

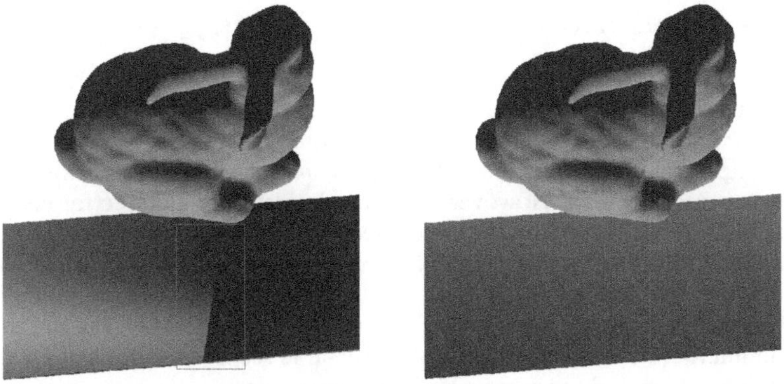

Fig. 3. The synthesized images for a scene consisting of a Bunny and a plate. The area in rectangle of the left image highlights the incorrect rendering on the plate, which is resulted from the normal map generated by just the classical averaging method, while the employment of B-spline surface fitting based method removes the problem.

3.3 Texture Encoding

The generated hierarchical octree needs to be encoded generally into a plain 2D texture due to the lack of flexibility of memory structure in GPU shader. Lacoste et al. [1] proposed an efficient encoding scheme (Figure 4), in which a BFS traversal is applied to pack the hierarchy and the representative normals are calculated by a ray-casting based method that requires searching the entire octree. Hence although it is not required for the final rendering, an entire intermediate octree has to be built first before encoding in their method, consuming vast memory storage which is needed usually for large scale scene mesh.

Internal Node

R	G	B	A	R	G	B	A
First Child Offset			Child Mask	Nx	Ny	Nz	Kind Mask

Leaf Node

R	G	B	A
Nx	Ny	Nz	Child Mask

Fig. 4. The encoding scheme of hierarchical octree in [1]. *First Child Offset* defines how far the parent node is from its first child in the texture, N_x, N_y *and* N_z define the representative normal. *Child Mask* identifies if the node has children and *Kind Mask* identifies the children as internal or leaf nodes if existing.

We adopt their encoding scheme in our method. However, since the calculation of representative normal in our method is localized into the surface patch belonging to the processing node, the advantage enable us to carry out the subdividing and encoding simultaneously in a single BFS construction pass. The intermediate octree nodes are released just after their information is packed into the 2D texture, saving the unnecessary storage for the whole octree. The representative normals of internal nodes, which are used when volumetric mipmapping or filtering is applied, are calculated by the method introduced in Section 3.2 if they are needed.

4 Exploiting Access Coherence in Filtering

The generated octree normal maps are uploaded onto GPU to recover geometric detail in render pass. In general, the filtering is applied to complete the final synthesization to improve overall rendering quality. The commonly used filtering algorithm is trilinear interpolation [21] that takes 8 samples around the current position and finds a weighted average of them. However, 8 traversal passes of an octree for each fragment could induce a significant drop in frame rate.

Since the 8 sampling points in trilinear interpolation are usually near to each other, which implies that all these samples share the same traversal path beginning from the root of octree to a certain internal node. Therefore, during sampling of the first sample point, an internal node *N* on the path of traversal is recorded as the common entrance node for the traversal of the remaining 7 sample points.

There are situations when one or more sample points lie outside the bounding box of N. In that case, the sampling is done in one of two ways depending on the distance of the sample point from the viewpoint. If the distance is larger than a pre-defined threshold η, the representative normal of the internal node *N* is used directly without further traversal. Although inaccurate, the rendering quality is acceptable since the distance is comparatively far. Additionally, it saves much traversal time.

When the viewpoint is close to the model, such inaccuracy is not longer acceptable. Instead, the outlying samples are re-traversed from the root to get the accurate values. However, doing so will significantly drop the performance. Therefore, to reduce the rate of sample points failing out of the bounding box of *N*, an entrance node with large bounding box is employed. We usually select the nodes on the level of half the maximum depth of the octree for *N*. If the traversal paths are shorter than that, the root node will be used instead.

5 Results

The described construction algorithm has been implemented on an Intel Core2 2.8GHz CPU with 3GB memory. The fragment shader is written in GLSL and run on an NVIDIA Geforce GTX260 graphics card with 896MB memory.

Various models with triangle counts from 1M to 10M with different topologies are tested. The quadratic error metrics approach proposed by Garland et al. [22] is used to generate the coarse meshes.

Our method is compared to Appearance Preserving Octree-textures (APO), which is a ray-casting based framework rendeing on GPU context. Due to the employment of the same texture encoding scheme, both methods run at the same speed during rendering pass while the quality is improved visibly in our method. Figure 5 shows the results.

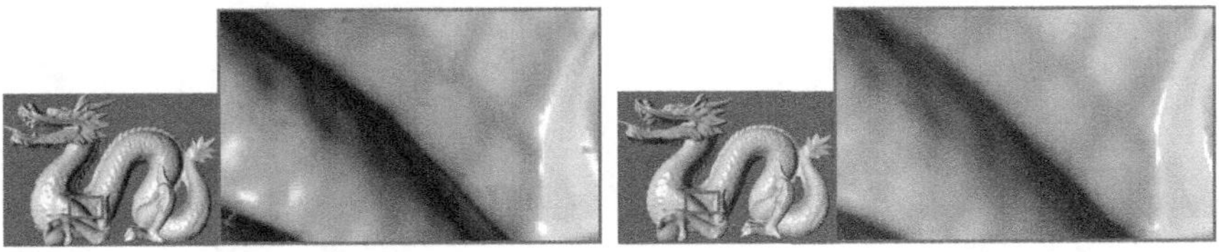

Fig. 5. The comparison of our approach with APO. There exist distinguishable artifacts when view-point is close to the model in APO while the image synthesized by our method is with good quality.

Figure 6 shows the synthesized images using our octree normal maps. Table 1 lists the parameters of tested models as well as the settings and construction time of the employed octree normal maps. The numbers of triangles in the simplified models have been drastically reduced to verify the effectiveness of our geometric detail recovering method. The total memory demand for resultant normal maps and simplified model is much less than that of original model while the quality of the synthesized image is comparable to the later thanks to the advantage of our method (see Figure 6). For the construction time, ours is slower than that of APO owing to the dynamic management of memory for octree nodes, while the memory demand for our building is low in turn since those nodes that are already packed into texture are released instantly.

The speed gain of the access coherence based filtering scheme is illustrated in Figure 7.

Table 1. The data of tested models and octree normal maps. *hiNum*, *hiSize*, *lowNum* and *lowSize* correspond to the number of triangles and storage size(MB) of M_h and M_l respectively, *maxD* and ε are the maximum depth of octree and the threshold defining the variant of normals in each leaf node, *mapSize* and *cTime* refer to storage size(MB) and construction time(Min) of our octree normal maps. All models are in *.ply* format except the dense version of *Neptune* and *Terrain*, for which *.off* is used..

Model	*hiNum*	*hiSize*	*lowNum*	*lowSize*	*maxD*	ε	*mapSize*	*cTime*
Neptune	4,007,872	161.13	10,000	0.317	10	0.01	6.66	18.12
Statue	10,000,000	181.20	15,000	0.463	10	0.25	9.07	36.29
Terrain	4,580,543	151.21	10,000	0.328	11	0.05	10.32	13.09

6 Conclusion and Future Work

The paper presents a new method for recovering geometric detail to synthesize good quality images for models with extremely high number of polygons. A variant of loose octree scheme is applied to optimally capture geometric detail. The classical averaging method enhanced with a B-spline surface filtering is employed to sample the mesh normals, solving the problem of thin plate. The memory saving scheme with BFS order enable the construction of octree normal maps for large scale scene geometry. An access coherence based fast filtering method is proposed to improve performance.

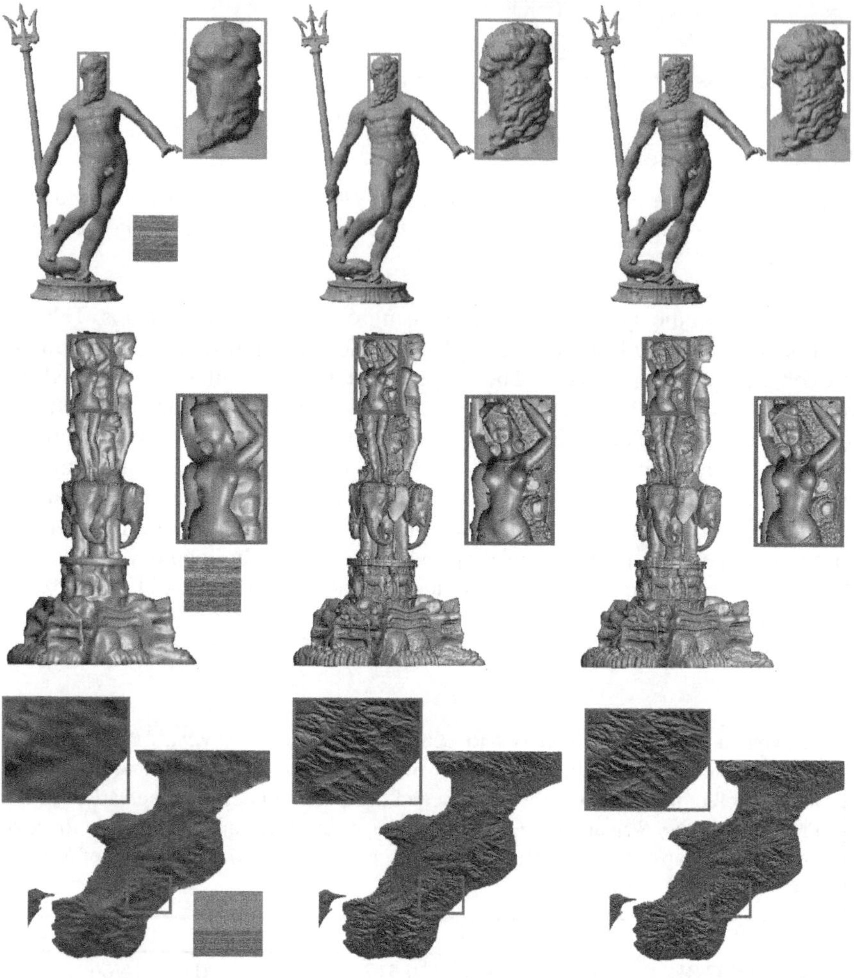

Fig. 6. Our synthesized images, *Neptune* (top row), *Statue* (middle row) and *Terrain* (bottom row). The left columns show the coarse meshes and the normal textures, the center column shows the synthesized images and the right column shows the original models. The frame rates for rendering the original dense *Neptune*, *Statue* and *Terrain* models are 7, 3 and 8 respectively, while our method archives 30, 28 and 31.3 FPS under the same viewpoint with much less memory usage. The window size is 1024*768 pixels.

With the characteristics of having good rendering quality, high frame rate and low storage demand, the proposed technique is suitable for quick view in real-time large scale models, which are required in plenty of applications. The method is also suitable for copyright-protected models. Since only the coarse models and the encoded normal maps are needed, the data of the original models can be protected.

The proposed method assumes that the coarse mesh closely approximate to its dense counterpart. However, if both meshes differ too much, our method may collapse at some point although so far we have not come across this case even when the models are simplified for several hundred times(667 times for Statue model).

Another limitation is from the practical maximum octree depth. It is possible in theory that there exist some nodes that contain extremely complex triangles set, where a single representative normal would be insufficient to represent the detail. The proposed method has the potential to solve this problem by applying a representative B-spline surface patch in each leaf node and it is what we want to try next.

Indirect access of octree on GPU considerably decreases performance. Therefore we are interested in porting our idea to the domain of perfect spatial hashing [23]. Accelerating the construction of our octree normal maps by some parallel scheme [24] is our next work as well.

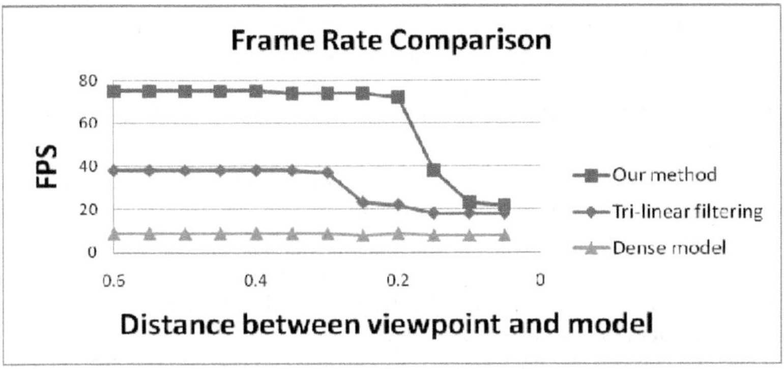

Fig. 7. Using *Neptune* model as an example, the performance of tri-linear filtering and our method is compared. The frame rates are recorded with a viewpoint moving slowly towards the model. The maximum extent of *Neptune* model is normalized to 1 and η is set to 0.5 in the test. The window size is 1024*768 pixels.

Acknowledgments. We thank Julien Lacoste for fruitful discussions on this subject and generously sharing the shader of APO. The Bunny, Dragon and Statue models are downloaded from Stanford 3D Scanning Repository. The Neptune and Terrain models are downloaded from AIM@SHAPE Shape Repository. The research was supported by Chinese 973 Program (2010CB328001), the National Science Foundation of China (61035002, 61003096) and the NSFC-JST Key Joint Funding Project (51021140004).

References

1. Lacoste, J., Boubekeur, T., Jobard, B., Schlick, C.: Appearance preserving octree-textures. In: Proceedings of the 5th International Conference on Computer Graphics and Interactive Techniques in Australia and Southeast Asia, pp. 87–93. ACM, New York (2007)

2. Benson, D., Davis, J.: Octree textures. In: Proceedings of ACM SIGGRAPH 2002, pp. 785–790. ACM, New York (2002)
3. DeBry, D., Gibbs, J., Petty, D.D., Robins, N.: Painting and rendering textures on unparameterized models. In: Proceedings of ACM SIGGRAPH 2002, pp. 763–768. ACM, New York (2002)
4. Hormann, K., Levy, B., Sheffer, A.: Mesh parameterization: theory and practice. In: Proceedings of ACM SIGGRAPH ASIA 2008 Courses, pp. 1–87. ACM, New York (2008)
5. Krishnamurthy, V., Levoy, M.: Fitting smooth surfaces to dense polygon meshes. In: Proceedings of the 23rd Annual Conference on Computer Graphics and Interactive Techniques, pp. 313–324. ACM, New York (1996)
6. Cohen, J., Olano, M., Manocha, D.: Appearance-preserving simplification. In: Proceedings of the 25th Annual Conference on Computer Graphics and Interactive Techniques, pp. 115–122. ACM, New York (1998)
7. Cignoni, P., Montani, C., Scopigno, R., Rocchini, C.: A general method for preserving attribute values on simplified meshes. In: Proceedings of the Conference on Visualization 1998, pp. 59–66. IEEE Computer Society Press, Los Alamitos (1998)
8. Cignoni, P., Montani, C., Rocchini, C., Scopigno, R., Tarini, M.: Preserving attribute values on simplified meshes by resampling detail textures. The Visual Computer 15, 519–539 (1999)
9. Sander, P.V., Gu, X.F., Gortler, S.J., Hoppe, H., Snyder, J.: Silhouette clipping. In: Proceedings of the 27th Annual Conference on Computer Graphics and Interactive Techniques, pp. 327–334. ACM, New York (2000)
10. Tarini, M., Cignoni, P., Scopigno, R.: Visibility based methods and assessment for detail-recovery. In: Proceedings of the 14th IEEE Visualization 2003 (VIS 2003), pp. 60–67. IEEE Computer Society, Washington, DC (2003)
11. Lefohn, A.E., Sengupta, S., Kniss, J., Strzodka, R., Owens, J.D.: Glift: Generic, efficient, random-access GPU data structures. ACM Transactions on Graphics 25, 60–99 (2006)
12. Lefebvre, S., Hornus, S., Neyret, F.: Octree textures on the GPU. In: Pharr, M. (ed.) GPU Gems 2, pp. 595–613. Addison-Wesley (2005)
13. Lefebvre, S., Dachsbacher, C.: TileTrees. In: Proceedings of the 2007 Symposium on Interactive 3D Graphics and Games, pp. 25–31. ACM, New York (2007)
14. Boubekeur, T., Heidrich, W., Granier, X., Schlick, C.: Volume-Surface Trees. Computer Graphics Forum 25, 399–406 (2006)
15. Cohen-Steiner, D., Alliez, P., Desbrun, M.: Variational shape approximation. In: Proceedings of ACM SIGGRAPH 2004, pp. 905–914. ACM, New York (2004)
16. Ulrich, T.: Loose octrees. In: DeLoura, M. (ed.) Game Programming Gems, pp. 444–453. Charles River Media, Rockland (2000)
17. Dierckx, P.J.: Curve and surface fitting with splines. Oxford University Press, New York (1993)
18. Lee, S., Wolberg, G., Shin, S.Y.: Scattered Data Interpolation with Multilevel B-Splines. IEEE Transactions on Visualization and Computer Graphics 3, 228–244 (1997)
19. Hjelle, Φ.: Approximation of scattered data with multilevel B-splines. Technical Report, SINTEF Applied Mathematics, Oslo (2001)
20. Flory, S.: Fitting curves and surfaces to point clouds in the presence of obstacles. Computer Aided Geometric Design 26, 192–202 (2009)

21. Trilinear interpolation,
http://en.wikipedia.org/wiki/Trilinear_interpolation
22. Garland, M., Heckbert, P.S.: Surface simplification using quadric error metrics. In: Proceedings of the 24th Annual Conference on Computer Graphics and Interactive Techniques, pp. 209–216. ACM, New York (1997)
23. Lefebvre, S., Hoppe, H.: Perfect spatial hashing. In: Proceedings of ACM SIGGRAPH 2006, pp. 579–588. ACM, New York (2006)
24. Sundar, H., Sampath, R.S., Biros, G.: Bottom Up Construction and 2:1 Balance Refinement of Linear Octrees in Parallel. SIAM Journal on Scientific Computing 30, 2675–2708 (2008)

Quad-Tree Atlas Ray Casting: A GPU Based Framework for Terrain Visualization and Its Applications

Jianxin Luo, Guiqiang Ni, Ping Cui, Jinsong Jiang, Yifeng Duan, and Guyu Hu

LMNT, Institute of Command Automation, PLA University of Science & Technology, Jiangsu, Nanjing, 210007, China
luojiaxin555@yahoo.com, ngq1966@163.com, acp420683@126.com

Abstract. We propose a novel framework for terrain visualization (We call it Quad-tree atlas ray casting). The main ideal of our framework is to lay the height field textures and the color textures of all visible terrain tiles in a big texture respectively, then use the single big height field texture and the single big color texture to perform ray casting to get the final image. The framework is very simple, but it is advantaged in many aspects, e.g., steady frame rate, effortless levels of detail, efficient out of core, easy vector data rendering and high image quality with screen space error below one.

Keywords: terrain, ray casting, visualization, rendering, level of detail.

1 Introduction

Real-time interactive terrain visualization has a wide application in video games, movie industry, virtual battlefields and Geographic Information Systems. But there is a challenging problem: the size of current datasets easily exceeds the capability of current hardware. Many researchers have attacked this problem and put forward various theories and algorithms. These methods can be categorized into two classes: ray-casting based approaches and rasterization-based approaches. In this paper, we focus on real-time rendering framework of terrain height-fields by ray casting.

Methods based on rasterization construct triangle meshes from elevation maps, using some error criteria to simplify the triangle meshes, and then send the simplified geometric data to graphic hardware for rasterization. These methods can be categorized into static-lod (level of detail) based techniques (e.g. Losasso and Hoppe[1]) and dynamic multi-resolution techniques (e.g. Lindstrom et al.[2];Pajarola[3]; Duchaineau et al.[4]). These methods achieve fast rendering rates and high image quality by using state-of-the-art graphics hardware and level-of-detail techniques.

Methods based on ray casting achieve terrain visualization by casting rays from view point, and then traversing the terrain height field to generate images.

Z. Pan et al. (Eds.): Transactions on Edutainment VII, LNCS 7145, pp. 74–85, 2012.

These methods can be categorized into incremental methods (e.g. Qu[5]; Dick et al.[6]) and hierarchical methods (e.g. Oh et al.[7]; Tevs[8]). The incremental methods trace rays in steps along intersections between rays and height field cell walls (i.e. vertical planes containing rows or columns of height field samples). Hierarchical methods are multi-resolution generalizations of incremental methods.

We present a novel framework for terrain visualization (We call it Quad-tree atlas ray casting). Our method provides a number of advantages over previous terrain rendering methods:

· **Simplicity.** Our ray casting method is a fixed incremental method, it's very easy to implement.

· **Efficiency.** Highly optimized texture and heightfield updating method makes the framework have a high efficiency.

· **Visual continuity.** Different level terrain tiles are seamlessly laid in a big atlas, there is no visual discontinuity.

· **Steady frame rates.** Terrain tiles are incrementally updated in the atlases, there is no big cost of CPU-GPU communication.

· **Efficient out of core.** Terrain tiles are culled before loading to GPU, only visible terrain tiles are rendered.

· **Effortless levels of detail.** Terrain tiles can adapt to match view point in the atlases.

· **Easy vector data rendering.** Vector data can be shown by directly drawing it on texture atlas, it is especially suitable for dynamic vector data rendering.

· **Unconstrained datasource.** The previous methods require that each tile consists of a heightfield texture and an orthographic color texture. Because the texture atlas and heightfield atlas are updated independently, we get rid of this limitation.

· **High precision.** Tiles are selected in a separated IO thread with screen error below one, ray casting technique can assure screen error below one rendering.

Besides, some disciplines or applications (e.g. GIS and military engineering) need to show accurate information on terrain. These applications require special terrain techniques to solve the difficulties. This paper also shows some applications of our algorithm ,including dynamic vector data rendering, valley detection and contour line drawing (Figure 10 shows the results). Our main contributions can be listed as:

1. An efficient texture and heightfield data updating method. (Section 3.1)
2. A fast incremental ray/heightfield intersection algorithm. (Section 3.2)
3. A novel GPU based ray casting framework for terrain virsualization. (Section 3)

Next section, we discuss the previous works. In section 3, we present the basic pipeline and the key algorithms in our terrain visualization framework. Some experiments and their results are shown in Section 4. Finally, we conclude with a discussion of our results and possible extensions in Section 5.

2 Previous Work

Early in the 70s and 80s of last century, there were research was conducted on ray casting for height field (e.g. Dungan[9]; Kajiya[10]; Musgrave[11]). These methods are constrained by the capability of hardware at that time; all of them are not suitable for real-time applications. By the end half of 90s, along with a series of highly efficient rasterization-based approaches appeared (e.g. Lindstrom et al.[2]; Duchaineau et al.[4]; Pajarola[3]; Hoppe[12]), researches on ray-casting based approaches decreased.

Along with the impressive improvements in graphics hardware both in terms of computation and communication speed, ray-casting based methods became a hot point in real-time computer graphics. Qu et al.[5] presented a GPU based ray-casting system for elevation data. Henning and Stephenson[13] used the run-length of the discrete lines to intersect larger bounding volumes with the height field data. Policarpo and Oliveira[14] used uniform stepping combined with binary search. Tatarchuk[15] referred the height profile for ray casting. But, these methods only use a fixed step size to trace over the height-field and thus may miss fine structures, producing only approximate results. To improve the approximation, Newton iterations were used on the GPU (e.g. Ohbuchi[16]) or the secant method was used (e.g. Risser et al.[17];) or in combination with precomputed self-occlusion information (e.g. Jeschke et al.[18]). To utilize both the GPU as well as the CPU power Balciunas et al.[19] presented a hybrid model method. In addition, Dick et al.[6] proposed an incremental approach by performing the ray trace in the local texel-space.

At the same time, the rasterization-based approaches have also advanced by using the GPU capability. Cignoni et al.[20] generalized the caching approach by combining regular and irregular triangulations on GPU. Losasso and Hoppe[1] proposed the geometry clipmap, which cached in video memory nested regular grids to create view-dependent approximations. Livny et al.[21] used the GPU-based projected grid to generate the continuous level of detail. Bruneton et al.[22] focused on real-time vector data edit and visualization. Dick et al.[23] proposed a highly optimized geometry compression method on GPU to reduce the bandwidth requirement in the rendering of large DEMs that have to be paged from disk.

The most recent published techniques for terrain visualization focus on hybrid techniques of rasterization and ray-casting , e.g., Lucas et al.[24]; Dick et al.[25], they both combine the rasterization and ray-casting for rendering, our framework belongs to this scope, but, different from their work, we only use ray-casting for rendering, rasterization in our framework is a speed up strategy. The ray casting part of our framework use a fix step size which similar to Policarpo [14] and Tatarchuk[15], but our method can provide accurate results.

3 Quad-Tree Atlas Ray Casting

Our system uses a tiled-based multiresolution to represent the terrain model and uses the quad tree structure to manage it. The basic pipeline of our quad-tree atlas ray casting framework is:(**Algorithm** 1)

1. Use atlas camera to render height field textures of all visible quad-tree nodes to get heightfield atlas, Section 3.1 gives the details.
2. Use the atlas camera to render color textures of all visible quad-tree nodes to get color texture atlas, Section 3.1 gives the details.
3. Cast rays from view point, transform the rays to atlas space, traverse the heightfield atlas to find a heightfield/ray intersections and fetch color from the color texture atlas. (details in Section 3.2).

For simplicity, we abbreviate the quad-tree atlas ray casting rendering framework to QTA.

3.1 Screen Space View Dependent Quad-tree Atlas

NVIDIA[26] described a technique for reducing batches caused by having to repeatedly bind different textures. Livny et al.[21] also used the technique, and they laid all clipmaps on a texture atlas. Niski et al.[27] and Döller et al.[28] introduced the tree structure to manage atlas, our atlas technique also use a tree structure, but our atlas has a view dependent layout, it is created wholly on GPU and it is fast and well suitable for real time rendering. The right part of Figure 1 shows the layout of our view dependent quad-tree atlas.

Quad tree atlas is generated by rendering all visible terrain tiles into screen space of atlas camera. But, what is the atlas camera? Figure 1 shows the locations of atlas camera and perspective camera. Atlas camera is an orthographic camera which face vertically down to the XY plane(ground), that means the view direction of atlas camera is the negative direction of z axis. The up vector of atlas camera is the horizontal component of the view direction of perspective camera. Why we take the horizontal component of the view direction as the up vector of atlas camera? Because, as shown in Figure 1, we must keep levels in the atlas increased from bottom to top, this can ensure that different levels are of the same size in screen space of perspective camera. Besides, we need to know

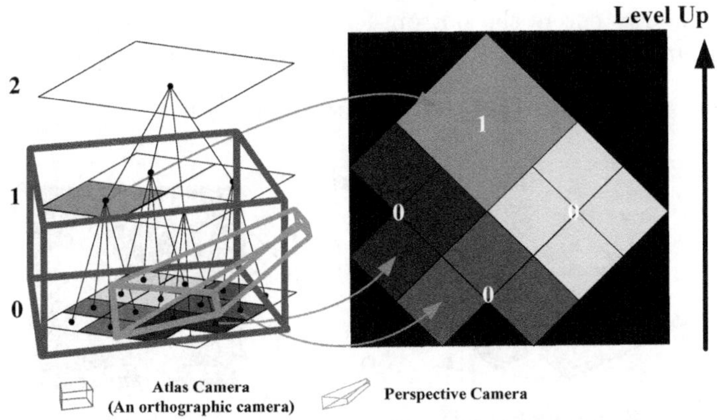

Fig. 1. Left: Locations of quad-tree, perspective camera and atlas camera. **Right**: the layout of quad-tree atlas.

how large area the atlas camera can see. As shown in the figure, we first cull the quad-tree nodes using perspective camera(green box), then, calculate the minimum bounding box(red box) that covers all the visible quad-tree nodes and take the bounding box as the perspective area of atlas camera.

In order to improve the precision and efficiency, we employ a series mipmap render targets to store atlases. In our implementation, we use three level atlases, the sizes are 2048×2048, 1024×1024 and 512×512 respectively. For each frame, we calculate the size of atlas and choose the closest render target. For example, if the size of atlas is 1000×600, we use the 1024×1024 render target, if the size is 1000×1500, we use the 2048×2048 render target.

3.2 Classification-Based Ray Casting Algorithm

After first two steps were done in algorithm 1, all needed texture and heightfield data are loaded in atlases. The work left is to visualize the data in the atlases, this section discuss the method.

As shown in Figure 2, O is view position, OE is one of the rays which are casted from view position O, E is on the ground plane, I is the first intersection of OE and heightfield. For the given ray OE, we need to find the intersection I. The fist step is to transform ray OE into atlas space, the process is: remove the vertical component of O to get O', then, calculate the intersection point S of $O'E$ and atlas frustum. The second step is to traverse height field cells to find the intersection point I. Before we discuss the traversing method, we first give some definitions. In the following discussion, we assume that X coordinate is the column cell(pixel) number in atlas space and Y coordinate is row cell(pixel) number in atlas space.

The classification of ray/heightfield intersection: Figure 3 shows the classification of intersections of a ray and four neighboring height field cells (pixels in atlas). It can be categorized into four classes by assuming slope is not bigger than 1 and the cell which ray enter is the bottom-left cell of four neighboring cells. We use mathematic language to describe the four classes:

Class A: The ray enters the bottom-left cell, travels through the top-left cell, and exits from the top-right cell. The math description is given by equation 1.

$$\lfloor y_{n+1} \rfloor = \lfloor y_{n+2} \rfloor = \lfloor y_n \rfloor + 1 \tag{1}$$

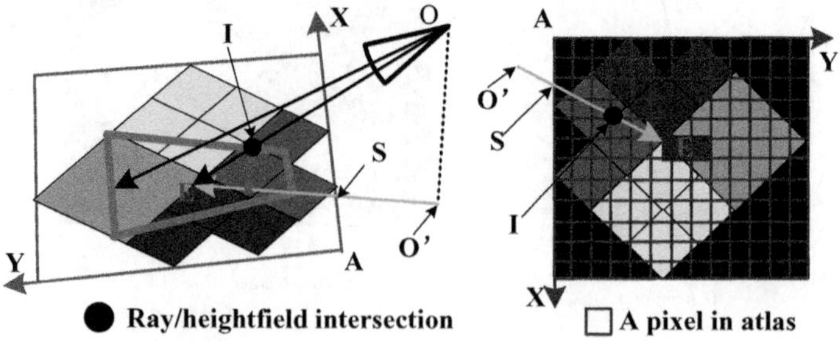

Fig. 2. Transform ray to atlas spaces

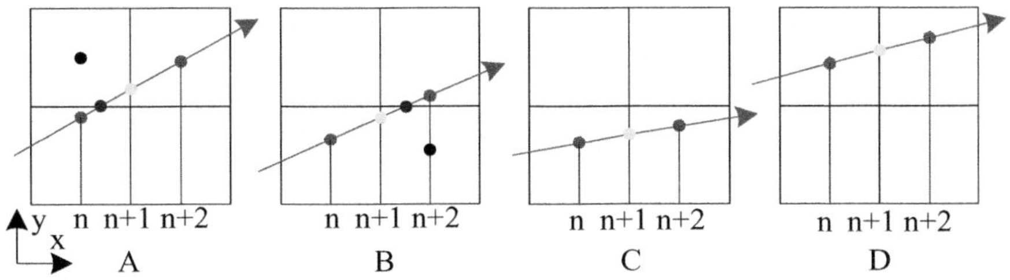

Fig. 3. By assuming slope is not bigger than 1, ray/heightfield intersections can be categorized into four types: **A, B, C** and **D**

Class B: The ray enters the bottom-left cell, travels through the bottom-right cell, and exits from the top-right cell. The math description is given by equation 2.

$$\lfloor y_{n+1} \rfloor = \lfloor y_n \rfloor = \lfloor y_{n+2} \rfloor - 1 \tag{2}$$

Class C: The ray exits from the bottom-right cell.
Class D: The ray enters the top-left cell (this situation is the same as **Class C**, since we can get rid of the bottom two cells and take the two cells above the ray into consideration). Class CD is described by equation 3.

$$\lfloor y_{n+1} \rfloor = \lfloor y_n \rfloor = \lfloor y_{n+2} \rfloor \tag{3}$$

Because the slope is not bigger than 1, the ray will not exit from the top-left cell. When the slope is bigger than 1, switching X and Y will get the same classification.

Calculation of the step number: We first project the ray on to X axis and Y axis to determine cell number $IterX$ in X direction and cell number $IterY$ in Y direction. Then the minimum step number is calculated by equation 4.

$$IterNum = Max(IterX, IterY) \tag{4}$$

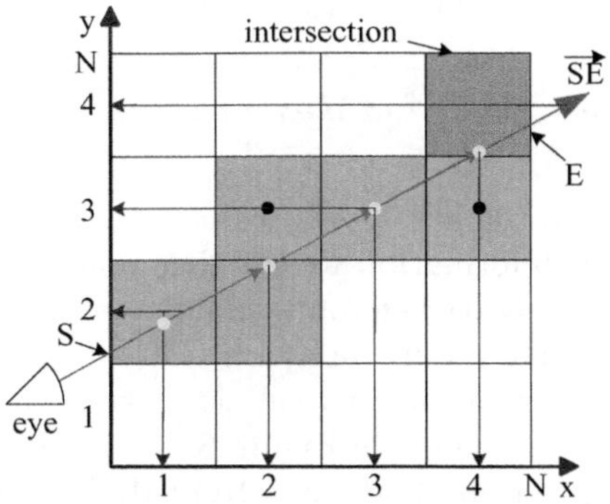

Fig. 4. Calculation of step number. The **black** points are the extra test positions.

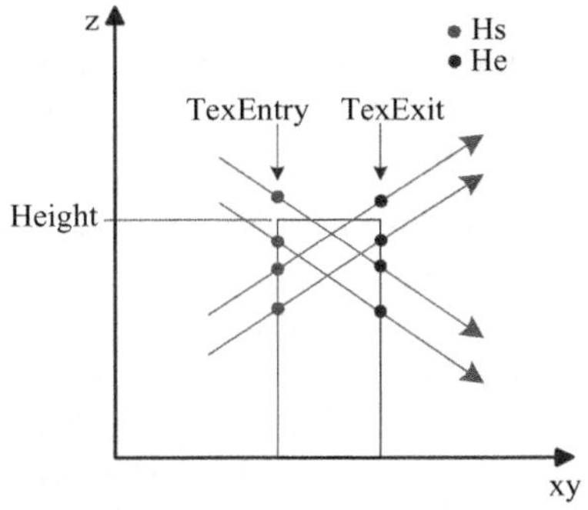

Fig. 5. Determination of intersection

Figure 4 shows a 4×4 atlas, where, $IterX = 4$ (the ray across four columns in X direction) and $IterY = 4\text{-}1{=}3$ (the ray across three rows in Y direction). So $IterNum = Max(IterX, IterY) = 4$. It is easy to see many test cells on the path where the ray travels will be lost, the cells contain a black point give some examples. We solve this problem by using the classifications determined by equation 1, 2 and 3 (see **Algorithm** 2 for details).

Determination of intersection: The intersection test is illustrated in Figure 5. Let $Height$ denote the height value of the current height field cell, Hs denotes the height of ray at TexEntry, and He denotes the height of ray at TexExit. We determine the intersection by using equation 5.

$$Hs \leq Height \quad \textbf{Or} \quad He \leq Height \tag{5}$$

Classification-based Ray Casting Algorithm **(CRC)**: Our algorithm implements in the fragment shader on GPU. We have discussed the key points of our ray casting algorithm, now, let us integrate them:(**Algorithm** 2)

1. Transform the ray into atlas space.
2. Compute the start cell coordinate S (Figure 4) in current quad-tree atlas; compute the end cell coordinate E in current quad-tree atlas.
3. Project the ray $\boldsymbol{SE}$ on to X axis and Y axis, which is shown in Figure 4, compute the minimum step number $IterNum$ using equation 4.
4. Compute y_n at current step position and y_{n+2} at next step position (red points in Figure 3); compute the middle position y_{n+1} (yellow points in Figure 3). Use equation 1, 2 and 3 to determine the class of the intersection. If the class is A or B, test the current cell for intersection, and test the extra cell, i.e., the cell that holds a black point in Figure 3 and Figure 4. If the class is C or D, we only need test the current cell for intersection. If an intersection is detected, break, the program is over, else, go to 5.Intersection is determined by Equation 5.
5. If $IterNum = 0$, break,
   else,$IterNum = IterNum - 1$, go to 4.

Thanks to the classification of ray/heightfiled intersection, our algorithm skips many unnecessary test cells, it has a fixed incremental value in the iteration and only need one conditional branch to determine the intersection, it is very fast.

3.3 GPU Vertex Displacement Coarse Mesh for Ray Casting Acceleration

Balciunas et al.[19] presented a method that, in the first pass, rasterizes a coarse mesh of terrain on GPU and uses the depth information as starting point for CPU-based ray-casting. Thanks to GPU vertex texture fetch technique and our quad-tree atlas technique, we generate the coarse mesh wholly on GPU. Unlike Balciunas et al.[19], we do not use the depth information, instead, we directly use the coarse mesh as the start positions of rays (red points in Figure 6).The coarse mesh can be generated by any rasterization based methods (e.g. ROAM[4]), but the simpler the better. In our implementation, a 128×128 uniform mesh which covers the whole visible terrain is used.

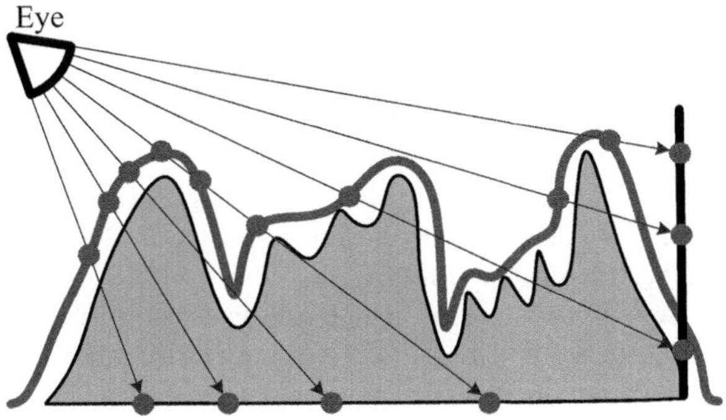

Fig. 6. Red line: the coarse mesh covers the entire terrain, it is the start points of rays

4 Experiments and Results

Our experiments were completed on a personal computer with an AMD Athlon™ 64 3200+ processor, 1GB memory. We use two graphics cards for testing, one is a Nvidia Geforce 8600 GT graphics card with 512MB texture memory, the other is a Nvidia Geforce GTX 260 graphics card with 1GB texture memory.

We have experimented with two data sets. One is Puget Sound $16K \times 16K$ data set, the other is world wind cached packs which is downloaded from , we use the SRTM (Shuttle Radar Topography Mission) heightfield data, BMNG (Blue Marble Next Generation) texture data and NLT Landsat7 (Visible Color) texture data as our second data set, the data size is about 9GB. Terrain tiles were selected in a separate I/O thread using the screen space error metric proposed by Cohen[29], the screen space error was set to 2/3 pixels. The view port was 1920×1080. The results of the second data set are listed in table 1. Our first experiment is to validate the framework of QTA, Image a) in Figure 10 shows a snapshot.

By comparison, Dick et al.[25] report an average frame rate of 60 frames/sec on NVIDIA Geforce GTX 280 card, Lucas et al.[24] report 43 frames/sec on the same card. As shown in Table 1, our QTA framework get a little fast rendering rate (63 frames/sec). Since most of the recent papers about terrain rendering have a high rendering rate, all of them are good for realtime rendering, we don't compare more about the rendering performance. Our framework can provide more efficient rendering in some applications, we focus our discussion on them below.

The QTA framework is significantly well for dynamic vector data edit and rending, the only thing to do is render the vector data in the pass of texture atlas updating (step 2 in **Algorithm** 1). Image b) in Figure 10 shows an example. It's a $230M\Delta$ polygons and 10M lines vector data.

The most recent and important work about dynamic vector data is presented by Bruneton [22], we implement their algorithm, and find that their dynamic vector data edit and rendering method have two limitations: 1) As shown in Figure 7), when rendering a text label which is wider than the quad-tree node, an error occurs (left), and our framework has no this limitation (right). 2) Bruneton

[22]'s algorithm perform well when editing vector data, but, not very well for rendering. Especially, when dynamic vector data is covering a large number of terrain tiles, lots of appearance textures in their algorithm need to be recreated, this leads to a huge cost, their algorithm sharply down to a very low performance. But, our algorithm draws dynamic vector data directly on texture atlas, there is no large data updating and no big performance loss, we have a constant frame rate. Figure 8 shows the comparison, the horizontal axis is the number of terrain tiles that dynamic vector data is moving on.

Terrain detection is an application which analyzes the terrain data and detects the relative terrain e.g. valley, peak, lake or river. In military engineering, in order to select the proper positions to construct the military buildings, it needs to detect the lowest part of terrain, that is, the valley floor. To our knowledge, no published techniques could achieve it in real time. The final experiment is about valley detection, our framework can directly implement valley(or peak) detection by scaling the height of coarse mesh, Image c) in Figure 10 shows an example result. The attached materials give you more details about the implementation.

For a given height field data, accurate rendering of contour lines is also a problem. Kriging methods are the most popular techniques to interpolate the value of height field in geostatistics [30]. Visualization of the results of kriging methods is usually based on polygon meshes, when drawing the contour line, the shaded polygon meshes introduce unwanted artefacts (left part of Figure 9). Our framework is significantly well for such an application. By combining the kriging methods with our ray casting framework(see attached materials for details), drawing of contour line avoids the artefacts (right part of Figure 9).

The attached materials give you more discussion and details, cg source codes of CRC are also provided for you.

5 Conclusion and Future Work

In this paper, we have proposed some new algorithms (quad tree atlas, CRC) and have implemented a novel framework for terrain visualization. Our framework provides some new features over previous framework, e.g, easy and efficient dynamic vector data, real time valley detection and accurate contour line drawing. However, there is still more work to do, including in these areas:

1. The quad-tree atlas would also make the rasterization based methods support dynamic vector data rendering. The method is: project the terrain mesh to atlas space using the atlas camera, calculate texture coordinates of mesh in atlas space and take the atlas as the texture input of terrain mesh. We will do extra experiments to validate this.
2. The scope of the ray casting is limited to problems involving surfaces that are functions z of two variables x and y. It is not easy to achieve spherical terrain visualization. So we will try to extend this to a spherical terrain.
3. We have also developed some techniques for true 3D terrain visualization (true 3D terrain visualization means the visualization shows the information underground, not only the surface of terrain, that is 2.5D). However, this area requires further work.

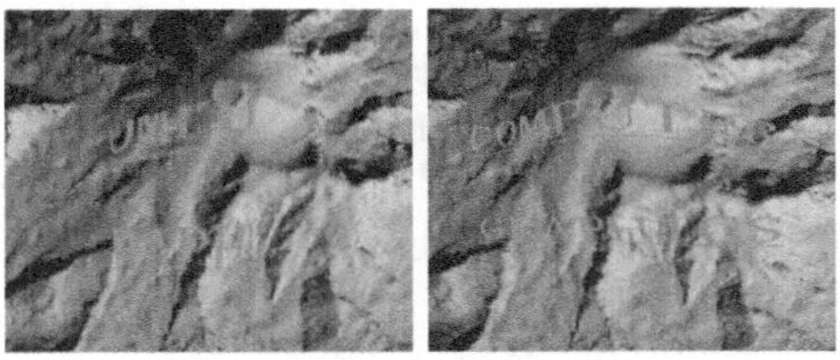

Fig. 7. Left: Bruneton [22]. Right: Our QTA.

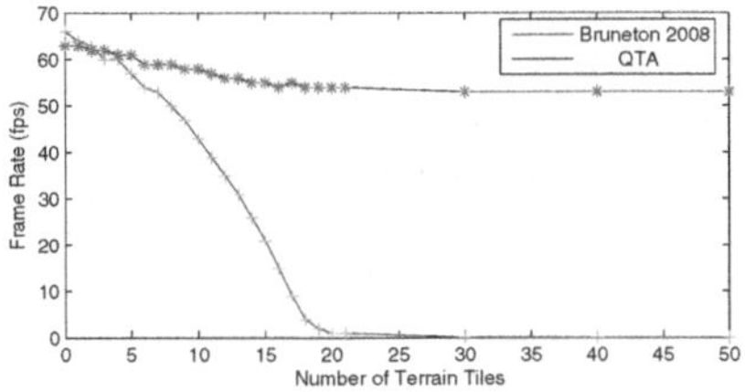

Fig. 8. Performance comparison on GTX 260 card

Fig. 9. Left: contour line drawing by polygon meshes. Right: contour line drawing by ray casting.

Table 1. Lists of the average frame rate on different graphics cards

Experiment Item	AMD Athlon™ 3200+	
	8600 GT	GTX 260
QTA	30fps	63fps
Vector Data	26fps	53fps
Valley detection	35fps	72fps
Contour line	31fps	63fps

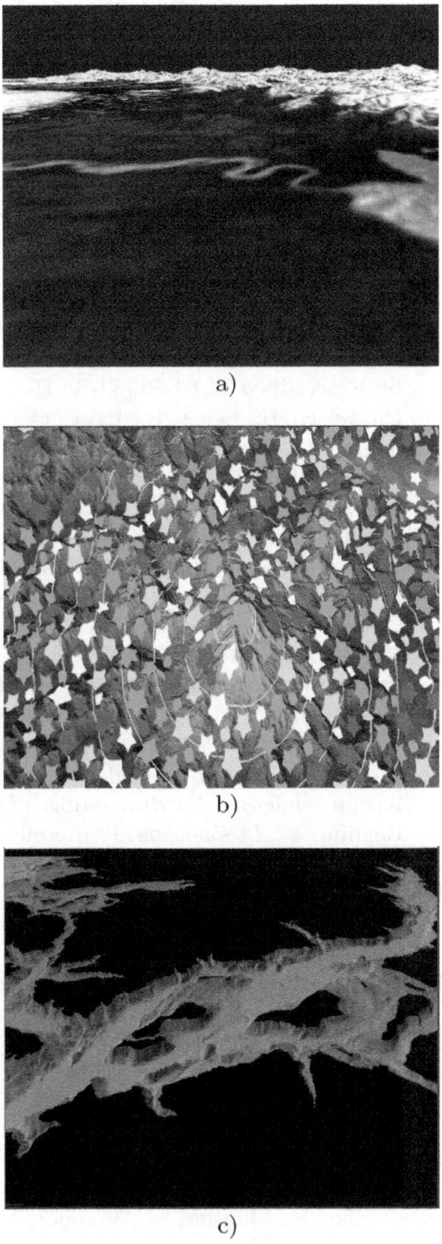

Fig. 10. Scenes rendered using our ray casting system

References

1. Losasso, F., Hoppe, H.: Geometry clipmaps: Terrain rendering using nested regular grids. In: Proceedings of ACM SIGGRAPH, pp. 769–776 (2004)
2. Lindstrom, P., Koller, D., Ribarsky, W., Hodges, L.F., Faust, N., Turner, G.A.: Real-time, continuous level of detail rendering of height fields. In: Proceedings of ACM SIGGRAPH, pp. 109–118 (1996)
3. Pajarola, R.: Large scale terrain visualization using the restricted quadtree triangulation. In: Proceedings of IEEE Visualization, pp. 19–26 (1998)
4. Duchaineau, M., Wolinsky, M., Sigeti, D.E., Miller, M.C., Aldrich, C., Mineev-weinstein, M.B.: ROAMing terrain: Real-time optimally adapting meshes. In: Proceedings of IEEE Visualization, pp. 81–88 (1997)
5. Qu, H., Qiu, F., Zhang, N., Kaufman, A., Wan, M.: Raytracing heigh fields. In: Proceedings of Computer Graphics International (2003)
6. Dick, C., Krüge, J., Westerman, R.: GPU ray-casting for scalable terrain rendering. In: Proceedings of EUROGRAPHICS, Areas Paper (2009)
7. Oh, K., Ki, H., Lee, C.H.: Pyramidal displacement mapping: A gpu based artifacts-free ray tracing through an image pyramid. In: Proceedings of ACM Symposium on Virtual Reality Software and Technology, pp. 75–82 (2006)
8. Tevs, A., Ihrke, I., Seidel, H.P.: Maximum mipmaps for fast, accurate, and scalable dynamic height field rendering. In: Proceedings of ACM Symposium on Interactive 3D Graphics and Games, pp. 183–190 (2008)
9. Dungan Jr., W.: A terrain and cloud computer image generation model. Computer Graphics 13(2), 143–150 (1979)
10. Kajiya, J.T.: New techniques for ray tracing procedurally defined objects. ACM Transactions on Graphics 2(3), 161–181 (1983)
11. Musgrave, K.: Grid tracing: Fast ray tracing for height fields. Technical report, Yale University, Department of Computer Science (1998)
12. Hoppe, H.: Smooth view-dependent level-of-detail control and its application to terrain rendering. In: Proceedings of IEEE Visualization, pp. 35–42 (1998)
13. Henning, C., Stephenson, P.: Accelerating the ray tracing of height fields. In: Proceedings of ACM GRAPHITE, pp. 254–288 (2004)
14. Policarpo, F., Oliveira, M.M.: Relief mapping of non-heightfield surface details. In: Proceedings of ACM SIGGRAPH 2005 Symposium on Interactive 3D Graphics and Games, pp. 55–62 (2006)
15. Tatarchuk, N.: Dynamic parallax occlusionmapping with approximate soft shadows. In: Proceedings of ACM Symposium on Interactive 3D Graphics and Games, pp. 63–69 (2006)
16. Ohbuchi, E.: A real-time refraction renderer for volume objects using a polygon-rendering scheme. In: Proceedings of Computer Graphics International, pp. 190–195 (2003)
17. Risser, E., Shan, M., Pattanaik, S.: Interval mapping. Technical report, University of Central Florida (2005)
18. Jeschke, S., Mantler, S., Wimmer, M.: Interactive smooth and curved shell mapping. In: Proceedings of Eurographics Symposium on Rendering, pp. 351–360 (2007)
19. Balciunas, D.A., Dulley, L.P., Zuffo, M.K.: GPU- assisted ray casting of large scenes. In: Proceedings of IEEE Symposium on Interactive Ray Tracing, vol. 31, pp. 95–103 (2006)

20. Cignoni, P., Ganovelli, F., Gobbetti, E., Marton, F., Ponchio, F., Scopigno, R.: BDAM - batched dynamic adaptive meshes for high performance terrain visualization. In: Proceedings of EUROGRAPHICS, pp. 505–514 (2003)
21. Livny, Y., Sokolovsky, N., Grinshpoun, T., El-sana, J.: Persistent grid mapping: A gpu-based framework for interactive terrain rendering. The Visual Computer (2007)
22. Bruneton, E., Neyret, F.: Real-time rendering and editing of vector-based terrains. In: Proceedings of EUROGRAPHICS, vol. 27, pp. 311–320 (2008)
23. Dick, C., Schneider, J., Westermann, R.: Efficient geometry compression for GPU-based decoding in realtime terrain rendering. Computer Graphics Forum 28(1), 67–83 (2009)
24. Ammann, L., Génevaux, O., Dischler, J.-M.: Hybrid rendering of dynamic heightfields using ray-casting and mesh rasterization. In: Proceedings of Graphics Interface 2010, pp. 161–168 (May 2010), http://lsiit-cnrs.unistra.fr/Publications/2010/AGD10
25. Dick, C., Krüger, J., Westermann, R.: GPU-aware hybrid terrain rendering. In: Proceedings of IADIS Computer Graphics, Visualization, Computer Vision and Image Processing 2010, pp. 3–10 (2010)
26. NVIDIA. Improve batching using texture atlases. SDK White Paper (2004)
27. Krzysztof, N., Budirijanto, P., Jonathan, C.: Multi-grained level of detail using a hierarchical seamless texture atlas. In: Proceedings of ACM Symposium on Interactive 3D Graphics and Games (2007)
28. Jürgen, D., Konstantin, B., Klaus, H.: Texturing techniques for terrain visualization. In: Proceedings of the 11th IEEE Visualization 2000 Conference (2000)
29. Cohen, D.: Appearance-Preserving Simplification of Polygonal Models. PhD thesis, University of North Carolina at Chapel Hill (1998)
30. WIKIPEDIA (2010), http://en.wikipedia.org/wiki/Kriging

Clustering Spatial Data for Aggregate Query Processing in Walkthrough: A Hypergraph Approach

Shao-Shin Hung[1], Chih Ming Chiu[2], Tsou Tsun Fu[3], Jung-Tsung Chen[4], Derchian Tsaih[5], and Jyh-Jong Tsay[2]

[1] Department of Computer Science and Information Engineering, WuFeng University, Taiwan
[2] Department of Computer Science and Information Engineering, National Chung Cheng University, Chiayi, Taiwan
[3] Department of Applied Digital Media, WuFeng University, Chiayi, Taiwan
[4] Department of Applied Game Technology, WuFeng University, Chiayi, Taiwan
[5] Department of Electronic Commerce Management, Nanhua University, Chiayi, Taiwan
hss@cs.ccu.edu.tw, zv@mail.stut.edu.tw, ttfu2004@gmail.com, jtchen@mail.wfu.edu.tw, dtsaih@mail.nhu.edu.tw, tsay@cs.ccu.edu.tw

Abstract. Nowadays, classical 3D object management systems use only direct visible properties and common features to model relationships between objects. In this paper we propose a new Object-oriented HyperGraph-based Clustering (OHGC) approach based on a behavioral walkthrough system that uses traversal patterns to model relationships between users and exploits semantic-based clustering techniques, such as association, intra-relationships, and inter-relationships, to explore additional links throughout the behavioral walkthrough system. The final aim consists in involving these new links in prediction generation, to improve performance of walkthrough system. OHGC is evaluated in terms of response time and number of retrieved objects on a real traversal dataset.

Keywords: walkthrough, data placement, hypergraph, prefetching, clustering.

1 Introduction

In the last decades, there is an increasing interest in developing techniques to deal with different 3D applications like MMOG models, 3D walkthrough. Many query processing techniques are proposed [1, 2, 3] to overcome the problems faced within the extensive scale of 3D applications. In WT, both the topological and geographical properties of the underlying network are important. The topological properties are usually represented as a finite collection of points, lines and surfaces. On the other side, efforts devoted for data layout on disks for efficient access have been proposed seldom. Especially, the layout can reflect semantic property is neglected and draw little attractions.

The remainder of this paper is organized as follows. Related works are discussed in Section 2. Section 3, describes the proposed hypergraph model and problem

Z. Pan et al. (Eds.): Transactions on Edutainment VII, LNCS 7145, pp. 86–98, 2012.

formulation. Section 4 and 5 explain the recommended clustering mechanism with illustrative examples. Section 6 then presents the experiment results. Conclusions are finally, drawn in Section 7, along with future research.

2 Related Works

In this subsection, we will briefly describe related works about virtual environments, sequential pattern mining and pattern clustering, respectively.

2.1 Prefetching and Caching Methods Based on Spatial Access Models

Most of the earlier researches have assumed that WT are memory resident. It is not until recently that managing large WT has become an active area [1, 2, 3]. Most of the works have adopted spatial indexes to organize, manipulate and retrieve the data in large WT.

The related work of prefetching and caching method involves in four aspects. First, *data-related*: it is concerned with the organization of objects, such as object partitioning, connectivity and block size. Like the level-of-detail (LOD) management [4, 11], hierarchical view-frustum and occlusion culling, working-set management (geometry caching) [4, 11] are these examples; Second, *traversal-related*: this focus on reduction of access times for objects. Traditional *cache-efficient* layouts [1, 5, 6] (also called *cache-aware*), based on the knowledge of cache parameters, utilize the different localities to reduce the number of cache misses and the size of the working set; Finally, another variation is *cache-oblivious* algorithms [1, 5]. Instead, they do not require any knowledge of cache parameters or block sizes of the memory hierarchy involved in the computation. In addition, large polygons of such highly complex scenes require a lot of hard disk space so that the additional data could exceed the available capacities [5, 6, 7, 8]. Moreover, the *semantics of data access* is more important in defining the placement policy [2, 3, 7, 8]. To meet these requirements, an appropriate data structure and an efficient technique should be developed with the constraints of memory consumption.

2.2 Hypergraph-Based Pattern Clustering Methods

The fundamental clustering problem is to partition a given data set into groups (clusters), such that data points in a cluster are more similar to each other (i.e., *intra-similar property*) than points in different clusters (i.e., *inter-similar property*) [9].These discovered clusters are used to explain the characteristics of the data distribution [9]. However, these schemes fail to produce meaningful clusters, if the number of objects is large or the dimensionalities of the WT (i.e., the number of different features) are diverse and relatively large.

3 Motivating Examples

Well known drawbacks of traditional geometric scene modelers make it difficult, and even sometimes impossible, intuitive design of 3D scenes [2-7]. In this section we will discuss on intelligent storage layout modeling, that is modeling using intelligent techniques during the designing process and thus allowing intuitive storage layout design. Based on the above discussions, the following subsections will explain our observations and motivations.

3.1 Motivations on Theoretical Foundations

Data mining [2, 3, 11], in artificial intelligence area, deals with finding hidden or unexpected relationships among data items and grouping the related items together. The two basic relationships that are of particular concern to us are:

- *Association*: states when one object occurs, it is highly probable that the other will also occur in.
- *Sequence*: where the data items are associated and, in addition to that, we know the order of occurrence as well.

Association rule mining [11] aims to extract interesting *correlations*, *frequent patterns*, *associations* or *casual* structures among sets of items in the transaction databases or other data repositories. Especially, a significant hidden relationship is the concept of *association*. More formally, let $I = i_1, i_2, \ldots, i_n$ denote a set of literals, called items, where a transaction T contains a set of items X if $X \subseteq T$. Let D represents a set of transactions such that $\forall T \in D, T \subseteq I$. A set $X \subseteq I$ is also called an *itemset*. An itemset with k items is called a k-itemset. An *association rule* is indicated by an implication of the form $X \Rightarrow Y$, where $X \subseteq I$, $Y \subseteq I$, and $X \cap Y = \varnothing$. A $X \Rightarrow Y$ is said to hold in transaction set D with *support* s in the transaction set D if s-% of transactions in D contain $X \cup Y$. The rule $X \Rightarrow Y$ has *confidence* c if c-% of the transactions in D containing X also contain Y. The thresholds for support and confidence are called *minsup* and *minconf*, respectively. The *support* of an itemset X, denoted $\sigma(X)$, is the number of transactions in which that itemset arises as a subset. Thus $\sigma(X) = |t(X)|$. An itemset is called a *frequent pattern* [1] if its support is greater than or equal to some threshold *minimum support* (*min sup*) value, i.e., if $\sigma(X) \geqq$ *min sup*.

3.2 Motivations on Practical Demands

Suppose that we have a set of data items $\{a, b, c, d, e, f, g\}$. A sample access history over these items consisting of five sessions is shown in Table 1. The request sequences extracted from this history with minimum support 40 percent are (a, f) and (c, d). The rules obtained out of these sequences with 100 percent minimum confidence are $a \Rightarrow f$ and $c \Rightarrow d$, as shown in Table 2. Two accessed data organizations are depicted in Figure 1. An accessed schedule without any intelligent preprocessing is shown in Figure 1a. A schedule where related items are grouped together and sorted with respect to the order of reference is shown in Figure 1b. Assume that the disk is spinning counterclockwise and consider the following client request sequence, $a, f, b, c, d, a, f, g, e, c, d$, shown in Figure 1. Note that dashed lines mean that the first element in the request sequence (counted from left to right) would like to fetch the first item supplied by disk. And directed graph denotes the rotation of disk layout in counterclockwise way. For this request, if we have the access schedule *(a, b, c, d, e, f, g)*, which dose not take into account the rules, the total I/O access times for the client will be *a*:5, *f*:5, *b*:3, *c*:2, *d*:6, *a*:5, *f*:5, *g*:1, *e*:5, *c*:6, *d*:6. The total access times is 49 and the average latency will be 49/11= 4.454. However, if we partition the items to be accessed into two groups with respect to the sequential patterns obtained after mining, then we will have {*a, b, f*}and {*c, d, e, g*}. Note that data items that appear in the same sequential pattern are placed in the same group. When we sort the data items in the same group with respect to the rules $a \Rightarrow f$ and $c \Rightarrow d$, we will have the sequences *(a, f, b)* and *(c, d, g, e)*. If we organize the data items to be accessed with respect to these sorted groups of items, we will have the access schedule presented in Figure 1b. In this case, the total access times for the client for the same request pattern will be *a*:1, *f*:1, *b*:1, *c*:1, *d*:1, *a*:3, *f*:1, *g*:4, *e*:1, *c*:4, *d*:1. The total access times is 19 and the average latency will be 19/11= 1.727, which is much lower than 4.454.

Table 1. Sample database of user requests

Session No	Accessed Request
1	e, a, f
2	b, d
3	c, d, a, f, g
4	b, a, f, g
5	c, d, a, f

Table 2. Sample association rules

Rule	Support	Confidence
$a \Rightarrow f$	80%	100%
$c \Rightarrow d$	40%	100%

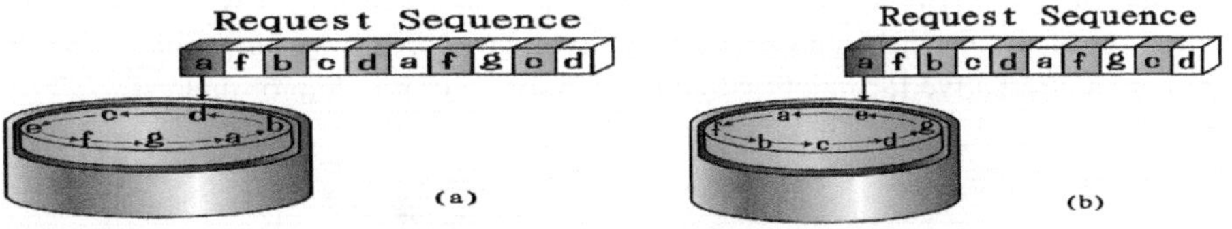

Fig. 1. Effects on accessed objects organization in disk. (a): without association rules; (b) with association rules.

Another example that demonstrates the benefits of rule-based prefetching is shown in Figure 2. We demonstrate three different requests of a client for consideration. Based on the obtained association rules, the prediction can be achieved. The current request is *c* and these is a rule stating that, if data items *c* is requested, then data items *d* will be also be requested (i.e., association rule $c \Rightarrow d$). In Figure 2a, data item *d* is absent in the cache and the client must spend more waiting time for item *d*. In

Figure 2b, although the item *d* is also absent in the cache, the client still spend one disk latency time for item *d*. In Figure 2c, the cache can supply the item *d* and no disk latency time is needed.

3.3 Motivations on Intertwined Relationship Demands

In essence, this can be classified into two different relationships. Under the concern of *intra-similarity*, every *object* represents some importance. For example, the support for frequent pattern *abcd* is 5, but the supports for the object *a*, *b*, *c*, *d* are 5, 6, 7, 8, respectively. Under the concern of *inter-similarity*, shown in Figure 3, every *frequent pattern* represents some importance. For example, the support for frequent pattern *abcd* is 5, but the supports for the object *abe*, *abcde*, *cd*, *df* are 5, 4, 6, 8, respectively. From the above observations, these patterns are intertwined with the relationships and should be properly and efficiently managed. Therefore, those observations also motivate us to adopt the HG model for representing the relationships.

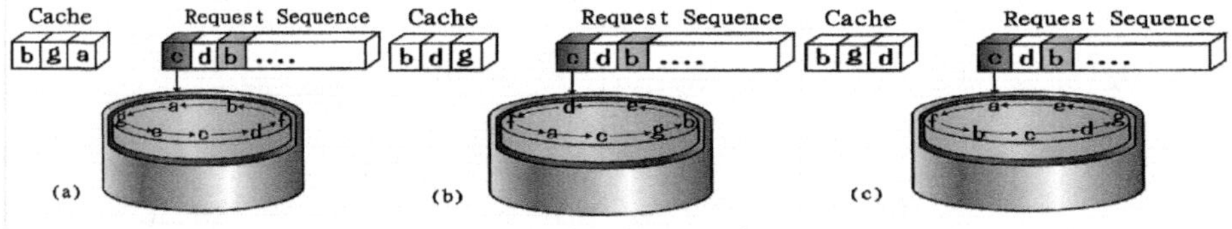

Fig. 2. Effects of prefetching

4 Problem Formulation and Graph-Based Model

In this section, we present a novel application of hypergraph partitioning to automatically determine the computation and I/O schedule. We begin with a definition of the problem and explain the hypergraph partitioning problem. We then present an alternative formulation that better solves our problem of interest.

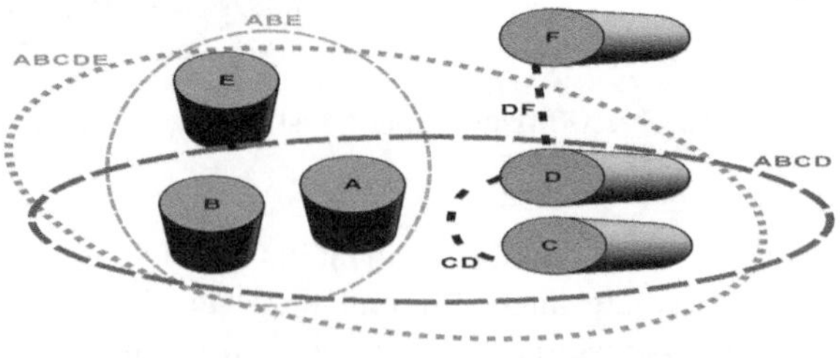

Fig. 3. Demonstration for intra-/inter-relationships among the frequent patterns

4.1 Hypergarph Partitioning Problem

A *hypergraph* $\Gamma=(V, N)$ [12, 13] is defined as a set of *vertices* V and a set of *nets* (*hyper-edges*) N among those vertices. Every net $n_j \in N$ is a subset of vertices, i.e., $n_j \subseteq V$. The size of a net n_j is equal to the number of vertices it has, i.e., $s_j = | n_j |$. Weight (w_j) and cost (c_j) can be assigned to the vertices ($v_j \in V$)) and edges ($n_j \in N$) of the HG, respectively. $\mathcal{K} = \{V_1, V_2, \ldots, V_\kappa\}$is a $\mathcal{K}$-way partition of $\mathcal{H}$ and satisfies the following conditions: (1) each partition is a nonempty subset of V, (2) partitions are pairwise disjoint, and (3) union of $\mathcal{K}$partitions is equal to V.

In our model, we assign every object to one vertex, and every frequent pattern is represented by one hyper-edge (net). As shown in Figure 3, according to how many objects involved, object *a*, *b*, *c*, *d*, *e*, and *f* are circled together in different line form, respectively. Since there are *five different patterns* (i.e., *cd, df, abe, abcd, abcde*), we plot *five different nets* for demonstration.

Finally, we will define our problem in two phases. Phase I: given a frequent pattern set $P = \{p_1, p_2, \ldots, p_n\}$, we design a efficient formulation scheme to bridge two different domain knowledge (i.e., P and HG model); phase II: in order to reduce the disk access time, we distribute P into a set of clusters, such that minimize inter-cluster similarity and maximize intra-cluster similarity.

5 1BData Layout Algorithm Based on Hypergraph Structure

Several studies [10, 12, 13] have shown that using these correlations can significantly improve the storage system performance. In this section, we describe a direct application of hypergraph partitioning to the disk I/O minimization problem. The construction of the hypergraph is described, followed by the partitioning procedure to derive a valid object layout and I/O schedule.

5.1 Object- Centric Clustering Scheme

First, as mentioned previously, let the object corresponds to a vertex, and a frequent pattern also corresponds to a hyperedge. The weight ψ_e of a hyperedge e is defined as $1/|e|$, which is inversely proportional to the number of objects that are incident to the hyperedge. Inspired by the main concepts of [13, 14], we propose our semantic-based hypergraph clustering scheme. Let two objects u and v are given, the similarity score $d\ (u,v)$ for between u and v is defined as

$$d(u,v) = \sum_{e \in E|u,v \in e} \frac{\psi_e}{(m(u)+m(v))} \tag{1}$$

Where e is a hyperedge connecting objects u and v. ψ_e is a corresponding edge weight, and $m(u)$ and $m(v)$ are the some interesting measures of u and v, respectively. As Han. *et. al.* [9] cited that the support measure is not a proper measure used in a hypergraph model. Therefore, in our experiments, shown in next section, the confidence measure was used. The similarity score of two objects is directly proportional to the total sum of edge weights connecting them and is inversely proportional to the sum of their measures. Suppose N_u is the set of neighboring objects to a given object *u*. We define the *closest* object to *u*, denoted *c(u)*, as the neighbor object with the *highest similarity score* to *u*, i.e., $c(u) = v$ such that $d(u,v) = \text{Max}\{d(u,z) \mid z \in N_u\}$.

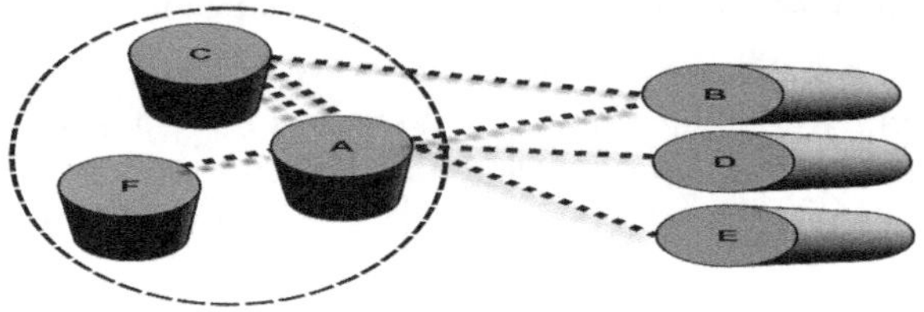

Fig. 4. The initial condition

In Figure 4, the dot lines denote which vertexes are connected in the hyperedges. The circle is especially for represented one hyperedge {*A*, *C*, *F*}. Since the multiplicity of hyperedge {*A*, *C*} is two. Therefore, there are two hyperedges between vertex *A* and *C*. The following is the pseudo codes of object-based hypergraph clustering algorithm.

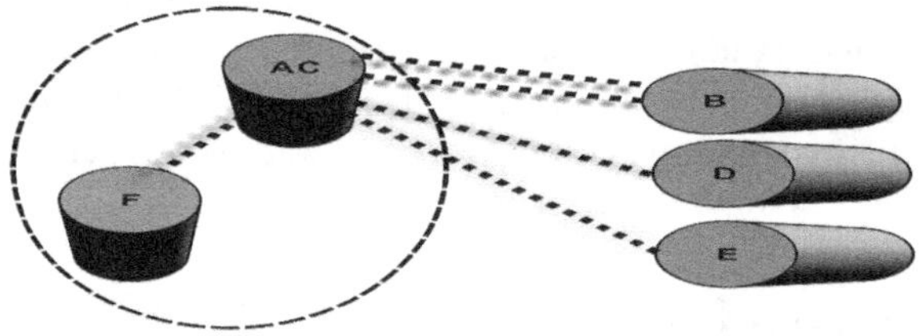

Fig. 5. After the computation of step1 to step4, the vertex *C* was chosen and merged with vertex *A*

Example 1 (*OHGC*). Assume that the system has 6 objects and 8 frequent patterns. Let *Obj* = {*A, B, C, D, E, F, G*} and frequent patterns ser $P = \{P_1 = AB;\ P_2 = AC;\ P_3 = AD;\ P_4 = AE;\ P_5 = AF,\ P_6 = AC,\ P_7 = BC, \text{and } P_8 = ACF\}$. Note that the multiplicity of hyperedge {*A,C*} is two. This is one of main differences between other methods and ours. We set up the *level-wise threshold* for the *multiplicity* of frequent patterns. For example, if the support of P_i is less than some fixed constant, say α, then the multiplicity of *Pi* is set up to be 1; otherwise if the support of P_i is less than or equal to some fixed constant 2α but great than α, then the multiplicity of P_i is set up to be 2. This idea will alleviate the complexity of HG-model for future partitioning. The initial conditions are shown in Figure 4 and final result was shown in Figure 5.

```
Object-oriented Hypergraph-based Clustering (OHGC) Algorithm
// D denotes the database. P indicates the set of frequent
patterns. Obj is the set of frequent patterns. T represents the
set of clusters, and is set to empty initially.
Input: D, P, Obj, and T.
Output: T
Begin
// Phase 1: Initialization step for Priority_Queue (PQ)
While (let each object u∈ Obj and Obj is not empty) do
Begin
Find closest object v, and its associated similarity score d;
 Insert the tuple (u, v, d) into PQ with d as key;
End;       // while in Phase 1
// Phase 2: Hypergraph Clustering based on PQ
 While (user-defined cluster number is not reached or top
  tuple score d >0) do
  Select top tuple (u, v, d) from PQ;
  Cluster u and v into new object u' and update the T;
  Find closest object v' to u' its associated similarity
   score d';
  Insert the tuple (u'' v', d') into PQ with d' as key;
  Update similarity score of all neighbors of u;
End;       // while in Phase 2
```

$P_1=\{5A, 6B, C\}$, $P_2=\{3A, 2B, 5C, 8D\}$, $P_3=\{5C, 8D\}$

$New\text{-}Jaccard(P_1,P_2) = \frac{\|\{3A,2B,1C\}\|}{\|\{5A,6B,5C,8D\}\|} = \frac{6}{24} = \frac{1}{4} = 0.25$	$New\text{-}Jaccard(P_1,P_3) = \frac{\|\{1C\}\|}{\|\{5A,6B,5C,8D\}\|} = \frac{1}{24} = 0.04$	$New\text{-}Jaccard(P_2,P_3) = \frac{\|\{5C,8D\}\|}{\|\{3A,2B,5C,8D\}\|} = \frac{13}{18} = 0.72$
$Old\text{-}Jaccard(P_1,P_2) = \frac{\|\{A,B,C\}\|}{\|\{A,B,C,D\}\|} = \frac{3}{4} = 0.75$	$Old\text{-}Jaccard(P_1,P_3) = \frac{\|\{C,D\}\|}{\|\{A,B,C,D\}\|} = \frac{2}{4} = 0.50$	$Old\text{-}Jaccard(P_2,P_3) = \frac{\|\{C,D\}\|}{\|\{A,B,C,D\}\|} = \frac{2}{4} = 0.50$

Fig. 6. Illustration between two different concerns about the Jaccard mechanisms

5.1 Quantity-Based Jaccard Function

The Jaccard index [14], also known as the Jaccard similarity coefficient, is a statistic used for comparing the similarity and diversity of sample sets. However, if the quantity for each element involved, this similarity can not reflect the following conditions. For example, let frequent pattern $\alpha=$ {(*A, B, C*) (*B, C*) (*B, D*)} can be abstracted as $\beta=$ {*A, B, C, D*} or $\gamma=$ {*1A, 3B, 2C, 1D*}. But these two different abstractions have different semantic but hidden meanings. In order to maintain this semantic property, we should retain them as much as possible. Here, let us consider three different frequent patterns, P_1, P_2, and P_3: P_1 = {*5A, 6B, C*}, P_2 = {*3A, 2B, 5C, 8D*}, P_3 = {*5C, 8D*}. Here take P_1 for an example, *5A* means there are *five* elements for object with type *A*. Similarly, *6B* means there are *six* elements for object with type *B*, and *1C* means there is *one* element for object with type *C*. As shown in Figure 6, the new *jaccard* similarity mechanism (i.e., *quantity-based Jaccard similarity* formula) can capture more semantic meanings than the old one.

Definition 1: Mapping relationships between 3D objects and items
First, according the *occupied size*, *visibility* and *ease of processing* constraints, we divide the 3D scene into many different objects with different sizes. If the object is too huge to process, we can split the object into several smaller sub-objects. Therefore, we assign different ID to every object as its *tag*. This tag is called the "*name*" of the item. For example, let we have one scene consisted of three components (i.e., α, β, γ). If the component α is too big to handle, we split the component α into four sub-objects. We assign four tags for the four sub-objects as $\{a, b, c, d\}$. The remaining components β, γ are assigned to $\{e\}$, $\{f\}$, respectively. Therefore, we get one mapping (i.e., $\{a, b, c, d, e, f\}$) for this 3D scene. Similar approaches are also applied to other 3D scenes.

Definition 2: View-radius
Inspired by the idea of *view importance* [10], Firstly, to obtain the efficient computation cost, we propose a simple but effective distance to measure the number of observable objects. Secondly, according to the distance threshold given by users, we define *view radius* in order to choose representative objects. For the comparison purposes, we divide the different intervals among the view-radius. The detailed data was shown in Table 3.

6 Experimental Evaluation

This section presents a progression of experiments for the effectiveness of predictive-prefetching mechanism in the storage systems. We begin by explaining the set-ups for experimental environments, included the experimental setups. Next, under different constraints, we show that HG-based clustering approach can outperform the other schemes. Besides, in order to compare with knowledge-based tree-like data structures [4], the mechanism of *Access Path Predictor* (APP) was implemented for performance comparisons.

Since the APP scheme share some similar properties with our approaches. For examples, APP claims that the most common access pattern within a dataset is the *frequent appearance* of the same *predecessor-current-successor* patterns [7]. This pattern represents a section of a *path* along which one application *navigates* through its data. As far as the intra- relationship be concerned, this type of patterns are similar our frequent sequential patterns. However, some significant limitation was posed on the APP scheme. Because the *correlated relationships* cover both the intra-relationship and inter-relationship [22, 25]. The APP scheme only considered their pattern inferred by intra-relationship only hidden in the same path. In other words, the inter-relationships across the different paths were neglected in the APP scheme. On the contrary, both of them were considered in our HG-based clustering approach. Based on the above discussions, we adopt the APP scheme for performance evaluation.

Table 3. Information on radius and average number of objects in one view

View Radius	Average Objects in One View
2000	15
4000	26
6000	46
8000	63
10000	81
12000	114

6.1 Implementation Setup

The experiments were conducted on a machine with a 1.6GHz Pentium 4 processor, 1GB main memory, running Microsoft Windows 2003 server. All algorithms were implemented in Java.

6.2 Results and Performance

We conduct several experiments to determine the performance of our proposed OHCG approach. In all four experiments, we test the performance of proposed technique for our traversal trace data using the mentioned clustering measures, Hypergraph and quantity-based Jaccard similarity.

Furthermore, we perform the same set of experiments for three other prediction techniques namely, Without-Clustering approach, APP approach, and quantity-based Jaccard approach. Without-Clustering approach is monitored and managed by operation system, where the prediction computation is deferred until LRU-like mechanism works. The APP approach uses tree-like data structure, a mechanism that calculates a probability by counting the frequency of values and combinations of values in the historical data. On the other side, quantity-based Jaccard approach focuses on selecting the most similar frequent patterns for a given patterns by combing both the co-occurrence and quantity principles. The final output of the hypergraph-based clustering is partitioned via pattern-based hypergraph model, where OHGC determines the best partition to place objects into the storage system for future accesses. This helps to explore the hidden relationships and estimate future fine-grained placements, leveraging the most effective predictive mechanism for each situation. Note that HG-Clustering represents our OHGC clustering scheme.

In particular, we focused on the following metrics, namely *demanded total objects, response time (in ms),* and *number of retrieval files.* The demanded total objects indicates that the percentage of request which can be met without accessing the out-of-core storage. The response time metric is the time interval elapsed that a clustering algorithm was required to load data form the disk. The number of retrieval files metric indicates that the effect of correlated relationships.

We carry out our experiments to compare four algorithms in the traversal database mainly on total objects/total files, response time, and number of retrieval files. Moreover, we vary the support threshold (between 70% and 10%). Similarly, we also vary the view radius threshold (between 2000 and 12000).

In the experiments of *total objects/total files*, as the figure 7 shown, it represents demanded total objects for the algorithms comprising points in a spherical volume. Besides, we have the following observations: firstly, the number of representative semantic patterns by OHCG is much more than those of the other three algorithms. It implies there are huge access time reductions during the retrieval of objects; secondly, in the algorithm of OHCG, we can obtain the dominating clusters which include the most representative sequential patterns. In addition, to verify the effectiveness of OHCG we proposed in our work, we also make the experiments on number of retrieval files which are shown in figures 8-10. Moreover, in the experiments of response time, as the figure 8 and figure 10 shown, the response time of OHCG is much less than the other three algorithms, and APP is very close to the time of quantity-Jaccard. This is because that the clustering mechanism can accurately support prefetching objects for future usage. Not only the access time is cut down but also the I/O efficiency is improved.

7 Conclusions and Future Works

This paper studies how to effectively and efficiently cluster frequent patterns from traversal database. To the best of our knowledge, the problem of clustering the semantic objects in 3D walkthrough has not been well studied in existing work.

Inspired by ideas of speedup of accessing semantic patterns, firstly, to obtain the high-quality clustering, we design a novel hypergraph-based model to measure the associations which shows the similarity between frequent patterns. Since the problem of retrieving 3D objects is equivalent to minimizing the number of frequencies for accessing 3D objects, we develop an algorithm, OHCG, including an efficient partitioning strategy. On the other side, Quantity-Jaccard is more flexible, due to its easy adaptation and implementation. This opens a new era for inducing the concepts of data mining to discover the hidden but valuable knowledge to improve the performance of the system.

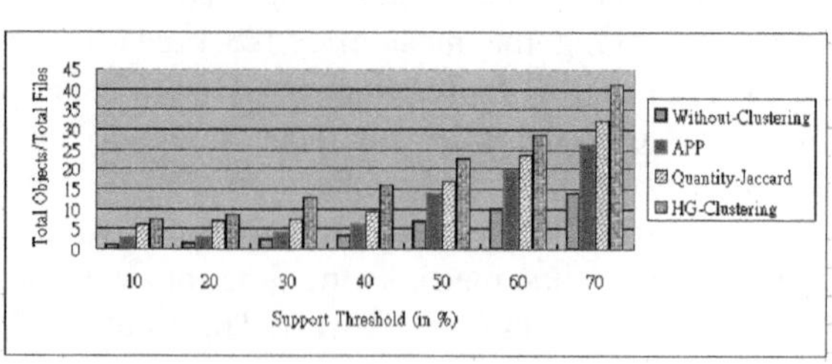

Fig. 7. Comparison of different algorithms on the number of objects retrieved

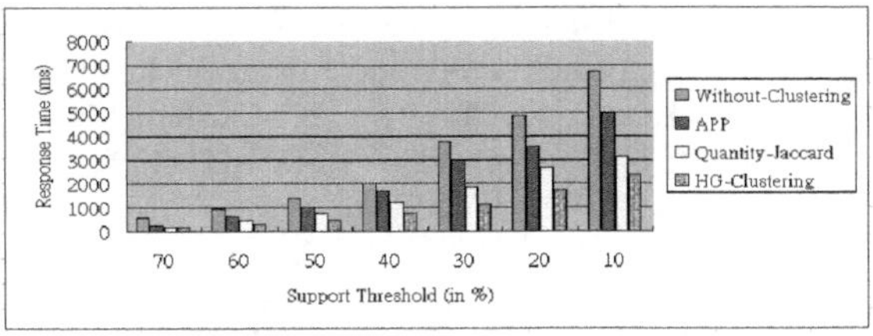

Fig. 8. Comparison of different algorithms on system response time

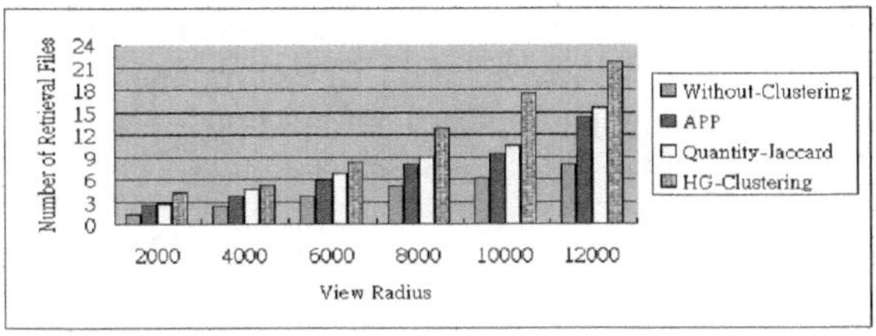

Fig. 9. Comparison of different algorithms on the number of files retrieved

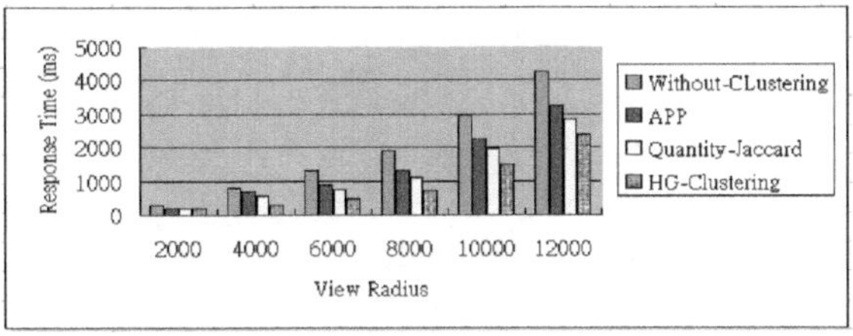

Fig. 10. Comparison of different algorithms on system response time

References

1. Sajadi, B., et al.: A Novel Page-Based Data Structure for Interactive Walkthroughs. In: ACM SIGGRAPH Symposium on Interactive 3D Graphics and Games, I3D (2009)
2. Bertini, E., Lalanne, D.: Investigating and Reflecting on the Integration of Automatic Data Analysis and Visualization in Knowledge Discovery. ACM SIGKDD Exploration 11(2), 9–18 (2009)
3. Plemenos, D., Miaoulis, G.: Visual Complexity and Intelligent Computer Graphics Techniques Enhancements. Springer, New York (2009)
4. Zhu, Y.: Uniform Remeshing with an Adaptive Domain: a New Scheme for View-Dependent Level-of-Detail Rendering of Meshes. IEEE Transactions on Visualization and Computer Graphics 11(3), 306–316 (2005)
5. Yoon, S.E., Manocha, D.: Cache-Efficient Layouts of Bounding Volume Hierarchies. Eurographics 25(3), 507–516 (2006)
6. Chisnall, D., Chen, M., Hansen, C.: Knowledge-based Out-of-Core Algorithms for Data Management in Visualization. In: EG/IEEE-VGTC Symposium on Visualization (2006)
7. Hung, S.S., Liu, D.S.M.: Using Predictive Prefetching to Improve Interactive Walkthrough Latency. CAVW Journal 17(3-4), 469–478 (2006)

8. Sivathanu, M., et al.: Arpaci-Dusseau. Semantically-Smart Disk Systems. In: Proceedings of the Second USENIX Conference on File and Storage Technologies (2003)
9. Han, E.-H., Karypis, G., Kumar, V., Mobasher, B.: Clustering based on Association Rule Hypergraph. In: Workshop on Research Issues on DMKD (1997)
10. Chim, J., et al.: CyberWalk: A Web-based Distributed Virtual Walkthrough Environment. IEEE Transactions on Multimedia 5(4), 503–515 (2003)
11. Agrawal, R., Imielinski, T., Swami, A.N.: Mining Association Rules between Sets of Items in Large Databases. In: Proceedings of the ACM SIGMOD International Conference on Management of Data, pp. 207–216 (1993)
12. Nam, G.-J., et al.: A Fast Hierarchical Quadratic Placement Algorithm. IEEE Trans. on Computer-Aided Design of Integrated Circuits and Systems 25(4), 678–691 (2006)
13. Demir, E., Aykanat, C., Cambazoglu, B.B.: Clustering Spatial Networks for Aggregate Query Processing: A Hypergraph Approach. Information Systems 33, 1–17 (2008)
14. Jaccard, P.: The Distribution of the Flora of the Alpine Zone. New Phytologist, 37–50 (1912)

Skin-Detached Surface for Interactive Large Mesh Editing

Yujian Gao, Aimin Hao, and Qinping Zhao

State Key Laboratory of Virtual Reality Technology and Systems,
Beihang University, Beijing, China
{gaoyj,ham,zhaoqp}@vrlab.buaa.edu.cn

Abstract. We propose a method for interactive deformation of large detail meshes. Our method allows the users to manipulate the mesh directly using freely-selected handles on the mesh. To best preserve surface details, we introduce a new surface representation, the skin-detached surface. It represents a detail surface model as a peeled "skin" added over a simplified surface model. The "skin" contains the details of the surface while the simplified mesh maintains the rough shape. The deformation process consists of three steps: first, the "detached skin" is precomputed according to the detail mesh at the loading stage. Then we deform the simplified mesh following the nonlinear gradient domain mesh editing approach to satisfy the handle position constraints. Finally the "detached skin" is remapped onto the simplified mesh, resulting in a deformed detail mesh. We investigate the advantages as well as the limitations of our method by implementing a prototype system and applying it to several examples.

Keywords: deformation, simplification, multi-resolution, gradient domain.

1 Introduction

The field of mesh deformation has attracted a lot of attention throughout recent years, and a variety of techniques have been developed and widely used in movie production, mesh editing tools and game engines. Existing mesh deformation techniques include: free-form deformation (FFD) [1, 2], RBF-based mesh deformation [3], curve-based deformation [4, 5], skeleton deformation [6], physical simulation [7] and gradient domain deformation. The computational load and memory consumption of all these approaches grow tremendously as the mesh complexity increases. With the development of 3D scanning techniques, people are becoming more and more critical about the detail level of 3D meshes, but it is difficult to edit and deform large meshes interactively using these methods on common PCs.

To achieve interactive editing of large meshes while preserving the geometric details, we propose a skin-detached mesh deformation scheme based on a new surface representation, the skin-detached surface. To put it simply, the skin-detached surface representation decomposes the mesh into a simplified mesh and a group of displacement detail coefficients, allowing global deformations with fine-scale detail preservation. This representation is inspired by the key idea of displacement mapping,

Z. Pan et al. (Eds.): Transactions on Edutainment VII, LNCS 7145, pp. 99–109, 2012.

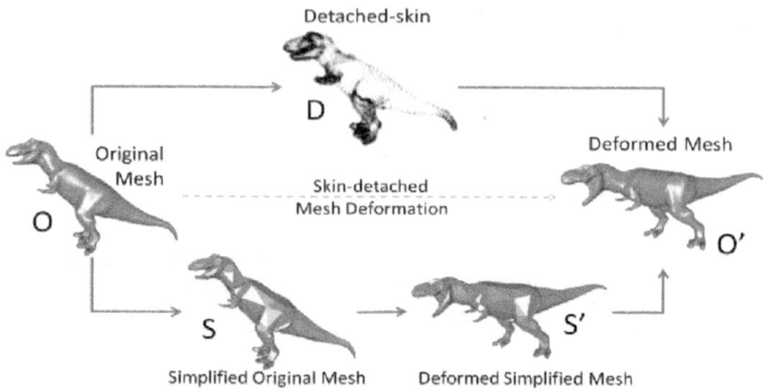

Fig. 1. The workflow of skin-detached mesh deformation

which was originally used for accelerating the rendering process of fine-scale detail on a mesh.

The whole deformation process is depicted in Figure 1. The main computational load of our skin-detached deformation scheme lies in extracting the displacement coefficients from the original surface in the precomputation step, and it is actually the simplified surface on which the deformation is applied, thus high performance and interactive editing on common PCs can be achieved using our method. In addition, our method completely separates the detail preservation mechanism from the mesh deformation process, resulting in an advantage that it can be easily combined with different mesh deformation approaches to satisfy various types of requirements while preserving the mesh detail.

In summary, there are two main contributions in this paper: 1. We introduce a new surface representation. This representation separates the details of the surface from the basic shape, and can be easily applied to the deformation of large meshes. The main challenge of designing the skin-detached surface representation lies in the diversity of mesh topologies. 2. We propose an efficient surface deformation scheme based on our surface representation, which integrates the strengths of the state-of-the-art deformation techniques and multiresolution techniques to achieve both detail-preserving deformation and high performance.

2 Related Work

Among the various existing mesh deformation approaches, gradient domain mesh deformation appears to be the one which can best represent the state-of-the-art deformation solutions. It directly encodes the geometric details into the Laplacian coordinates, and avoids the detail distortion by preserving the computed Laplacian coordinates. Another advantage of gradient domain mesh deformation is that it provides an intuitive way of mesh editing. Existing gradient domain deformation techniques can be categorized into two classes: linearization methods and nonlinear optimization techniques. Linearization methods dominated in the early stage development. This class generally includes Poisson mesh editing [8], harmonic propagation methods [9, 10], Laplacian mesh editing [11-13], as-rigid-as possible (ARAP) [14] methods, volume graph Laplacian [15] and multi-grid deformation algorithm [16]. Nonlinear methods tackle the limitation of solving large rotation in linearization methods by automatically deriving the rotation from pure translation. Current nonlinear methods include subspace gradient deformation [17], dual Laplacian coordinates method [18] and subdivision surface deformation method [19].

In recent years, with the development of 3D scanning techniques, highly detail surface models are becoming commonplace. This directly results in the emergence of an issue with current deformation techniques, i.e., how to achieve detail-preserved deformation for large meshes with high performance. To the best of our knowledge, this problem has not been solved well yet. To tackle this problem, our method combines the strengths of gradient domain techniques and displacement mapping technique to achieve visually pleasing deformation and high performance. Displacement mapping was introduced by Cook [20] as a rendering technique in computer graphics, and the idea of displacement mapping is now widely used in multiresolution techniques [21-23] and cage based deformation[24,25].One representative multiresolution technique is displaced subdivision surfaces [21]. In this technique, Lee et al. enhanced the expressive power of integrating displacement mapping into the subdivision framework. Based on Lee's work, Zhou et al. [19] proposed a GPU-based method for interactive deformation of subdivision surfaces, which upgrades the performance of the previous deformation methods. The difference between our deformation method and Zhou's method is that we maintain the original topology of the mesh and can recover the mesh details accurately. There are several advantages of maintaining the original topology of mesh: 1. The users can save the current deformation for further edit. 2. For textured models, the texture coordinates can be preserved after the deformation is applied. 3. The deformation results can be easily used for mesh interpolation or animation. In addition, the simplified mesh in our method has much lower complexity than the subdivision surfaces in Zhou's [19], which endows our method with higher performance.

3 Method Overview

As depicted in Figure 1, our method consists of the following steps:

- Mesh simplification ($O \rightarrow S$)

The first step of processing is mesh simplification which is done by system automatically without user's interaction. The simplified mesh will then be used for "skin" coefficients computation as well as actual shape deformation.

- Skin computation ($O \ominus S \rightarrow D$)

Computing "skin" coefficients based on the simplified mesh is a nontrivial task. The main challenge lies here is that all the geometric relationships of different meshes should be taken into consideration. We investigate whether it is possible to handle all of the cases automatically, and describe exceptional cases which are out of the capability of our algorithm.

- User-directed deformation (S → S')

The users can directly manipulate the handles on the mesh to achieve desirable results. We employ the nonlinear gradient domain deformation to deform the mesh according to the user-specified constraints.

- Detail reconstruction (S'⊕D → O')

After each iteration of the user's manipulation, we compose the "skin" coefficients with the simplified mesh to obtain the deformed detail mesh. This step is basically a reverse of the "skin" computation step. In the following sections, we elaborate each step of our method with more technical details.

3.1 Mesh Simplification

The mesh simplification step consists of a sequence of edge collapse transformations prioritized according to the quadric error metric which was first proposed by Garland and Heckbert [26]. To handle the case in which one vertex has multiple set of displacement coefficients (see the next section), we restrict some of the candidate edge collapses. We set the main objective as ensuring that the resulting simplified mesh should have a locally similar space of normals with the original mesh. We borrow the 1-ring neighborhood test method introduced by Aaron et al. [21] for this task. If the test fails on any face in the 1-ring neighborhood, the edge collapse transformation is denied.

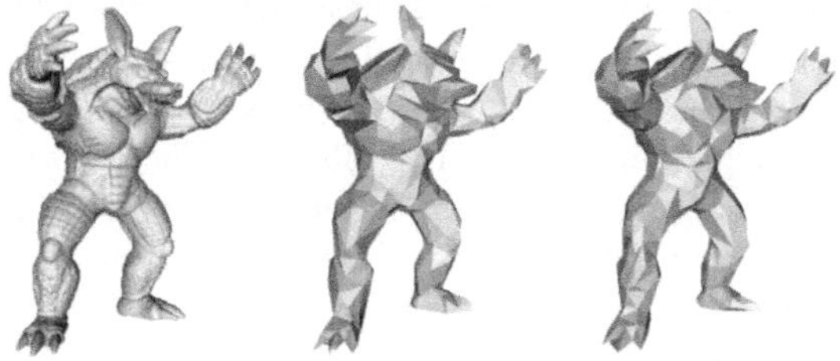

Fig. 2. Mesh simplification comparison

Figure 2(b) and Figure 2(c) give the simplified meshes of Armadillo model (Figure 2(a)) without and with 1-ring neighborhood test respectively, note that the claws and ears of Figure 2(c) are better simplified.

3.2 Skin-Detached Surface Representation

A skin-detached surface representation consists of a simplified mesh and a group of displacement coefficients (Figure 3). The large green triangle is one of the triangles in the simplified bunny mesh, and the blue mesh above it is the corresponding part of the detail bunny. Each vertex of the detail mesh is displaced from a specific droppoint (the black points) on the simplified triangle along the normal direction of the triangle.

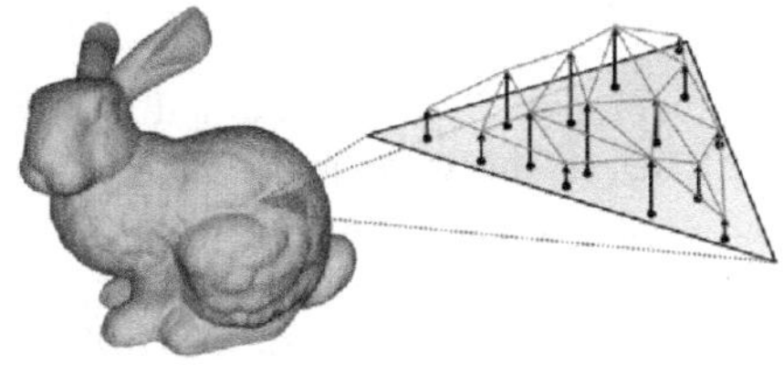

Fig. 3. Vertices' displacements from the triangle of coarse level

We define a set of displacement coefficients for a specific vertex V as:

- **Triangle index:** This parameter stores the index of the simplified triangle in which the vertex V falls along the normal direction. To put it iconically, it is the piece of flesh where the "skin" point V attaches.
- **UVW coordinates:** *UVW coordinates* define the position where the drop-point lies in the simplified triangle. Suppose P_1, P_2, P_3 are the three sequenced vertices of the simplified triangle, then the droppoint coordinates can be computed using $V' = u \cdot P_1 + v \cdot P_2 + w \cdot P_3$.
- **Distance:** The distance between the vertex V and the point of fall V'. Given the distance d and the triangle normal $\hat{n}$, we have $V = V' + d \cdot \hat{n}$.

Note that our method maintains the original topology of the mesh in the displacement coefficients which is different from the displaced subdivision surfaces, therefore the reconstruction of the detail mesh using our method is absolutely accurate. Figure 3 shows only the ideal relationship between the detail mesh and the simplified triangle, but the situation can be much more complex in practice. Therefore we study the diverse relationships between vertices of the detail mesh and triangles of the simplified mesh, and conclude them into three categories as following.

Case one

Figure 4(a) shows the 2D view of the first case. It is the ideal case that the vertex V of the detail mesh falls within one and just one triangle of the simplified mesh. The *normal volume* is a volume that is swept by the translated triangle along its normal direction. The vertex V of the detail mesh lies in and only in the *normal volume* of triangle 3.

Calculating the set of displacement coefficients for vertex V can be cast as a problem of Ray/Triangle intersection. We denote the triangle $\Delta P_1P_2P_3$ as T and the plane in which T lies as π (Figure 4(b)). The parametric equation of plane π is given by:

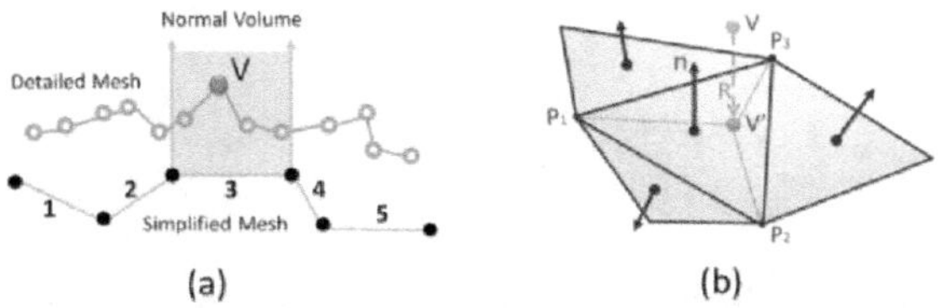

Fig. 4. (a)2D view of the 1st case; (b)3D view of the 1st case

$$V(s,t) = P_1 + s \cdot (P_2 - P_1) + t \cdot (P_3 - P_1) = P_1 + s \cdot \hat{u} + t \cdot \hat{v}, \quad (1)$$

where s and t are real numbers, and $\hat{u} = P_2 - P_1$ and $\hat{v} = P_3 - P_1$ are edge vectors of T. A point $V' = V(s,t)$ lies in the triangle T when $s \geq 0, t \geq 0$, and $s + t \leq 1$. Further, a point $V' = V(s,t)$ is on an edge of T if one of the conditions $s = 0, t = 0$, or $s + t = 1$ is true (each corresponds to one edge).

To solve for (s,t), we use a 3D generalization of Hill's *"perp-dot" product* [27]. For plane π with a normal vector n, and any vector a in the plane $(n \cdot a = 0)$, the *generalized perp operator* on π is: $a^{\perp} = n \times a$. Put $\widehat{w} = V' - P_1$, we want to solve the equation: $\widehat{w} = s \cdot \hat{u} + t \cdot \hat{v}$ for s and t. Take the dot product of both sides with $\hat{v}^{\perp}$ to get: $\widehat{w} \cdot \hat{v}^{\perp} = s\hat{u} \cdot \hat{v}^{\perp} + t\hat{v} \cdot \hat{v}^{\perp} = s\hat{u} \cdot \hat{v}^{\perp}$, and solve s. Similarly, t can be solved by taking the dot product with $\hat{u}^{\perp}$:

$$s = \frac{\widehat{w} \cdot \hat{v}^{\perp}}{\hat{u} \cdot \hat{v}^{\perp}} = \frac{\widehat{w} \cdot (\hat{n} \times \hat{v})}{\hat{u} \cdot (\hat{n} \times \hat{v})}, t = \frac{\widehat{w} \cdot \hat{u}^{\perp}}{\hat{v} \cdot \hat{u}^{\perp}} = \frac{\widehat{w} \cdot (\hat{n} \times \hat{u})}{\hat{v} \cdot (\hat{n} \times \hat{u})}, \quad (2)$$

where $\hat{u}^{\perp} = \hat{n} \times \hat{u} = (\hat{n} \times \hat{u}) \times \hat{u}$, $\hat{v}^{\perp} = \hat{n} \times \hat{v} = (\hat{n} \times \hat{v}) \times \hat{v}$. Since the intersection is computed frequently, we can achieve better performance by applying the *left association identity* instead of cross products (for any three vectors a, b, c, we have$(a \times b) \times c = (a \cdot c)b - (b \cdot c)a$ to the above equations, resulting in:

$$s = \frac{(\hat{u} \cdot \hat{v})(\widehat{w} \cdot \hat{v}) - (\hat{v} \cdot \hat{v})(\widehat{w} \cdot \hat{u})}{(\hat{u} \cdot \hat{v})^2 - (\hat{u} \cdot \hat{u})(\hat{v} \cdot \hat{v})}, t = \frac{(\hat{u} \cdot \hat{v})(\widehat{w} \cdot \hat{u}) - (\hat{u} \cdot \hat{u})(\widehat{w} \cdot \hat{v})}{(\hat{u} \cdot \hat{v})^2 - (\hat{u} \cdot \hat{u})(\hat{v} \cdot \hat{v})}, \quad (3)$$

where the denominators only need to be calculated once. Since we precompute and store the normal vectors for all triangles, this ray/triangle intersection algorithm is very efficient. After obtaining the (s,t), the UVW coordinates can be simply computed by $u = 1 - s - t, v = s, w = t$. The *triangle index* and *distance* coefficients are very easy to obtain.

Case two

Figure 5(a) shows the 2D view of case two. In this case, the vertex V does not fall within any triangle. This case usually happens when the vertex V is near to a summit of the mesh. We tested several ways of selecting associated triangle for V, e.g., associating the vertex with one of the closest triangles, but none of them achieves pleasing results. Therefore we adopt a strategy that associates the vertex V with multiple triangles. We first traverse over the simplified mesh to find the vertex P_3 which is the closest to vertex V (Figure 5(b)), then we associate vertex V with all the neighbour triangles of P_3.

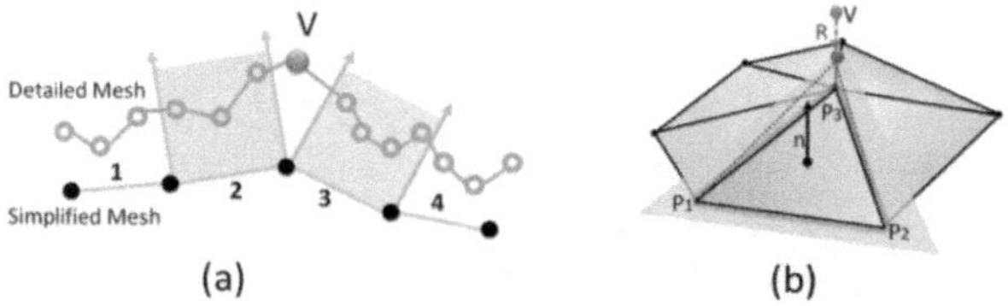

Fig. 5. (a)2D view of the 2nd case; (b)3D view of the 2nd case

As illustrated in Figure 5(b), we take the highlighted triangle $\Delta P_1P_2P_3$ (T) as an example. First, we emit a ray from vertex V along the normal direction of T, and compute the intersection point V' on the extended plane of T (the big blue triangle) by applying the same Ray/Triangle intersection scheme introduced in case one. Since the intersection vertex V' lie outside of T, it must be one of the following cases: $s \leq 0$ or $t \leq 0$, or $s + t \geq 1$. Note that we can still compute the UVW coordinates by $u = 1 - s - t, v = s, w = t$($uvw$ could be negative). In this way, we associate vertex V with triangle T. The other neighbour triangles are associated in the same way, resulting in multiple set of displacement coefficients for one vertex.

Case Three

Figure 6 shows the 2D view of the third case. In this case, vertex V falls within multiple triangles along their normals. This case usually happens when the vertex V is near to a concave part of the mesh. It is actually the general case of the first case, and we only need a scheme for selecting triangles to associate.

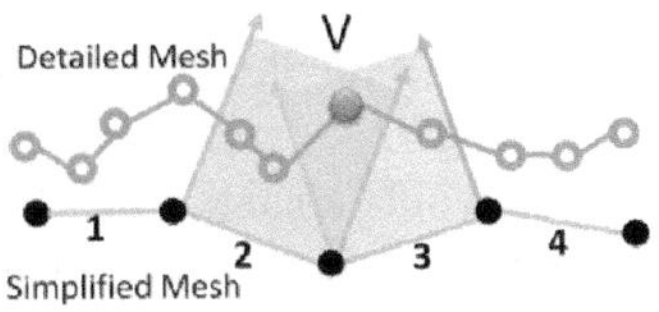

Fig. 6. 2D view of the 3rd case

To avoid associating triangles far from V, we sort triangles according to their corresponding *distance* coefficients. Suppose the shortest *distance* is d_{min}, we then associate V with triangles whose *distance* coefficient are less than $(2 \times d_{\min})$. The rest of the computation is same with the first case, and we also store multiple sets of displacement coefficients for one vertex like the second case.

3.3 Dual Laplacian Mesh Deformation

To ease the users' manipulation of mesh deformation, we employ the dual Laplacian mesh deformation technique proposed by Au et al. [18]. The dual Laplacian method encodes both the local parameterization and geometric details in the dual mesh domain, thus it can reduce the distortion caused by large angle deformation or the translations of handles.

3.4 Detail Mesh Reconstruction

The detail mesh reconstruction is basically a reverse procedure of the skin-detached surface computation. Given a deformed simplified mesh and the "skin" coefficients, we can efficiently compute the deformed position of vertex V of the detail mesh. For the first case, V can be calculated as:

$$V_{deformed} = u \cdot P_{i,1} + v \cdot P_{i,2} + w \cdot P_{i,3} + d \cdot \hat{n}_i, \tag{4}$$

where i, uvw and d are the displacement coefficients of vertex V. $(P_{i,1}, P_{i,2}, P_{i,3})$ and $\hat{n}$ are vertices and normal of triangle i from the deformed simplified mesh.

For the other two cases, we adopt a weighted mean value scheme to reconstruct the deformed vertex V. The weight of each set of displacement coefficients is determined by the area of the corresponding simplified triangle:

$$V_{deformed} = \frac{u \cdot P_{i,1} + v \cdot P_{i,2} + w \cdot P_{i,3} + d \cdot \hat{n}_i}{\sum_{i=1}^{n} S_{\Delta_i}}, \tag{5}$$

where n stands for the count of corresponding triangles and S_{Δ_i} is the area of the ith corresponding triangle of the simplified mesh.

4 Experiment

We implemented a prototype system of the described algorithm on a 3.0 Ghz PC with 2GB of memory using OpenGL and C++. At the precomputation stage, the system first simplify the mesh to a customizable coarse level (1000 triangles as default in our implementation), then computing the "skin" based on the simplified mesh. During editing stage, each time the users drop the handle, the system reconstructs the detail mesh according to the deformed simplified mesh. Since the simplification, decomposition and reconstruction are hided in a black box, it appears to the users as if they are editing the detail mesh directly. Figure 7 shows the deformation results of four large detail meshes using our system. With conventional gradient domain mesh deformation techniques, the computation of these meshes would be complex and time-consuming. This makes the deformation work quite difficult for the artists. But with our method, the artists can edit large meshes interactively and achieve visually pleasing deformation results.

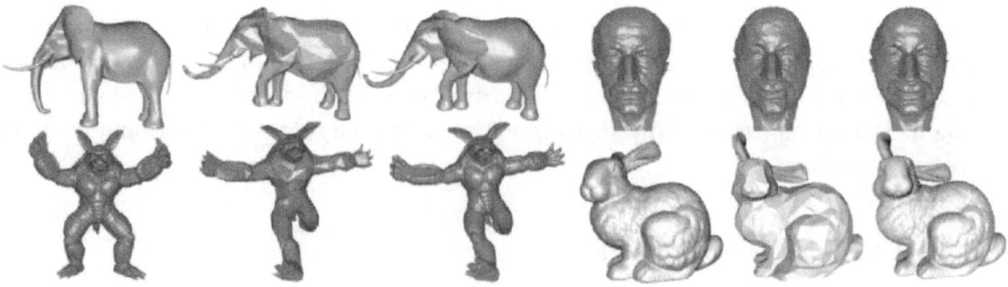

Fig. 7. Original meshes/ Deformed simplified meshes/ reconstructed detail meshes

Table 4 provides performance statistics for the four examples in Figure 7. For models of this scale, traditional methods typically take several seconds or longer for a single manipulation of moving one handle, and take even longer for the recomputation each time when the users change the handles. But we can see that our skin-detached mesh deformation system can achieve real-time performance. Note that if the users change handles, we need to re-compute the inverse for some matrices and the frame rate will decrease. Fortunately these matrices' dimensions are proportional to the complexity of the simplified mesh, but not the detail one. For all the above examples, this recomputation took less than one second.

Table 1. Experimental performance statistics

Model	$V_{simplified}$	$V_{detailed}$	Frames per Second	Precomputation Time
Elephant	700	157,160	86fps	21_{min}
Max-Planck	5,000	398,043	34fps	64_{min}
Armadillo	1,000	331,904	75fps	52_{min}
Detail Bunny	500	277,804	92fps	44_{min}

Note that the real performance bottleneck of our method lies in the precomputation step of generating skin-detached surface representation. In its last column, table 1 also provides the precomputation time of each model. Although the precomputation takes relatively long time for large models, it is acceptable since we only need to compute them once, and then save them for further usage

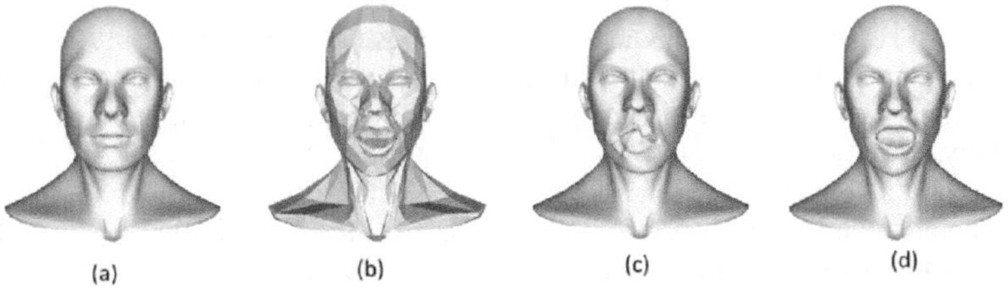

Fig. 8. (a) Original model; (b) Deformed simplified model; (c) Reconstructed detail model; (d) Desired result

During our experiment, we found that there are some exceptional cases such as shown in Figure 10. Figure 8(a) shows the original head model with mouth closed. Figure 8(b) and 8(c) show the deformed simplified model and the reconstructed detail model whereas Figure 8(d) shows the desired result (made by artists). When we tried to drag the lower lip from the upper lip, the shape of mouth was heavily distorted. The reason for this phenomenon is that some vertices of the upper lip were mistakenly attached to the simplified lower lip during the "skin" computation, and vice versa. Therefore, when we reconstructed the detail mesh of the head, these vertices were determined by improper simplified triangles and then the distortion happened. This limitation should be improved in the future work.

5 Conclusions and Future Work

We have described a method for interactive deformation of large detail mesh. With our method, the user can directly manipulate large meshes using freely-selected surface points as handles. The most important feature of our algorithm is that it combines the strengths of the nonlinear gradient domain mesh deformation techniques and the multiresolution techniques to achieve both visually pleasing deformation and high performance. Specifically, by separating the detail recovering mechanism from the mesh deformation procedure, our system achieves the advantage that it can be easily combined with different mesh deformation approaches to satisfy various requirements. As a topic of future research, we plan to explore the solution to the exceptional cases of our system. Besides, we are also interested in developing techniques for multi-component models or non-manifold models.

References

1. Sederberg, T.W., Parry, S.R.: Free-form deformation of solid geometric models. In: SIGGRAPH 1986, vol. 20(4), pp. 151–160 (1986)
2. Botsch, M., Kobbelt, L.: An intuitive framework for real-time freeform modeling. In: SIGGRAPH 2004, pp. 630–634. ACM, New York (2004)
3. Mario, B., Leif, K.: Real-time shape editing using radial basis functions. Computer Graphics Forum 24(3), 611–621 (2005)
4. Karan, S., Eugene, L.F.: Wires: A geometric deformation technique. In: Proceedings of SIGGRAPH 1998, Computer Graphics Proceedings, pp. 405–414 (July 1998)
5. Peng, Q.S., Jin, X.G., Feng, J.Q.: Arc-length-based axial deformation and length preserved animation. In: CA 1997: Proceedings of the Computer Animation, p. 86. IEEE Computer Society, Washington, DC (1997)
6. Lewis, J.P., Cordner, M., Fong, N.: Pose space deformation: a unified approach to shape interpolation and skeleton-driven deformation. In: SIGGRAPH 2000, pp. 165–172. ACM Press/Addison-Wesley Publishing Co., New York, NY (2000)
7. Terzopoulos, D., Platt, J., Barr, A., Fleischer, K.: Elastically deformable models. In: SIGGRAPH 1987, pp. 205–214. ACM, New York (1987)
8. Yu, Y.Z., Zhou, K., Xu, D., Shi, X.H., Bao, H.J., Guo, B.N., Shum, H.Y.: Mesh editing with poisson-based gradient field manipulation. In: SIGGRAPH 2004, pp. 644–651. ACM, New York (2004)
9. Zayer, R., Rossl, C., Karni, Z., Seidel, H.P.: Harmonic guidance for surface deformation. Computer Graphics Forum 24(3), 601–609 (2005)
10. Popa, T., Julius, D., Sheffer, A.: Material-aware mesh deformations. In: SMI 2006: Proceedings of the IEEE International Conference on Shape Modeling & Applications, p. 22. IEEE Computer Society, Washington, DC (2006)
11. Alexa, M.: Local control for mesh morphing. In: SMI 2001: Proceedings of the International Conference on Shape Modeling & Applications, p. 209. IEEE Computer Society, Washington, DC (2001)
12. Lipman, Y., Sorkine, O., Cohen-Or, D., Levin, D., Rossl, C., Seidel, H.P.: Differential coordinates for interactive mesh editing. In: Proceedings of Shape Modeling International, pp. 181–190. IEEE Computer Society Press (2004)

13. Sorkine, O., Lipman, Y., Cohen-Or, D., Alexa, M., Rossl, C., Seidel, H.P.: Laplacian surface editing. In: Proceedings of the Eurographics/ACM SIGGRAPH Symposium on Geometry Processing, pp. 179–188. Eurographics Association (2004)
14. Igarashi, T., Moscovich, T., Hughes, J.F.: As-rigid-as-possible shape manipulation. ACM Transaction on Graphics 24(3), 1134–1141 (2005)
15. Zhou, K., Huang, J., Snyder, J., Liu, X.G., Bao, H.J., Guo, B.N., Shum, H.Y.: Large mesh deformation using the volumetric graph laplacian. ACM Transaction on Graphics 24(3), 496–503 (2005)
16. Shi, L., Yu, Y.Z., Bell, N., Feng, W.W.: A fast multigrid algorithm for mesh deformation. ACM Transaction on Graphics 25(3), 1108–1117 (2006)
17. Huang, J., Shi, X.H., Liu, X.G., Zhou, K., Wei, L.Y., Teng, S.H., Bao, H.J., Guo, B.N., Shum, H.Y.: Subspace gradient domain mesh deformation. ACM Transaction on Graphics 25(3), 1126–1134 (2006)
18. Oscar, K.C., Tai, C.L., Liu, L.G., Fu, H.G.: Dual Laplacian editing for meshes. IEEE Transaction on Visualization and Computer Graphics (TVCG) 12(3), 386–395 (2006)
19. Zhou, K., Huang, X., Xu, W.W., Guo, B.N., Shum, H.Y.: Direct manipulation of subdivision surfaces on gpus. ACM Transaction on Graphics 26(3), 91 (2007)
20. Cook, R.L.: Shade trees. In: SIGGRAPH 1984, pp. 223–231. ACM, New York (1984)
21. Lee, A., Moreton, H., Hoppe, H.: Displaced subdivision surfaces. In: Proceedings of ACM SIGGRAPH 2000, pp. 85–94 (July 2000)
22. Oscar, K.C., Tai, C.L.: Sampling-sensitive multiresolution hierarchy for irregular meshes. Vis. Comput. 20, 479–493 (2004)
23. Fu, H.B., Tai, C.L., Zhang, H.X.: Topology-free cut-and-paste editing over meshes. In: Geometric Modeling and Processing 2004, pp. 173–182 (2004)
24. Ju, T., Zhou, Q.Y., Van de Panne, M., Cohen-Or, D., Neumann, U.: Reusable skinning templates using cage-based deformations. ACM Trans. Graph. 27, 122:1–122:10 (2008)
25. Joshi, P., Meyer, M., DeRose, T., Green, B., Sanocki, T.: Harmonic coordinates for character articulation. ACM Trans. Graph. 26 (2007)
26. Garland, M., Heckbert, P.S.: Surface simplification using quadric error metrics. In: SIGGRAPH 1997, pp. 209–216. ACM Press/Addison-Wesley Publishing Co., New York, NY (1997)
27. Hill Jr., F.S.: The pleasures of "perp dot" products. In: Graphics Gems IV, pp. 138–148 (1994)

Physically Based Simulation of Solid Objects' Burning

Shiguang Liu[1,2,*], Tai An[1], Zheng Gong[3], and Ichiro Hagiwara[3]

[1] School of Computer Science and Technology, Tianjin University, Tianjin 300072, China
[2] State Key Lab of Virtual Reality Technology and System, Beihang University, Beijing 100191, China
[3] Department of Mechanical Science and Engineering, Tokyo Institute of Technology, Tokyo 152-8550, Japan
lsg@tju.edu.cn

Abstract. This paper presents a novel method for realistic simulation of solid objects' burning. The temperature field is first constructed based on combustion theories. Then, a temperature field motivated interaction model (TFMI) is proposed to simulate the interactions between the fire and the objects during burning. In TFMI, the decomposition of the objects is modeled by improving the level set method and the spreading of fire is calculated using the updated temperature field at each time step. Our method can deal with varied topologies of different objects during burning. The fire is simulated by adopting stable fluid method and integrated into the whole burning scenes. Finally, various solid objects' burning scenes are rendered automatically using the above model. The experiment results show the validity of our method.

1 Introduction

Realistic simulation of nature scenes automatically has become one of the research hotspots in computer graphics in recent years. Among them, burning simulation draws more and more attentions which can be found wide applications such as computer games, special effects, fire disaster prevention and rescue, virtual reality, etc. However, most previous works focus on the simulation of fire in burning scenes. How to simulate the interactions between fire and burning objects realistically remains an open problem for computer graphics researchers.

It is well known that the combustible object will begin to burn when the temperature reaches its ignition temperature. During burning, the object will decompose due to the propagation of the temperature in the environment. On the other hand, the process of objects' decomposition will also lead to heat release and thus influence the temperature field. The above physics principles should be considered to simulate a burning scene realistically.

Based on the combustion theories, we present a novel method to simulate solid objects' burning. A temperature field motivated interaction model which is called TFMI in this paper is proposed to model the interactions between the fire and the burning objects. TFMI can be used to simulate the objects' decomposition and the fire spreading for complex burning scene. It can also deal with complex varied topologies. The dynamics of the fire is modeled by the stable fluid method. The simulation of the

* Corresponding author.

Z. Pan et al. (Eds.): Transactions on Edutainment VII, LNCS 7145, pp. 110–120, 2012.

fire and the objects' deformation is modeled in the same 3D space and integrated as a whole framework. The main contributions of our paper can be summarized as follows:

- A novel physically based simulation framework for solid objects' burning is proposed which can deal with various dynamic burning scenes.
- TFMI is specially designed to model the interactions between the fire and the objects during burning.
- Our method can deal with complex varied topologies during burning which is also easy to implement.

The rest of the paper is organized as follows. In Section 2 we give a brief survey of relative works. Then we propose the method of modelling the temperature field in Section 3. Section 4 describes TFMI which is adopted to simulate the interactions between the fire and the object during burning. The implementation and rendering results are discussed in Section 5. Conclusions and future works are at last.

2 Related Work

Recently, more and more attention has been paid to realistic simulation of burning scenes. However, extensive studies are conducted on the simulation of fire phenomena without considering its interactions with the burning objects.

For fire simulation, the existed methods belong to two categories: heuristic methods and physics based methods. Heuristic methods are fast and easy to implement, including particle systems, cellular automata, etc. Physically based methods can simulate more realistic fire scenes but need more computational times. In 1983, Reeves [1] adopted particle systems to simulate fire which was the first fire model in computer graphics. This method is simple and easy to implement. A large amount of particles are needed to generate a realistic scene and the motion of fire is also hard to control by this method. Supposing that fire consisted of some simple cellular, Pakeshi et al. [2] used the theory of Cellular Automata to model fire. By combining the cellars into different patterns, this method can control the motion of fire easily. Wang et al. [3] proposed a unified framework for modeling and animating fire using geometric constrains such as curves, surfaces, etc. To achieve more accurate fire scenes, many physics based fire models are proposed. Rushemeier et al. [4] described the visualization method for fire by using data from pool fires. In 1995, Stam et al. [5] simulated the dynamics of fire by a finite difference scheme. This method can generate realistic motion of fire. However, the solution is not stable. Nguyen et al. [6] introduced a Navier-Stokes equations based fire model. By adopting level set method to track the blue core of the fire, this method can model complex fire with realistic shapes at the cost of a large amount of computations. Considering the physical and chemical theories, Ishikawa et al. [7] presented a novel method to simulate the fire spread. Hong et al. [8] tried to simulate fire with more detailed features like flame wrinkling and cellular patterns using the DSD (Detonation Shock Dynamics) framework. Explosion is the results of instant fire in a limited space, which was also simulated [9, 10] in computer graphics in recent years. Though the above methods can simulate the dynamics and the shapes of the fire realistically, they can not be used to simulate the interactions between fire and the burning objects. Until now, there are only a few works for the simulation of realistic burning scenes considering the interactions between fire and the objects.

Burning solids into gases was simulated by Losasso et al. [11] using a remeshing method. This model doesn't consider the burning object's influence on the motion of the fire and can not generate fine-scale decomposition structures. Melek et al. [12, 13] proposed an interactive method to simulate the objects' decomposition and deformation during burning. However, their method did not consider the object's property such as the calorific value and the specific heat capacity, etc. Also, they suppose the deformation direction of the object as the opposition to the normal. The similar method [14] was also adopted to simulate the bending and crumpling effects of simple objects such as matches and paper. Just recently, Liu et al. [15] proposed a novel unified framework for simulating burning phenomena of thin-shell objects such as paper, cloth, etc. However, this method is difficult to be extended for the simulation of solid objects' burning. In this paper, we propose a novel method for simulation of solid objects' burning, which can simulate the interactions between fire and burning objects realistically. Our method can also capture the fine scales of decomposition for solid objects when they are burning.

3 Temperature Field

During objects' burning, the temperature in the space will vary due to the motion of fire. Meanwhile, the updated temperature field will influence the propagation of the fire. For example, the diffusion of the temperature can make more vertexes' temperature reach their ignition temperature and thus begin to burn. So, calculation of the temperature field is the basis to model the interactions between fire and the object. Figure 1 shows the framework of our temperature field motivated burning simulation.

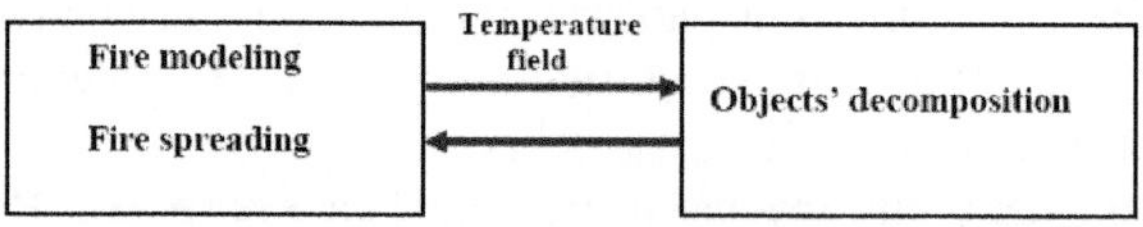

Fig. 1. Temperature field motivated burning simulation

The propagation of temperature will be different for different vertexes in the space. We calculate the temperature for the outer vertexes (including the boundary vertexes) and the interior vertexes, respectively. For the outer vertexes, the temperature will be advected by the velocity field and spread to its six neighboring vertexes. As the object will release heat during burning, new thermal energy will add to the temperature field. We model the temperature of the boundary vertexes as follows:

$$T_t = -(\vec{u} \cdot \nabla)T + K_T \nabla^2 T + T_{add} \, , \tag{1}$$

where T is the temperature to be calculated, T_t is the time differentiation of the temperature with respect to time, $\vec{u}$ represents the velocity of the fire, K_T is the diffusion coefficient which is varied with the position, T_{add} denotes the added temperature due to the heat release of the objects. T_{add} is a function of the calorific value and the specific heat capacity of the object, which can be expressed as follows:

$$T_{add}(\vec{x}) = \begin{cases} \frac{q}{c \cdot f_{total}} \cdot \frac{\partial}{\partial t} S(\vec{x}), T(\vec{x}) > T_{thres}, f_{left} > 0 \\ 0, T(\vec{x}) < T_{thres} \end{cases}, \quad (2)$$

where $S(\vec{x})$ is the amount of the released fuel of vertex $\vec{x}$ which will be detailed in Section 4, $T(\vec{x})$ is the temperature of vertex $\vec{x}$, f_{total} is the total amount of the fuel, T_{thres} represents the self-pyrolysis temperature of the object, and f_{left} is the amount of the left fuel. In our method, $S(\vec{x})/f_{total}$ is used to control the intensity of the temperature's variation, q and c are the calorific value and the specific heat capacity of the object, respectively.

Fig. 2. The varied temperature field of a bunny model at different time

For the interior vertexes, the spread of the temperature is only caused by the diffusion process. We calculate it by $T_t = K_T \nabla^2 T$. By introducing the signed distance field which will be expressed in the following section, we can divide the vertexes into the boundary vertexes, the outer vertexes and the interior vertexes easily. Then, the temperature for different kind of vertexes will be calculated using the above model, respectively. Figure 2 shows the result of the varied temperature field of a bunny model at different time. The ignition point is at the bottom of the model. The color shows the magnitude of the temperature, that is, red represents the highest and white represents the lowest.

4 Temperature Field Motivated Interaction Model (TFMI)

4.1 The Overview of TFMI

Figure 3 shows the sketch map of TFMI. When the object burns, its temperature will increase. The object will decompose when the temperature reaches its self-pyrolysis temperature. At the same time, the object will release heat and influence the temperature field. On the other hand, the object will also be converted into hot gaseous product during its burning, and thus increase the source fuel of the fire. This converted source value can be calculated as follows:

$$\frac{\partial}{\partial t}S(\vec{x}) = \begin{cases} S(\vec{x},t)\cdot 2^{\frac{1}{10}\frac{\partial T}{\partial t}}, \vec{x}\in\partial\Omega, T(\vec{x}) > T_{thres}, f_{left} > 0, \\ 0, otherwise \end{cases} \tag{3}$$

where a is an adjustment parameter, $|\vec{u}|$ is the modulus of the velocity, $\partial\Omega$ represents the boundary of the object, ρ and μ are the density and the viscosity, respectively. As the object converts into hot gaseous product during burning, the left fuel will decrease gradually. The time differentiation of the amount of the fuel of vertex $\vec{x}$ can be expressed as $\frac{\partial}{\partial t}f_{left}(\vec{x}) = -\frac{\partial}{\partial t}S(\vec{x})$.

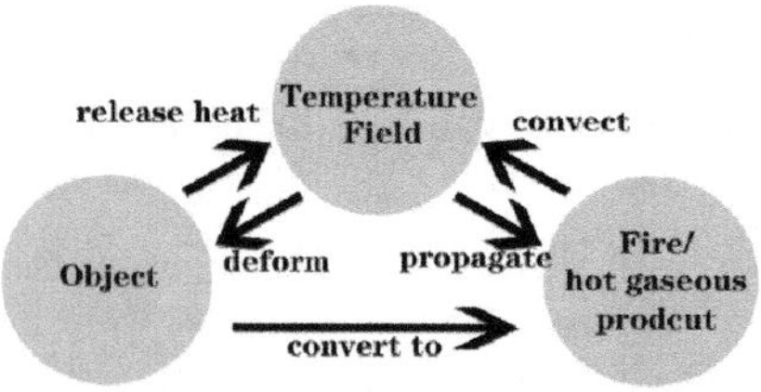

Fig. 3. The overview of TFMI

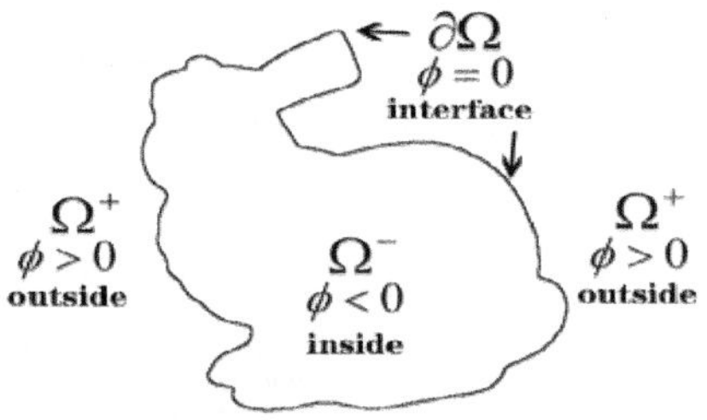

Fig. 4. The isocontour surface in our method

4.2 Level Set Based Object Decomposition

When the temperature reaches the object's self-pyrolysis temperature, it will decompose. In most cases, the object will be burned into pieces. We introduce the physics of burning into the level set method to model the complex process of the object's decomposition.

Level set method is widely used to trace the dynamic interfaces in computer graphics and image processing [16-18]. In our method, the interface between the fire and the object is simulated as one side of an isocontour of a signed distance field, ϕ. The interface $\partial\Omega$ is defined by $\phi = 0$ isocontour with $\phi < 0$ representing the inside of the object Ω^- and $\phi > 0$ representing the outside of the object Ω^+, respectively (see Fig. 4).

The signed distance $d(\vec{x})$ of a vertex $\vec{x}$ is defined as the minimum length from $\vec{x}$ to the interface, that is, $d(\vec{x}) = \min(|\vec{x} - \vec{x}_I|)$, where $\vec{x}_I \in \partial\Omega$. The sign of $d(\vec{x})$ is positive, zero and negative when $\vec{x}\in\Omega^+$, $\vec{x}\in\partial\Omega$ and $\vec{x}\in\Omega^-$, respectively. Until now, there are some methods to calculate the signed distance field in 3D space [19-24]. Here, we introduce the method of pseudo normal [25], which can design the signed distance field from the triangle meshes. The interface is dynamically evolved in space and time according to the velocity field $\vec{u}$. This process is expressed by the following equation:

$$\phi_t + \vec{u} \cdot \nabla \phi + n | \nabla \phi | = b \kappa | \nabla \phi |, \tag{4}$$

where ϕ_t is the partial derivative of ϕ with respect to time, ∇ is the gradient operator, κ is the curvature, n denotes the velocity on the direction of the normal, b is a coefficient. During burning, the maximum deformation direction of the object is opposite to the normal. So, Equation (4) can be converted as follows:

$$\phi_t - D(\vec{x}) | \nabla \phi | = 0, \tag{5}$$

where $D(\vec{x})$ is the magnitude of the decomposition of vertex $\vec{x}$ which is a function of the position, the temperature, the property of the object such as the self-pyrolysis temperature, density, etc. We calculate $D(\vec{x})$ as the following:

$$D(\vec{x}) = \begin{cases} (a(T(\vec{x}) - T_{\text{air}}) / \rho | \vec{u} |^2), \vec{x} \in \partial\Omega, T(\vec{x}) > T_{thres}, f_{left} > 0, \\ 0, otherwise \end{cases} \tag{6}$$

where a denotes the intensity of the combustion of the object, T_{air} is the average temperature of the air. As Equation (5) satisfies the condition of the signed distance field, it can be discreted as $\phi^{n+1} = \phi^n + D(\vec{x})\Delta t$, here Δt is the time step. This method can deal with complex varied topology during burning. Figure 5 shows the topology variation of a dog model constructed by our method.

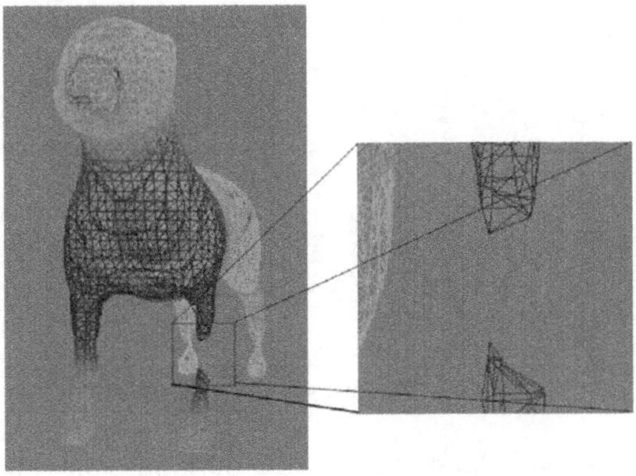

Fig. 5. Topology construction for a dog model during burning

4.3 Fire Spreading

To simulate the spreading of fire, we will first initialize the position of the ignition points. Then, according to the updated temperature field at each time step, we determine which vertexes will reach the combustion conditions. We divide the vertexes into three categories: burning vertex, unburned vertex and burned vertex. Figure 6 shows the results of the spreading of the burning areas. In Figure 6, the black part represents the burned area.

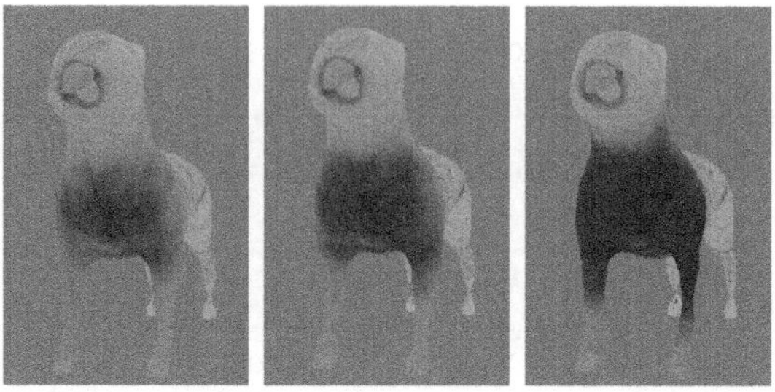

Fig. 6. Results of the spreading of the burning areas

5 Implementation and Rendering Results

Based on the above model, we have rendered various burning scenes of solid objects. All simulations were run on a Pentium IV with 3.0G RAM, nVidia 7800 display card. In our experiments, the time step dt is 0.25, and the values of T_{air} and $T_{\max}$ are $25.0^{\circ}C$ and $600.0^{\circ}C$, respectively. The rendering rates are about 1 second per frame. More meaningful parameters of the different examples are showed in Table 1. RES is the resolution of the space to calculate level set equations.

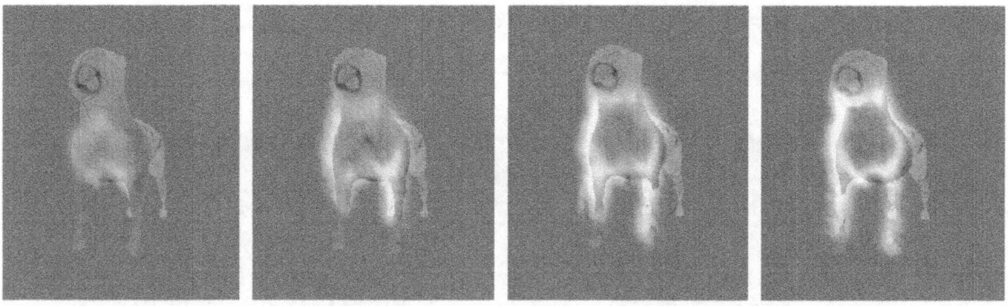

(a) (b) (c) (d)

Fig. 7. Burning results of a dog model

Figure 7 shows the simulation results of a burning bunny model using our method. The ignition point is in the front part of the model. We can see that the burning process and the decomposition of the model from Figure 7(a) through 7(d). Our method can deal with the varied topology of the burning model as shown in Figure 7(c) and 7(d). Figure 8 is the burning results of a monster model. Our method can also simulate the burning phenomena generated by multiple ignition points. Figure 9 (a) through 9(f) shows the burning process of a bunny model generated by only one ignition point which lies on the lower part. We can see that the fire spreads upward along the surface of the model accurately. Figure 10 shows the burning results generated by two ignition points. In Figure 10, one ignition point lies on the lower part and the other lies on the upper part. We can see that the two groups of fire spread according to their own paths first and then convergence into one when they meet. At the same time, the decomposition of the bunny model gets faster. In addition, our method can be used to simulate the burning phenomena of very complex models such as a tree, a house, etc. Figure 11 shows the simulation results of a burning tree. In this experiment, we improve the resolution of the simulation space to $200\times200\times200$ to get accurate results. The fine details of the burning of little branches are showed in Figure 11(a) through 11(d). The varied topologies of the tree model during burning are also simulated accurately.

6 Conclusions and Future Works

In this paper, we proposed a novel method to simulate the burning phenomena of solid objects automatically. This method adopted TFMI to model the interactions between the fire and the objects. The decomposition of the burning object is simulated by introducing the combustion theory into level set method. The decomposition of the object will be converted into hot gaseous product and add influence the fire on the contrary. Our method can also model the above process by calculating the temperature field accurately. This new method can deal with complex objects and varied topologies during the burning process.

Our method can be integrated into current popular simulation software to add more details of various burning scenes. However, since we don't consider the animation of the burning model, the dynamics of the burning is less realistic. We will improve it in future work by introducing the advanced animation techniques into our simulation framework. By considering the properties of different objects, our method can be extended to simulate the phenomena of melt, explosion, etc. Our future work will also include acceleration and optimization of the algorithms. For example, the adaptive method to calculate the level set equations and the optimization of the reconstruction of signed distance field may accelerate the rendering. Modern graphics hardware will also be used to achieve real time simulation in our future work.

Table 1. The parameters and their values in our experiment

Figures	RES	$c\ (J/(Kg\cdot{}^{\circ}C))$	$q\ (J/Kg)$	K_{mat}	$T_{thres}\ ({}^{\circ}C)$
Fig.7	80×80×80	2.1×10^3	0.8×10^7	0.1520	185.0
Fig.8	80×80×80	2.6×10^3	1.0×10^7	0.1250	205.0
Fig.9/10	100×100×100	1.7×10^3	1.2×10^7	0.3750	196.4
Fig.11	200×200×200	3.0×10^3	0.4×10^7	0.0625	260.0

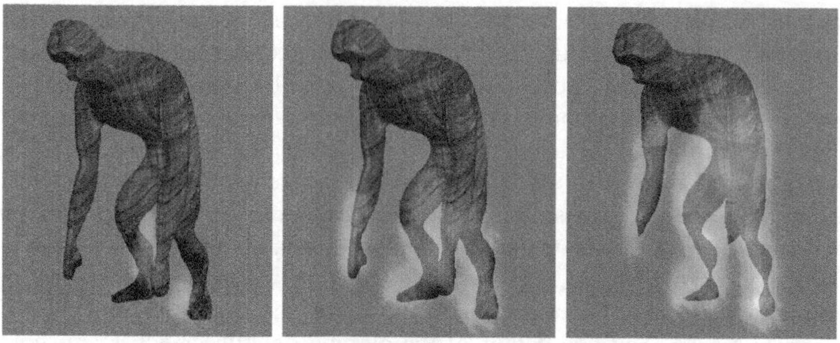

(a) (b) (c)

Fig. 8. Burning results of a monster model

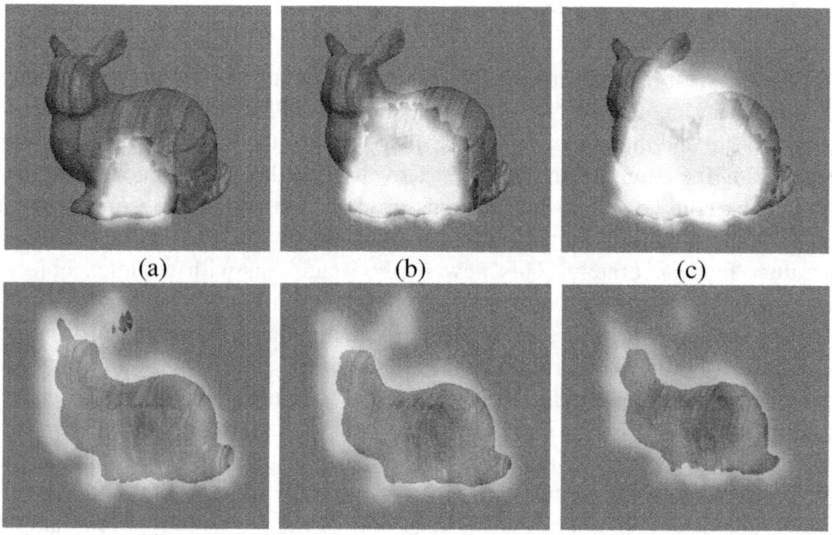

(a) (b) (c)

(d) (e) (f)

Fig. 9. Burning results of a bunny model with one ignition point

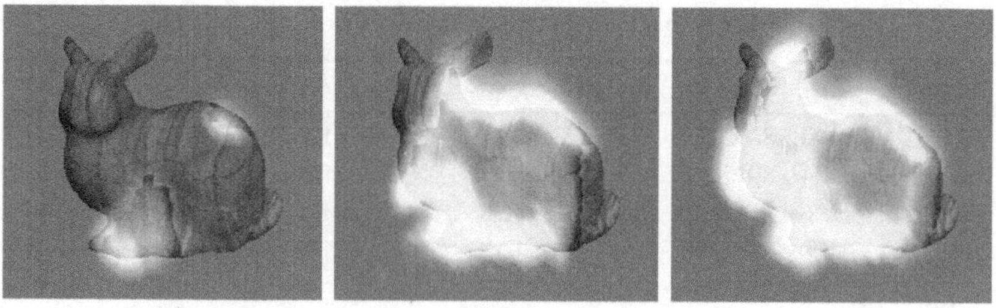

(a) (b) (c)

Fig. 10. Burning results of a bunny model with two ignition points

Fig. 11. Burning results of a tree mode

Acknowledgments. This work was supported by Natural Science Foundation of China under Grant No. 60803047 and 61170118, the Specialized Research Fund for the Doctoral Program of Higher Education of China under Grant No. 200800561045, the Open Project Program of the State Key Laboratory of Virtual Reality Technology and System, Beihang University under Grant No. BUAA-VR-10KF-1, the Open Project Program of the State Key Lab of CAD&CG, Zhejiang University under Grant No. A1210. The authors would also like to thank the reviewers for their insightful comments which greatly helped improving the manuscript.

References

1. Reeves, W.T.: Particle Systems-a Technique for Modeling a Class of Fuzzy Objects. In: Proceedings of SIGGRAPH, pp. 359–376 (1983)
2. Pakeshi, A., Yuz, K., Nakajima, M.: Generating Two Dimensional Flame Images in Computer Graphics. IEICE Transactions 74(2), 457–462 (1991)
3. Hong, Y., Zhu, D., Qiu, X., Wang, Z.: Geometry-Based Control of Fire Simulation. The Visual Computer 26 (2010)
4. Rushmeier, H.E., Hamins, A., Choi, M.Y.: Volume rendering of pool fire data. In: Proceedings of IEEE Conference on Visualization, pp. 382–385 (1994)
5. Stam, J., Fiume, E.: Depicting Fire and Other Gaseous Phenomena Using Diffusion Processes. In: Proceedings of SIGGRAPH, pp. 129–136 (1995)
6. Nguyen, D., Fedkiw, R., Jensen, H.W.: Physically based modeling and animation of fire. In: Proceedings of SIGGRAPH, pp. 721–728 (2002)
7. Ishikawa, T., Miyazaki, R., Dobashi, Y., Nishita, T.: Visual simulation of spreading fire. In: Proceedings of NICOGRAPH International, pp. 43–48 (2005)
8. Hong, J., Shinar, T., Fedkiw. R.: Wrinkled flames and cellular patterns. In: Proceedings of SIGGRAPH, pp. 47.1–47.6 (2007)
9. Yngve, G.D., O'Brien, J.F., Hodgins, J.K.: Animating explosions. In: Proceedings of SIGGRAPH, pp. 29–36 (2000)
10. Feldman, B.E., O'Brien, J.F., Arikan, O.: Animating suspended particle explosions. ACM Transactions on Graphics 22(3), 708–715 (2003)
11. Losasso, F., Irving, G., Guendelman, E., et al.: Melting and burning solids into liquids and gases. IEEE Transactions on Visualization and Computer Graphics 12(3), 343–352 (2006)

12. Melek, Z., Keyser, J.: Interactive simulation of burning objects. In: Proceedings of Pacific Graphics, pp. 462–466 (2003)
13. Melek, Z., Keyser, J.: Driving object deformations from internal physical processes. In: Proceedings of the ACM Symposium on Solid and Physical Modeling, pp. 51–59 (2007)
14. Melek, Z., Keyser, J.: Bending burning matches and crumpling burning paper. In: Proceedings of SIGGRAPH Poster (2006)
15. Liu, S., Liu, Q., An, T., Sun, J., Peng, Q.: Physically based simulation of thin-shell objects' burning. The Visual Computer 25(5-7), 687–696 (2009)
16. Osher, S., Fedkiw, R.: Level Set Methods and Dynamic Implicit Surfaces. Springer, New York (2002)
17. Fedkiw, R.: Geometric Level Set Methods in Imaging, Vision and Graphics. Springer, New York (2003)
18. Mitchell, I.M.: The flexible, extensible and efficient toolbox of level set methods. Journal of Scientific Computing 35(2-3), 300–329 (2007)
19. Sethian, J.A.: Level Set Methods and Fast Marching Methods. Cambridge University Press, New York (1999)
20. Strain, J.: A fast modular semi-lagrangian method for moving interfaces. Journal of Computational Physics 161(2), 512–536 (2000)
21. Sethian, J.: A fast marching level set method for monotonically advancing fronts. Proceedings of the National Academy of Sciences 93, 1591–1595 (1996)
22. Hugues, H., Tony, D., Tom, D., John, M., Werner, S.: Surface reconstruction from unorganized points. Computer Graphics 26(2), 71–78 (1992)
23. Desbrun, M., Meyer, M., Schroder, P., Barr, A.H.: Implicit fairing of irregular meshes using diffusion and curvature flow. In: Proceeding of SIGGRAPH, pp. 317–324 (1999)
24. Ken, M., David, E.B., Ross, T.W., Alan, H.B.: Level set surface editing operators. In: Proceedings of SIGGRAPH, pp. 330–338 (2002)
25. Aanaes, H., Baerentzen, J.A.: Pseudo-normal for signed distance computation. In: Proceedings of Vision, Modeling and Visualization, pp. 407–413 (2003)

Tunneling Blasting Simulation for Digital Mine

Chao Wang[1,2], Yu Wu[1], Tingting Zhu[2], Hongbo Li[1], and Mingliang Xu[2]

[1] Institute of Web Intelligence, Chongqing University of Posts and Telecommunications, Chongqing, 400065, China
[2] State Key Lab of CAD&CG Zhejiang University, Hangzhou, 310027, China
wcfairytale@hotmail.com, wuyu@cqupt.edu.cn, ttingzhu@gmail.com, lihongbo@cqupt.edu.cn, develop_game@yahoo.com.cn

Abstract. Tunneling blasting is a major component of digital mine simulation, with the high cost, dangerous and irreversible features of blasting, it is difficult to design tunneling blasting scheme in real world. The paper simulates tunneling blasting by combining blasting animation of computer graphics with mining empirical formulas. A connected voxel model is used to represent rocks and their failure mechanism. This simulation helps engineers test and adjust blasting scheme before real operation.

Keywords: Digital Mine, Blasting, Simulation, Voxel.

1 Introduction

Digital mining related techniques and construction schemes have become a hot research topic [1]. Currently tunneling relies mainly on blasting, however, blasting design requires highly technical skills. The blasting scheme not only affects the blasting quality directly, but also, even more importantly, threats the operators' safety if the blasting scheme is wrongly chosen. Due to irreversibility of blasting, it's unable to test the feasibility of blasting scheme in real world. Therefore, it is imperative to implement a computer simulation to reflect the blasting results helping engineers to adjust and optimize blasting scheme.

There are up to 400 GIS software commonly used in the world now, such as Dimine, Micromine, Geocom, Datamine, etc [2]. However, in the field of simulation of tunneling blasting, existing work only made some efforts on post-process animation, while real-time 3D animation with controllable parameters is not yet seen.

The paper combines blasting animation of computer graphics with mining empirical formulas and sets up a method of tunneling blasting simulation. Users can adjust blasting scheme with key parameters such as drilling hole pattern and explosive charge. Blasting animation is determined by the scheme and generated in real-time. At the same time, key parameters of blasting result are calculated and presented to users as a sheet of report. The paper firstly introduces the key parameters of blasting scheme, then discusses the theories and techniques of blasting animation in details, at last gets result by experimental results with different parameters.

Z. Pan et al. (Eds.): Transactions on Edutainment VII, LNCS 7145, pp. 121–128, 2012.

2 Previous Work

In the field of computer graphics, previous efforts on blasting animation have focused on the graphical representation modeling explosive products while less work has done on objects effects around the blasting environment.

Pioneering work was done by Reeves [3] who proposed an explosion model using particle system. Particle system is good at simulating fuzzy objects such as fire and smoke, nevertheless inadequate to the behavior modeling of rocks under shockwaves because the adjacent debris connects with each other while particles are independent entities. Moreover, rock fragments are the variants of original rocks that they are not generated from an emitter as Reeves' particle system.

Some progress has been made in simulating influence on surrounding objects caused by shockwaves through shockwave propagation model. Neff and Fiume [4] generate cracks in a planar surface in a form similar to recursion. Mazarak chooses an ideal blast wave model and proposes a connected voxel representation of object to model the fracturing and splashing process of objects being pressed by a shockwave [5]. Based on Mazarak's work, Martins [6] extends the concept of voxel by allowing arbitrary scaling along any axis which enhances the performance of graphics. Rami [7] introduces geology into the terrain model and takes reflection of shockwaves between layers of the terrain into consideration and finally implements a simulation of cratering and fragmentation of the terrain.

In the field of high realistic simulation of fracturing and explosive products, Brien uses finite element method to model brittle and ductile fracture [8, 9]. Yngve and Sewall model complex shockwave interaction rather accurately and at the same time simulate high realistic flames. Due to the complexity of computing mechanisms of these methods, the time expense goes too high for a real-time application [10, 11].

Since underground blasts should consider the stone lithology, drilling hole pattern, detonating network, explosive charge and so on, to get an exactly accurate model of blasts remains a challenging work. Time consumption is another factor to take into consideration. The paper cares more about the visual perception, so connected voxel model is adopted to obtain a tradeoff between accuracy and realistic visualization.

3 Tunneling Blasting Design

When a dynamite is set off in a rock mass with moderate depth, we can see cracking, plumping up and throwing away on free face, which is shown in Fig. 1. As a result, a turbinate pit will occur at free surface named *blasting crater* [12]. The factor which mostly impact the blasting animation in the paper is the explosive charge which can be determined by drilling hole pattern and condition of tunnel.

3.1 Drilling Hole Pattern

The parameters relative to drilling hole pattern includes diameters, depths, numbers, spacing (space between holes and holes) and angles (from the normal of free face) of blast holes [13, 14, 15]. In China, the diameter of a traditional dynamite pack is $32 \sim 35mm$, and the diameter of a blast hole is $4 \sim 6mm$ bigger than that of the dynamite pack.

The depth of a blast hole is related to the tunnel's width:

$$l = (0.5\sim0.7)B \tag{1}$$

B is the width of a tunnel. An important parameter W called *least resistance line*, which is the minimum distance between pack's center and free face, can be calculated according to the hole depth:

$$W = Kl \tag{2}$$

K is the influence coefficient varying by the rock features, which is generally set to $15\sim30$, the bigger value for harder rocks. Then we can use least resistance line to obtain hole spacing a (horizontal) and row spacing b (vertical):

$$a = (0.8\sim2.0)W \tag{3}$$

$$b = (0.8\sim1.2)W \tag{4}$$

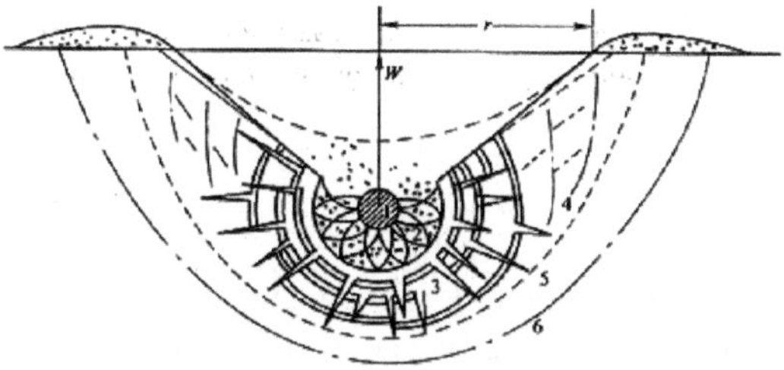

Fig. 1. Blasting effect schematic diagram 1-dynamite source; 2-compression circle; 3-fragmentation circle; 4-fissured circle; 5-permanent deformation circle; 6-elastic vibration circle; W-least resistence line; r-crater radius

3.2 Charge Calculation

Explosive charge Q can be obtained by influence coefficient K, hole spacing a, row spacing b and hole depth l:

$$Q = 0.33Kabl \tag{5}$$

4 Modelling and Animation

4.1 Blast Wave Theory

We adopt Friedlander equation [16] which is able to accurately describe the propagation of a shockwave's peak overpressure. At the beginning of an explosion, a cloud of gas with high temperature and high pressure is formed. This cloud of gas violently pushes the air nearby and generates a series of compressed wave which propagates all around and finally stacks into a shock.

Before the shock front reaches a given point, the ambient pressure is p_o. At arrival time t_a, the pressure rises sharply to the peak value. The difference between peak value and p_o is p_{so} which is called *peak overpressure*. Within time T_d pressure drops to ambient pressure and keeps dropping to a partial vacuum, then in a given time eventually returns to the ambient pressure. The Friedlander equation described the pressure profile curve $p(t)$ as:

$$p(t) = p_o + p_{so}\left(1 - \frac{t}{T_d}\right)e^{-bt/T_d} \tag{6}$$

t is the time passed from arrival time t_a.

Yang synthesizes previous work and gets a relation between peak overpressure p_{so} and scaled distance Z [17]:

$$p_{so} = \begin{cases} \dfrac{0.084}{Z} + \dfrac{0.270}{Z^2} + \dfrac{0.70}{Z^3}, & Z \leq 1 \\ \dfrac{0.076}{Z} + \dfrac{0.255}{Z^2} + \dfrac{0.65}{Z^3}, & 1 < Z \leq 15 \end{cases} \tag{7}$$

The scaled distance Z is defined as:

$$Z = R/Q^{\frac{1}{3}} \tag{8}$$

R is the distance between a given point and the center of blast. Q is the TNT mass.

The expressions of t_a and T_d are:

$$t_a = 0.34R^{1.4}Q^{-0.2}/C_a \tag{9}$$

$$T_d = 0.0005R^{0.72}Q^{0.16} \tag{10}$$

C_a is the speed of sound in air.

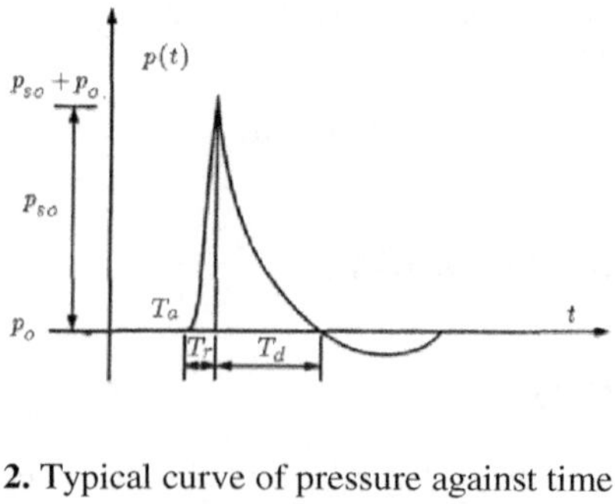

Fig. 2. Typical curve of pressure against time

4.2 Modelling

Rocks are modeled with connected voxels which represent fragments that can't be subdivided any more. Adjacent voxels are connected by links that store those voxels' adjacent information. Links could be regarded as springs with no elasticity. Connected voxels are relatively still to each other and can be grouped into more complex structures called *bodies*. The position and orientation of a voxel is determined by the body it belongs to.

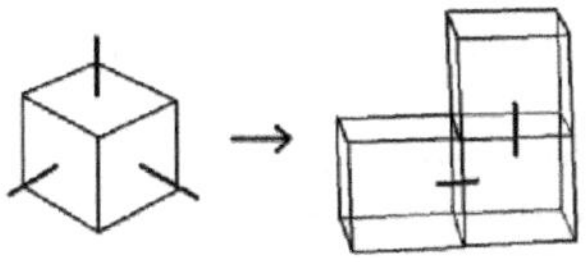

Fig. 3. Connected voxels make up a body

Identical and homogeneous voxels can't represent the irregular contour of the objects, so we choose three basic voxel shapes according to the common shapes of the rock fragments. They are 8-vertices voxel, 6-vertices voxel and 4-vertices voxel. Disturbance variables are introduced on every vertex of a voxel along three axis and a random scaling is performed to the whole voxel so that generated voxels have different shapes and sizes.

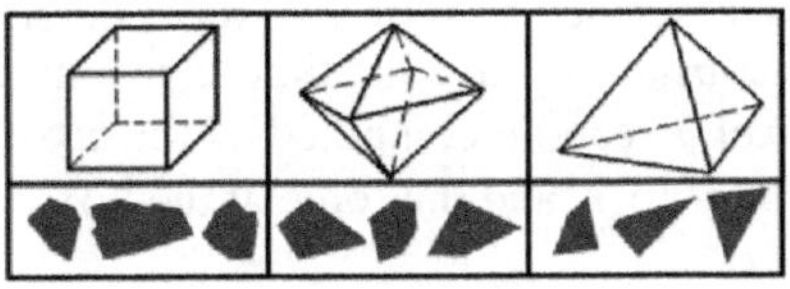

Fig. 4. 8-vertices voxel (left); 6-vertices voxel (middle); 4-vertices voxel (right)

When blast wave reaches to a rock, huge pressure differentials cause it break. In connected voxel model, this effect is simulated by breaking links of voxels. Initially, the entire scene is presented as a connected graph, the nodes of which are voxels, edges of which are links. Every connected component of the graph is a body that represents a rock. As links being broken by shockwave, connected graph changes and new connected components are generated. Original bodies split into smaller bodies which represents original rocks split into smaller fragments.

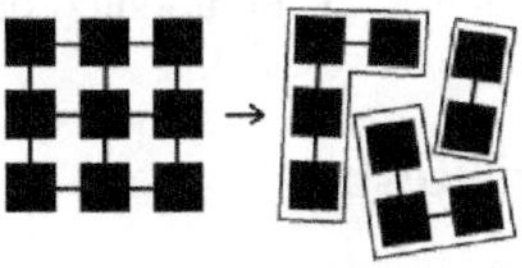

Fig. 5. Initial body(left); Fracture (right)

Every link has a yield limit which is the maximum pressure a link can endure. Once the pressure exceeds this limit, the associated link breaks. In reality, compressive resistance varies in different position inside a rock. To simulate this, a disturbed value is added on the mean yield limit of every link:

$$yield_{limit} = yield_{mean} \pm rand(yield_{var}) \tag{11}$$

4.3 Animation

The blast wave not only causes rocks to fracture, but also causes the rock fragments to rotate and splash by changing their velocity and angular via force and torque. Since the shapes and sizes are different, calculating the forces at the vertices of each voxel is more accurate than at the center of the voxel. The resultant force of a voxel is calculated as the average force at each voxel.

The force at a given vertex $\vec{F}$ is determined by the blast wave pressure $p(t)$ and the area of the voxel projected onto the surface of the shock front A. The direction of vector $\vec{R}$ is from explosive source to the vertex:

$$\vec{F} = p(t) \cdot A \cdot \frac{\vec{R}}{\|\vec{R}\|} \tag{12}$$

Because the projected surface area of a voxel is determined mainly by the voxel's size, so A is set to be constant to save the time-consuming cost.

The torque on a voxel $\vec{T}$ can be computed as the cross product of its relative position of the body it belongs to $\vec{r}$ and the force at the voxel $\vec{F}$:

$$\vec{T} = \vec{r} \times \vec{F} \tag{13}$$

Resultant force of a body is the sum of all the forces of the voxels within the body, while the torque is the sum of all torques within it:

$$\vec{F}_{body} = \sum \vec{F}_{voxels} \tag{14}$$

$$\vec{T}_{body} = \sum \vec{T}_{voxels} \tag{15}$$

Currently generated bodies keep their velocity and angular velocity in accordance with Newton law of inertia. According to each body's resultant force and torque, the position and orientation of each body are updated between animation frames.

5 Experiments and Results

Based on the above work, we implement the tunneling blasting simulation in which users can make blasting scheme by adjusting key parameters of blasts. The result blasting animation is generated in real-time which simulates the process of rocks fracturing and rock fragments splashing. By walking through the scene, users can check the blasting result conveniently. And a report is generated listing key parameters of blasting results in details.

Fig. 6 and Fig. 7 show simulation results with different TNT equivalence in a same tunnel scene while all other parameters keep the same. From left to right, top to bottom, the first picture shows the scene when blast has been set off for $1000ms$ and each picture afterwards has a time interval of $1000ms$. Last picture shows the final scene at stationary state. We can see that the influence of blasting parameters on simulation result is significant and the simulation is believable.

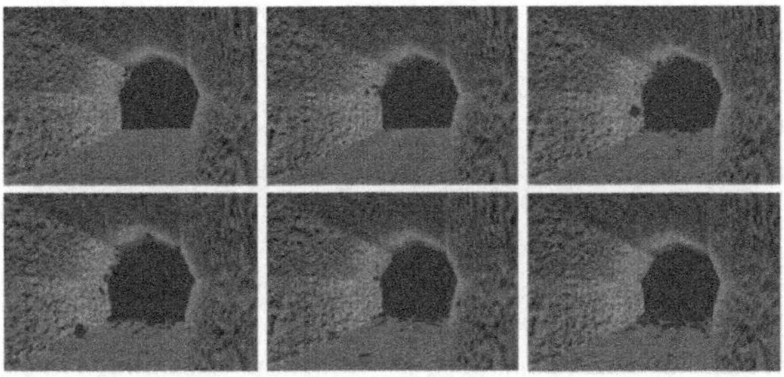

Fig. 6. An explosive force equivalent to 1 ton of TNT

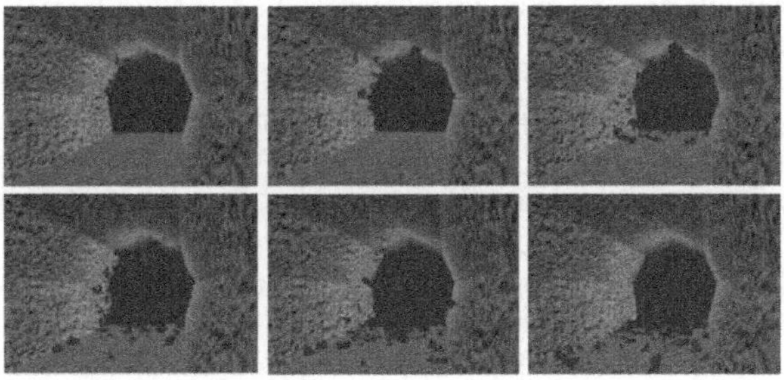

Fig. 7. An explosive force equivalent to 2 tons of TNT

6 Conclusion

Digital mining simulation has positive significance on enhancing scientificity, improving safety and increasing efficiency of the industry. In our work, key parameters of tunneling blasting are extracted based on mining empirical formulas and the blasting result is presented as animation which uses graphics techniques of explosion simulation. Believable animation combined with a sheet of report helps engineers adjust and optimize blasting scheme interactively.

Our future work is to complete the process of blasting design which includes drilling hole pattern, charging and detonating network by implementing human-computer interface for each key link of the process. And further research on visual simulation of influence by blasts is still desirable.

Acknowledgments. The project was supported in part by National High-tech R&D 863 Program (Grant No. 2009AA062704) and National Natural Science Foundation of China (Grant No. 60970076).

References

1. Lu, X., Yin, H.: Definition, Connotations and Progress of Digital Mine. Coal Science and Technology 38(1), 48–52 (2010)
2. Fang, Z., Wang, L., He, Y.: DIMINE-based Research and Realization of True 3D Mining Method Design. Metal Mine 5(395), 129–130 (2009)
3. Reeves, W.T.: Particle System—a Technique for Modeling a Class of Fuzzy Objects. ACM Transactions on Graphics 2(2), 91–108 (1983)
4. Neff, O., Fiume, E.: A Visual Model for Blast Wave and Fracture. In: Proceeding of Graphics Interface 1999, pp. 193–202 (1999)
5. Mazarak, O., Martins, C., Amanatides, J.: Animating Exploding Objects. In: Proceeding of Graphics Interface 1999, pp. 211–218 (1999)
6. Martins, C., Buchanan, J., Amanatides, J.: Animating Real-Time explosions. The Journal of Visualization and Computer Animation 13(2), 133–145 (2002)
7. Rami, N., Proctor, M.D.: Real Time Physically-Based Modeling and Simulation of Cratering and Fragmentation of Terrain. Simulation 83(12), 830–841 (2007)
8. O'Brien, J.F., Hodgins, J.K.: Graphical Modeling and Animation of Brittle Fracture. In: Proceeding of ACM SIGGRAPH 1999, pp. 137–146 (1999)
9. O'Brien, J.F., Bargteil, A.W., Hodgins, J.K.: Graphical Modeling and Animation of Ductile Fractrue. In: Proceeding of ACM SIGGRAPH 2002, pp. 291–294 (2002)
10. Yngve, G.D., O'Brien, J.F., Hodgins, J.K.: Animating Explosions. In: Proceeding of ACM SIGGRAPH 2000, pp. 91–95 (2000)
11. Sewall, J., Galoppo, N., Tsankov, G., Lin, M.: Visual Simulation of Shockwaves. In: Proceeding of ACM SIGGRAPH 2008, pp. 19–28 (2008)
12. Cheng, K., Zhu, W., Wang, Q.: Geotechnical Excavation Engineering Blasting. Wuhan University of Technology Press (2008)
13. Lin, D.: Mining Blasting Engineering. Metallurgical Industry Press, Beijing (1993)
14. Терпигорев, A.M.: Mining Handbook. Metallurgical Industry Press, Beijing (1954)
15. Liu, D., Yang, S.: Blasting Engineering Practical Handbook. Metallurgical Industry Press, Beijing (2004)
16. Baker, W.E.: Explosives in Air. University of Texas Press (1973)
17. Yang, X., Shi, S., Cheng, P.: Forecast and Simulation of Perk Overpressure of TNT Explosion Shock Wave in the Air. Blasting 25(1), 15–18 (2008)

Massively Multiplayer Online Games Developed with Agents

Gustavo Aranda[1], Tomas Trescak[2], Marc Esteva[2], Inmaculada Rodriguez[3], and Carlos Carrascosa[1]

[1] Universitat Polit'ecnica de Valencia,
DSIC, Camino de Vera sn 46022 Valencia, Spain
{garanda,carrasco}@dsic.upv.es
[2] Artificial Intelligence Research Institute (IIIA)
Spanish National Research Council (CSIC)
Campus Universitat Autonoma de Barcelona
08193 Bellaterra, Catalonia, Spain
tomi.trescak@gmail.com, marc@iiia.csic.es
[3] Applied Mathematics Department,
UB Barcelona, Spain
inma@maia.ub.es

Abstract. Massively Multiplayer Online Games (MMOGs) are online videogames played at the same time by a huge number of players experiencing together the same virtual world. MMOGs are an important focus of research, not only because they are economically attractive, but also because a MMOG involves many technologies (3D graphics, networking, AI) and a large amount of data that is generated by the interactions of many individuals in an inherently distributed scenario, forming a complex problem. Previous work in this line of research introduced the architecture called the "Massively Multiplayer Online Games based on Multi-Agent Systems", an effort to develop a system to design, and later deploy, MMOGs using agent technologies. In this paper, we present the model and method behind this architecture, paying special attention to the definition and design of the **"Game Zones"**, the representation of the virtual environment. Also, we detail the components and steps to follow in the design of MMOGs based on organizations.

Keywords: Multi-Agent Systems, MAS, Massively Multiplayer Online Games, MMOG, Multi-user/multi-virtual-agent interaction, Environments, organizations and institutions, Agent development techniques, tools and environments.

1 Introduction

A typical MMOG (Massively Multiplayer Online Game, such as World of Warcraft^{TM}[1] or Aion^{TM}[2], two successful games of this kind) gathers a large

[1] http://www.blizzard.com
[2] http://eu.aiononline.com/en/

Z. Pan et al. (Eds.): Transactions on Edutainment VII, LNCS 7145, pp. 129–138, 2012.

community of concurrent players in a persistent virtual game world. These players take part in a common game which has no foreseeable end (i.e. the game is never completed or finished) and, along with some synthetic characters and creatures driven by AI, they populate the virtual world and create an online society with its own rules, landscape, economy and idiosyncrasy.

Massively Multiplayer Online Games development involves 3D modeling, advanced graphics, networking and artificial intelligence technologies. As a consequence to achieve an integrated, consistent and seamless development process performed by inter-disciplinary stakeholders is an interesting topic of research that may give fruitful results to the gaming industry. In particular, in the field of AI to model such systems and its dynamics has been a very relevant task [1][2][3] that has been mostly centered in the intelligent capability of individuals (non-player characters) instead of groups. In MMOGs, many players interact to compete or collaborate and achieve individual and collective outcomes. An organizative Multi-Agent System allows to regulate the activities of the agents, and an MMOG can take advantage of this feature.

The key idea behind this research is to apply existing organizative Multi-Agent Systems technologies (agent organizations, institutions, agreement technologies, etc ...) to design and deploy MMOGs and virtual worlds with high participation: the concept of "MMOG based on MAS" (MMOGboMAS) [4].

Section 2 presents some of the related work in this research line. Next, section 3 introduces the method of development behind MMOGboMAS. Later, section 4 formally defines **Game Zones**. Following, section 5 explains the actual implementation of **Game Zones** using Virtual Institutions[5]. Finally, section 6 presents some conclusions and future work.

2 Related Work

This research follows in the footsteps of previous research efforts by different authors like [6], [7], [4], [8], [9] and [10] in which games in general, and MMOG in particular, are researched as natural scenarios for agents and MAS. These works work around an architecture that can be used to build MMOGs. This architecture is based on Multi-Agent System concepts, taking advantage of agent technology's features to better suit the particular needs of MMOGs.

2.1 MMOG Based on MAS Architecture

A MMOG (like most complex systems) can be seen as a system split into several layered subsystems, with each layer being relatively independent and taking care of one aspect of the whole MMOG experience. From the perspective of this work, a MMOG is split into three layers: the HCI Layer (Human-Computer Interface, the client software), the IVE layer (Intelligent Virtual Environment, a distributed simulator) and the MMOG layer (Game logic). A detailed description of each layer is outside the scope of this article and can be found in [8,4].

The MMOG Layer: Agent Taxonomy The **MMOG Layer** is essentially a dedicated, open MAS which runs the game. This MAS uses agent technologies like agent services, Electronic Institutions[11,12] and Agent Organizations[13,14,15] to model some game mechanics. It solves the common issues found in MMOGs using classic software agent features, such as agent interactions, agent communication protocols (like auctions or call-for-proposals), service-oriented computing, event-driven behaviors, role models, etc. We consider the following type of agents: **ProfileAgent**, the personal profile of each player in the system; **AvatarAgent and NPCAvatarAgent**, virtual avatars representing player characters and non-player chacters in the game world; **GameZoneAgent**, implements the logics of the game environment and works as a nexus between the *MMOG Layer* and the simulation. For a more detailed description of these types, the reader is refered to [7].

2.2 Virtual Institutions

Virtual Institutions are 3D Virtual Worlds with normative regulation of interactions [16]. This concept appeared as a combination of Electronic Institutions [17] and 3D virtual worlds. In this context, Electronic Institutions are used to specify the rules that govern participants' behaviors, while 3D virtual worlds are used to facilitate human participation in the institution. The design of Virtual Institutions is divided in two separate steps: i) specification of the institutional rules, and ii) generation of the virtual world [9].

Virtual Institutions are one of the key elements of the MMOGboMAS architecture, as they are used to implement the Game Zones, as seen in section 5, and serve as the game environment.

3 The Method behind MMOGboMAS

Designing and deploying a whole MMOG or any multi-user virtual environment is a complex task. Notice that most MMOGs can be seen as a kind of open systems, thus an organizative MAS approach becomes quite useful to build them[13]. The MMOG based of MAS architecture extends agent technologies to be used in interactive virtual environments or MMOGs. Each functionality of the system (e.g. the player representation, the player profile, a player clan, etc.......) is implemented by a dedicated type of agent or by an agent organization. Of course, depending on actual implementation details, some functionalities could end up being offered by the same agent or organization in order to simplify some processes.

In order to properly use this architecture, game designers should follow a design method which involves some sequential phases (as illustrated by figure **??**). This method is an iterative life-cycle where each phase's products are the next phase's inputs, and where designers can return to a previous phase to add or modify elements at any given time. It is based in the iterative life-cycle of software as seen in classic software engineering. The phases that compose this method are:

1. **Role definition**. The first phase is to define the roles that the agents of the system will play (i.e.define which types of agents will be in the system). The MMOGboMAS architecture provides a core set of agent roles that should be used as the starting point. Each role is specified with an identifier (i.e. a name) and a set of attributes. Attributes define the properties that the agents playing that role must have (e.g. "Money", "Game Score", "Health Points", etc...). Roles are not isolated and are related to each other using a hierarchy. The pre-defined set of agent roles (or agent types) is designed to provide the basic features that any MMOG should have, and those roles serve as the root types of the system (e.g. Non-Player Characters, player avatars, profile managers ...). These root types can be extended by the game designers to offer new features to the game system, normally creating new agent roles that fulfill the custom needs of each particular new game. The architecture also makes extensive use of agent organizations to represent players and choral player behaviour (i.e. "player clans").
2. **Activities and Services.** This phase defines agents' activities within the game. Defining the activities of the system means defining what the agents within the game, that is, sequences of atomic actions (i.e. interactions) that the agents perform in the system. Each activity has a set of preconditions, consequences and a process flow detailing the atomic actions that are performed. **Services** are activities that are invoked from an agent ("client") but that are really performed by another agent ("server"). Of course, as part of this step, the atomic actions that conform activities and services must be defined too. For instance, one could define the "Fishing" activity, which would be a combination of the atomic actions *"Use fishing rod"*, *"Use bait on fishing rod"* and *"Throw bait to sea"*. The preconditions for this activity would be for the agent to have a fishing rod and some bait (in its inventory), and the consequences (if successful) would be for the agent to catch a fish (and add it to its inventory).
3. **Game Zones**. The virtual locations where the game takes place are called **Game Zones**, and are defined as virtual environments with some added properties. **Game Zones** are the main focus of this paper and are covered in more detail in subsequent sections.
4. **Quests.** Once the virtual world and its set of "what-can-be-done"s and "what-cannot-be-done"s are defined by the previous phases, quests represent the real flow of the game: the objectives, stories and challenges that players expect from these kind of games. Quests make use of roles, locations, activities, etc... So they can only be well defined once everything else has been set up. The development of quests for MMOGboMAS is a subject of research onto itself and has been extensively covered in [10].

While in the process of following this method and as a mixed output of all its phases, a designer is compiling a game specification. Thus, at the end of each phase, the designer would have compiled the specification of that phase. This specification contains information about roles, activities, actions, services, locations, objectives as relevant game elements. The specification is a set of all the meaningful elements in each relevant game category and it is organized as a hierarchical thesaurus. In order to ease the development of these specifications, a common "starting point" ontology has been developed called the "MMOG ontology". It has been constructed using the OWL-S[18] semantic language and the Protégé[3] tool. The idea is to use this MMOG Ontology as the foundation for building the new ontologies while developing an MMOGboMAS. More information on the MMOG Ontology can be found in [19].

Let's propose an example of this phases to help clarify the method. Let's think of a game designer who is thinking about designing a MMOG featuring a classic medieval *"Sword and Sorcery"* set piece: castle, taverns, knights and evildoers, dungeons and so on. following the phases of the method. Regarding **roles**, let's say that the players play the role of the knights and that the tavern will act as a hub to draw players, put them in contact and allow them to perform certain in-game activities, such as to purchase in-game goods from the tavern owner and its employees. Also, let's say that the game specification contains a generic role for all the player agents called "Player" with some basic attributes like: "Money", the amount of virtual currency that the player has; "Hours", the amount of hours the player has been playing the game. Moreover, let's say that there is a generic role for all non-player agents called "NPC" with an attribute called "Faction" that identifies wether the character is on the knights' side, on the evildoers side or it's neutral.

Regarding **Activities**, apart from the "Fishing" activity defined earlier, the designers want the avatars to be able to fight, so they define the "Fight" activity as a process that involves the "Attack", and "Defend" basic actions. Regarding services, the designers want the avatars to be able to order drinks and food from in tavern, so they define the "Order food and drinks" service which is an activity that will be performed by an employee of the tavern (a NPCAvatar) by request of a player avatar.

Regarding **Game Zones**, the designers want to keep the flow of the game simple, so they define three major **Game Zones**: the castle, which will act as the initial zone for all players (it is where their avatars will be spawned in the virtual world) and it is the zone where the designers hope to introduce the game to new players; the dungeon, which is where the evildoers lurk and where players will go to fight them and obtain rewards; and the tavern, which will serve as the hub for the players as stated earlier. The tavern **Game Zone** is explained in more detail in section 4.

Regarding **Quests**, the designers want to add new quests to the game as time goes on, but for starters, they define an introductory quest for all players which involves going to the tavern to learn of a treasure inside the dungeon, form a clan, and actually going to the dungeon to retrieve the treasure. It is a narrative device to introduce the players to all the **Game Zones** present in the game, introduce the concept of creating a clan, and reward the players for doing so. Quest definition and deployment is extensively explained in [10].

[3] http://protege.stanford.edu

After having passed through all four design phases, the designers of the game have defined a game specification that gives a big picture and clear idea of what the game is about and how it works in terms of design structure. Section 4 explains in more detail how to model and design a **Game Zone**.

4 Game Zones

A **Game Zone** is essentially a segment of the virtual game world with its own name, theme and regulations. **Game Zones** work in a very similar way as Virtual Institutions do: there are entry and exit points to the zone, interconnected *Areas* (or subzones), requirements for entering certain areas, crowd limitations, AI-controlled inhabitants that play different roles, etc. The whole game world is envisioned as a set of interconnected (or *federated*) **Game Zones**. The main zone of the game world and the main starting point for the game is usually called the *"Free Zone"*, a Game Zone with relaxed constraints and where the Player Clans may be formed. It acts as a hub for other zones as it hosts many entry points connected to them.

Formally, a **Game Zone** is defined as follows:

$$GZ = (R, L, A, O)$$

- **R**: Is the set of ***Roles*** an avatar agent (AvatarAgent or NPCAvatarAgent, see section2.1) can play in the zone.
- **L**: Is the graph of connected ***Locations*** that form the zone. This locations can be either **Areas** or entire **sub-Game Zones**.
- **A**: Is the set of ***Activities*** that can be performed inside the zone.
- **O**: Is the set of valid graphical outlines and styles for each zone.

Let's explain the major factors in more detail. R is defined as a hierarchy of roles that the agents can play. It is a subset of all the roles that the agents can play in the whole game (as seen in section 3). Any agent within a game zone must be playing one of its roles. This role is normally assigned to the agent (whenever it enters the zone) by the **GameZoneAgents** (see section 2.1 and [7]) ruling the zone. However, certain zones may allow the agents to choose their own role from a set of available ones. Of course, depending on the role an agent plays, its capabilities inside the zone change, as the dynamics of the zone may dictate what a role is allowed or not to do inside the zone (see below).

L is the graph of connected **locations** that represent the Game Zone. This graph can be either a graph of connected **Areas** or a graph of connected **sub-Game Zones**, which are the two supported location types. This approach allows the game designers to define as much or as less complexity as desired when developing a Game Zone. A sub-Game Zone is a Game Zone which is contained within another, larger, Game Zone. It has all the traits of a regular Game Zone. The concept of **sub-Game Zones** existing within **Game Zones** exists as a way to let designers delegate, split and organize complex locations in pieces. The concept of **Area** represents the minimal virtual space that conforms a zone.

An area has a name, a set of entry points and, optionally, a shape. An **Area** cannot contain **sub-Areas** inside of it, **sub-Game Zones** should be used for that matter.

A is a subset of all the activities and services that can be performed in the **Game Zone**. This way, game designers can restrict which activities can and cannot be performed inside each **Game Zone**.

O represents a set of graphical outlines which are valid floorplans for the **Game Zone**, since different outlines can be adequated for a **Game Zone**. It also represents a set of graphical theme styles or "looks" that go well with a zone. Later, in runtime, many **Game Zones** may be instantiated from the same **Game Zone** specification, each one with a different floorplan outline and a different look.

Let's continue with the example from section 3: A **Game Zone** from this game represents a tavern where players can meet to chat, tell stories, get involved into further quests, order virtual beverages, etc.... The entry point for this zone would be the main door of the bar, and the exit point would be the rear door (which could be connected to another **Game Zone** representing a back alley, etc...).

The set of roles that can be played in this zone are:

- *"Owner"* is a role that should be played by a **NPCAvatarAgent** or an **AvatarAgent** from a player who owns the place.
- *"Client"* is a role played by a player **AvatarAgent** who enters the Tavern to perform activities and is not one of the owners.
- *"Waiter"* is a role played by **NPCAvatarAgents** who accept commands from the *"Owner"*. Also they interact with the *"Clients"* to get their orders and talk to them.

Note that there are no evildoer roles in the hierarchy, since the game designers do not want enemies to be present in this zone. This is a zone for players and *positive* Non-Player characters, and the way to enforce this is to restrict the roles that can be played in the zone.

Regarding **locations**, the tavern is split into two floors. Each floor is a **sub-Game Zone**, so the main location graph connects both floors. The second floor is small as it is just composed by a few **Areas**: a couple of bedrooms separated by a corridor. The first floor has many different **Areas** that are connected following the graph shown in figure **??**.

Regarding **Activities** and **Services**, as stated earlier, this zone is for players to chat, form clans and trade. So, for instance, the "Fishing" or "Fight" **Activities** make no sense here. Thus, they are not in the list of **Activities** for this zone. The "Order food and drinks" Service however is perfectly fine and can be performed in the zone.

When it comes to outlines and style, the game designers devise a single outline and define a couple of styles called *"Wood"* and *"Marble"* that describe two different graphical themes that could go well with the tavern. The true meaning and content of these styles is left for the game artists responsible for creating and painting the graphical assets that conform each location.

And essentially, that is the definition and specification of a **Game Zone**. Game designers can use a specification like this as a reference to instantiate one or many taverns, depending on the actual implementation of the game.

5 Implementing Game Zones

In this section, the use of the VI framework and tools to develop **Game Zones** for the MMOGboMAS is explained. The approach followed in this work is to formally specify Game Zones using VIs, which is a process supported by Islander. The Islander tool was developed as a user-friendly graphic interface for specifying Electronic and Virtual Institutions and has already been used to specify quests in the same architecture [10]. In order to successfully implement a Game Zone, the following points need to be taken care of: be able to define the hierarchy of roles; be able to represent the specification and attributes of the zone and its inhabitants; and be able to represent the environment.

Regarding the role hierarchy, VIs have a great feature called the Social Structure as part of their Dialogical Framework. It is defined using the Islander editor, which allows designers to define roles and subroles that the agents are going to play once inside the institution. This tool can be used to implement the role hierarchy of the zone into the VI.

Regarding the specification and attributes, as stated in section 2.2, VIs define the concept of Information Models, which represent the attributes of roles at run-time and keep track of them while the institution is active. This way, attributes attached to roles that have been specified by the designers (e.g. in section 3 the examples were "Money", "Game Score" and "Health Points") become typed attributes of the Information Models representing those roles.

Regarding the environment, there are two key elements: the main element is the Performative Structure of VIs which, as seen in section 2.2, is essentially a directed graph that connects scenes through transitions. Although they are different concepts, a Performative Structure and a locations graph share the same kind of graphic representation. In fact, a locations graph may be seen as a subset of a whole Performative Structure, which contains all the connections that any agent can follow through the zone at any given time.

The second key element is the generation and representation of the graphical environment of the zone. This is where the Virtual World component of VIs comes into play. As the locations graph is defined using a Performative Structure, it's feasible to build a 3D Virtual World representation of the Game Zone using the tools of the VIs, namely, the Virtual World Builder Toolkit [9]. This tool supports the definition and execution of Virtual World Grammars, an extension of shape grammars, for the automatic generation of virtual worlds from a Performative Structure. In our case from the performative structure specification. Using these tools, the designers can automatically generate a 3D representation of the **Game Zone** that complies both with the graphical outline associated with the zone and the (optional) shapes associated with each **Area**.

The most important implication from the relation between **Game Zones** and Virtual World Grammars and Interpreters is the way in which **Game Zone** specifications can be seen as *"blueprints"* that generate an arbitrary number of **Game Zones** which are different from each other. This is possible by relaxing the restrictions when defining **Game Zones** (e.g. use different outlines and shapes, provide more than one entry to **Areas**, etc...) and also by adding many valid graphical looks (see section 4) both to the specifications and to the Virtual World. This way, a designer can potentially generate dozens of **Game Zones** parting from the same specification and customizing the Virtual World generation process. All these **Game Zones** would be identical in terms of game logic (i.e. the same roles, **Activities**, etc...) but would be different in terms of graphical style and spatial topology, giving players the feeling that they are playing in a completely different zone. This is a very attractive way of saving time and effort to game designers and artists, removing the need of "hand-crafting" every single piece of the game environment.

6 Conclusions

The main contribution of this paper has been the method of defining a game using the MMOG based on MAS architecture, paying special attention to the definition and design of **Game Zones**, which are the most integral part of this architecture. The relation of this architecture and the Virtual Electronic Institutions has been established, and a novel method for implementing **Game Zones** using Virtual Electronic Institutions has been introduced. Moreover, with the use of Virtual World Grammars and Interpreters, this method allows for a game designer to generate a whole Virtual World specifying only a few **Game Zones** that serve as *"blueprints"* for the environment.

Acknowledgements. This work is partially funded by OVAMAH (TIN2009-13839-C03-01), EVE (TIN2009-14702-C02-01 / TIN2009-14702-C02-02) and AT (CONSOLIDER CSD2007-0022) projects, EU-FEDER funds, the Catalan Gov. (Grant 2005-SGR-00093) and M. Esteva's Ramon y Cajal contract.

References

1. Matskin, M.: Scalable Agent-Based Simulation of Players in Massively Multiplayer Online Games. In: Eighth Scandinavian Conference on Artificial Intelligence: SCAI 2003 (2003)
2. Ducheneaut, N., Yee, N., Nickell, E., Moore, R.J.: Alone together?: exploring the social dynamics of massively multiplayer online games. In: Proceedings of the SIGCHI Conference on Human Factors in Computing Systems, pp. 407–416 (2006)
3. Guyot, P., Honiden, S.: Agent-based participatory simulations: Merging multi-agent systems and role-playing games. Journal of Artificial Societies and Social Simulation 9(4) (2006)
4. Aranda, G., Botti, V., Carrascosa, C.: Mmog based on mas: The mmog layer (extended abstract). In: Decker, Sichman, Sierra, Castelfranchi (eds.) Proc. of 8th Int. Conf. on Autonomous Agents and Multiagent Systems (AAMAS 2009), pp. 1149–1150 (2009)

5. Bogdanovych, A., Rodriguez, J.A., Simoff, S.J., Cohen, A.: Virtual Agents and 3D Virtual Worlds for Preserving and Simulating Cultures. In: Ruttkay, Z., Kipp, M., Nijholt, A., Vilhjálmsson, H.H. (eds.) IVA 2009. LNCS, vol. 5773, pp. 257–271. Springer, Heidelberg (2009)
6. Aranda, G., Carrascosa, C., Botti, V.: Intelligent agents in serious games. In: Fifth European Workshop On Multi-Agent Systems (EUMAS 2007). Association Tunnisienne dIntelligence Artificielle (2007)
7. Aranda, G., Carrascosa, C., Botti, V.: Characterizing Massively Multiplayer Online Games as Multi-Agent Systems. In: Corchado, E., Abraham, A., Pedrycz, W. (eds.) HAIS 2008. LNCS (LNAI), vol. 5271, pp. 507–514. Springer, Heidelberg (2008)
8. Aranda, G., Carrascosa, C., Botti, V.: The MMOG Layer: MMOG Based on MAS. In: Dignum, F., Bradshaw, J., Silverman, B., van Doesburg, W. (eds.) Agents for Games and Simulations. LNCS, vol. 5920, pp. 63–78. Springer, Heidelberg (2009)
9. Trescak, T., Esteva, M., Rodriguez, I.: A Virtual World Grammar for automatic generation of virtual worlds. The Visual Computer 26(6), 521–531 (2010)
10. Aranda, G., Trescak, T., Esteva, M., Carrascosa, C.: Building Quests for Online Games with Virtual Institutions. In: Dignum, F. (ed.) Agents for Games and Simulations II. LNCS, vol. 6525, pp. 192–206. Springer, Heidelberg (2011)
11. Esteva, M., Rosell, B., Rodriguez-Aguilar, J.A., Arcos, J.L.: AMELI: An Agent-Based Middleware for Electronic Institutions. In: Proceedings of the Third International Joint Conference on Autonomous Agents and Multiagent Systems, vol. 1, pp. 236–243 (2004)
12. Bogdanovych, A., Berger, H., Simoff, S.J., Sierra, C.: Narrowing the Gap Between Humans and Agents in e-Commerce: 3D Electronic Institutions. In: Bauknecht, K., Pröll, B., Werthner, H. (eds.) EC-Web 2005. LNCS, vol. 3590, pp. 128–137. Springer, Heidelberg (2005)
13. Garcia, E., Argente, E., Giret, A.: Issues for organizational multiagent systems development. In: Sixth International Workshop From Agent Theory to Agent Implementation, AT2AI-6 (2008)
14. Criado, N., Argente, E., Julian, V., Botti, V.: Organizational services for spade agent platform. In: IWPAAMS 2007, vol. 1, pp. 31–40. Universidad de Salamanca (2007)
15. Argente, E., Palanca, J., Aranda, G., Julian, V., Botti, V., Garcia-Fornes, A., Espinosa, A.: Supporting Agent Organizations. In: Burkhard, H.-D., Lindemann, G., Verbrugge, R., Varga, L.Z. (eds.) CEEMAS 2007. LNCS (LNAI), vol. 4696, pp. 236–245. Springer, Heidelberg (2007)
16. Bogdanovych, A., Simoff, S.J., Esteva, M.: Virtual institutions prototype. In: 8th International Joint Conference on Autonomous Agents and Multiagent Systems (AAMAS 2009), Budapest, Hungary, May 10-15, vol. 2, pp. 1373–1374 (2009)
17. Esteva, M.: Electronic Institutions: From Specification to Development. PhD thesis, Artificial Intelligence Research Institute (IIIA-CSIC), Spain (2003)
18. Martin, D., Burstein, M., Hobbs, J., Lassila, O., McDermott, D., McIlraith, S., Narayanan, S., Paolucci, M., Parsia, B., Payne, T., et al.: OWL-S: Semantic Markup for Web Services. W3C Member Submission, 22 (2004)
19. Aranda, G., Carrascosa, C., Botti, V.: Mmog based on mas: A game-independent ontology. In: GAME-ON 2008, vol. 20, pp. 141–146. EUROSIS (2008)

A Novel Skeletonization and Animation Approach for Point Models

Zhiying He, Xiaohui Liang, and Qinping Zhao

State Key Lab. of Virtual Reality Technology and Systems,
School of Computer Science and Engineering, Beihang University,
Beijing, 100191, P.R. China
hezhy@vrlab.buaa.edu.cn

Abstract. It is hard to extract skeletons using geometric models with limited information such as point models without topology and models with low resolution. This paper proposes a novel skeleton-extracting and animation approach for point models, which explores the differential properties of point models without triangulating the discrete points. First, this paper gives definitions of the attributes of surface and tangency, and then uses these attributes to iteratively contract the model to get the skeleton. At last the point models animation driven by the resulting skeleton is presented. Results show that our approach can get good skeletons even if the model is lacking connection information and in low resolution. Also, it can obtain good animation results and make the animation more convenient since the binding of skeleton points and skin is obtained.

Keywords: point models, skeleton extraction, low-resolution, animation.

1 Introduction

The skeleton is a simple and efficient representation of a 3D model and therefore is widely used in many areas, such as data analysis, animation, deformation, shape matching, etc.

There are extensive methods for extracting skeletons. In general, they can be divided into two categories. The first category is "topology and extraction based", which uses topological and intrinsic information of geometry model to extract skeleton; the other is "example and learning based", which uses many examples to learn skeleton. Either of them has its own advantages and disadvantages. The former is memory saving and efficient but needs some constraints while the latter is robust but time- and memory-consuming. Our method belongs to the former and we lay emphasis on how to deal with geometry models with limited information.

Most of algorithms in the first category are dealing with closed polygonal meshes [1][2][3]. Ref. [4] constructs Laplacian matrix based on the topology, and then contracts the geometry according to the operation in the differential field. This method can get good result, but only works for closed mesh models with manifold connectivity. In addition, it cannot generate fine skeletons for very coarse model (less than 5000 vertices).

Z. Pan et al. (Eds.): Transactions on Edutainment VII, LNCS 7145, pp. 139–150, 2012.

There are also some methods for discrete models [5], such as thinning and boundary propagation [6][7], distance field [8], and general-field functions [9][10]. But these methods are mainly based on volume data, and require clear knowledge about the interior information of models. Thus, they are not appropriate for point surface models.

The approaches for directly treating point surface models are mainly geometric ones, such as Voronoi diagram [11], and Reeb-graph-based [12][13] method. These methods are usually sensitive to noise, and cannot well express the geometry and topology of models. Ref. [14] extracts the skeleton from incomplete point clouds based on recursive planar cuts and local ROSA construction. But it is designed to model generally cylindrical regions of a shape. Recently, [15] expands [4] to make use of Laplacian matrix on point models. However, it still needs to do local Delaunay triangulation to compute the Laplacian matrix. In essence, [15] uses the mesh method, without considering the characteristics of point models.

Point models have no topology information. Though one can reconstruct the triangular mesh and extract skeleton using methods which are typical used for mesh models. Nevertheless, it is not preferable because it is not only time consuming but also easy to introduce errors. Thus, how to directly use the approach of differential geometry to extract the skeleton for point models should be further studied. In addition, low resolution point models are useful in many real-time applications, such as real-time animation, transmission and rendering on mobile devices [16]. But as mentioned earlier, many skeleton extraction methods cannot get good result on low resolution models because of limited information. Therefore, how to get the skeletons on low resolution models should also be researched.

In this paper, we present a novel skeleton extraction approach that can get better result even if the model is lacking in connection information and in low resolution. First, we give the definition of attributes of surface and tangency (AST). Then, we control the geometry contraction by the two attributes. According to the attribute of surface which is obtained from surface neighborhood, this method can obtain similar effect to that of Laplacian smoothing contraction but without rebuilding the connection of vertices nor constructing the Laplacian matrix. Furthermore, we add the attraction of geodesic tangency neighborhood, and then approximate the skeleton gradually by iterative calculation. The effect of these two attributes of AST provides enough information when extracting the skeleton. So we can also get a good skeleton even in low resolution.

At last, we give animation of point models driven by the resulting skeleton of our approach. It is more convenient since the skeletonization process gets the binding relationship between the skeleton points and their corresponding skin points (the corresponding tangency neighborhood points).

Experiments show that our skeletonization approach maintains the geometry and topology of original model, is insensitive to noise, and applicable to multi-resolution point models. Even if the model is in low resolution (less than 5,000 vertices), our method can also get good result. The animation results also demonstrate the performance of our approach.

In section 2, we give the definition of AST and the core idea of the AST-based skeletonization. Based on the theory of AST, section 3 gives the implementation process of skeletonization and animation for point models. Section 4 gives the results.

2 The Principle of AST Based Skeletonization

2.1 Surface Neighborhood and Geodesic Tangency Neighborhood

Point model consists of a set of discrete points. Thus, the way to express the information of topology is important. This paper proposes the use of surface neighborhood and geodesic tangency neighborhood to represent the basic information of a point p_i in a model.

Let $Nei(p_i)$ be the surface neighborhood of p_i. It is the set of the n-nearest neighborhood points of p_i on the surface.

$$Nei(p_i) = \{p_{N_1}, p_{N_2}, \ldots p_{N_n}\} \tag{1}$$

Let $Tan(p_i)$ be the geodesic tangency neighborhood of p_i. It is a set of points that have the same geodesic distance to the benchmark point p_{head} as p_i and in the same connected component.

$$Tan(p_i) = \{p_{T_j} \mid g(p_{T_j}, p_{head}) = g(p_i, p_{head}), p_{T_j} \in C_i\} \tag{2}$$

where C_i denotes the connected component containing p_i, and $g(p_i, p_{head})$ denotes the geodesic distance between point p_i and the benchmark point p_{head}.

2.2 Attributes of Surface and Tangency

Surface neighborhood contains basic information of the surface. Geodesic tangency neighborhood involves the relationship between points and skeleton. Through a specific function transformation of these two neighborhoods, we can obtain the corresponding attribute of surface (AS) and attribute of tangency (AT) as follows:

$$AS_{Pi} = f_{AS}(Nei(p_i)) \tag{3}$$

$$AT_{Pi} = f_{AT}(Tan(p_i)) \tag{4}$$

The attribute of surface can provide a strength of smooth contraction and at the same time maintain the geometric shape. It can receive similar effect to that Laplacian smoothing contraction in differential field without triangulation.

The essence of Laplacian smoothing contraction is to let the curvature of surface tend to zero. To get the same contraction effect on point models, we give formula (5) to compute the operator f_{AS}. Assume point p_i' is the point after p_i contraction. Let AS minimum means making the sum of the differences between p_i' and neighborhood

Nei(p_i) in direction of *a* smallest, as shown in formula (5)(6). It means making the point p_i' and neighborhood *Nei(p_i)* in a plane as far as possible.

$$f_{AS}(Nei(p_i)) = \sum_{j=1}^{n} (\langle a, p_{N_j} \rangle - \langle a, p_i' \rangle)^2 \tag{5}$$

$$min(f_{AS}(Nei(p_i))) \tag{6}$$

When the point model is simple and the branches are in one direction, we can use the following simplified modality of f_{AS}, regardless of the direction.

$$f_{AS-d}(Nei(p_i)) = \sum_{j=1}^{n} (\| p_{N_j} - p_i' \|^2) \tag{7}$$

The attribute of tangency can provide an attractive strength that attracts the points to the center. This paper uses the minimum squared-distance between the center of *Tan(p_i)* and contracted point p_i' to express the function f_{AT} as follows:

$$f_{AT}(Tan(p_i)) = \| p_i' - (\sum_{j=1}^{n} p_{T_j}) / n \|^2 \tag{8}$$

$$min(f_{AT}(Tan(p_i))) \tag{9}$$

2.3 Geometry Contraction Based on AST

The key of skeleton extraction is to maintain the geometry and topology of original model, and makes it insensitive to noise. From the effect of AS, we can get similar result to Laplacian smoothing contraction, and make it maintain the basic structure of model and insensitive to noise. The key of skeleton extraction in low resolution is to get enough information to ensure the effectiveness of skeleton extraction. Influenced by the AT and AS, the approach of AST can ensure that there is enough information to do skeleton extraction on low resolution models.

The energy field obtained by the function of AT and AS is expressed as:

$$Energy = W_S * AS_{Pi} + W_T * AT_{Pi} \tag{10}$$

$$W_S^{t+1} = l_s * W_S^t \tag{11}$$

$$W_T^{t+1} = l_T * W_T^t \tag{12}$$

where W_S and W_T are weighted values representing the influential factors of each attributes. They will update after each contraction. $W_S^0, W_T^0 \in [0, 10], l_S, l_T \in [0, 10]$.

Substituting (3)(4)(5)(8) into (10), we have

$$Energy = W_S * (\sum_{j=1}^{n}(\langle a, p_{N_j}\rangle - \langle a, p_i'\rangle)^2) + W_T * (\| p_i' - (\sum_{j=1}^{n} p_{T_j})/n \|^2) \quad (13)$$

$$p_i' = argmin_{p_i'}(Energy) \quad (14)$$

According to the above analysis, to achieve the effect of the geometry contraction, we should let the energy field obtained by AS and AT reach the minimum. This means that p_i, $Nei(p_i)$ and $Tan(p_i)$ are known. Then we compute the point p_i' that satisfy the equation (14).

Referring to the calculating method in [17], we adopt the energy field and the vector field to compute. Firstly, find an optimal direction a_{best} from all directions. Secondly, compute the point p_i' that makes the energy minimum in the optimal direction. a_{best} is the direction that through the point p_i and the energy function value is minimum. It is usually the normal direction.

The contraction is done iteratively and it finally attracts all the points approximately to the skeleton. Then the centers of tangency neighborhoods can be considered in the skeleton. By connecting the centers, we get the skeleton.

3 Implementation of Skeletonization and Animation

Figure 1 shows the process of skeletonization and animation for point models based on AST, where the yellow data is the input data.

In the process of skeletonization, after obtaining the surface neighborhood and tangency neighborhood, we iteratively contract the model until the diameter of tangency neighborhood is less than a certain threshold or an end operation is given. Then the center of tangency neighborhood can be considered in the skeleton. We define the centers as skeleton points. Connecting these points, we get the skeleton.

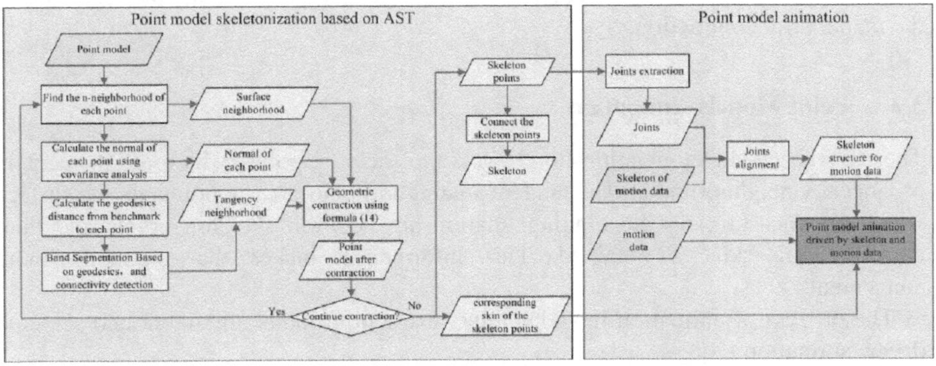

Fig. 1. The process of skeletonization and animation for point models based on AST

After skeletonization, the skeleton points and their corresponding skin (the corresponding tangency neighborhood points) are obtained. Thus, we can use motion data which has its own skeleton structure to drive the point model animation. The process is shown on the right of figure 1. First, we extract joints and align them to the skeleton of motion data. Then, according to the relationship between the skeleton points and skin which has been obtained in the skeletonization process, we can drive the point model animation.

3.1 Point Models Skeletonization Based on AST

In the paper, we use kdtree to accelerate the neighborhood finding, and use covariance analysis [18][19] to obtain the normal which is the eigenvector of the smallest eigenvalue in the covariance matrix.

Then, a solution based on the relationship between neighborhood points is presented to calculate the geodesic distance. The geodesic distance of p_{head} is set to 0, and the geodesic distance of its one ring neighborhood point is set to the Euclidean distance between the two points. Neighborhood of neighborhood is traversed, and the geodesic distance is iteratively calculated, until all points have been traversed. In the paper, the benchmark point p_{head} is set as the point that has the maximum or minimum value in one axis direction, which means it is the extreme in one direction. Different p_{head} will lead to different initial tangency neighborhoods. But our approach is a iteratively contraction process which adjusts the tangency neighborhood gradually in the contraction, thus when contracting to a thin shape, we can finally get similar tangency neighborhood even using different p_{head}.

Band segmentation means classifying the points that have the same geodesic distance or in a range of the geodesic distance as a band. However, the same band may contain several connected components. So we need to detect connectivity by using the neighborhood relationship.

Through the above steps, we can get the $Nei(p_i)$ and $Tan(p_i)$. Subsequently, the method described in subsection 2.3 is used to do geometry contraction. By equation (14), we can get the point p_i' that makes the energy value minimum, and hence obtain the model after contraction.

3.2 Point Models Animation

The AST based skeletonization finally gets the skeleton points which are the centers of tangency neighborhoods. The tangency neighborhoods are the points on the surface which are the skin. So the binding relationship between skeleton points and their corresponding skin is obtained. This information makes the animation more convenient.

The process of animation includes joints extraction, joints alignment and skeleton driven animation.

(1) Joints extraction

After obtaining the skeleton points by AST method, we should further do the joints extraction for subsequent point models animation. Obviously, the branch points are the main joints. However, besides the main joints, there are also many other joints, such as ankle joint. Considering the bone is straight, if there is a clear bend in the skeleton, there may be a joint. Thus, we use the following decision rules to extract the joints:

Rule 1: Branch point is the joint.

Rule 2: If the curvature of a skeleton point exceeds a certain threshold, then it is a joint.

In this paper, we do the curvature decision by calculating the deviation of angle. Assume there is a skeleton point S, whose left and right adjacent skeleton points are S_l and S_r respectively. The deviation of angle θ between vector SS_l and SS_r is given by

$$\theta = arccos((SS_l \bullet SS_r)/(|SS_l| \bullet |SS_r|)) \quad (15)$$

When θ of a skeleton point S exceeds a certain threshold, we define the S as a joint.

However, if the limb is straight, we cannot extract the joints, such as elbow joint, by curvature. In this case, the limb joints can be selected according to the characteristic proportions of human.

(2) Joints alignment and animation

To make an object move, we need to know the location of each joint at any time. The classic methods for obtaining the motion data include physical simulation and motion capture. Motion capture data can present realistic and high quality motion, so it has been widely used in animation. However, the data always has its own skeleton structure. Thus, using the motion capture data to drive our resulting skeleton to move, we should do a joint alignment between the skeleton of this paper and the motion data skeleton.

After the joints alignment, we can use the motion data to drive our skeleton to move. And then we need to use the skeleton to drive the point model for animation.

In order to drive the point model by skeleton, the binding of the joints and skin should be known. The AST based skeletonization algorithm finally gets a set of skeleton points which are the centers of tangency neighborhood when the iteration is finished. Thus, the corresponding skin of the skeleton points is its corresponding tangency neighborhood points. Thus, when the skeleton points move, they can drive their corresponding skin to move.

4 Results and Discussion

In order to validate the effectiveness of the AST method for skeleton extraction in low resolution, models with less than 5000 points are adopted to do experiments. Using the algorithm of ref. [19] to simplify the large amount of point data, we get some low resolution models. In the experiments, the initial value in formulae (11) and (12) W_S^0, W_T^0 is set to 1, $l_S=2$, $l_T=1.8$. For the selection of f_{AS}, the model male uses $f_{AS\text{-}d}$ because its branches are basically in the Y-axis direction. Other models use the normal f_{AS} function.

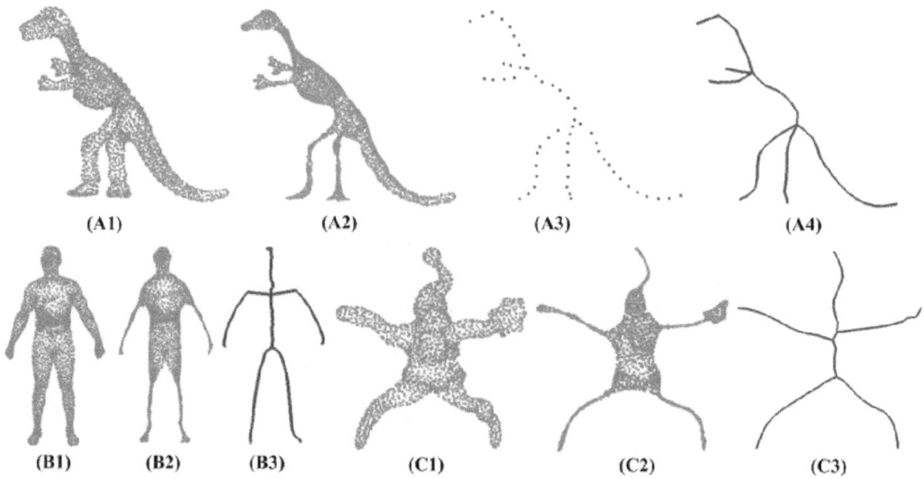

Fig. 2. The skeleton extraction process of AST method. (A) dinosaur model (3075 points). (A1) original model. (A2) the process of iterative contracting. (A3) the centers of tangency neighborhoods obtained after the contraction ends. (A4) the skeleton after connecting the centers. (B) male model (4333 points). (C) santa model (2525 points).

4.1 Results of Skeletonization

Figure 2 shows the skeleton extraction process of AST method. Input point model just needs the position of points. Iterative contraction is done based on AST method. After the iteration, the center of tangency neighborhood can be considered as the skeleton point. Connecting these centers, we get the skeleton. From figure 2 we can see that the resulting skeleton well expresses the geometry and topology of original model.

In order to verify the sensitivity of this algorithm to the noise, we add some noises to dinosaur model, as shown in figure 3(A). And then we do skeleton extraction for the noise model. The result is shown in figure 3(B). As is evident in the figure, the AST method is insensitive to noise. Figure 3(C) shows that the noise is smooth after contraction because the attribute of surface can get similar effect to that of Laplacian smoothing.

Our method can achieve good result for low resolution models. In figure 2(C), the model data is only 2525 points, and in figure 2(A) the model data is only 3075 points. But the skeletons obtained with this data can still well reveal the geometry and topology of original model.

In order to verify the quality of AST method, this paper makes a comparison between the method of ref. [4] and ours. The experiments on the method of [4] are performed using the executable program provided by Au et al. The low resolution mesh models are simplified by using the Rapidform software.

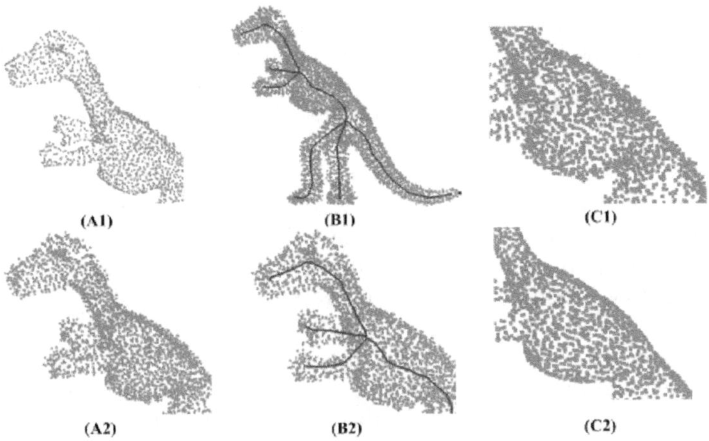

Fig. 3. Skeleton extraction for noise model. (A1) The partial figure of original dinosaur model (3075 points). (A2)The partial figure of dinosaur model with noise added (6150 points). (B1)The skeleton obtained from noise model. (B2) The local enlarge figure of B1. (C1) The original noise model for pre-contraction. (C2) The noise model after contraction.

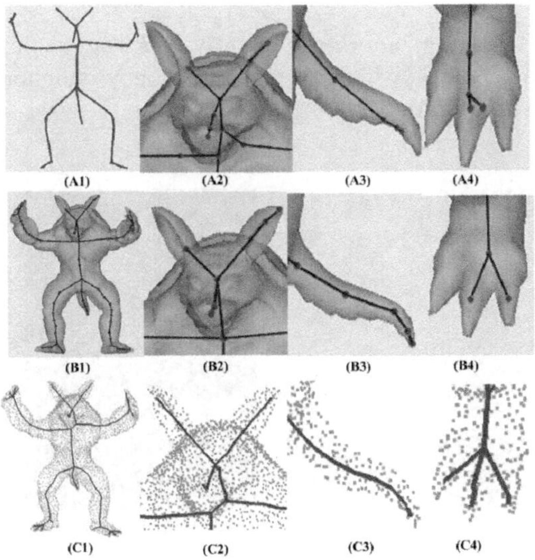

Fig. 4. The extracted skeleton using different methods for low resolution model. (A)(B)Simplified mesh model (4,755 vertices, 9,506 faces).(C)Simplified point model (4,713 points). (A)The extracted skeleton obtained by Laplace contraction of ref. [4]. (B)The final skeleton obtained after embedding refinement of ref. [4]. (C) The extracted skeleton obtained by AST method.

Figure 4 is a comparison of different methods for low resolution models whose vertexes are less than 5000 in number. From the figure, we can see that the skeleton obtained by the method of ref. [4] which uses Laplace contraction is too straight. In the tail, it is a straight line, so it cannot reveal the change in surface very well. The centrality is also poor. Even after optimizing embedding refinement, the final skeleton is still too straight and poor in centrality, as shown in figure 4(B). It misses some part of skeleton in the ears and toes. In the tail, the skeleton is too straight and poor in centrality. In the chest, it misses the changes of details. Our AST method can obtain better skeletons in centrality. Moreover, it can express the geometry shape of model for the same low resolution model more precisely, even with less connection information.

It is noticeable that in the step of finding the optimal direction, if using covariance analysis to compute the normal, and using it as a_{best}, it will not contract well when dealing with some particular models that close to flat. The special part will be contracted to a plane and no longer contract. Because the normal that get from covariance analysis is close to the plane normal, in the direction, when contracting to the plane the energy is minimum. Thus, when dealing with these special parts, the optimal direction a_{best} should be recalculated, and use the direction making the energy function value minimum as the optimal direction.

4.2 Results of Animation

The AST based skeletonization can finally get the skeleton points and their corresponding skin points which are the tangency neighborhood points. Some examples are shown in figure 5(A1).

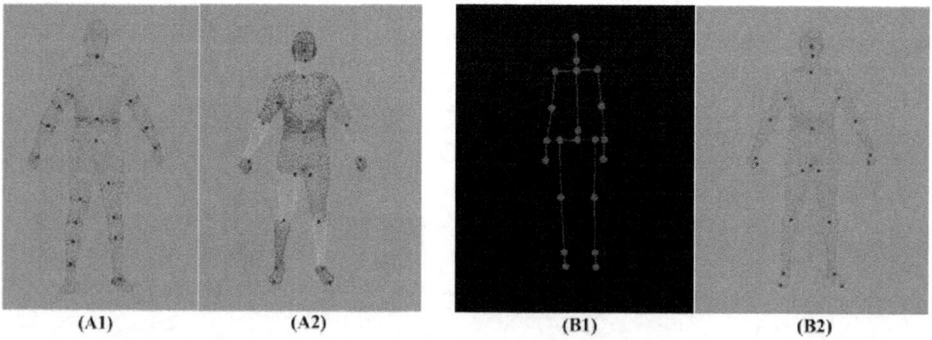

Fig. 5. (A) The binding relationship. A1: skeleton points and their corresponding tangency neighborhood points (red skin points are corresponding to the blue skeleton point). A2: the binding of the joints and skin. (B) Joints extraction and alignment. B1: the skeleton of motion data. B2: joints extraction and alignment result of our skeleton.

We use the approach of subsection 3.2 to do the joints extraction and alignment. Since the skeleton of motion data has large variation, we may need do some manual adjustments. Figure 5(B) is the final result of joints extraction and alignment.

In order to drive the point model by skeleton, the binding of the joints and skin should be known in advance. Fortunately, from the relationship between skeleton points and skin shown in figure 5(A1), we can easily get the binding of the joints and skin. Figure 5(A2) shows the result.

Then, we use our skeleton and the motion data to drive the point model animation. Figure 6 shows that our approach can get flexible animation results.

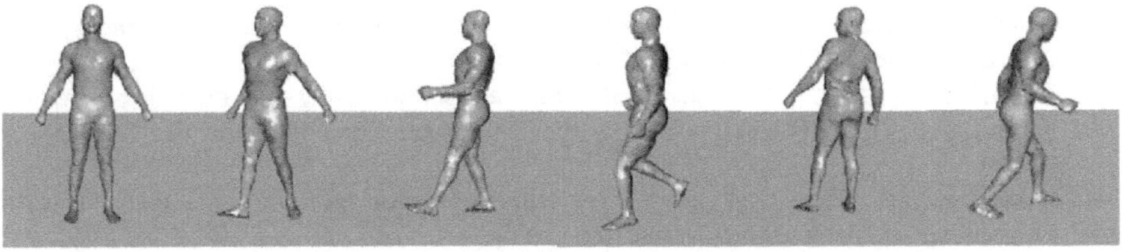

Fig. 6. The animation results of the point model

5 Conclusions and Future Work

At present, approaches for directly dealing with point surface models either cannot obtain good skeleton or have special requirements on the models. Better algorithms always deal with closed polygonal meshes and not applicable to low resolution models. With respect to this issue, this paper presents a skeleton extraction approach based on attributes of surface and tangency for point models. First, the definition of attributes, the method of calculating attribute functions and the principle of geometry contraction are given. Second, the implementation of skeletonization and animation is described based on the AST theory. Finally, experiments analysis and comparison are made to validate the effectiveness of AST method. Experiment results show that the skeleton extracted from AST approach can well express the geometry and topology of original models, insensitive to noise and able to implement animation easily. Besides, it can get good skeleton even in low resolution.

Since AST method should update neighborhood and normal information after every contraction, when dealing with large-scale data, it has to do a large quantity of calculations. In the future work, we should make optimization of this algorithm so as to reduce the computational complexity. In addition, in order to get more realistic animation, the elastic deformation should be further explored.

Acknowledgments. This paper is supported by the National Natural Science Foundation of China under Grant No. (61170186, 60873159), the Beijing Municipal Natural Science Foundation under Grant No. 4112032.

References

1. Dey, T.K., Sun, J.: Defining and computing curve skeletons with medial geodesic function. In: Proceedings of the 4th Eurographics Symposium on Geometry Processing, pp. 143–152 (2006)

2. Chuang, J.H., Ahuja, N., Lin, C.C., Tsai, C.H., Chen, C.H.: A potential-based generalized cylinder representation. Computers & Graphics 28, 907–918 (2004)
3. Aujay, G., Hetroy, F., Lazarus, F., Depraz, C.: Harmonic skeleton for realistic character animation. In: Proceedings of Eurographics/ACM SIGGRAPH Symposium on Computer Animation, pp. 151–160 (2007)
4. Au, O.K.C., Tai, C.L., Chu, H.K., Cohen-Or, D., Lee, T.Y.: Skeleton extraction by mesh contraction. ACM Transactions on Graphics (SIGGRAPH 2008) 27, 44:1-44:10 (2008)
5. Cornea, N.D., Silver, D., Min, P.: Curve-skeleton properties, applications, and algorithms. IEEE Transactions on Visualization and Computer Graphics 13, 530–548 (2007)
6. Lohou, C., Bertrand, G.: A 3d 12-subiteration thinning algorithm based on p-simple points. Discrete Applied Mathematics 139, 171–195 (2004)
7. Wang, Y.S., Lee, T.Y.: Curve skeleton extraction using iterative least squares optimization. IEEE Transactions on Visualization and Computer Graphics 14, 926–936 (2008)
8. Hassouna, M.S., Farag, A.A.: Robust centerline extraction framework using level sets. In: Proceedings of CVPR 2005, pp. 458–465 (2005)
9. Chuang, J.H., Tsai, C.H., Ko, M.C.: Skeletonization of three-dimensional object using generalized potential field. IEEE Transactions on Pattern Analysis and Machine Intelligence 22, 1241–1251 (2000)
10. Cornea, N.D., Silver, D., Yuan, X., Balasubramanian, R.: Computing hierarchical curve-skeletons of 3d objects. The Visual Computer 21, 945–955 (2005)
11. Amenta, N., Choi, S., Kolluri, R.K.: The power crust. In: Proceedings of the 6th ACM Symposium on Solid Modeling and Applications, pp. 249–260 (2001)
12. Verroust, A., Lazarus, F.: Extracting skeletal curves from 3d scattered data. The Visual Computer 16, 15–25 (2000)
13. Xiao, Y., Siebert, P., Werghi, N.: A discrete reeb graph approach for the segmentation of human body scans. In: Proceedings of the 4th International Conference on 3D Digital Imaging and Modeling, pp. 378–385 (2003)
14. Tagliasacchi, A., Zhang, H., Cohen-Or, D.: Curve skeleton extraction from incomplete point cloud. ACM Transactions on Graphics (SIGGRAPH 2009) 28, Article 71, 9 pages (2009)
15. Cao, J.J., Tagliasacchi, A., Olson, N., Zhang, H., Su, Z.X.: Point cloud skeletons via laplacian-based contraction. In: Proc. of IEEE Conf. on Shape Modeling and Applications, pp. 187–197 (2010)
16. Liang, X.H., Zhao, Q.P., He, Z.Y., Xie, K., Liu, Y.B.: A point-based rendering approach for real-time interaction on mobile devices. Science in China Series F: Information Sciences 52, 1335–1345 (2009)
17. Amenta, N., Kil, Y.: Defining point-set surfaces. ACM Transactions on Graphics (Proceedings of SIGGRAPH 2004) 23, 264–270 (2004)
18. Pauly, M., Gross, M., Kobbelt, L.P.: E±cient simplification of point-sampled surfaces. In: Proceedings of the Conference on Visualization, pp. 163–170 (2002)
19. He, Z.Y., Liang, X.H.: A novel simplification algorithm based on mls and splats for point models. In: Computer Graphics International 2009 (CGI 2009), pp. 40–47 (2009)

View-Dependent Line Drawings for 3D Scenes

Xin Zhang, Zi'ang Ding, Chuan Zhu, Wei Chen*, and Qunsheng Peng

State Key Lab. of CAD&CG, Zhejiang University, Hangzhou, P.R.China,
{zhangxin,dingziang,zhuchuan,chenwei,peng}@cad.zju.edu.cn

Abstract. We present a novel density control algorithm to achieve interactive line drawing of 3D scenes. The kernel of our approach is a line selection method that considers both the geometry property of lines and the view-dependent line density in the image space. The latter is measured as a combination of a local entropy and a global entropy subject to the information theory. The view-dependent line drawing is fulfilled by leveraging two entropies, facilitating the preservation of details in important regions. We demonstrate our new approach with a variety of examples and provide comparisons with recent approaches.

Keywords: line drawing, view-dependent, information entropy.

1 Introduction

Visual cues of our real world can be greatly enhanced by means of line-art illustrations [1]. Nowadays 3D computer generated line drawing has emerged as an attractive tool, which seeks to represent and render the models in a scene with abstractive lines [2]. One crucial problem of line drawings from 3D scenes is the control over the abstraction, that is, the generated lines should exhibit conceivably effective cues for shape depiction at an appropriate scale [3]. The expressiveness of the abstraction can be achieved by the use of aesthetic line styles, fine-grained feature line extractions, and interactive user adjustments [4,5,6]. Among them, the control of line density and contrast is of great importance to remove visual clutter and achieve appealing results [7,8]. As such, distinctive emphasis may be imposed on visually important regions, yielding higher line density in regions than those with low saliency.

The line drawing may vary according to the form of data and the desired application. When 3D line drawings are zoomed in or out, how to preserve shape and stroke density is a primary issue. There are two main challenges in the abstraction of line drawings. First, when the view changes, the sensitive region in a scene may also change. In order to properly exhibit effective cues for scene understanding, it is necessary to choose lines that best depict the salient regions in the new view. The second challenge concerns the issue of line density: too many lines may result in unreadable pictures, while too few lines can not convey enough information of the scene.

* Corresponding author.

Z. Pan et al. (Eds.): Transactions on Edutainment VII, LNCS 7145, pp. 151–160, 2012.

Alternatively, one can control the line density in the image space with the projected lines, or say, 2D strokes. The 2D strokes naturally tend to be much easier collected, modified and manipulated than 3D lines. Many existing approaches directly adjust the number of drawn strokes based on the measured density in the image space[7,8,9,10]. In [11], local control of line density is accomplished by leveraging two secondary off-line buffers to compute the line visibility and vary the line width. In contrast, geometric line simplification algorithms seek to merge dense strokes, and replace them with fitted strokes. Recent progress [12,13] has demonstrated its advantages over other schemes.

In this paper, we introduce a new simplification method for line drawing to control the line density in the image space. First, the local entropy of each line is computed based on the entropy theory [14] and its geometric property. Second, inspired by [11], we consider the global property of each line that is estimated by measuring effectiveness in the image space. By combining both local and global properties of lines, we are able to depict 3D scenes in an uncluttered yet expressive fashion.

The rest of this paper is organized as follows. The related work is summarized in Section 2. The overview of our algorithm is explained in Section 3. In Section 4, we introduce our view-dependent line drawing algorithm, followed by the detailed results in Section 5. We discuss and conclude this paper in Section 6 and Section 7.

2 Related Work

There has been many efforts dedicated to various types of automatic real-time NPR line drawing synthesis by means of image-space or object-space techniques. For simplicity, we roughly categorize these methods into three classes: line extraction, line clustering and line simplification.

Line extraction from 3D Models is the process of generating a set of lines to represent the input model meanwhile providing as much as possible visual cues [15,16]. Over the past decades, a variety of line types have been discussed, including hidden lines [17], silhouettes [5,9], suggestive contours [18], ridge-valley lines [19], apparent ridge [20], abstracted shading lines [6] and PELs [21]. For efficient visual clarification, relevant issues on how to achieve stylized illustration [10], coherent rendering [22], detail control [8,23,24,11] as well as task-adaptable shading [25] have also been addressed. A detailed review on the line extraction algorithms can be found in [3].

Line clustering denotes the classification of lines into groups so that lines in the same cluster seems more similar to each other than lines from different clusters. The primary task of line clustering is the definition of a distance measure, or the so-called spatial proximity. Varied schemes were proposed depending on different applications [26,27,28,29], including the closest point measure [29], the Hausdorff distance [30], the Frechet distance [31], the mean of closest distances [30], and the mean of thresholded closest distances [32].

Essentially the line clustering can be regarded as either a statistical data analysis issue [33] or a computational geometry problem [34]. For the former, representative data clustering algorithms [35] include hierarchical single linkage, K-means, ordering points, and density based approaches. In contrast, geometry-inspired line clustering relies more on the intrinsic properties of curved lines. For instance, the ϵ-group technique [12] makes use of the morphological property of lines and defines an ϵ-group as a cluster. The work presented in [13] employs a divide-and-conquer approach to evaluate the proximity of 2D strokes and to dynamically group lines at run-time.

Line simplification can be easily conducted after clustering. Rather than simplifying the point distribution in a line, its basic task is to select or generate a representative one from a set of clustered lines. For instance, an ϵ-line can be quickly retrieved with the pre-computed ϵ-group [12]. The complicated structure of ϵ-group makes dynamic and interactive simplification difficult. Recently Shesh and Chen [13] introduced a new data structure, called $1+\epsilon$ deformable spanner, for run-time line simplification that simultaneously preserves the proximity and continuity of lines.

This paper introduces a new method to deal with the simplification issue. We propose a density control algorithm to generate line drawings for arbitrary 3D scenes without requiring user adjustment. Our approach can produce visually effective depiction of 3D scenes while preserving details in important regions.

3 Overview

Our approach determines the line density by considering the viewing configuration and the model characteristics itself. The pipeline works fully in the 2D image space with three stages:

- Initially, the input is an unordered set of 3D line strokes. We first sample each stroke uniformly (in terms of its length) into a set of points and then represent each line with these points. Each point stores its position in 2D image space.
- An *occupancy buffer* is set up by projecting all the lines from the previous stage onto this buffer. Intuitively, the *occupancy buffer* is used to indicate which regions of the screen have higher line density, and vice versa.
- In the third stage, we remove the lines that may cause visual clutter. Based on the *occupancy buffer* and the line-specific property, we first compute the local entropy of each line. Figure 1(b) shows the result after removing lines with lower local entropy at the current condition. Then, the global entropy is computed for each line by considering its overall effectiveness in the entire image space. Lines with higher global entropy are shown in Figure 1(c). By combing both local and global entropies of each line, we are able to determine the lines to be removed while maintaining a high visual accuracy, as shown in Figure 1(d).

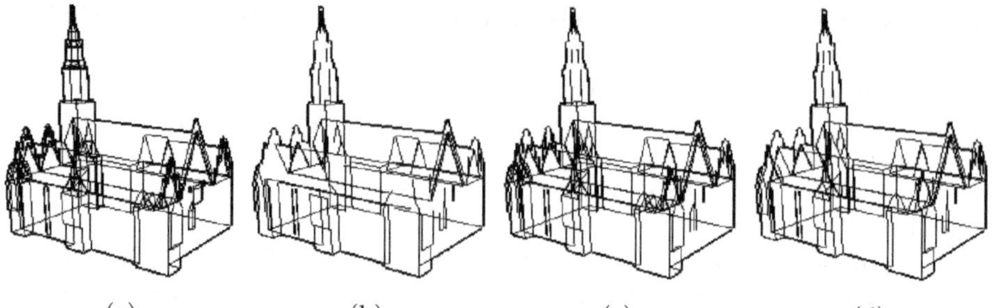

Fig. 1. Overview of our approach. (a) the input data; the line removal result with the local entropy (b) and the global entropy (c); (d) shows the final result by combining both the local and global entropies together.

4 View-Dependent Line Drawing

4.1 Computing the Occupancy Buffer

The first step of our algorithm is to build a so-called *occupancy buffer*. This buffer is a screen-sized view-dependent buffer in which each point is associated with the number of lines projecting to the neighborhood of this point. In our experiments, we set the size of the neighborhood as 3×3. The occupancy buffer will be used to evaluate the line density in the image space.

To compute this occupancy buffer, we first project all the lines from the input data onto an empty buffer, as shown in Figure 2. Notice that we do not take self-cross into account. The pixel value records the number of lines that pass the pixel, and may exceed 1 if multiple lines covers it. A line is counted only once to avoid discarding some critical lines that are curvy and are highly occluded in other viewpoints. In this way, we do not take the line self-cross into account and use the actual screen-space footprint instead.

4.2 View-Dependent Line Removal

Our view-dependent line removal algorithm starts from the input data and determines which lines should be drawn according to a view-dependent criterion. We therefore need a criterion to select the candidate lines from the line set. This criterion should take into account both the geometry property of a line and also its expression effectiveness in the screen space. We first introduce multiple criteria that are to combined together to obtain a robust metric.

The lines generated by the input model are evaluated based on the information entropy. Information entropy [13] has been already applied in several works on optimal viewpoint selection [36]. Inspired by these work, we define the information entropy E_L of a line as follows:

$$E_L = -\frac{1}{\log_2 m} \sum_{i=0}^{m-1} \frac{D_i}{L_S} \log_2 \frac{D_i}{L_S} \tag{1}$$

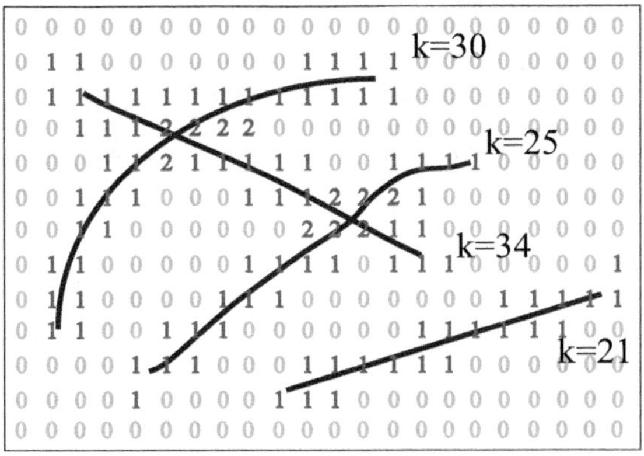

Fig. 2. The *occupancy buffer* computation

where m is the number of segments of a line, D_i is the length of the ith segment on the screen (in our experiments, we set D_i to be 10 pixels uniformly), and L_S is the total length of the line. Using this value E_L, we can evaluate all the lines by taking the local length of each line into account, as shown in Figure 1(b). Thus, we call the E_L as the local property of a line. However, if only the local entropy of a line is accounted for, some overall information, such as long lines may be lost. Therefore, we also define the global effectiveness for each line in the 2D image space. A new metric is yielded, which quantifies the effectiveness of a line in the line set:

$$E_G = -\frac{L_S}{L_M}\log_2\frac{L_S}{L_M} \tag{2}$$

where L_M is the maximal length of the entire line set in the 2D image space. This global property can convey the amount of the length effectiveness in the whole screen, and therefore be useful for revealing the structure information of a 3D model or scene, as shown in Figure 1(c).

The last criterion used by our metric is the overlapping ratio. Intuitively, this value quantifies the density of lines inside a region. By projecting the line onto the screen and reconstructing the occupancy information for each line, we are able to determine the degree of overlapping for each line. For that, we compute the footprint of each line and fetch the corresponding values in the *occupancy buffer*. From a series of overlapping numbers o_i over k pixels, we compute the average overlapping ratio:

$$O = \frac{\sum_{i=1}^{k} o_i}{k} \tag{3}$$

Once we know the local and global entropies and the occupancy value for each line, we can compute the metric for the line selection. It is the weighted sum of the local and global entropies divided by the average occupancy. Thus, we can select the lines that possess interesting properties avoid generating over-dense line distribution:

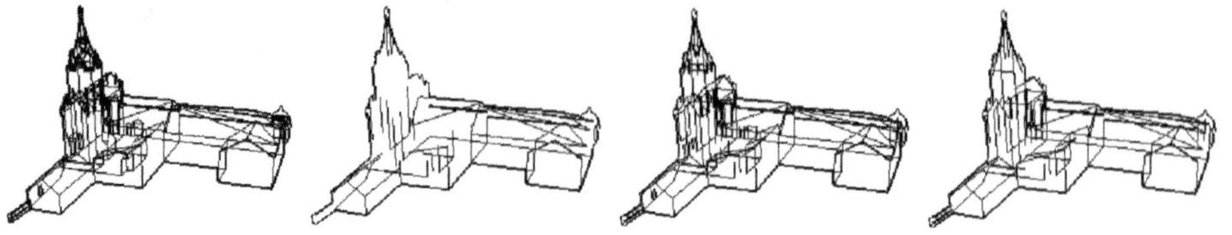

(a) (b) (c) (d)

Fig. 3. Three steps of our approach on the *Rathausblock* model. (a) the input data; the line removal result with either local entropy (b) or global entropy (c); (d) our final result with $\alpha = 0.5$ and $\beta = 0.5$.

$$C = \frac{\alpha E_L + \beta E_G}{O} \tag{4}$$

where α and β are user-controlled parameters. The lines with low values computed from Equation 4 are removed. Finally, we can obtain the line drawing with a lower threshold or a given number of target lines, as shown in Figure 1(d).

5 Results

We implemented the proposed approach on a PC equipped with Intel Core 2 Quad Q9550 2.83 GHz CPU, 4G host memory and Nvidia WinFast GTX 280 graphics card. Table 1 reports the experimental statistics, including the number of lines (#L), resolution (#R) and the time for handling (TS) the models presented in this paper. Figure 3 shows the results of three steps in our algorithm

Table 1. Performance statistics for a sequence of models

Data	#L	#R	TS(fps)
Ratusz w Poznaniu	1051	512×512	19.1
Rathausblock	1370	512×512	17.5
New York City Hall	811	512×512	20.1

on the *Rathausblock* model. The local entropy effectively reduces the clutter of the line drawing (Figure 3(b)), while the global entropy is helpful to preserving the important features (Figure 3(c)). Therefore, we can obtain the result with both of them when combining the local and global properties together, as shown in Figure 3(d).

Figure 4 displays two sets of line drawings on the *New York City Hall* model with and without an account for line visibility. We use the method introduced in [37] to detect the visibility of each line. The results clearly demonstrate that our algorithm is suitable for both cases.

Figure 5 illustrates another line drawing of *Ratusz w Poznaniu* model with different distances. Our algorithm can reduce the clutter whenever the viewpoint is zooming in or out, and meanwhile preserve the overall shape of the model.

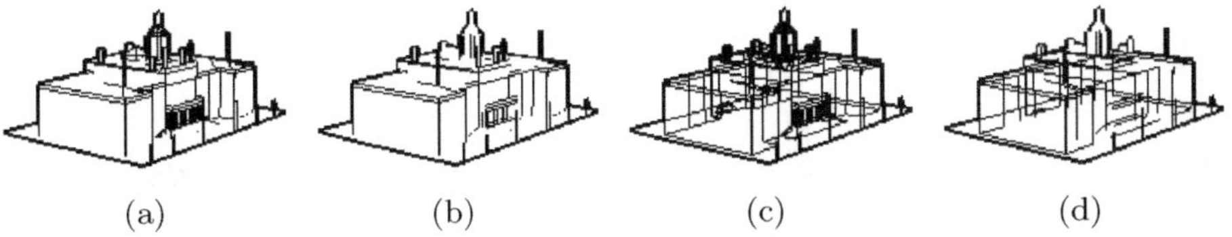

Fig. 4. Line drawings with and without using line visibility. (a) and (c) the input data; (b) and (d) our results. In both cases, the effects are implemented with $\alpha = 0.5$ and $\beta = 0.5$.

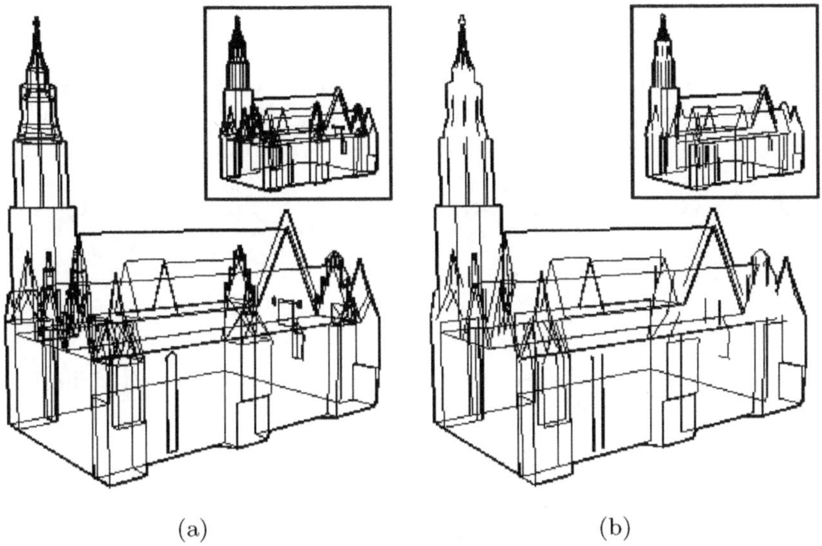

Fig. 5. Line drawings with different distances. (a) the input data; (b) our result with $\alpha = 0.4$ and $\beta = 0.6$.

6 Discussion

We have shown that the proposed line drawing approach achieve high quality line density control at a low computational cost. In Figure 6, we present a comparison of our algorithm with the *priority buffer* approach introduced in [11]. It is apparent that our approach can reduce more clutter. That is because that the *priority buffer* in [11] is computed by considering the length effectiveness of each line in image space, which plays a similar role as the global entropy. We additionally employ the occupancy-based local entropy to clarify highly dense region, yielding visually pleasing results, as shown in Figure 6.

Our approach shows some limitations though. First, some important information could also be reduced in our line selection scheme. In Figure 7, the structure information in the red rectangle can not be detected and is reduced by our line selection scheme. Therefore, we plan to incorporate the *Human Visual System* into our framework to select more meaningful information in the future work.

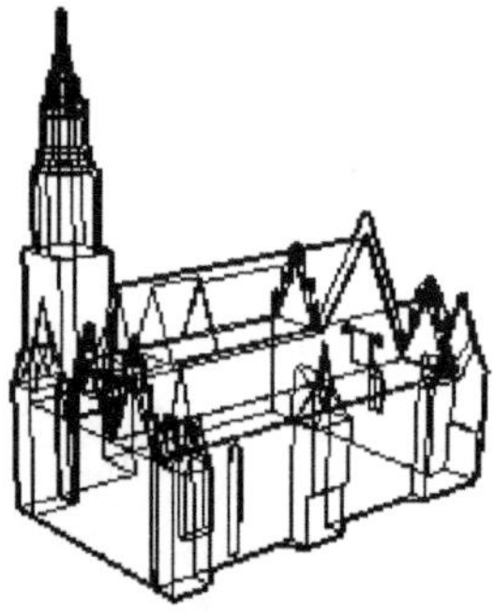

(a) (b) (c)

Fig. 6. Result comparison for the *Ratusz w Poznaniu* model. (a) the initial line drawing; (b) the result generated by [11]; (c) our result with $\alpha = 0.3$ and $\beta = 0.7$.

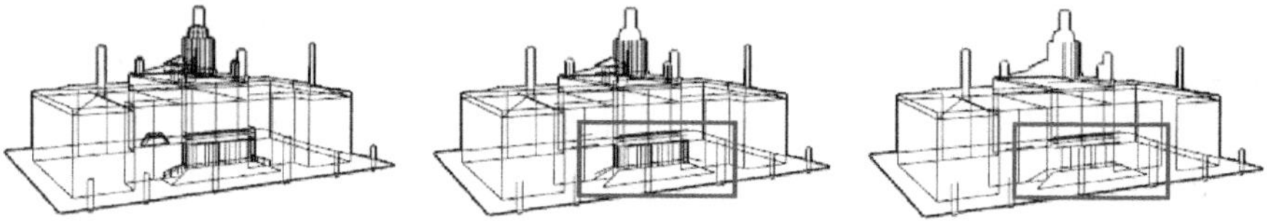

(a) (b) (c)

Fig. 7. Result comparison for the *New York City Hall* model. (a) the initial line drawing; (b) the result generated by [11]; (c) our result.

Second, the line selection scheme can be improved, especially on the criterion of local entropy. We plan to incorporate the curvature information into the local entropy by computing the angular variation along a line. We believe that it may lead to more plausible results. Third, the temporal coherence can not be ensured by our algorithm. We intend to define a similarity metric between successive frames to achieve temporal coherence, and leave it for future work.

7 Conclusions and Future Work

We have presented a density control algorithm to achieve an interactive line drawing of 3D scenes. Challenges in this include how to select meaningful lines to reduce clutter and how to achieve visually effective results. Whether our results demonstrate a promising line drawing may be a matter of taste. But the experimental results do indicate that our results greatly improves the readability of line drawings without requiring user interaction, and that it is probably intractable to get the similar results with existing line drawing methods.

There are some interesting topics valuable for future exploration. The current metric for measuring the local entropy is independent of curvature. Additional consideration of the curvature configuration may lead to more plausible results. Moreover, we would like to incorporate temporal coherence into our framework.

To achieve temporal coherence, we intend to use a similarity metric to pair some lines at the current frame with ones at the previous frame. We could thereby have a temporal coherent set of lines and use it to transition smoothly from one frame to the next.

Acknowledgments. This research is supported by National Grand Foundation Research 973 Program of China under Grant No. 2009CB320802, National Natural Science Foundation of China Under Grant No. 60970020 and No. 60873123. We would like to thank Mr. Guanyu Xing and Ms. Xiaoyan Cui for their help.

References

1. Elber, S.: Line illustrations in computer graphics. The Visual Computer 11(6), 290–296 (1995)
2. Gooch, B., Gooch, A.: Non-Photorealistic Rendering. A. K. Peters (2001)
3. Rusinkiewcz, S., Cole, F., Decarlo, D., Finkelstein, A.: Line drawings from 3D models. In: Proceedings ACM SIGGRAPH Classes (2008)
4. Isenberg, T., Brennecke, A.: G-strokes: A concept for simplifying line stylization. Computers & Graphics 30, 754–766 (2006)
5. Hertzmann, A., Zorin, D.: Illustrating smooth surfaces. In: Proceedings ACM SIGGRAPH, pp. 517–526 (2000)
6. Lee, Y., Markosian, L., Lee, S., Hughes, J.F.: Line drawings via abstracted shading. ACM Transactions Graphics 26(3) (2007)
7. Grabli, S., Durand, F., Sillion, F.: Density measure for line-drawing simplification. In: Proceedings of Pacific Graphics, pp. 183–192 (2004)
8. Wilson, B., Ma, K.-L.: Rendering complexity in computer-generated pen-and-ink illustrations. In: Proceedings of International Symposium on Non-Photorealistic Animation and Rendering, pp. 129–137 (2004)
9. Isenberg, T., Freudenberg, B., Halper, N., Schlechtweg, S., Strothotte, T.: A developer's guide to silhouette algorithms for polygonal models. IEEE Computer Graphics and Applications 23(4), 28–37 (2003)
10. Kalnins, R.D., Davidson, P.L., Markosian, L., Finkelstein, A.: Coherent stylized silhouettes. ACM Transactions on Graphics 22(3), 856–861 (2003)
11. Cole, F., DeCarlo, D., Finkelstein, A., Kin, K., Morley, K., Santella, A.: Directing gaze in 3D models with stylized focus. In: Eurographics Symposium on Rendering, pp. 377–387 (June 2006)
12. Barla, P., Thollot, J., Sillion, F.X.: Geometric clustering for line drawing simplification. In: Proceedings of Eurographics Workshop on Rendering, pp. 183–192 (2005)
13. Shesh, A., Chen, B.: Efficient and dynamic simplification of line drawings. Computer Graphics Forum 27(2), 537–545 (2008)
14. Shannon, C.E.: A mathematical theory of communication. Bell System Technical Journal 27, 379–423, 623–656 (1948)
15. Elber, G.: Line art rendering via a coverage of isoparametric curves. IEEE Transactions on Visualization and Computer Graphics 1(3), 231–239 (1995)
16. Cole, F., Golovinskiy, A., Limpaecher, A., Barros, H.S., Finkelstein, A., Funkhouser, T., Rusinkiewicz, S.: Where do people draw lines? ACM Transactions Graphics 27(3) (2008)

17. Elber, G., Cohen, E.: Hidden curve removal for free form surfaces. In: Proceedings of ACM SIGGRAPH, pp. 95–104 (1990)
18. DeCarlo, D., Finkelstein, A., Rusinkiewicz, S., Santella, A.: Suggestive contours for conveying shape. ACM Transactions Graphics 22(3), 848–855 (2003)
19. Ohtake, Y., Belyaev, A., Seidel, H.-P.: Ridge-valley lines on meshes via implicit surface fitting. ACM Transactions Graphics 23(3), 609–612 (2004)
20. Judd, T., Durand, F., Adelson, E.: Apparent ridges for line drawing. ACM Transactions Graphics 26(3) (2007)
21. Xie, X., He, Y., Tian, F., Seah, H.-S., Gu, X., Qin, H.: An effective illustrative visualization framework based on photic extremum lines (PELs). IEEE Transactions on Visualization and Computer Graphics 13(6), 1328–1335 (2007)
22. DeCarlo, D., Finkelstein, A., Rusinkiewicz, S.: Interactive rendering of suggestive contours with temporal coherence. In: Proceedings of International Symposium on Non-Photorealistic Animation and Rendering (NPAR), pp. 15–24 (June 2004)
23. Jeong, K., Ni, A., Seungyong, L., Markosiana, L.: Detail control in line drawings of 3D meshes. The Visual Computer 21(8-10), 698–706 (2005)
24. Ni, A., Jeong, K., Lee, S., Markosian, L.: Multiscale line drawings from 3D meshes. In: Proceedings of ACM Symposium on Interactive 3D Graphics and Games, pp. 133–137 (2006)
25. Lum, E., Ma, K.-L.: Expressive line selection by example. The Visual Computer 21(8-10), 811–820 (2005)
26. Rosion, P.L.: Grouping curved lines. In: Proceedings of British Machine Vision Conference, pp. 625–644 (1994)
27. Agrawala, M., Stolte, C.: Rendering effective route maps: improving usability through generalization. In: Proceedings of ACM SIGGRAPH, pp. 241–249 (2001)
28. Engbers, E.A., Smeulders, A.W.M.: Design considerations for generic grouping in vision. IEEE Transactions on Pattern Analysis and Machine Intelligence 25(4), 445–457 (2003)
29. Moberts, B., Vilanova, A., van Wijk, J.J.: Evaluation of fiber clustering methods for diffusion tensor imaging. In: Proceedings of IEEE Visualization, pp. 65–72 (2005)
30. Corouge, I., Gouttard, S., Gerig, G.: Towards a shape model of white matter fiber bundles using diffusion tensor MRI. In: International Symposium on Biomedical Imaging, pp. 344–347 (2004)
31. Alt, H., Godau, M.: Computing the frechet distance between two polygonal curves. International Journal of Computational Geometry and Applications 5, 75–91 (1995)
32. Zhang, S., Demiralp, C., Laidlaw, D.H.: Visualizing diffusion tensor MR images using streamtubes and streamsurfaces. IEEE Transactions on Visualization and Computer Graphics 9(4), 454–462 (2003)
33. Duda, R.O., Hart, P.E., Stork, D.G.: Pattern Classification, 2nd edn. Wiley Interscience (2000)
34. Pottmann, H., Wallner, J.: Computational Line Geometry. Springer, Heidelberg (2001)
35. Han, J., Kamber, M.: Data Mining: Concepts and Techniques. Morgan Kaufmann (2006)
36. Takahashi, S., Fujishiro, I., Takeshima, Y., Nishita, T.: A feature-driven approach to locating optimal viewpoints for volume visualization. IEEE Visualization 23-25, 495–502 (2005)
37. Cole, F., Finkelstein, A.: Two fast methods for high-quality line visibility. IEEE Transactions on Visualization and Computer Graphics 16(5), 707–717 (2010)

Propositions for Innovative Forms of Digital Interactive Storytelling Based on Narrative Theories and Practices

Nicolas Szilas, Monica Axelrad, and Urs Richle

TECFA, FPSE, University of Geneva, 40 boul Pont-d'Arve 1205 Geneva, Switzerland
{nicolas.szilas,monica.axelrad,urs.richle}@unige.ch

Abstract. This paper takes a look at narrative forms as of yet unexplored in the field of digital interactive storytelling, and proposes methods for how they can be used in engaging ways for the user. Digital Interactive Storytelling, while nearly two decades old as a field of research, has yet to produce a tool capable of producing masses of narratively interesting and engaging pieces for the end user. Although the various prototypes available produce several different story genres, they stem from the same classic narrative form. With this paper, we aim to introduce narrative techniques that have successfully been used in cinema, literature and the gaming world, and show how they can be adapted to DIS. We believe that by presenting these techniques authors can gain a better understanding of how to use existing systems.

1 Introduction

A hybrid between computer games and storytelling, the field of Digital Interactive Storytelling (DIS) aspires to deliver a new reading experience to its audience. By putting the reader in control of one character (at a time) and allowing him to make decisions that not only guide, but generate the plot, DIS aims to ultimately provide a unique story experience with each reading of the story [1, 2, 3, 4]. While early day adventure games such as Leisure Suit Larry in the Land of the Lounge Lizard that came out in 1987 [5] or Infocom's Hitch Hiker's Guide to the Galaxy adventure game [6] are a good example of what a basic DIS piece can look like, mixing story and user interaction, they hardly provide a comprehensive overview, nor do they go far enough into the possibilities of what DIS aims to achieve today. Recent adventure games have a strong cinematographic influence with nicely crafted stories, but leave little choice to the user to influence the story. These games generally use a storyline as a means to advance the actions [7], DIS would like to advance the storyline through actions. Modern adventure games provide players with a setting to perform actions and revert to cut scenes where the player gets presented the new scene which advances the storyline from which he will continue to perform basically the same actions as before. Most DIS systems today present the player with an unfolding story and will systematically present the player with a scene where he can take action from which the storyline will continue to advance.

Z. Pan et al. (Eds.): Transactions on Edutainment VII, LNCS 7145, pp. 161–179, 2012.

An overview of approximately 25 DIS system prototypes can be found here [8]. Looking through the various systems it becomes clear that the DIS community has not yet achieved its goal of providing the reader with a high quality story experience while at the same time providing him with a key role in affecting the outcome of said story. Several challenges still obstruct this goal, and these can be divided into two categories; technical feasibility and creative contributions - or authoring as it is referred to within the DIS community [9]. DIS must generate story fragments based on a user's actions and insure that their addition to the current story keeps the latter coherent. Or, as C. Crawford puts it "In Interactive Storytelling, the story engine must be able to generate stories on the fly, based on user feedback, without relying on pre-scripted action or a hardwired series of events" [10]. And this is not easy. Writing a story that will be completed only once it is read is a difficult task for authors. Finding the balance between giving the reader enough control so that he feels he is taking an active part in the story's development, and keeping enough control to produce a coherent story, is one of the main challenges of DIS.

Taking a look at the various types of stories implemented with current DIS prototypes, we find children's fairytales [11, 12, 13], greek tragedies [14, 15], classical literature [16], adventures [17, 18, 19, 20], sitcom [21], soap opera [12], family drama [22], whodunit [2], political fiction [23]. While these works are varied, they all stem from classical and established, literature or drama, narrative forms.

Except for the user's ability to influence the story, the existing DIS pieces don't explore the large palette of expressive means offered by the computer. This is certainly explained by a certain immaturity of the domain, and the technical difficulties regarding the dynamic generation of narrative, that need to be solved first. Many of (if not all) the stories mentioned above were not designed by professional writers, but by the system designers, who naturally started simple. It could thus be argued that one should wait for the domain to gain maturity and for professional authors to get comfortable with the DIS approach, systems and authoring tools. However, this is a typical chicken and egg problem as explained in Spierling and Szilas [9]: artists wait for mature DIS systems, but DIS need artists' guidance to evolve in an appropriate and innovative direction.

In light of the current situation, this paper explores new possibilities of expression that advanced DIS research could offer authors. We are basing our exploration on technology, considering that engines capable of dynamically generating narrative actions according to a user's actions are available. Promising narrative engines such as Mimesis [24], IDtension [17], Gadin [12] or Storytron [23] are already developed and are examples of such technology. Then, taking inspiration from both theoretical work in narratology and practical creative narrative work, we explore what could be achieved in the future. While one could consider that these propositions go far beyond the current technological state of the art, several of the propositions below are already feasible with current technology. Our approach is profoundly interdisciplinary, mixing technology, narrative theories and art.

To limit the field of exploration of this paper, we have defined a set of constraints on how the user can interact with the DIS artefact:

- The only means for the user to act upon the fictional world is via a character's actions. This excludes letting the user act as in a god-game style, such as adding a prop in the stage, but does however include other out of character actions at the discourse level, as long as the story is untouched. (Here we refer to the classical distinction between story and discourse in narrative theories [25].)
- There is only one user.
- The interacting device does not play a role in the exploration of expressive possibilities, that is the classical keyboard and mouse interface will be sufficient for interacting with these future works. Of course, many innovations can be investigated regarding interaction devices combined with our propositions, but we leave these aside for future work.

2 Multiple Actualisations

In classical narrative, a text (understood in its generic meaning) triggers a multitude of possible worlds, which are constantly created by the reader, according to "clues" provided by the author [26]. These worlds correspond to alternatives that the reader imagines while reading. But only one of these worlds is finally actualised to create the story. While the story can vary a bit according to each reader and depending on the degree of openness of a work [27], each reader reconstructs a single story.

Things are different in less classical forms in which several alternative routes, representing alternative worlds from a narratological point of view, are included in the same work. Various movies have explored this form, for example: *It's a Wonderful Life* (F. Capra), *Smoking / No Smoking* (A. Resnais), *Lola Rennt* (T. Tykwer), *Sliding Doors* (P. Howitt). In these movies, two or more alternative worlds are actualised.

With current DIS systems, although the user may be given choices at several points within the story (choice points), only one route is finally explored. If the user replays, he can explore another route, but each reading is distinct, and previous readings are not accessible during the current reading.

How can the possibility of multiple actualisations be better exploited in DIS? As the user interacts via a character (see the first scope limitation defined in the introduction), the only way to create alternative worlds is through a character's choice points. Thus, this opens the possibility that when interacting with a story via a choice point, the user can, not only actualize one of his choices, but also explore other alternative routes.

Before going further in this investigation, it is convenient to represent these routes as a tree: the root node is the start of the story, each node represents a choice point, a bifurcation corresponds to the creation of an alternative route and world from an existing one, the leaves represent the world in the state the user left it, and finally a storyline or route is a full trajectory from the root node to a leaf (see Figure 1).

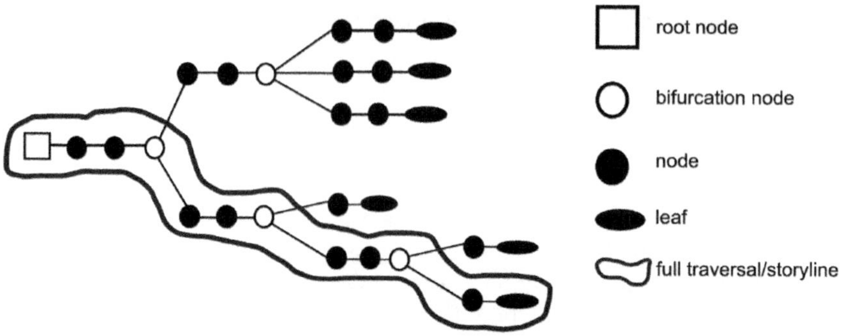

Fig. 1. Multiple Actualisations

Although this tree representation evokes the concept of a hypertext, it is radically different. In a hypertext, the tree is built by the author, in multiple actualisation based DIS, the tree would be dynamically generated by the user. In fact, a main property of DIS is that the largest explorable tree is gigantic.

We can then further refine this potential form, according to three criteria.

The bifurcation point chooser: Who decides where the bifurcation points are, the user or the computer? Four cases can be distinguished:

- **Free choice:** Any user interaction point can be a bifurcation point, leaving the user the possibility to create as many alternative worlds desired.
- **Computer-constrained:** The computer filters the user interaction points to keep only a part of them, among which the user is free to choose.
- **Computer-proposed:** According to the current state of the story, the computer proposes several bifurcations points that the user is free to accept or not. Typically, the computer is able to calculate causal dependencies between events and it proposes to "replay the past to modify the present".
- **Computer-imposed:** The computer decides which bifurcation points must be explored by the user.

The moment of bifurcation point choice: When the user decides that a bifurcation point is worth exploring.

- When played: after encountering a certain choice point, the user decides that this moment in the story should create two possible worlds to be played. Then, in most cases (but see part 6) the user will explore one of them, leaving the alternative world for later (in playing time).
- Retrospectively: the user, when at a leaf of the story, decides/selects one or more bifurcation points, and either explores one of them (the most natural case) or continues with the current storyline route.

The navigation between alternative worlds: how does the user stop exploring the current world and go back to a previous (in playing time) alternative world?

- **Totally free:** the user can go towards any bifurcation point, either continuing an already started storyline at its leaf or directly starting another branch from an existing bifurcation point to create a new alternative world.
- **To any leaf:** The user can continue any already started storyline at its leaf.
- **At a subset of leaves:** The computer restricts which leaves can be continued.
- **At the previous leaf:** To simplify the user's representation of storyline imbrications, the user can only go back to the storyline he came from.

When combined, these different criteria can produce many different subforms of multiple actualisations. All these forms enable navigation at the discourse level on top of navigation at the story level, managed by the narrative engine.

Let us provide a few examples of combinations of the above criteria:

- Free choice of the bifurcation point, retrospective bifurcation, going back to another alternative world at the previous leaf: The user plays his story and can decide at any moment to stop the current storyline to explore another branch from any previously played storyline. At any moment, he can also stop the current storyline to go back to the previous storyline's leaf he quit to join the current storyline.
- Computer-proposed bifurcation point, retrospectively chosen, going back to another alternative world at a subset of leaves: During his interaction in a storyline, the user is prompted by the computer: "apparently, your choice to [...] three months ago had serious consequences. Do you want to replay this previous scene?". If the user clicks "no", he simply continues the current story, but if he clicks "yes", he replays the past decision point and chooses another option. He then explores the consequences of this choice. When the equivalent situation to the previous leaf is played, the computer prompts the user: "which story would you like to explore further?". The user can then either continue the first storyline, or the second one.
- Free choice of the bifurcation point, chosen when played, going back to another alternative world at any leaf: While playing the story, the user has the possibility to mark some of his decision points. Later, he can choose which among the marked decision points will constitute a bifurcation point, from which another storyline will be explored. He can quit the current storyline to continue any other previously started storyline.

Technically, since the worlds do not interact with each other, there is no specific challenge requiring advanced AI for implementing these forms. The main difficulty is to keep a memory of the different narrative states.

These forms rely on a Graphical User Interface (GUI) that enable the choice of bifurcation point (if not computer-imposed) and the navigation to and from these bifurcation points. The tree representation already mentioned above is certainly to be reused in this GUI. The user would visualize the globality of his multiple storyline current exploration and navigate through it. This GUI, and the concept of navigation through alternative worlds is clearly a breach in the search of immersion. By quitting a world to re-enter another one, the user is in a more distant, position regarding the fictional world. This contrasts with the "Hamlet on the Holodeck" [28] point of view on DIS but promotes a more reflexive and critical approach regarding the story.

Finally, it should be stressed that such multiple actualisation forms are not so far from certain existing functionalities in digital media. In particular, the saving mechanism in video games is, implicitly at least, a form of multiple storyline exploration. By saving a game, the player stores a specific game's state (choice of the bifurcation point when played) that he will be able to explore later. Note that there exists a multitude of variants of the saving mechanisms in video games: automatic save points (the game is automatically saved when a given stage is reached), in-game (diegetic) save points (the possibility of saving is represented in the fictional world by a specific artefact), manually vs. automatically labelled saved games, constrained or unconstrained number of saved games, etc. However, the saving mechanism in games is primarily a tool allowing both to enable to play a game in several sessions and to manage the reaching of the game's success in the most efficient manner (that is without having to replay a large part of the game) [29]. The saving mechanisms in video games are rarely used as a narrative device. An interesting exception is the game *The Last Express* [30], in which the user can go back in time in the current storyline via a rewinding clock metaphor, to explore another branch (but the previous leaf becomes no longer accessible). Four such clocks are available in the game, constituting four saved games.

3 Embedded Stories

In classical narrative, an embedded story is a fiction in a fiction. Within a first fictional world, the embedding world, a boundary is crossed and the reader/audience is transported into another world, the embedded world [31]. Typically, a character tells a story to another character. An exemplary form of embedded stories is the *1001 Arabian Nights*, in which Sheherazade is constantly embedding new stories within the current story as a narrative strategy to extend the narration. Embedded stories are a common device, both in literature and drama. According to Todorov, the embedded narrative is a "narrative within a narrative". The embedding narrative provides the contextual theme for the embedded narrative [32]. In movies, there are several examples of "film/play in a film" which also constitute embedded stories: for example *La Nuit Américaine* (F. Truffaut) or *Deathtrap* (S. Lumet).

Embedded stories applied to DIS would consist in letting the user act in both the embedding and the embedded worlds. A Non Playing Character (NPC) would "tell" an embedded story in a participative way, since the user would play one character in the embedded story. Depending on what crosses the boundary between the two worlds, several cases can be distinguished.

- **Separate worlds:** The embedding and embedded worlds are totally separate. The user goes into the embedded worlds and what happens in that world does not have any influence on the embedding world that he comes back to later. The two stories can only be thematically linked.

Fig. 2. Separate Worlds: Embedding and embedded worlds that are only thematically linked

Knowledge connected worlds: Some knowledge crosses the boundary between the two worlds. Typically, the embedded stories would serves as a metaphor to inform about something that is relevant in the embedding world. For example, a NPC, instead of convincing the user via a dialogue based argumentation, would let the user play a relevant embedded story, announced in a sentence such as "Imagine yourself in this situation" and the boundary would be crossed.

Fig. 3. Knowledge Connected Worlds: The embedded world serves as a metaphor to inform about something relevant in the embedding world

- **Materially connected worlds:** The embedding and embedded worlds recognise a change; the absence of the user or introduction of a new object. For example, as is nicely illustrated in the movie *The Purple Rose of Cairo* (W. Allen), when the character leaves the film in the movie theatre to enter the audience's world, the rest of the cast in the movie becomes stuck because they cannot finish the movie. With materially connected worlds, the character physically travels from one world to the other, not just the user's point of control. We can further distinguish between three kinds of material connections:
  - **Absence:** A minima, the character is missing in one world, which might have some consequences, as illustrated in the above example of *The Purple Rose of Cairo*.

- **Object transfer:** The user's character can cross the boundary with objects. If the two stories are happening in different periods in history, this can create humoristic anachronisms, as is often seen in time travel movies.
- **NPC transfer:** In this case, a NPC can cross the boundary, either on its own initiative or being invited by the user to do so. This situation is technically harder to implement, since one needs to model not only the reaction of the "travelling" NPC to the other world but also the reactions of other NPCs to the "stranger" character.

Fig. 4. Materially Connected Worlds: There is a recognised change in both the embedding and embedded world

Furthermore, the navigation to/from an embedded world can:

- occur at the user's initiative
- be proposed by the computer, typically a NPC
- be imposed by the computer

Finally, we would like to discuss two more complex cases of interactive embedded worlds.

Strange loops: As described by Marie-Laure Ryan [31], in some rare cases, within the embedded world one finds elements from the embedding world itself. An example of this is the movie *Stranger than Fiction* (M. Forster), where the main character happens to be the character of a book being written by another character in the same world. In DIS, it would mean that while moving from world A to world B, then again from world B to world C, one would strangely be back in world A. It is hard to predict how this would be perceived by the user, but such a form would certainly be worth exploring by an author.

NPC's role playing: In all previous cases of interactive embedded stories, only the user could play two characters in two different worlds. Going back to the example of the "movie in the movie" (e.g. *La Nuit Américaine*), one could imagine a situation where the user meets a NPC, and they both decide to go to an embedded world where they would each respectively play a new character. When the user meets the NPC's new character, it can actually be considered a double encounter since he has knowledge of the NPC's original role. When the user goes back to the embedding world, both "actors" can refer to the embedded experience during their conversations. Because the process of embedding is recursive (A can play character B who can play character C, etc.), one could imagine triple encounters, quadruple encounters, etc.

These last two examples show that the possibility of interactive embedded stories are very rich, and that we are far from having exhausted the possibilities of artistic explorations for these new kinds of forms.

4 Modal Worlds

In Section 2, we discussed the notion of possible worlds as various, alternative, future worlds imagined by the audience while experiencing the narrative. Frequently within a story, one of these worlds is explicitly mentioned by a character, according to different modalities. For example, when a character says "if you do that then..." or "if I had not done that, ..." or "I wish this could happen and...", it corresponds to specific narrative acts studied in narratology. In particular, we refer to T. Todorov [32, 33], who distinguishes four modes that can be attached to an action or state:

- Motivation-based modes
  - **Obligative:** What must be true in a society: "You have to respect the law: tell them the truth"
  - **Optative:** What characters desire: "I want that... "
- Hypothetical modes
  - **Conditional:** if something becomes true the character will do something: "If you give me a rose, I will kiss you"
  - **Predictive:** What could happen if something were true: "If it rained, people in this country would be happy"

To each of these four worlds corresponds a type of possible world that when explored with DIS techniques opens new narrative forms. Before giving examples of such narrative forms, let us extend the four previous modes with the work of M.L. Ryan [31], who adds the following worlds:

- **K-worlds, worlds of knowledge:** The knowledge a character has of the fictional world is in itself a possible world. Of course, if this knowledge is true, this K-world is not particularly interesting because the possible world and the fictional world are the same. But if it is wrong, then the beliefs of a character can constitute a separate and relevant possible world to explore. Example: "We know that the world is flat: if you walk in that direction, then there is nothing".
- **Pretend worlds:** In this case, the possible world presented by a character is deliberately wrong. This is very common in narrative, two excellent examples are the movies *The Usual Suspects* (B. Singer), where a large part of the movie happens to be a pretend world or *Big Fish* (T. Burton) where most of what is recounted is embellished to the point where the audience is brought to believe it is pretend.
- **F-Universes, mind's created worlds:** The possible world is simply imagined by the character. This case includes dreams, hallucinations, fantasies and fictional stories. Example: "I dreamed that...". This case resembles the case of embedded

stories, with the difference that the worlds "creator" might not be aware of the fact that this is a different world.

Applied to DIS, the idea consists in letting the user act in a possible world created during a given dialogue. We denote the Initiating Dialogue Act the precise dialogue line which triggers the possible world. It can be considered a generalization of the embedded worlds case discussed in Section 3, where the relation between the embedding world and the embedded world can vary in nature. Let us shortly review what kind of narrative forms this could take, depending on the above narratological discussion:

- **Obligative interactive world:** The user would enter in the NPC's "obligative logic" to live what it means, in this context, to respect what must be respected. This case has something special in that the user's possibility of acting would be constrained: each time he would select a non correct action, he would be reminded that it is not the way to proceed and the action would be blocked. This interactivity management might seem odd and contrary to the principle of DIS, however, it can provide a powerful expressive means. For example, the game Real Lives [33] uses a similar mechanism: it puts the user in the life of a person in the developing world and explicitly shows impossible choices to express the idea that some actions cannot be taken. It is contrary to the basic ergonomic principle of control but still provides a narrative effect.
- **Optative interactive world:** In this case, the user would enter an alternative world, bifurcating from the current situation. However, this alternative world that would not follow the natural property of the fictional world but it would be biased by what the uttering character wishes. If the wish is a NPC's one, then a branch would be explored by the user, as described in Section 2 regarding multiple actualisation, with the difference of status: this new branch must be tagged as a character's wish, rather than as a mere fictional possibility. It might be the case that one storyline evolves according to that wish, but it could also be the case that all storylines that the user would explore according to the multiple actualisation system described in Section 2 will never conform to the wished storyline.

Note that if we wanted to have the user interact with his own wished world, a situation that is similar to the concept of an awake dream in real life, then the user would need to be given direct access to the rules governing the fictional world. This would violate our initial scope (user's intervention is restricted to character-based intervention)

- **Conditional and predictive worlds:** We group these two modes, since the latter is in fact a generalization of the former [32]. This case is already covered by Section 2: case where the bifurcation is proposed by a NPC in a dialogue and the navigation back to the original storyline necessarily gets to the initial dialog.
- **Knowledge world and pretend world:** It is a variation of the embedded story case, but the embedded world is 1) introduced by a NPC in a dialogue 2) similar to the embedding world, with specific knowledge differences (a mistake or a lie).
- **Mind's created worlds:** See embedded worlds (See Section 3).

Finally, we found that a hypothetical mode, missing in the narratological work we referred to, should be added: the past conditional mode, to follow a grammatical metaphor, or the retrospective extension of K-Worlds, to follow M.-L. Ryan's classification. It consists in assertions such as "If I had done this...". This mode is related to the multi-actualised world forms discussed in Section 2. Let the parent world be the world where the dialogue takes place and the child world the world that is referred to during this dialogue. Two sub cases are worth considering:

- The child world is played before the parent world, and the initiating dialog act is performed by the user: The user plays a first storyline, then, according to the mechanism discussed in Section 2, he goes back to another alternative storyline. At some point in this second storyline, during a dialogue, the user can refer to the previous storyline, and utter: "If I had done this, then ...". Such a sentence would be generated from the GUI used for the navigation through the different alternative worlds.
- The child world is played after the parent world, and the initiating dialog act is performed by a NPC: The user is prompted by a NPC, with a dialogue line such as: "let's suppose you had...". Then the user would play an alternative branch and go back later in the initial dialogue. It is a similar situation than one of the cases discussed in Section 2, except that the navigation occurs via a dialogue, which increases the feeling of immersion. Furthermore, another case is also possible, if the choice point used as a bifurcation point is not a user choice point but a NPC or a happening: "let's suppose he had...", "let's suppose it had not rained that day".

This exploration of novel interactive forms based on possible world interaction in dialogues gives us a multitude of possibilities for DIS that we have certainly only partially covered in this section.

5 Ellipsis

An ellipsis is a frequently used narrative device in literature [26] and film [35] to condense time or to create space for free imagination. By omitting a portion of a sequence, it becomes up to the audience to fill in the narrative gaps. This can simply be used to shorten the telling of an action like standing up, walking through the room, opening the door and going out. The reader of a story or the viewer of the film understands the action by simply showing the standing up and the coming out of the door. A second function of an ellipsis is to create a metaphorical parallel between two different instants in a story. A great example is given by Stanley Kubrick in his film *2001* where he uses an ellipsis to create a metaphorical relationship between the first tool used in the history of humans (a bone) and the latest in the near future (a space station).

Ellipses are rarely used in DIS and even less so in games, simply because they do not fit with the idea of real-time interaction. While real-time interaction is absolutely necessary for action-based games, it is less true for adventure games and interactive narratives. In this section, we want to explore how ellipses could be used in DIS. We won't discuss scripted ellipses imposed by the computer (for example between levels or scenes in a video game) but rather ellipses triggered by the current situation and the user. Such triggering by the user is an action at the discourse level, contrary to the action taken as a character.

Let us define the concepts of the ellipse-start time as the time in the story when the first scene stops, the ellipse-stop time as the time in the story when the second scene begins just after the ellipsis and the ellipsed period, the time section between the ellipse-start time and the ellipse-stop time (by definition not seen by the user). Three cases are worth being distinguished:

- **The ellipsed period contains no narrative action:** the ellipsis is just a way to speed up the narrative and eliminate "empty" bits, like for example movement in a room. (Of course, these bits are only empty from the narrative progression point of view.)
- **The ellipsed period contains NPC actions only:** the system calculates some actions that are played by the NPCs. The user will (or will not) discover these actions after the ellipsis. Such an ellipsis is similar to the kind of ellipses found in movies.
- **The ellipsed period contains player character's actions:** this implies that the user let's his character act autonomously during the ellipsed period. This is a loss of control from the user towards his character, who becomes semi-autonomous [36]. How will the user's character behave? Either automatically or according to the user's instruction. Metaphorically, the character goes into an "auto-pilot" mode. This evokes the movie *Click* (F. Coraci), in which a character discovers a remote control able to skip some of the boring bits of his life... but soon, the remote control decides what to skip and goes out of control.

The key issue in the proposed ellipses management is the balance of control between the user and the computer. Among the three types of ellipsis mentioned above, the type chosen can be defined within the form of the narrative. But also, it could be possible to give the user the choice to define what type of ellipsis he wants at a given moment; he can decide if his character and other NPCs can act in the ellipsed period or not.

In the case where semi-autonomy of the user's character is not allowed, the ellipse-stop time is calculated by the computer, according to the current situation (we assume here, to keep things simpler, that this discourse-based interaction does not modify the story level; action will not magically stop or slow down because there is an ellipsis going on).

Computer-decided ellipses have a great potential but need to be implemented with subtlety. The ellipsis should not be felt as a loss of control ("Okay, whatever I do, I get the same end scene anyway!"), but instead as a device creating narrative tension ("Well, how did all this finally end?").

6 Parallelism

Parallel narrative structures often refer to cases where a story has more than one causal chain of events. Stories that deal with parallel structures are not confined to having these unfold in the same time space and can just as easily mix past and present as is done in the film *Julie and Julia* (N. Ephron) or mix contemporary story lines like in Armstead Maupin's *Tales of the City* series of books or K. Kwapis' film *He's Just Not That Into You.* However, we will consider parallelism relevant for DIS in the cases when the multiple causal chains that make up a complete story can be experienced simultaneously at various points throughout the narrative, regardless if they occur at the same time story wise. Additionally, the parallelism we are interested in, is used only when the actions that unfold are disjoint and not split just for reasons of geography (i.e. watching a telephone conversation between two people with each half of the screen displaying the character's apartment). Simultaneous visioning of different scenes can be done using a split screen and can be seen in examples such as *Timecode* (M. Figgis), *24* (J. Surnow and R. Cochran) or the internet fiction *HBO Imagine* [37] (see Figure 5). Usually, the use of simultaneous viewing is temporary, since for comprehension it is difficult to focus on several scenes at the same time, especially if there is dialogue because divided attention and the cocktail-party effect comes into play [38, 39]. In a split screen scenario, the screen is divided to show multiple action settings unfolding at the same time. For example in *24*, the viewer sees 4 scenes unfolding until the focus settles on one. This gives the viewer a sense of what is going on with the other characters in the drama while watching what unfolds for only one. The switch screen is when several scenes unfold simultaneously but only a subset of those can be seen and the user can control which ones are visible. This is demonstrated in the scene cubes The Affair and The Art Heist in *HBO Imagine* (see Figure 5) where the viewer selects the scenes to watch in any order.

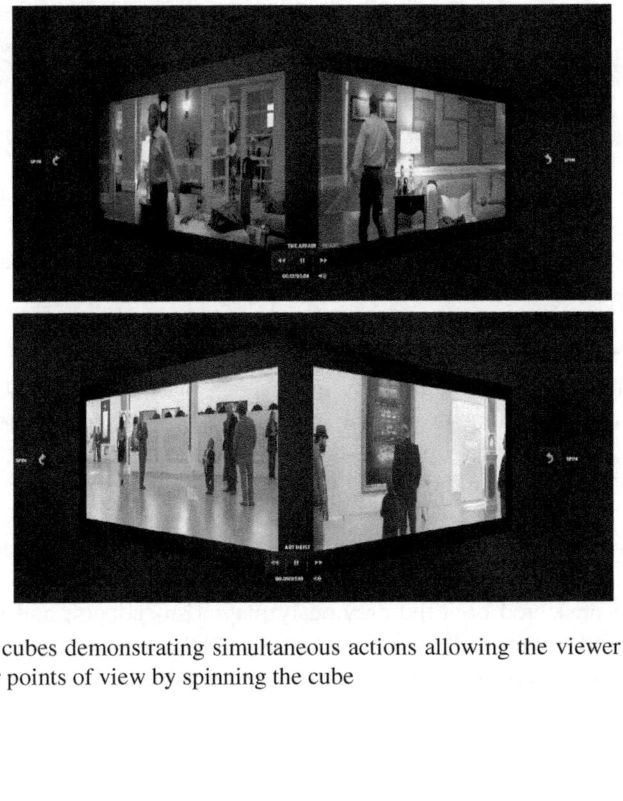

Fig. 5. 2 scene cubes demonstrating simultaneous actions allowing the viewer to see the same scene from four points of view by spinning the cube

When considering simultaneity of causal chains, it is important to note that this is not limited to a visual modality as in the examples mentioned above. Simultaneous viewing can be done with text as well. For example, the children's book *Milo and the Magical Stones* [40] contains pages which are horizontally cut, the top pages representing the happy version of the story, while the bottom pages represent the unhappy version (see Figure 6). The format clearly encourages a parallel reading of two alternative stories.

Fig. 6. A paper implementation making use of a parallel storyline with simultaneous viewing

Parallelism and multiple views can be exploited in DIS whenever it appears relevant for an author to give two or more perspectives at the same time. Parallelism is most interesting when coupled with other narrative methods mentioned in the previous sections. In what follows, we will analyse the coupling of multiple views with multiple actualisations, but the reader is free to extrapolate how it could also be applied to embedded stories and modal worlds.

Multiple views on multiple actualisation means that the user sees two (or more) actualised worlds unfolding in two (or more) parts of the screen; the screen would effectively be split in as many parts as there are actualised worlds. Three cases can be distinguished, depending on the user activity during these phases.

- Passive user: Suppose the user chooses to create an alternative storyline from a bifurcation point whose one branch has already been actualised (see Fig. 1). The user is then presented both the previously played storyline(s) and the current one that is currently being following, until the next choice point, where the multiple viewing stops. This provides a transition between paths.

- Active user on one storyline: This cases starts like the passive user case, but when a new choice is provided to the user, the previously played alternative storyline continues. This case is harder to handle for the user, as the alternative views might disrupt the interaction. Note also that this case is technically challenging, as it requires some form of synchronisation between the storylines. In particular, if the type of interaction freezes the world, the alternative storylines might need to be stopped as well, to maintain synchronisation.
- Active user on two storylines (we restrict the case of two storylines, for the sake of simplicity): In this case, the user is able to start two alternative storylines at the same time. In a bifurcation node, the user chooses not one but two choices and two parallel views start. When an interaction is required in one of the parallel actualisations, the other actualisation continues, or, if needed, waits for synchronisation reasons. When two interactions are required at the same time, it is of course not possible to interact on both views at the same time. In this case, the time must be frozen on both storylines, and the user must choose the actions successively, before the parallel stories can restart.

It is also possible to view two storylines that correspond to different times in the story. This mechanism is potentially interesting for choosing a bifurcation point in retrospect. During the experience, the user is simultaneously shown the current action he is involved in and a previous action of the same storyline that is relevant given the current situation. He can mark a bifurcating node from it or even start exploring the alternative storyline.

Different sub-cases can be further distinguished depending on how and when the user is proposed parallel scenes. The user can be offered the choice to see the multiple views and select between them at will, or only during specific moments:

- **User decides:** The user selects when he wants to be presented with simultaneous scenes from which to choose one to follow.
- **Computer proposed:** The computer offers the user the choice to select a new scene.
- **Computer imposed:** The user must select one of several simultaneous scenes at moments decided by the computer.

7 Point of Action

We've looked at situations where several causal chains construct the whole narrative. Here, we will consider the case where the same causal chain of actions seen through various perspectives provides a different narrative experience. For example, the film *A la folie, pas du tout* (L. Colombani) uses two perspectives on the same chain of events to tell two very different stories. Similarly, the films *Rashômon* (A. Kurosawa) or *Courage Under Fire* (E. Zwick) recount the same scenario from several perspectives, recounting a slightly different story each time. The interactive drama, *Three Angry Men* [41] allows a user to experience the same scene from the point of view of three very different characters, thus giving the scene a different interpretation from each perspective.

In DIS systems, the user not only reads or watches the story; he interacts with a given fictional world. So if the user chooses a point of view in the fictional world he chooses not only the viewpoint but also the starting point of his interaction, we call this the *point of action*. Each point of action will then have a different impact on the user's choices and decisions and consequently create a different story.

Applying the model of changing the point of view on DIS gives two types of possible points of action:

- Changing the point of action by changing the character: a DIS system would give the user the possibility to change the point of view on the fictional world by changing the character. This opens the opportunity for the user to choose the point of action with respect to the identity of the selected character. By switching between characters he becomes a kind of story-master with multiple identities. The system then has to be more open and less prescriptive. This option exists in the video game Farenheit [42], an adventure game where the user is offered the possibility to change the character he is playing with. Note however that these changes are scripted, in the sense that the user cannot influence the course of the story by freely changing the point of action.
- Changing the point of action by "taking a mask": A second type of changing the point of view is given, if the user has the possibility to test a character "under cover", that means if he can be masked or if he can play a second character by keeping its identity of the first character. This kind of exchanging identities has been explored in literature and film for example in "Face/Off" (J. Woo, 1997) where a FBI agent and a terrorist assume the physical appearance of one another. A second example is "Freaky Friday" (M. Waters, 2003 - The novel of the same name by Mary Rodgers) where a mother and daughter experience each other's lives by exchanging bodies, but not identities. They can see the life and the world through their respective realities. For DIS this experience would add a second level of role-playing: the user plays the role of a character and his character plays the role of another character of the fictional world. This concept intersects with the NPC's Role-playing case discussed in Section 3, with the difference that the role-playing happens in the same fictional world.

A further question is who decides at which point to change the point of action. Similar to the question about the bifurcation point chooser we can distinguish four cases:

- **Free choice:** the user chooses at the beginning or during the story construction to change his point of action by selecting the type of point of action (in character or mask exchange) and the selected character.
- **Computer constrained:** the system can constrain the user to choose a specific point of action. This constraint can be related to other setting definitions like time, space, number of characters, etc.
- **Computer proposed:** the system can propose a certain number of point of actions without any constraint or preference. But the propositions can be related to user choices or bifurcation points for example.
- **Computer imposed:** in this case the computer decides which point of action must be accomplished at which moment.

Points of action make narratives multidimensional. A given fictional world can be seen in different ways, it can be influenced in different ways and it can be constructed in different ways starting from different points of action.

8 Conclusion

The exploration of several distinct narrative devices; multiple actualisations, embedded stories, modal worlds, ellipsis, parallel worlds and points of action, exposes innovative narrative forms for DIS that can open new horizons for both researchers and creative authors.

The narrative forms presented here represent the mere tip of the iceberg of possibilities to be explored within the field of DIS, especially when one considers the endless mixing, matching and imbrications that could be done. While we realise that the technical feasibility is still a hurdle, we postulate that an equivalent hurdle facing the field is its tendency to follow traditional linear narrative forms. As well, as we mentioned in the introduction, systems do exist today with the technical capacity to produce stories using some of the narrative forms presented in this article. What systems are lacking are authors [9] who can use them to produce interesting stories. With the various narrative forms presented in this article, we hope to provide insight into the possibilities DIS can become.

Acknowledgments. This work has been funded (in part) by the European Commission under grant agreement IRIS (FP7-ICT-231824).

References

1. Bates, J.: Virtual Reality, Art, and Entertainment. Presence: The Journal of Teleoperators and Virtual Environments 1(1), 133–138 (1992)
2. Weyhrauch, P.: Guiding Interactive Drama, Ph.D. Dissertation, Tech report CMU-CS-97-109, Carnegie Mellon University (1997)
3. Szilas, N.: Interactive Drama on Computer: Beyond Linear Narrative. In: Papers from the AAAI Fall Symposium on Narrative Intelligence, Technical Report FS-99-01, pp. 150–156. AAAI Press, Menlo Park (1999), `http://nicolas.szilas.free.fr/research/aaai99.html`
4. Crawford, C.: Assumptions underlying the Erasmatron interactive storytelling engine. In: Proc. AAAI Fall Symposium on Narrative Intelligence, North Falmouth, MA. AAAI Press, Menlo Park (1999)
5. Sierra Entertainment, Leisure Suit Larry - In the Land of the Lounge Lizards (December 2011), `http://www.mobygames.com/game/leisure-suit-larry-in-the-land-of-the-lounge-lizards`
6. Infocom, Hitch Hiker's Guide to the Galaxy (December 2011), `http://www.douglasadams.com/creations/infocom.php`
7. Crawford, C.: Chris Crawford on Game Design. New Riders Publishing (2003)
8. IRIS Wiki (December 2011), `http://tecfalabs.unige.ch/mediawiki-narrative/index.php/Interactive_Storytelling_and_Narrative_Theories`

9. Spierling, U., Szilas, N.: Authoring Issues Beyond Tools. In: Iurgel, I.A., Zagalo, N., Petta, P. (eds.) ICIDS 2009. LNCS, vol. 5915, pp. 50–61. Springer, Heidelberg (2009)
10. Crawford, C.: Chris Crawford on Interactive Storytelling. New Riders Games (2004)
11. Prada, R., Machado, I., Paiva, A.: TEATRIX: Virtual Environment for Story Creation. In: Gauthier, G., VanLehn, K., Frasson, C. (eds.) ITS 2000. LNCS, vol. 1839, pp. 464–473. Springer, Heidelberg (2000)
12. Barber, H., Kudenko, D.: Dynamic Generation of Dilemma-based Interactive Narratives. In: Proceedings of the Artificial Intelligence and Interactive Digital Entertainment Conferance - AIIDE 2007. AAAI Press, Menlo Park (2007)
13. Riedl, M., Stern, A., Dini, D., Alderman, J.: Dynamic Experience Management in Virtual Worlds for Entertainment, vol. 3(1), pp. 23–42 (2008)
14. Sgouros, N.M.: Dynamic Generation, Management and Resolution of Interactive Plots. Artificial Intelligence 107(1), 29–62 (1999)
15. Seif El-Nasr, M.: A User-Centric Adaptive Story Architecture – Borrowing from Acting Theories. In: International Conference on Advances in Computer Entertainment Technology ACE 2004, June 3-5 (2004)
16. Pizzi, D., Cavazza, M.: Affective Storytelling Based on Characters' Feelings. In: AAAI Fall Symposium on Intelligent Narrative Technologies, Arlington, Virginia (2007)
17. Szilas, N.: A Computational Model of an Intelligent Narrator for Interactive Narratives. Applied Artificial Intelligence 21(8), 753–801 (2007)
18. Swartjes, I., Theune, M.: The Virtual Storyteller: story generation by simulation. In: The Proceedings of the 20th Belgian-Netherlands Conference on Artificial Intelligence (BNAIC 2008), pp. 257–264. University of Twente, The Netherlands (2008)
19. Mott, B.W., Lester, J.C.: U-director: a decision-theoretic narrative planning architecture for storytelling environments. In: Proceedings of the Fifth International Joint Conference on Autonomous Agents and Multiagent Systems, AAMAS 2006, Hakodate, Japan, May 08-12, pp. 977–984. ACM, New York (2006)
20. ISRST IS (December 2011), `http://arturo.prendingerlab.net/isrst/wyhtoargument.html`
21. Cavazza, M., Charles, F., Mead, S.J.: Characters in Search of an Author: AI-Based Virtual Storytelling. In: Balet, O., Subsol, G., Torguet, P. (eds.) ICVS 2001. LNCS, vol. 2197, pp. 145–154. Springer, Heidelberg (2001)
22. Mateas, M., Stern, A.: Integrating Plot, Character and Natural Language Processing in the Interactive Drama Façade. In: Proceedings of the 1st International Conference on Technologies for Interactive Digital Storytelling and Entertainment (TIDSE 2003), Darmstadt, Germany (2003)
23. Storytron (December 2011), `http://www.storytron.com/`
24. Riedl, M., Saretto, C.J., Young, R.M.: Managing interaction between users and agents in a multiagent storytelling environment. In: The Proceedings of the Second International Conference on Autonomous Agents and Multi-Agent Systems (2003)
25. Genette, G.: Figures III. Le Seuil, Paris (1972)
26. Eco, U.: Lector in Fabula, Milan, Bompian (1979)
27. Eco, U.: L'oeuvre ouverte. Le Seuil, Paris (1965)
28. Murray, J.: Hamlet on the Holodeck. The future of narrative in the cyberspace. Free Press, New York (1997)
29. AMATO (December 2011), `http://hypermedia.univ-paris8.fr/seminaires/semaction/seminaires/txt01-02/seance1/sauvegarde.htm`

30. Broderbund Software, The Last Express (December 2011), `http://www.mobygames.com/game/last-express`
31. Ryan, M.L.: Possible Worlds, Artificial Intelligence, and Narrative Theory. Indiana University Press (1991)
32. Todorov, T.: Poétique de la prose, choix, suivi de Nouvelles recherches sur le récit, Paris, Seuil, Points (1978)
33. Donikian, S.: De l'écriture à la réalisation d'une fiction interactive: simplification de la chaîne allant de la création à l'adaptation. In: Créations de Récits Pour les Fictions Interactives, Hermès (2006)
34. Education Simulations Corporation, Real Lives (December 2011), `http://www.educationalsimulations.com`
35. Durand, P.: Cinéma et montage – un art de l'ellipse. Cerf, Paris (1993)
36. Portugal, J.-N.: Environnement narratif: une approche pour la fiction interactive, appliquée au jeu The Insider. In: Conference Imagina 1999 (1999)
37. HBO Imagine (April 2010), `http://www.youtube.com/watch?v=v-dGkc6g9_A`
38. Arons, B.: A review of the cocktail party effect. Journal of the American Voice I/O Society 12(7), 35–50 (1992)
39. Stifelman, L.J.: The cocktail party effect in auditory interfaces: A study of simultaneous presentation. In: MIT Media lab technical report (1994)
40. Herbert, M.P.: Milo and the Magical Stones. NorthSouth (1999)
41. MacIntyre, B., Bolter, J.D., Vaugh, J., Hannigan, B., Gandy, M., Moreno, E., Haas, M., et al.: Three Angry Men: An Augmented-Reality Experiment in Point-of-View Drama. In: Proc. International Conference on Technologies for Interactive Digital Storytelling and Entertainment (TIDSE 2003), pp. 230–236 (2003)
42. Atari, Fahrenheit (December 2011), `http://www.atari.com/fahrenheit`

A Virtual Informal Learning System for Cultural Heritage

Shengnan Chen[1,2], Zhigeng Pan[1,3], and Mingmin Zhang[1]

[1] State Key Lab of CAD&CG, Zhejiang University
310027 Hangzhou, China
[2] Zhejiang Textile & Fashion College
315211 Ningbo, China
[3] Digital Media & HCI Research Center, Hangzhou Normal University
310012 Hangzhou, China
{Chenshengnan,Zgpan,Zmm}@cad.zju.edu.cn

Abstract. Computer graphics and digital technologies have opened up a myriad of ways for both preservation and transfer of cultural heritage information. The digital storage systems, digital lab notebooks and virtual museums are all examples. VR technology development has made it possible to construct large, immersive and interactive virtual environment for the cultural heritage content. The users could achieve learning outcome by the interactions and immersions in the digital cultural heritage which is reconstructed from the scene no longer in existence. This paper presents a virtual informal learning system for the famous ancient painting of "Qing-ming Festival by the Riverside". Innovative multi-screen projection and interaction techniques are also presented.

Keywords: Cultural heritage, Informal learning, User immersion.

1 Introduction

The cultural heritage has been handed down from generation to generation during the long human history as universal treasures. Most of them include rich learning information. Advanced developments of computer graphics and digital technologies such as immersive VR system, image indexing and impainting support cultural heritage preservation and transmission in various approaches. A diverse range of cultural heritages have been attempted by digital preservations [1], online exhibitions and virtual explorations [2]. These applications improved the steps of cultural heritage preservations.

Informal learning is a semi-structured process and independent from the instructor leading programs. It usually occurs in a variety of places outside schools, such as the museums and exhibition centers as well as while learning at home, working, visiting and via the daily interactions with other people. Perez et al. proposed their opinions on the integrated level within heritage education [3]. They claimed that the approach to heritage is interdisciplinary and holistic. In terms of education, the heritage is considered as the objective content and specific resource which facilitates the more comprehensive and meaningful view of teaching. The heritage is based on the

Z. Pan et al. (Eds.): Transactions on Edutainment VII, LNCS 7145, pp. 180–187, 2012.

constructivism principles which are characterized by a social and investigative mode of education. The conceptual, procedural and attitudinal contents are fully integrated in the cultural heritage education. The ultimate aim of heritage education tends to be the development of critical thinking ability, and the appreciation and conservation of the heritage which confers identity.

Adopting informal learning theory in a cultural heritage museum matches education and entertainment, and brings a new era for the museums by enhancing the immersion, visualization and preference. The advanced technologies such as the virtual and augment reality techniques, human computer interaction and story-telling approaches make the learning process effective and enjoyable. Creating fully immersive 3D virtual environment provides users with the new approaches to informal learning by experiencing and interacting with the cultural heritages. Previous research on immersion has been scattered in several different areas such as virtual learning, game research, heritage studies and interface design. Immersion is the subjective impression that one is participating in a comprehensive, realistic experience [4]. Immersion in a digital experience involves the willing suspension of disbelief and the design of immersive learning experiences that induce this disbelief by drawing upon the sensory, action and symbolic factors [5]. Virtual reality research has an interesting perspective on the immersive experience. Studies have shown that immersion in the virtual environment can enhance education in at least three ways: by allowing multiple perspectives, situated learning, and transfer. Dede concluded that immersion could foster learning experiences and draw on a powerful pedagogy through multiple perspectives, and lower degree of immersion can still provide situated learning [6]. Swing attempted to add immersion to a collaborative tool in a 3D world where each user was represented with an avatar [7]. Jacobson explored whether students benefited from an immersive panoramic display in heritage learning that is visually complex and information-rich. He executed experiments of learning experiences of middle-school students in the Virtual Egyptian Temple and Gates of Horus, and concluded that the immersive display provides better supports for learning activities in virtual heritage [8]. Apostolellis and Daradoumis investigated the potential learning benefit of integrating audience interaction with gaming environments in the immersive space of a dome theater [9].

The aim of this study was to implement a virtual informal learning system for the cultural heritage by the natural user interaction based on gesture recognition. The system design was approached in two respects, one is to manage the multi-screen projection, and the other one is to implement the user interactions with virtual characters by their implicit relationship. In section 2, the design and development of the informal learning system is introduced and followed by section 3 which describes the implementation and early results of the system. The conclusion and future work are given in section 4.

2 System Design and Development

The main sections for the system design include the content organizing, basic 2D impainting and 3D modeling, animation creating for both of the virtual environment and virtual characters, multi-screen projection and gesture interactions with the system. The following describes each section in more detail.

2.1 Qing-Ming Festival by the Riverside

The famous ancient painting "Qing-ming Festival by the Riverside" was painted by Zhang Zeduan in the Northern Song Dynasty about 1000 years ago. It is a rare realistic artwork and considered as a world-class cultural relic. As one of the most important traditional Chinese festivals, Qing-ming Festival is granted an intangible cultural heritage. It has a long history of more than two thousand years, and was called March Festival in the old times. People celebrated it with various actions, such as worshipping ancestors, outing, swinging and planting trees.

Fig. 1. A part of the original painting

The painting was completed from a panoramic view with detail scenes of Qing-ming Festival along a river. It gives the audiences a bird's eye view of the prospering scene of Bianliang City which was the capital of the Northern Song Dynasty. This painting covers dozens of miles along the river and includes more than 500 human figures, 60 animals, 100 trees, 30 constructions, 20 wooden boats and many other characters. The origin version of this painting, which is about 500 centimeters long and 25 centimeters wide, is kept in the National Palace Museum in Peking, China. One part of this painting is showed as Fig. 1. This system aimed to exhibit the famous Chinese painting on a large display wall dynamically and provide the users with the natural interactions to the virtual characters.

2.2 Image-Based Animation

In order to illustrate the locomotive 3D objects on a 2D background picture, the image-based animation [10] was employed. This technique improved the real-time rendering speed and makes the scene more alive. First, a professional artisan was invited to repaint the painting of "Qing-ming Festival by The Riverside", maintaining the details from the original artwork as well as the perspective relationship. Second, certain objects from the background picture were extracted and animated. The inanimate objects were translated and rotated while skeleton-based characters were applied to objects representing humans and animals. Third, a Tour into Picture method [11] was employed to create animations and narrations to enable the viewpoint to move back and forth when the animation was going on. As the final step, textures, lights and shadows were created and imposed on the scenes to harmonize the locomotive 3D objects on the 2D background picture (Fig. 2).

Fig. 2. A screenshot of the animated painting

2.3 Multi-screen Projection

The main purpose of the system was to implement a real time informal learning approach for the users to experience the Qing-ming Festival by dynamically interacting with the virtual character and also have a virtual navigation in the famous ancient Chinese painting on a large display wall which was used as a big screen [12]. In order to display this painting dynamically and keep its artistic appeal at the same time, a multi-screen projection system was implemented for the Grand Canal Museum. The museum specially arranged a huge hall for this system. There was a wall with 6 meters high and 12 meters long in the hall which is used as a large screen. A multi-screen based projection system was designed in terms of the size of the wall. The wall surface was specially treated so that it can give good diffuse reflection. Therefore a PC-based multi-channel VR projection system was employed in order to project a high resolution storytelling video on the large display wall.

C/S architecture was used in this projection system. Each frame was segmented into 30 tiles in the PC server, and each segmented tile was transmitted to the corresponding client PC through synchronous switching. Each client PC connected with a projector was responsible for rendering one tile and projecting this tile to the proper position on the large wall. The architecture of projection system used in the system is shown in Fig. 3. The animation "Qing-ming Festival by the Riverside" was projected on the display wall. The music and commentary were played synchronously as the video went on so that the flourishing scene of the capital of Song Dynasty showed vividly before the users as if they were standing right in the street by the river. In order to achieve deeper user immersion, this system was further developed into a more interactive facet that the users could interact with the virtual characters and also have real time navigation by gestures.

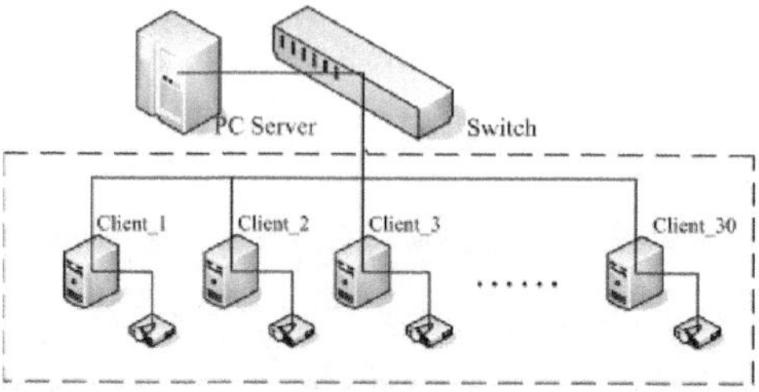

Fig. 3. The projection system architecture

2.4 Personalized 3D Avatar Creation

A personalized 3D avatar was employed in order to enhance the realistic behavior of the users and connect the users and virtual environment. Personalization has become a novel topic recently. Studies reported that personalization positively impacts human-computer relationships because of its ability to provide a better user experience in the virtual environments [13]. However, existing studies about personalization have largely focused on the parameters setting for the users' custom while this system integrated personalization with an avatar construction. The avatar was personalized with a photo-based 3D face model construction method, and the users were empowered to customize and manipulate their avatar. The avatar can walk to virtual objects of user interest, as well as observe the objects or trigger an interaction process. Furthermore, the avatar may receive feedback generated from the task implementation.

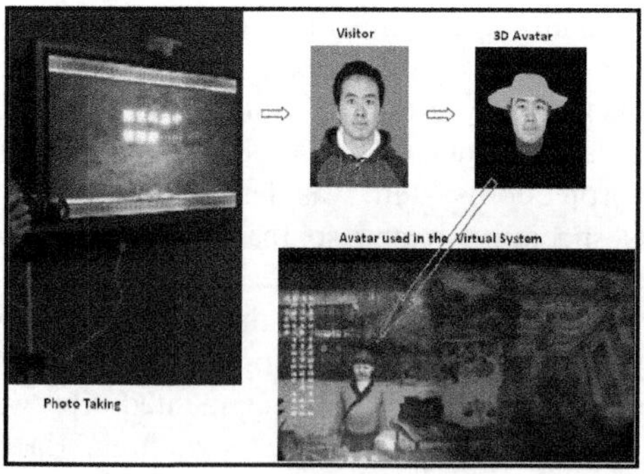

Fig. 4. The personalized 3D avatar construction method

A photo-based 3D face model construction method was used to reconstruct the user's 3D face model and implement the customized avatar. The application method is shown in Fig. 4. This method included two steps: first, extracting the characteristics from the user's photo, and second, reconstructing the face model according to extracted characteristics. For a new input image, the face region was detected first. This was followed by searching for the feature points in a local area through rotation and scaling operations to determine the actual feature points that were closest to the provided points in the template. For the grid deformation, a RBF-based (Radial Basis Function) interpolation method was employed [14].

2.5 Gesture-Based Interaction

A robust real-time hand tracking and hand posture recognition method was proposed in this system. This method allowed the user to interact with their customized avatar by natural gestures, they could also interact with the constructions in the system and observe the specific models and navigate in the virtual constructions by gestures. In order to trigger the hand tracking and hand posture recognition, a multi-cue method based on modified census transform [15] was used to firstly detect the specific posture. It's based on velocity weighted features and color cue, and applied to track the hand robustly with a single camera and distinguish it from the complex background. The method could also deal with large space with the objects of skin color due to its high detection rate. It was used to detect hand for triggering the system in the first frame. Then the hand is accurately segmented using both Bayesian skin-color model [16] and the hand tracking result. Finally hand posture was recognized by the feature based on density distribution. (Fig. 5).

This method enforced the robustness of hand posture recognition because of its scale-invariance and rotation-invariance, and also provided the users with much more natural interactions. The users could control the direction and manipulate their navigation in the system by gestures.

Fig. 5. The real time hand tracking and hand posture recognition method

3 Results

In this system, the visitors interact with the painting by waving their hands at the avatar in the system, and the avatar is able to respond to the users by the tracking technology. Since we created 3D virtual scenes from the 2D painting, the users could interact with virtual objects or characters. These two interactions also improved the connection between the avatar and the virtual world by giving those objects in the environment with semantic information.

Adopting virtual characters generally had two main functions: first, the virtual characters could gain the publicity effect because their lovely appearance draw more attraction from the audiences and bring the public recognition to the system; second, the virtual characters could make the users gain authentic experience. Additionally we integrated the avatar personalization idea in this system, which was different from the traditional interaction methods. With the photo-based 3D face model construction method, the avatar can be customized to enhance the realistic behavior of either the virtual human or the users. It provided better immersive experience in the virtual environment and positively impacted on the human-computer interactions.

4 Conclusions and Future Work

Both of the cultural heritage environment and human figures with the interactions were presented in this system. We rebuilt the constructions, shipping, water transportation tools, horses and human figures, and digitally repainted the background, and then constituted an interactive environment by joining all the space, objects and colors together. Additionally, a multi-screen projection and adaptive virtual character were applied to the system. This paper explored on these immersion impacts in virtual informal learning of cultural heritage for enhancing the system usability. As we've implemented and evaluated the system, we learnt about some open problems that still remain and can be applied to the development of the future work. The questions include how much immersion is enough for learning cultural heritage, how to design the system in terms of different respects which are supporting informal learning for the cultural heritage? In other words, how can this immersion be operated, and how to enhance the user immersion efficiently?

Acknowledgments. Project supported by China 863 Project (Grant No. 2009AA062704 and 2007AA10Z224-1), and the National NSF projects (Grant No: 61170318). The authors would like to acknowledge Zhi Li, Kangde Guo and the support from colleagues of the project group for their contributions.

References

1. Charles Olson's Melville Project, `http://charlesolson.uconn.edu/Works_in_the_Collection/Melville_Project/index.htm`
2. Brewster, S.: The Impact of Haptic 'Touching' Technology on Cultural Applications. In: EVA Conference, pp. 1–14. Academic Press, UK (2001)

3. Perez, R.J., Lopez, J.M.C., Listan, D.: Heritage Education: Exploring the Conceptions of Teachers and Administrators from the Perspective of Experimental and Social Science Teaching. Teaching and Teacher Education: An International Journal of Research and Studies 26(6), 1319–1331 (2010)
4. Stanney, K.M.: Handbook of Virtual Environments. Erlbaum, New Jersey (2002)
5. Dede, C., Salzman, M., Loftin, R.B., Ash, K.: The Design of Immersive Virtual Learning Environments: Fostering Deep Understandings of Complex Scientific Knowledge. In: Jacobson, M., Kozma, R. (eds.) Innovations in Science and Mathematics Education: Advanced Designs for Technologies of Learning, pp. 361–414. Erlbaum, Mahwah (2000)
6. Dede, C.: Immersive Interfaces for Engagement and Learning. Science 323(5910), 66–69 (2009)
7. Swing, E.: Adding Immersion to Collaborative Tools. In: 5th Symposium on Virtual Reality Modeling Language (Web3D-VRML), pp. 63–68. ACM, New York (2000)
8. Jacobson, J.: Ancient Architecture in Virtual Reality: Does Immersion Really Aid Learning. PhD thesis, School of Information Sciences, University of Pittsburgh (2008)
9. Apostolellis, P., Daradoumis, T.: Audience Interactivity as Leverage for Effective Learning in Gaming Environments for Dome Theaters. In: Wolpers, M., Kirschner, P.A., Scheffel, M., Lindstaedt, S., Dimitrova, V. (eds.) EC-TEL 2010. LNCS, vol. 6383, pp. 451–456. Springer, Heidelberg (2010)
10. Pan, Z., Liu, G., Li, Z.: Virtual Presentation and Animation of Qingming Festival by the Riverside. In: Second Workshop on Digital Media and its Application in Museum & Heritage, pp. 102–105. IEEE Computer Society Press, Los Alamitos (2007)
11. Cao, Z.: Image Based TIP Method. M. S. thesis, Computer Science Dept., Zhejiang University (2005)
12. Pan, Z., Chen, W., Zhang, M., Liu, J.: Virtual Reality in the Digital Olympic Museum. IEEE Computer Graphics and Applications 29(5), 91–95 (2009)
13. Sung, J., Grinter, R., Christensen, H.: Pimp My Roomba: Designing for Personalization. In: 27th International Conference on Human Factors in Computing Systems, pp. 193–196. ACM, New York (2009)
14. Zhang, M., Xiang, N., Wang, K., Pan, Z., Yuan, H., Liu, H.: Avatar-based Intelligent Navigation for Online Shanghai Expo. International Journal of Virtual Reality 9(3), 39–45 (2010)
15. Pan, Z., Li, Y., Zhang, M., Sun, C., Guo, K., Tang, X., Zhou, S.Z.: A Real-time Multi-cue Hand Tracking Algorithm Based on Computer Vision. In: IEEE Virtual Reality 2010, pp. 219–222. IEEE Computer Society Press, Los Alamitos (2010)
16. Weng, C., Li, Y., Zhang, M., Guo, K., Tang, X., Pan, Z.: Robust Hand Posture Recognition Integrating Multi-cue Hand Tracking. In: Zhang, X., Zhong, S., Pan, Z., Wong, K., Yun, R. (eds.) Edutainment 2010. LNCS, vol. 6249, pp. 497–508. Springer, Heidelberg (2010)

Multi-samples Texture Synthesis for Dynamic Terrain Based on Constraint Conditions

Xingquan Cai*, Jie Li, Haiyan Sun, and Jinhong Li

College of Information Engineering, North China University of Technology,
100144 Beijing, China
xingquancai@126.com

Abstract. In this paper, we provide an efficient multi-samples texture synthesis method for dynamic terrain based on constraint conditions. We initialize a multi-samples texture system, including the texture data for every sample and the texture data for the noise. Then, we figure out the constraint conditions parameters according to the characteristics of dynamic terrain effects, and we deal with every pixel in a raster scan ordering. We get the value of every result pixel and update the value to the result texture. In this way, we can rapidly synthesize the different textures for different dynamic terrain effects. The results prove that our method is feasible and high performance. Our method can be used in simulation system based dynamic terrain effects, such as fighting games with advanced weapons explosions, animation with terrain deformation, etc.

Keywords: Dynamic terrain; Multi-samples texture synthesis; Constraint condition; Raster scan ordering.

1 Introduction

In the past decade, effects such as the tires of vehicles did not leave ruts in area with soft soil and explosions did not alter the surface of the terrain by creating craters. This limited the training value of ground-based visual simulation systems. Dynamic terrain has become an increasingly important requirement for realistic ground-based simulation systems, such as some training system, some fight games and some battle simulation systems.

Terrain deformation can be divided into terrain height field deformation and terrain texture alteration. Most researches have presented the method to simulate the terrain height field deformation [1],[2], but they have not focus on the terrain texture alteration. As we all know, terrain texture alteration also is the most important part of dynamic terrain effects. However, the texture for dynamic terrain effects has regular

* Supported by National Natural Science Foundation of China(No. 51075423), PHR(IHLB) Grant (PHR20100509, PHR201008202), Funding Project of Beijing Outstanding Academic Human Resource Program (No. 20081D0500200114), and Funding Project of Beijing Municipal Education Committee (No. KM201010009002).

Z. Pan et al. (Eds.): Transactions on Edutainment VII, LNCS 7145, pp. 188–196, 2012.

aspects, such as the craters close to half-ellipsoid and the ruts approximate along the center axes, and the texture for dynamic terrain also has the irregular aspects, like the size of craters not the same, the margin of ruts with some random sawteeth, etc. So it is not easy to generate the texture for dynamic terrain.

In this paper, we provide an efficient multi-samples texture synthesis method for dynamic terrain based on constraint conditions. We initialize a multi-samples texture system, including the texture data for every sample and the texture data for the noise. Then, we compute the constraint conditions parameters according to the characteristics of dynamic terrain effects, and we deal with every pixel in a raster scan ordering. We get the value of every result pixel and update the value to the result texture. In this way, we can rapidly synthesize the different textures for different dynamic terrain effects. The results prove that our method is feasible and high performance. Our method can be used in simulation system based dynamic terrain effects, such as fighting games with advanced weapons explosions, animation with terrain deformation, etc.

In this paper, after exploring the methods for texture synthesis and analyzing the existing algorithms, we provide our multi-samples texture synthesis method for dynamic terrain based on constraint conditions. Then, we show the results using our method. Finally, we draw the conclusion and give the future work.

2 Related Work

Usually, texture synthesis is an alternative way to create textures. It is general and easy to use, as the user only needs to supply an input exemplar and a small set of synthesis parameters. The output can be made to be of any size without unnatural repetition. Existing 2D texture synthesis methods fall into five basic categories [3],[4], including procedural methods, statistical feature matching methods, neighborhood matching methods, patch based methods, and optimization based methods.

Procedural methods synthesize textures as a function of pixel coordinates and a set of tuning parameters. Among all procedural methods, the most used in Computer Graphics is Perlin Noise [5]. Perlin noise is a smooth gradient noise function that is invariant with respect to rotation and translation and is band-limited in frequency. Perlin noise has been widely used in various applications, such as rendering water waves, fire, or realistic-looking marble or crystal. Procedural methods can be efficiently used in randomness domains, but they can not be used in texture synthesis for dynamic terrain because of the regular aspect of terrain texture alteration.

Statistical feature-matching methods mainly capture a set of statistical features or abstract characteristics from an exemplar image and transfer them to a synthesized image. Heeger et al [6] used an image pyramid to capture statistical properties in the exemplar image at different resolution levels. Portilla et al [7] extended this method and worked well on stochastic textures, but their quality can degrade if the example texture is structured. So statistical feature-matching methods can not be used in texture synthesis for dynamic terrain.

Neighborhood-matching methods mainly enforce and deploy the relation between the pixel color and its spatial neighborhood. After an initial phase of training, where each pixel of the example texture is correlated to its neighborhood kernel, the target image is synthesized pixel by pixel. The synthesis step consists in substituting each pixel with the one that has the most similar neighborhood, chosen from the example texture [8]. Wei and Levoy [9] extended this algorithm in a multi-resolution fashion using Gaussian pyramids. In 2005, Lefebvre [10] improved Wei's method and performed order-independent synthesis on GPU. Neighborhood-matching methods are so higher performance, and we are inspired to provide the method to create the texture of dynamic terrain.

Patch based methods divide the example texture into a set of patches, which will be rearranged in the output image. Efros et al [11] used an overlap region between adjacent patches to appropriately quilt them, and made sure they all fit together. They chose patches that minimized an overlap error step-by-step randomly from a set of candidates, and iteratively placed the patches over the synthesized image. Then, they quilt the overlap region appropriately to minimize the error. In 2006, Wang et al [12] optimized the parameters for patch-based texture synthesis. In 2010, Chen et al [13] provided reusing partially synthesized textures for real-time synthesis of large textures. So patch based methods can rapidly generate the new texture, but can not be used in texture synthesis for dynamic terrain.

As to optimization based method, Kwatra et al [14] firstly provided the texture optimization method for example-based synthesis. Kwatra's method relied on a global optimization framework to synthesize a new texture. This global optimization framework consisted essentially of minimizing an energy function that considered all the pixels together. This energy function measured the similarity with respect to the example texture and it was locally defined for each pixel. The local energy contributions coming from pixels were merged together in a global metric that is minimized. In 2006, Xue et al [15] provided one method for texture synthesis using variant Self-Organizing Feature Maps. We can optimize our method using these ways.

The texture for dynamic terrain effects has regular aspects, such as the craters close to half-ellipsoid and the ruts approximate along the center axes. The texture for dynamic terrain also has the irregular aspects, like the size of craters not the same, the margin of ruts with some random sawteeth, etc. It's not easy to deal with it and the existing methods are not fit for create the texture for dynamic terrain. So we should provide a new method to synthesize the textures to show the regular and irregular of dynamic terrain textures.

3 Multi-samples Texture Synthesis for Dynamic Terrain Based on Constraint Conditions

3.1 Principle of Our Algorithm

Usually, texture synthesis uses a single sample texture. The application area of result textures is restricted and these methods can not be used in dynamic terrain texture synthesis. So we thought whether textures could be synthesized from multi-samples.

The problem of texture synthesis from multi-samples could be described as Equation (1). In Equation (1), $I_1, I_2, \cdots, I_n$ are different sample textures, and R is the synthesized texture result. In this method, we can control the percentage of every sample, but we can not control the location of every sample in texture synthesis result. So the texture synthesis result is full of randomness, although it is self similarity.

$$R = I_1 + I_2 + \cdots + I_n \ . \tag{1}$$

We decide to add some constraint conditions to multi-samples texture synthesis method. Here the constraint condition means that users could specify the proportion and location of sample textures in the synthesized texture. Maybe we have several constraint conditions in our practical applications. So we can add several constraint conditions. Just as Equation (2) shows, $C_1, C_2, \cdots, C_m$ are the constraint conditions.

$$R = I_1 + I_2 + \cdots + I_n + C_1 + C_2 + \cdots + C_m + N \ . \tag{2}$$

Some time we need to add some noise to multi-samples texture synthesis method, in order to make the texture look natural. We can select the Gaussian Noise and the Perlin Noise. In this paper, we use the Perlin Noise. As Equation (2) shows, N is the Perlin Noise.

Table 1. Symbols list

Symbol	Meaning
I_i	Input texture sample
I_o	Output texture image
p_i	An input pixel in I_i
p	An input pixel in I_o
c_i	Constraint parameter of pixel
N	Noise pixel
R_p	R value of pixel p
G_p	G value of pixel p
B_p	B value of pixel p

When synthesizing the texture based multi-samples, we should keep the basic shape of texton, maintain seamless connection and smooth transition between each texton and synthesize the right texton in right location according to the constraint conditions. So we divide our method into six steps. The symbols we used are showed in Table 1.

Step 1: Initialize the data. We should load the samples, initialize the parameters of constraint conditions and fill the output texture with random Perlin Noise.

Step 2: Compute the value of every pixel. We should deal with them pixel by pixel in a raster scan ordering.

Step 3: Determine the value of p_i. To compute pixel value of $p(x, y)$, we should determine the value of $p_i(x\%w, y\%h)$. w is the width of texture sample and h is the height of texture sample. In this way, we can get the RGB value of pixel p_i.

Step 4: Figure out the constraint value c_i of p_i.

Step 5: Calculate the value of $p(x, y)$ according to Equation (3).

Step 6: Compute all pixels value by step 2 to step 5.

In this way, we can synthesize the texture for dynamic terrain. And we can synthesize several type textures by changing the constraint conditions.

$$\begin{cases} R_p = \sum_{i=0}^{n-1} R_i \cdot C_i + R_N \\ G_p = \sum_{i=0}^{n-1} G_i \cdot C_i + G_N \ , \quad where \sum_{i=0}^{n-1} C_i = 1 \ . \\ B_p = \sum_{i=0}^{n-1} B_i \cdot C_i + B_N \end{cases} \tag{3}$$

3.2 Constraint Conditions for Dynamic Terrain

As we all know, in our real world, the texture of terrain is changed, soil, grass, rock, snow, and so on. So we select the right basic textures in our multi-samples system. We need a structure to hold all the samples information. The structure is defined as *STextureMultiSamples*. In this structure, *m_textureSample* stores the data for every sample, *m_noise* stores the Perlin Noise data, *m_regions* provides the arguments to compute the constraint conditions, and *m_fConstraint* will store the constraint condition parameters for every sample.

```
struct STextureMultiSamples {
  CImage m_textureSample[NUM];
  CImage m_noise;
  STextureRegion m_regions[NUM];
  float m_fConstraint[NUM];
}
struct STextureRegion {
  float m_fHigher;
  float m_fHigh;
  float m_fLow;
  float m_fLower;
}
```

We observe and study the craters on the grass. Usually, the gradation of craters on the grass can be divided into four regions, including charring region, adust region, soil region and grass region, just as Fig.1a. Between two regions, there is smooth transition. So we select the distance from current point to the center of radius as the constraint condition parameter, as Equation (4) shows, and Equation (5) gives the constraint method.

$$d = dist(p, O) \ . \tag{4}$$

$$C(d)=\begin{cases} 0 & d \le m\_fLower \\ \dfrac{d-m\_fLower}{m\_fLow-m\_fLower} & m\_fLower < d \le m\_fLow \\ 1 & m\_Low < d \le m\_fHigh \\ \dfrac{d-m\_fHigh}{m\_fHigher-m\_fHigh} & m\_fHigh < d \le m\_fHigher \\ 0 & d > m\_fHigher \end{cases} . \tag{5}$$

$$Color = Noise + \sum_{i=0}^{Num} texSamples[i]\cdot C_i(d)) \quad where \sum_{i=0}^{Num} C_i(d)) = 1 \ . \tag{6}$$

$$d = dist(p, CenterLine) \ . \tag{7}$$

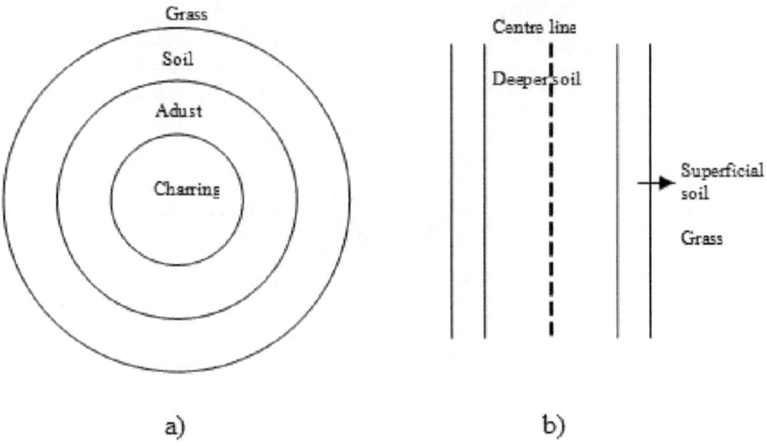

Fig. 1. Gradations of craters and ruts on the grass

We use Equation (6) to compute each pixel color of texture and the following shows out process.

```
Begin
  Read pixel value in every texture
  Compute constraint condition parameter
  Synthesize new color
  Write color to result texture
  Proceed with next pixel
End
```

As to the ruts, we observe and study the ruts on the grass. Usually, the single rut is symmetrical along the centre line. As Fig.1b shows, from the centre line to the outside, there are three regions, including deeper soil, superficial soil, and grass. Between two regions, there is smooth transition. We select the distance from current point to the center line as the constraint condition parameter, just as Equation (7) shows. We also use Equation (5) and (6) to synthesize the texture for rut.

In this way, we can define the constraint conditions and synthesize the different textures for dynamic terrain.

4 Results

We have implemented our method to synthesize the different textures for different dynamic terrain effects. Our implementations are running on a Intel Core2 Duo 3.0GHz computer with 2GB RAM, and NVIDIA GeForce 8400SE graphics card with 256M RAM, under Windows 7 system, VC++ 8.0, and OpenGL environment. The rendering system has a real viewport size of 1024×768.

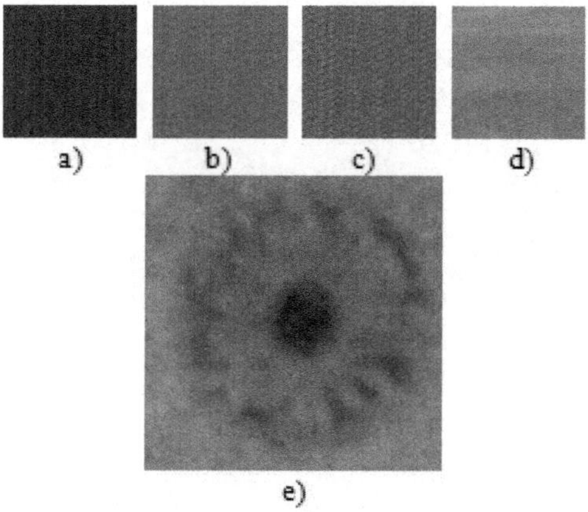

Fig. 2. Synthesizing crater texture on the grass

4.1 Synthesizing Texture for Craters and Ruts

In order to test and verify our method, we implement one system to synthesize the texture for craters. To get the crater texture on the grass land, we select four textures in our multi-samples system, including charring texture, adust texture, soil texture and grass texture. Just as Fig.2 shows, a) is the charring texture, b) is the adust texture, c) is the soil texture, d) is the grass texture and e) is the result texture for crater.

We also synthesize the complex textures. Fig.3 shows craters texture and ruts texture on the grass and on the sand.

4.2 Using Our Method in Practical Projects

Our method has also been used in the practical projects, and the systems are running smooth and high performance. Fig.4a shows the craters on the grass. Fig.4b presents one car running on the grass. The textures getting from our method increase the sense of reality of the practical projects.

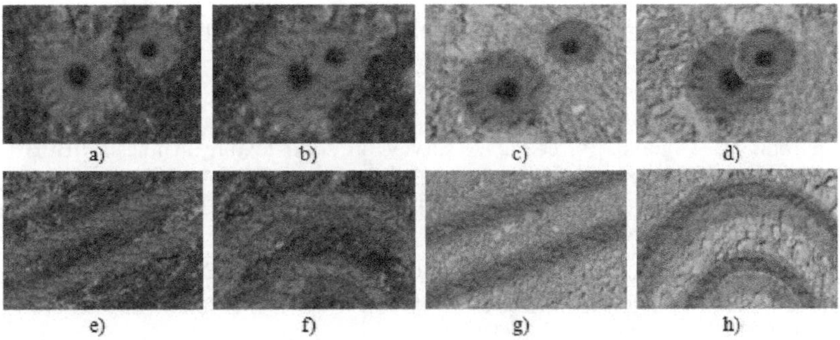

Fig. 3. Synthesizing crater texture and rut texture on the grass and sand

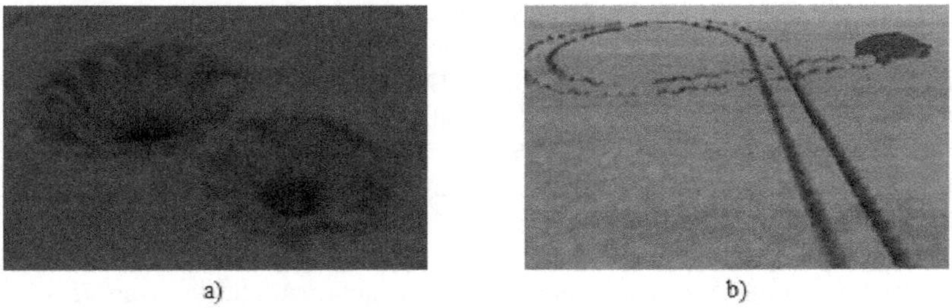

Fig. 4. Using craters texture and ruts texture in practical projects

5 Conclusions and Future Work

In this paper, we provide an efficient multi-samples texture synthesis method for dynamic terrain based on constraint conditions. We initialize a multi-samples texture system, including the texture data for every sample and the texture data for the noise. Then, we compute the constraint conditions parameters according to the characteristics of dynamic terrain effects, and we deal with every pixel in a raster scan ordering. We get the value of every result pixel and update the value to the result texture. In this way, we can rapidly synthesize the different textures for different dynamic terrain effects. The results prove that our method is feasible and high performance. Our method can be used in simulation system based dynamic terrain effects, such as fighting games with advanced weapons explosions, animation with terrain deformation, etc.

As a future possibility, we are working on bringing forward other types of dynamic terrain effects, optimizing our multi-samples texture synthesis method, using CG technology to quicken up our method, and extending our method to other simulation systems.

References

1. Sumner, R.W., et al.: Animating Sand, Mud, and Snow. Computer Graphics Forum 18(1), 3–15 (1999)
2. He, Y., et al.: Real-time Extendible resolution Display of On-line Dynamic Terrain. In: Proceedings of Graphics Interface 2002, pp. 151–160 (2002)
3. Pietroni, N., Cignoni, P., et al.: A survey on solid texture synthesis. IEEE Computer Graphics and Applications 30(4), 74–89 (2010)
4. Wei, L., Lefebvre, S., et al.: State of the Art in Example-Based Texture Synthesis. In: Eurographics 2009, State of the Art Report (2009)
5. Perlin, K.: An Image Synthesizer. Computer Graphics 19(3), 287–296 (1985)
6. Heeger, D.J., Bergen, J.R.: Pyramid based texture analysis synthesis. In: Proceedings of SIGGRAPH 1995, pp. 229–238 (1995)
7. Portilla, J., et al.: A parametric texture model based on joint statistics of complex wavelet coefficients. International Journal of Computer Vision 40(1), 49–70 (2000)
8. Efros, A., Thomas, K.L.: Texture synthesis by non-parametric sampling. In: Proceedings of International Conference on Computer Vision 1999, pp. 1033–1038 (1999)
9. Wei, L., Levoy, M.: Fast Texture Synthesis Using Tree-Structured Vector Quantization. In: Proceedings of SIGGRAPH 2000, pp. 479–488 (2000)
10. Lefebvre, S., Hoppe, H.: Parallel Controllable Texture Synthesis. In: Proceedings of SIGGRAPH 2005, pp. 777–786 (2005)
11. Efros, A., Freeman, W.T.: Image Quilting for Texture Synthesis and Transfer. In: Proceedings of SIGGRAPH 2001, pp. 341–346 (2001)
12. Wang, Y., et al.: Optimizing the parameters for patch-based texture synthesis. In: Proceedings of ACM Virtual Reality Continuum and Its Applications, pp. 75–82 (2006)
13. Chen, X.: Reusing Partially Synthesized Textures for Real-Time Synthesis of Large Textures. Chinese Journal of Computers 33(4), 765–774 (2010)
14. Kwatra, V., Irfan, E., et al.: Texture Optimization for Example-Based Synthesis. In: Proceedings of SIGGRAPH 2005, pp. 795–802 (2005)
15. Xue, F., Zhang, Y., et al.: Synthesizing Texture Using Variant SOM. Journal of System Simulation 18(3), 581–585 (2006) (in Chinese)

PCA and FLD in DWT Domain

Zhicheng Liu[1] and Zhijun Fang[2]

[1] Dept. of Information Engineering, Hunan Railway Professional Technology College, Zhuzhou, Hunan, 412001

[2] Institute of Digital Media, School of Information Technology, Jiangxi University of Finance & Economics, Nanchang, Jiangxi, 330013

liuzc518@163.com, zjfang@foxmail.com

Abstract. In this paper, we prove that the principal component analysis (PCA) and the linear discriminant analysis (LDA) can be directly implemented in the wavelet cosine transform (DWT) domain and the results are exactly the same as the one obtained from the spatial domain. In some applications, compressed images are desirable to reduce the storage requirement. For images compressed using the DWT in JPEG2000 or MPEG4 standard, the PCA and LDA can be directly implemented in the DWT domain such that the inverse DWT transform can be skipped and the dimensionality of the original data can be initially reduced to cut down computation cost. Finally, It is verified by infrared face recognition based on PCA and LDA in DWT domain through our infrared face database.

Keywords: Infrared face recognition, compression, DWT, PCA, FLD.

1 Introduction

With the continuous development of the information society, face recognition technology, as intuitive, passive and non-invasive advantages, is widely used in the fields of some identity authentication, such as customs, banks and some public security areas. With the development of face recognition technology, the database capacity is also growing fast, the demand for storage devices is becoming more sophisticated. In some sense, the image compression is applied to the face recognition system inevitably. Avoiding compression decoding and re-encoding process, it is directly operating on the image in the compressed domain [1]. These not only reduces the amount of data processing to save memory space, but also acquire better data processing results by using the properties of compressive domain data. In recent years, the idea of image compression applied to face recognition systems is one of the hottest topics in the relative international field.

Recent studies have showed that: local information on IR face recognition plays an important role, while the wavelet theory (such as haar, db2, db4 and etc) is recently the most widely used for most effective analysis of local information. It reflects the two-dimensional signal space position, orientation and spatial frequency information, which can get the characteristics of scale, location and differences and so on. In particular, this description for the time-varying signal has a good robustness. Even in

Z. Pan et al. (Eds.): Transactions on Edutainment VII, LNCS 7145, pp. 197–204, 2012.

the case of stable equilibrium, because of the bodies self-adaptive, the human body is also a small-scale change in biological characteristics, so it is suited to use wavelet theory to extract the local temperature information.

From the experimental results of many researchers who have done a lot work in the DWT domain [2], we known that the performance of face recognition is merely reduce in compressions, in some cases, improving recognition performance. These studies lead us to realize achieving face recognition in the compressive domain is feasible. As effectively removing the unimportant image information using DWT, the performance of face recognition can improve under certain conditions.

In our survey, we find that most of the current face recognition systems are based on the study of visible light images, which are influenced by posture, light, shadow, make-up and other factors, while recognising using the infrared images can be avoided from the above-mentioned factors. In the face recognition technology, the most representative feature extraction method is PCA [3], FLD [4], and Fisherface[5]. PCA and FLD methods which are widely used in face recognition systems have been developed in the literature [6], where has proved that transforming domain for PCA or FLD in the DCT has the same result as in the spatial domain.

Inspired by these studies, we try to transform from a theoretical analysis of the original image to the wavelet domain through the PCA, LDA transform of the projection results and the projection in the spatial domain to be the same result, and to be verified in experiments in the experiment. Under such circumstances, face images in the database formatted in JPEG2000 or MPEG4, its wavelet coefficients can be directly used for feature extraction. It has a very important practical significance of reducing the storage capacity and computational complexity.

2 PCA and LDA in DWT Domain

In this section, we first argue that the orthogonal transformation of data PCA projection result is unchanged. After that, we demonstrate that DWT is an orthogonal transformation, and PCA can be achieved directly in the DWT domain. Similarly, we can demonstrate LDA can be directly implemented in the DWT domain.

2.1 PCA in Orthonormal Transformation Domain

Let $X=\{x_1,x_2,\cdots,x_n\}^T$ denote an n-dimensional random vector. The mean of the random vector X is denoted by $\overline{X}=E[X]$ and the covariance matrix of the random vector X is defined as $C_X=E[(X-\overline{X})(X-\overline{X})^T]$. The PCA projection matrix A can be obtained by feature analysis of the covariance matrix C_X, is that

$$C_X a_i=\lambda_i a_i, i=1,2,...,m \tag{1}$$

Where a_i is the i-th largest eigenvector of C_X, m < n and $A=[a_1,a_2,...,a_m]\subset R^{n\times m}$. We have the following projection result:

$$Y=A^T(X-\overline{X}) \tag{2}$$

Let us assume that the original data are transformed by using an nxn orthogonal matrix Q, is that, $Z = Q^T X$. The mean of the transformed random vector Z is given by

$$\overline{Z} = E[Q^T X] = Q^T E[X] = Q^T \overline{X} \tag{3}$$

We may obtain the covariance matrix C_Z of the transformed random vector Z as follows:

$$\begin{aligned} C_Z &= E[(Z-\overline{Z})(Z-\overline{Z})^T] \\ &= E[(Q^T X - Q^T \overline{X})(Q^T X - Q^T \overline{X})^T] \\ &= Q^T E[(X-\overline{X})(X-\overline{X})^T]Q \\ &= Q^T C_X Q \end{aligned} \tag{4}$$

Similarly, the PCA projection matrix

$\widetilde{A} = [\widetilde{a}_1, \widetilde{a}_2, ..., \widetilde{a}_m] \subset R^{m \times n}$ For the orthonormally transformed data can be obtained by eigenanalysis of

$$C_z \widetilde{a}_i = \lambda_i \widetilde{a}_i, i = 1, 2, ..., m \tag{5}$$

Substituting (3.7) into (3.8), we have

$$Q^T C_X Q \widetilde{a}_i = \lambda_i \widetilde{a}_i \tag{6}$$

Since Q is an orthogonal matrix, i.e., $Q^T = Q^{-1}$,
Eq. (6) can be rewritten as

$$C_X Q \widetilde{a}_i = \lambda_i Q \widetilde{a}_i \tag{7}$$

Eq. (7) shows that the covariance matrices C_X and C_Z have exactly same eigenvalues and the relation of their eigenvectors is $a_i = Q\widetilde{a}_i$, Therefore, the PCA projection matrices A and $\widetilde{A}$ also satisfy $\widetilde{A} = Q^T A$. The projection result of Z is as follows:

$$\widetilde{Y} = \widetilde{A}^T (Z - \widetilde{Z}) = A^T Q (Z - Z^T) = A^T (X - \overline{X}) = Y \tag{8}$$

From (8), we can conclude that for the PCA subspace projection, orthonormal transformation of the original data will not change the projection result.

2.2 LDA in Orthonormal Transformation Domain

For the LDA, the between-class scatter matrix S_b and the within-class scatter matrix S_w are respectively defined as:

$$S_b = \sum_{i=1}^{C} ni(\overline{X}_i - \overline{X})(\overline{X}_i - \overline{X})^T \tag{9}$$

$$Sw = \sum_{i=1}^{C} \sum_{X_j \in C_i} (X_j - \overline{X}_i)(X_j - \overline{X}_i)^T \tag{10}$$

Where C is the number of classes, and ni is the number of samples in class C_i and $\overline{X} = \frac{1}{C}\sum_{k=1}^{C}\overline{X_k}$ is the mean of class C_i, and $\overline{X} = \frac{1}{C}\sum_{k=1}^{C}\overline{X_k}$ is the mean of all samples. The optimal subspace projection is determined as follows:

$$E_{OPT} = \arg\max_{E} \frac{|E^T S_b E|}{|E^T S_w E|} = [e_1, e_2, ..., e_m] \tag{11}$$

Where $[e_1, e_2, ..., e_m]$ is the set of generalized eigenvectors corresponding to the $m(m \leq C-1)$ largest generalized eigenvalues $\lambda_i, i = 1, 2, ..., m,$ i.e.,

$$S_b e_i = \lambda_i S_w e_i, i = 1, 2, ..., m \tag{12}$$

So, the projection results is

$$Y = E_{OPT}^T X \tag{13}$$

Let us assume that the original data is transformed using an orthogonal matrix Q, is that $Z = Q^T X$.

$$\overline{Z} = E[Q^T X] = Q^T E[X], \overline{Z_i} = Q^T \overline{X_i}$$

$$\begin{aligned}\widetilde{S_b} &= \sum_{i=1}^{C} ni(Q^T \overline{X_i} - Q^T \overline{X})(Q^T \overline{X_i} - Q^T \overline{X})^T \\ &= Q^T \sum_{i=1}^{C} ni(\overline{X_i} - \overline{X})(\overline{X_i} - \overline{X})^T \\ &= Q^T S_b Q\end{aligned} \tag{14}$$

$$\begin{aligned}\widetilde{Sw} &= \sum_{i=1}^{C} \sum_{X_j \in C_i} (Q^T X_j - Q^T \overline{X_i})(Q^T X_j - Q^T \overline{X_i})^T \\ &= Q^T \sum_{i=1}^{C} \sum_{X_j \in C_i} (X_j - \overline{X_i})(X_j - \overline{X_i})^T Q \\ &= Q^T S_w Q\end{aligned} \tag{15}$$

The between-class and within-class scatter matrices for Z are obtained as follows:

$$\widetilde{S_b} = Q^T S_b Q \tag{16}$$

$$\widetilde{Sw} = Q^T S_w Q \tag{17}$$

$$\widetilde{E_{OPT}} = \arg\max_{E} \frac{\left|\widetilde{E}^{T}\widetilde{S_b}\widetilde{E}\right|}{\left|\widetilde{E}^{T}\widetilde{S_w}\widetilde{E}\right|} = [\widetilde{e_1}, \widetilde{e_2}, \ldots, \widetilde{e_m}] \tag{18}$$

$$\widetilde{S_b}\widetilde{e_i} = \lambda_i \widetilde{S_w}\widetilde{e_i}, i = 1, 2, \ldots, m \tag{19}$$

Substituting (16) and (17) into (19), we have

$$S_b Q\widetilde{e_i} = \lambda_i S_w \widetilde{Qe_i}, i = 1, 2, \ldots, n \tag{20}$$

Comparing to (12), we can see that the generalized eigenvalues are the same and the generalized eigenvectors satisfy $e_i = Q\widetilde{e_i}, i = 1, 2, \ldots, m$. Since Q is orthogonal, the optimal projection matrix satisfies $\widetilde{E_{OPT}} = Q^T E_{OPT}$. Therefore, the projection result of Z is as follows:

$$\widetilde{Y} = \widetilde{E}^T Z = (Q^T E_{OPT})^T Z = E_{OPT}^T QZ = E_{OPT}^T X = Y \tag{21}$$

Then, we can conclude that for the LDA subspace projection, orthonormal transformation of the original data will not change the projection result.

2.3 Two-Dimensional Orthogonal Wavelet Transformation

The wavelet function that we constructed is orthogonal wavelet. Therefore, the wavelet transformation is orthogonal wavelet transformation. See the two-dimensional orthogonal wavelet transform algorithm [7] for more details.

The transformation matrix which we proceed the two-dimensional orthogonal wavelet transform in image is orthogonal matrix. So we obtain conclusions as follows: for the sub-space projection of PCA and LDA, the image after two-dimensional orthogonal wavelet transform did not change the projection result of PCA and LDA.

3 Experimental Test Results and Analysis

As there haven't yet unified infrared face database in the international by far, the infrared database we used is taken by ourselves, the IR data were captured by an IR camera Thermo Vision A40 supplied by FLIR Systems Inc. This camera, which uses an uncooled microbolometer sensor with resolution of 320×240 pixels and operates in the spectral response of 7.5 ~ 13 microns, is specially designed for accurate temperature measurement. The sensitivity is as high as 0.08°C. One of its prominent features is the function of automatic self-calibration to cope with the temperature drift. The database comprises 1000 thermal images of 50(i.e. each person have 20 thermal images.)individuals which were carefully collected under the similar conditions: i.e. environment under air-conditioned control with temperature around 25.6~26.3 °C, and each person stood at a distance of about one meter in front of the camera. As glass is opaque to long-wavelength IR, subjects are required to remove their eyeglasses in database collection. After detecting face, the face image is normalized to size of 80 × 60。 The database is separated into two sets, one is for training samples which comprising 500 thermal images (i.e. 50 persons and each have 10 images), and the other is for testing samples (i.e. 50 persons and each have 10 images).

3.1 The Experimental Results and Analysis of PCA in DWT Domain

From the experimental results in figure 1, we can see that the recognition rates of PCA in DWT domain are also different using the different basis. And when choosing the wavelet basis of haar, the recognition rate is the best. When we apply the haar wavelet basis in the experiment, it even reaches to 93.6%. As for the question how to select wavelet basis, there is no unified view and the related research is still under way.

From the figure 2, we can see that the curves of PCA and PCA in DWT domain are almost coincident. And this shows that the results of PCA projection aren't changed almost using the method PCA in DWT domain, which confirms our previous theoretical analysis, that is, when the original images are transformed by DWT, the results will not change the PCA projection subspace. In addition, the recognition rate of PCA in DWT domain should be slightly higher than PCA. Because the original images are decomposition using DWT, discarding the high-frequency part and just leaving the low-frequency part with more concentrated energy in the experiment. While losing some useful information, it doesn't reduce the dimensionality of the image and but also remove the bad factors of feature extraction, such as noise and so on. From the experimental results, we can conclude in another side that discarding the high frequency part of the images will not reduce the recognition rate, but slightly increase it in some cases. Therefore it indicates that the method which extracts feature values after retaining the lower-frequency wavelet is effective, and also shows that the method based on DWT domain is effective.

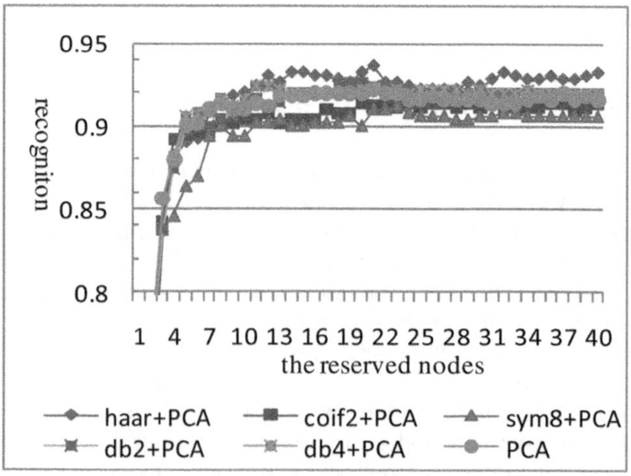

Fig. 1. The results of PCA and PCA based on the different wavelet basis

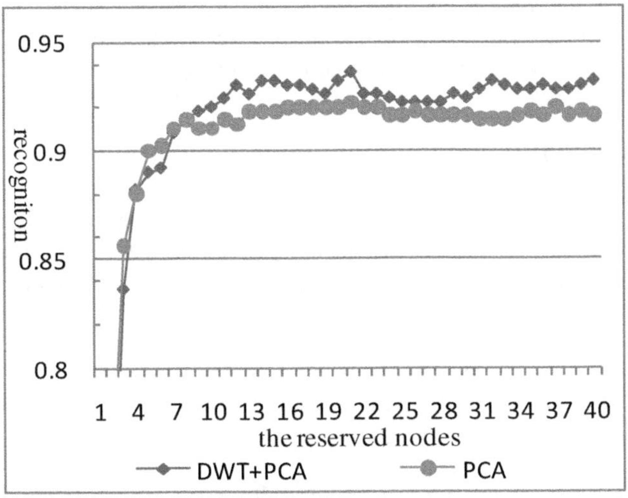

Fig. 2. The comparison between PCA and PCA in DWT(haar) domain

3.2 The Experimental Results and Analysis of LDA in DWT Domain

Table 1. The highest recognition rate comparison of which based on the different thermogram wavelet basis in the wavelet domain LDA

Method (number)	Recognition rate
DWT (Haar) + LDA	84%
DWT (Db2) + LDA	84%
DWT (Db4) + LDA	84.8%
DWT (Sym8) + LDA	85.6%
DWT (Coif2) + LDA	85.4%

From Table 1, we can see from the table, choose a different wavelets obtained recognition results are different, but the difference between them is small, the biggest difference is 1.6 percentage points. When it shows based on different wavelet bases in the wavelet domain LDA method the results obtained are similar.

From Table 1, we can also see that the approach of LDA in DWT domain, when selecting the different wavelet basis, the recognition rates is almost the same. In addition, in this experiment, we can not test based on the thermogram LDA approach, because it consumes a large amount of memory required, which also shows the dimensionality of the original image is reduced, the LDA feature extraction is not feasible and unrealistic. And when putting the image using orthogonal discrete wavelet transformations, we solve this problem. After the discrete wavelet transformation, the dimensionality of the images has been reduced, and the images are also smaller, while from the analysis above we conduce that the method based on DWT domain will not change the projection results of the LDA.

4 Conclusion

Based on storage requirements and computational complexity, in this paper, we try to apply compressed images to the infrared face recognition system, a method of infrared face recognition based on DWT domain combined PCA and FLD is proposed . At the same time, we analyze the project subspace of the PCA and the LDA from theory that after 2D orthogonal wavelet transform the original image will not change the project results. At last, our theoretical analysis are verified in the experiments results and the recognition rate based on DWT domain are slightly improved than the spatial domain.

Acknowledgments. This work was partially supported by the National Natural Science Foundation of China (60862002), the Scientific Research Project of Higher Education of Hunan Province, China (10C0229).

References

1. Liu, Y., Li, H.-D.: Image and Video Processing Techniques in the DCT Domain. Journal of Image and Graphics 8(2), 121–128 (2003)
2. Delac, K., Grgic, S., Grgic, M.: Blood perfusionImage Compression in Face Recognition - a Literature Survey models in Recent Advances in Face Recognition. IN-Tech Publishing, Refer to `http://intechweb.org`
3. Turk, M., Pentland, A.: A face recognition using eigenfaces. In: Proc. IEEE Conf. on Computer Vision and Pattern Recognition, pp. 586–591 (1991)
4. Martinez, A.M., Kak, A.C.: PCA versus LDA. IEEE Trans. Pattern Analysis and Machine Intelligence 23(2), 228–233 (2001)
5. Belhumeur, P.N., et al.: Eigenfaces vs. Fisherfaces: Recognition using class specific linear projection. Pattern Analysis and Machine Intelligence 19(7), 711–720 (1997)
6. Chen, W., Er, M.J., Wu, S.: PCA and LDA in DCT Domain image. Pattern Recognition Letters 26(15), 2474–2482 (2005)
7. Wang, G., Cheng, Z.X.: On the Vector-Space Algorithm of Two-dimensional Orthonormal Wavelet Transform. Journal of Nanjing University (Natural Sciences) 41(1), 71–76 (2005)

Area Measurement Method of Paint Bubble Based on Computer Vision

Shidu Dong[1,2], Xiaofan Yang[1], Huaqiu Wang[2], Xiang Liu[2], and Hengyang Liu[2]

[1] College of Computer Science, Chongqing University, Chongqing, 400044, China
[2] College of Computer Science and Engineering, Chongqing University of Technology, Chongqing, 400054, China
dongshidu@yahoo.com.cn

Abstract. An area measurement method of paint bubble based on computer vision is proposed. Firstly, through a camera calibration, the lens distortion is removed and the mapping between image coordinate and real world coordinate is constructed. Secondly, a novel color image segmentation method based on graph-cut, whose seeds can be auto-marked, is proposed, and with the method, paint bubbles are extracted from image. Finally, with camera calibrated parameter, the size of segmented paint bubbles is figured out. Experiment result shows that the proposed method gains higher precision than classical graph-cut segmentation method and can figure out the area of the bubble automatically.

Keywords: Vision measurement, Graph-cut, Image segmentation, Paint bubbles.

1 Introduction

To evaluate the quality of a proper paint, paint samples are always exposed in terrible environment for a given period, and then its defects (such as bubble, crack, and rusting) are estimated. Area of the Bubble is an important factor [1]. It is known that manual area measurement is very time-consuming. For the purpose of relieving job stress, vision measurement, which always consists of camera calibration and image segmentation, is adopted.

Through camera calibration, intrinsic, extrinsic and lens radial distortion parameters, which is essential to figured out the area of object from image, are gained. In calibration method proposed by O. Faugeras [2], the calibration object usually consists of two or three planes orthogonal to each other. While in paper [3], plane undergoes precisely known translation. These approaches require an expensive calibration apparatus and an elaborate setup. The more flexible method presented by Z. Zhang only requires the camera to observe a planar pattern shown at a few (at least two) different orientation [4]. In order to solve intrinsic and extrinsic parameters, the plane should not be parallel to the other. Since paint sample always is planar, and measurement equipment is fixed, the more easy calibration method can be used.

Z. Pan et al. (Eds.): Transactions on Edutainment VII, LNCS 7145, pp. 205–213, 2012.

Classical image segmentation schemes such as region growing, and split-merge are fast due to their low complication algorithm, but unfortunately, they are not robust in practice, and prone to many problems, most notably, to "leaking " through week spots in object boundaries [5,6]. Such weak spots can be easy found in the image of paint bubble. In addition, kinds of paint are multitudinous and the pixel difference between bubble and other region is very little. As a result, the classical image segmentation method is not competent to segment bubbles of paints. Recently, the interactive image segmentation scheme is very popular. With certain pixels marked as "object" or "background" (seeds, for short), the object, which is not able to be segmented by classical method, can be segmented with the method based graph-cut proposed by Yuri Boykov [3,4]. But unfortunately, the color information are not utilized enough, further more, when the amount of the bubbles in paint is large, it is very time-consuming to mark seeds of all bubbles.

A computer vision measurement method for paint is proposed. Firstly, a camera is calibrated. Secondly, a paint bubble segmentation method based on graph-cut, whose weight of edge is figured from color distance and seeds are auto-marked, is proposed, and with the method, paint bubbles are extracted from image. Finally, with the camera calibrated parameters, the size of segmented paint bubbles is figured out.

The remainder of the paper is organized as follows: the main framework of the proposed scheme is introduced in next section, and camera calibration method is presented in section 3. The image segmentation scheme based on color graph cut, the auto-marking bubble scheme and the area calculation method of segmented bubble are proposed in section 4, 5 and 6 respectively. Experimental results are given in Section 7 and some conclusions are drawn in Section 8.

2 Main Framework

Fig. 1 plots the basic main framework of proposed scheme. First, the camera is calibrated, and camera parameters are gained. And then the paint defect image is collected and the seeds of a bubble are marked manually. With the seeds, the bubble is segmented by image segmentation scheme based on color graph cut. With the camera parameters and the segmented bubble, the area of the bubble can be figured out. Finally, other bubbles are detected with the features from the segmented bubble and their seed are marked. Repeating the processes, all bubbles are segmented and measured.

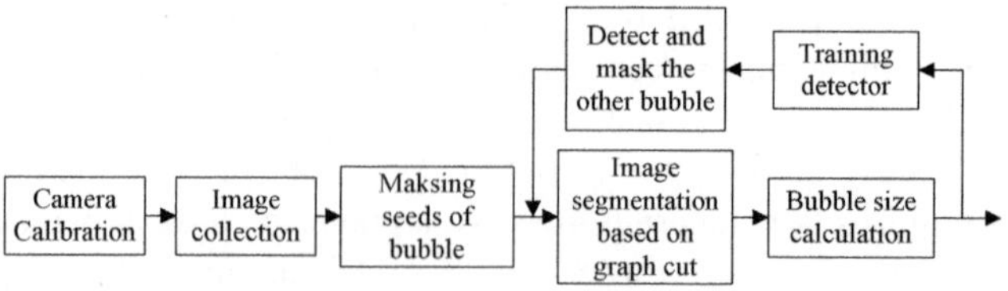

Fig. 1. Main framework

3 Camera Calibration

In general, the distance between the camera and plane is constant, through camera calibration, the size of the given object in image can be figured out.

The camera is modeled as following equation.

$$s\begin{bmatrix} u \\ v \\ 1 \end{bmatrix} = A\begin{bmatrix} r_1 & r_2 & r_3 & t \end{bmatrix}\begin{bmatrix} X \\ Y \\ Z \\ 1 \end{bmatrix}. \tag{1}$$

Without loss of generality, we assume the model plane is on Z=0 of the world coordinate system. From (1), we have

$$\begin{bmatrix} u \\ v \\ 1 \end{bmatrix} = \begin{bmatrix} h_1 & h_2 & h_3 \end{bmatrix}\begin{bmatrix} X \\ Y \\ 1 \end{bmatrix}. \tag{2}$$

Let's denote

$$H = [h_1 \quad h_2 \quad h_3] = s^{-1}A\begin{bmatrix} r_1 & r_2 & t \end{bmatrix}. \tag{3}$$

Let's m_j the coordinate of point P_j in image, and $\hat{m}_j$ the corresponding figured coordinate with Eq.(1). Without considering the lens distortion of a camera, H can be estimated by minimizing the following functional:

$$\min \sum_j \left\| m_j - \hat{m}_j(H, P_j) \right\|^2. \tag{4}$$

However, camera usually exhibits significant lens distortion, especially radial distortion. Assume (u,v) be the ideal pixel image (distortion-free) coordinates, $(\hat{u}, \hat{v})$ the corresponding real observed coordinate and d the distance between (u,v) and (u_0, v_0) the optical center .

$$\hat{u} = u + (u - u_0)\left[k_1 d^2 + k_2 d^4\right], \tag{5}$$

$$\hat{v} = v + (v - v_0)\left[k_1 d^2 + k_2 d^4\right]. \tag{6}$$

With the estimated H, the value of H and distortion parameters k_1 and k_2 can be solved by minimizing the following function:

$$\sum_j \left\| m_j - \hat{m}_j(H, k_1, k_2, P_j) \right\|^2. \tag{7}$$

Based on the previous discussions, we present a complete description of the calibration process as follows:

i. The pattern plane, (standard chessboard, as Fig.2-B) is printed, the size is measured and the coordinate of the corners is determined.

ii. The chessboard is placed on the plane of the equipment, its image is collected and the pixel coordinates of the corners are determined.

iii. Initial values of H are estimated by Eq.(4).

iv. Final values of H and radial distortion k_1, k_2 are solved by Eq.(2), (5), (6) and (7) with the Levenberg-Marquardt Algorithms[7].

Given the image of paint defect, the lens distortion is removed by Eq.(5) and Eq.(6). We assume that the x-axis and y-axis is vertical, and

$$\begin{bmatrix} X_h \\ Y_h \\ 1 \end{bmatrix} = \begin{bmatrix} h_1 & h_2 & h_3 \end{bmatrix}^{-1} \begin{bmatrix} 1 \\ 0 \\ 1 \end{bmatrix}. \tag{8}$$

As paint samples are planar, so the corresponding paint sample width of a pixel is

$$W_p = \sqrt{X_h^2 + Y_h^2}. \tag{9}$$

Similarly, the height of a pixel, H_p , can be figured. As a result, the corresponding area of pixel can be gained by following the equation

$$A_p = W_p \times H_p. \tag{10}$$

4 Color Graph-Cut Image Segmentation

Firstly, an image is transformed to graph $G = \langle V, E \rangle$, defined as a set of nodes or vertices V and a set of edges E connecting "neighboring" nodes.

$$G = < V, E > = < P \cup \{S, T\}, N \cup \{\{p, S\}, \{p, T\}\} >, \tag{11}$$

where, P corresponding to pixels in the image, and edge between P are called N-linking. There are two specially designated terminal notes S (source) and T (sink) that represent "bubble" and "background" labels. Another type of Edges, called T-linking, are used connect P to S or T [6,8]. The weight of edge denotes the cost of breaking the linking. Under condition of minimizing the cost, graph cut algorithm divides the nodes into two-part, i.e. bubble and background.

Color component, which contains more detailed information of image, can improve the accuracy of segmentation. Different from the scheme in the papers [6, 8], the weight of N edge is calculated with the color components of neighbor pixels.

By Eq.(12)-(14)[9], color components in HSV color space are gained.

$$h=\begin{cases}\arccos\left\{\dfrac{(r-g)+(r-b)}{2\sqrt{(r-g)^2+(r-b)(g-b)}}\right\} & b\le g\\ 2\pi-\arccos\left\{\dfrac{(r-g)+(r-b)}{2\sqrt{(r-g)^2+(r-b)(g-b)}}\right\} & b>g\end{cases}, \tag{12}$$

$$v=\frac{\max(r,g,b)}{255}, \tag{13}$$

$$s=\frac{\max(r,g,b)-\min(r,g,b)}{\max(r,g,b)}, \tag{14}$$

where r, g and b are color component in RGB space.

The color distance [10] between i^{th} pixel and j^{th} pixel is governed by

$$D_{(i,j)}=\left[\left(v_i-v_j\right)^2+\left(s_i\cosh_i-s_j\cosh_j\right)^2+\left(s_i\sinh_i-s_j\sinh_j\right)^2\right]^{\frac{1}{2}}. \tag{15}$$

The weight of edge (i,j) is get

$$B_{i,j}=\exp(-D_{i,j})/dist(i,j), \tag{16}$$

where dist(i,j) denotes the Euclidean distance between i^{th} pixel and j^{th} pixel.

The seeds of bubble and background, which denoted by O and B respectively, are marked by user. The weight of edge connecting the seeds to S or T is

$$R_{p\in O,S}=R_{p\in B,T}=1+\max_{p\in P}\sum_{q:\{p,q\}\in N}B_{p,q}. \tag{17}$$

The weight of edge between other pixel and S or T is

$$K=1+\max_{p\in P}\sum_{q:\{p,q\}\in N}B_{p,q}. \tag{18}$$

Let $L=(L_1,\cdots,L_i,\cdots,L_{|P|})$ be a binary vector whose components $L_i\in\{0,1\}$ represents either "object" or background. Then the cost function of segmentation which divides all nodes (or pixels) into "object" and "background" [5,6] is described by

$$B_{p,T}=\begin{cases}K & p\in B\\ 0 & p\notin B\end{cases}, \tag{19}$$

Where,

$$E(A) = \sum_{\{p,q\} \in N} B_{p,q} \cdot \delta_{L_p \neq L_q}, \tag{20}$$

$$\delta_{A_p \neq A_q} = \begin{cases} 1 & L_p \neq L_q \\ 0 & L_p = L_q \end{cases}. \tag{21}$$

The global minimum of cost function can be solved by the classical graph cut algorithm. In fact, in this paper, the novel algorithm proposed by Yuri Boykov [8], which is faster in computer vision application, is adopted.

5 Auto-Marking Seeds

The image segmentation scheme proposed in section 4 requires marking seeds of both bubble and background. When the amount of bubble is large, it is terrible job. A novel method for auto-marking seeds of bubble, which utilize the feature extracted from the segmented bubble, is proposed. For our purpose, entropy of intensity and HVS histogram are adopted as features.

The color component in HSV space is quantized firstly [11]. h component is quantized to $0 \sim 15$, s to $0 \sim 3$, and v to $0 \sim 3$. Thus, total 256 colors are gained. By Eq. (15), the distance, $a_{i,j}$, between the ith and j^{th} colors is figured out, and we get the matrix

$$A = \left(a_{i,j}\right), \tag{22}$$

where $0 \leq i \leq 255, 0 \leq j \leq 255$.

The histogram distance between region to be probed and the segmented bubble is represented as follows:

$$D_{hist} = (H_O - H_P)^T A (H_O - H_P), \tag{23}$$

where H_0 denotes the histogram of the segmented bubble and H_P denotes that of the region to be probed.

Entropy, which is used to describe the amount of information, is a texture measure widely used to quantify the smoothness of image texture. In addition, entropy does not depend on scale and direction of texture. Thus, entropy is chosen as a feature to detect bubble. Entropy is expressed by the following equation

$$E = \sum_{i=0}^{255} - p(i) \log p(i), \tag{24}$$

where $p(i)$ is the probability of occurrence of gray level i.

The distance of entropy between the bubbled and region to be probed is determined by

$$D_{entropy} = \left| E_O - E_P \right|. \tag{25}$$

So, if the entropy and histogram distances between the bubble and region to be probed are less than the given thresholds, new bubble are found, and seeds are marked as following equation.

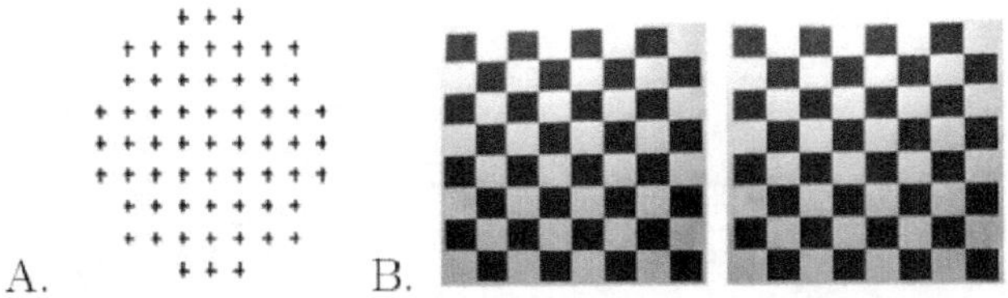

Fig. 2. A. Window shape and B. Distortion image and its undistorted image

$$M(i,j) = \begin{cases} 1 & D_{hist}(i,j) \le T_{hist} \quad and \quad D_{entropy}(i,j) \le T_{entropy} \\ 0 & others \end{cases}. \tag{26}$$

where (i,j) denotes the center of the region to be probed, and T_{hist} and $T_{entropy}$ denote thresholds of distance of histogram and entropy respectively.

Each pixel in the image is scanned. The local region to be probed is windows modeled as Fig.2-A, whose sizes is 65×65 , 33×33 , 17×17 and 9×9 . Each window is adopted ordered by the size until bubble is found.

6 Area Calculation

Through connect components labeling algorithm [2], each pixel of the ith segmented bubble is labeled as i. The pixel number of the ith bubble can be gained as following

$$N_i = \sum_j \delta_j \quad \delta_j = \begin{cases} 1 & L_j = i \\ 0 & other \end{cases}. \tag{27}$$

The area of the ith segmented bubble can be figured out by the following equation:

$$A_i = N_i \times A_p. \tag{28}$$

7 Experimental Result

Fig.2-B depicts the distortion image and its' undistorted image. From the images, the proposed camera calibration can remove lens distortion.

Fig.3 (left) illustrates the first bubble segmentation result with manual seeds, and the auto-marked seeds by detector using the features from the first segmented bubble. From the figure, it is shown that most bubbles are marked correctly.

Fig.4 plots segmentation result of the proposed method (left) which utilize color component to figure out the weights of N edges, manual (middle) and graph cut proposed by Yuri Boykov, with only intensity data, respectively. Comparing them, we can conclude that the proposed scheme is more approximate to the manual one.

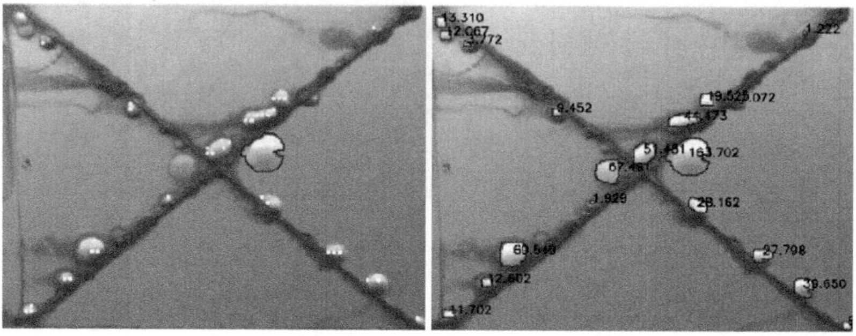

Fig. 3. (left)Auto-marked seeds(white dot) and (right)Measure result of bubble size (mm^2)

Let L_i^M denotes the label of ith pixel of manual segmentation, and L_i^c the label of the proposed segmentation method. The relative error rate of color-graph-cut segmentation method is

$$R_{CM} = \sum_{i \in P} (L_i^C \oplus L_i^M) / \sum_{i \in P} L_i^M , \tag{29}$$

and the absolute error is

$$R'_C = \sum_{i \in P} (L_i^C \oplus L_i^M) / |P| . \tag{30}$$

Tab.1 illustrates the error rates of the propose method and gray-graph-cut method. From the Tab.1, it is shown that the proposed method gains higher precision.

Fig. 3 (right) illustrates the measurement result of the segmented bubbles. The calculated value of theoretical measurement precision is $0.042865mm^2$. But it should be pointed out that real measurement precision is lower than the precision due to the error of segmentation and neighbor pixel disturbing.

8 Conclusion

An Area Measurement method of Paint Sample Bubble is proposed in this paper. The color image segmentation method based on graph cut, which utilized color components to calculate weights of edges, and an auto-marking seeds method with feature extracted from the previous segmented bubble, which can significantly decrease the workload of user, are proposed. In addition, through camera calibration, the area of segmented bubble can be figured out.

Table 1. The error rates of the proposed and gray-graph-cut methods(%)

	relative error rate	*absolute error*
The proposed	3.9	0.17
Gray-graph-cut	14.74	0.64

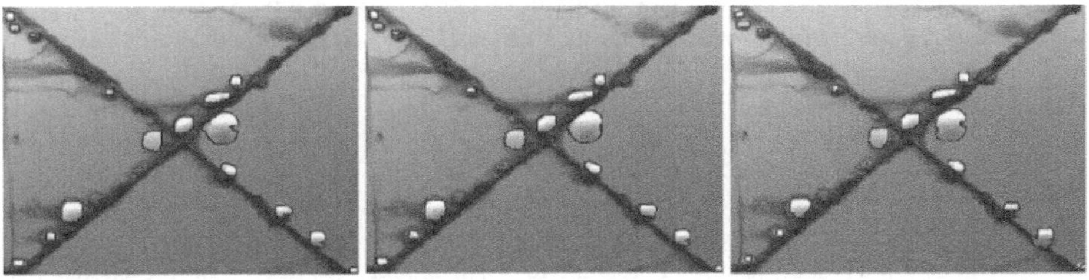

Fig. 4. Segmentation results of the proposed method (left) , manual (middle) and gray-graph-cut method(right)

Acknowledgments. The authors are grateful to the anonymous reviewers for their valuable comments and suggestions. This work is supported by Science and Technology Research Project of Chongqing's Education Committee (KJ110806).

References

1. GB/T 1766-1995, Paint and Vanish-Rating Scheme of Degradation of Coats (in Chinese)
2. Faugeras, O.: Three-Dimensional Computer Vision: a Geometric Viewpoint. MIT Press (1993)
3. Tsai, R.Y.: A versatile camera calibration technique for high-accuracy 3D machine vision metrology using off-the-shelf tv cameras and lenses. IEEE Journal of Robotics and Automation 3, 323–344 (1987)
4. Zhang, Z.: A flexible new technique for camera calibration. IEEE Transactions on TPAMI 22, 1330–1334 (2000)
5. Shapiro, L.G., Stockman, G.C.: Computer Vision. Prentice Hall (2001)
6. Boykov, Y., Funka-Lea, G.: Graph Cuts and Efficient N-D Image Segmentation. International Journal of Computer Vision 70, 109–131 (2006)
7. More, J.: The levenberg-marquardt algorithm, implementation and theory. In: Watson, G.A. (ed.) Numerical Analysis. LNM, vol. 630. Springer, Heidelberg (1977)
8. Boykov, Y., Kolmogorov, V.: An Experimental Comparison of Min-Cut/Max-Flow Algorithms or Energy Minimization in Vision. IEEE Transactions on PAMI 26, 1124–1137 (2004)
9. Zhang, Y.J.: Image Engineering(I) Image Processing, 2nd edn. Tsinghua university press (2006) (in Chinese)
10. Smith, J.R., Chang, S.-F.: VisualSEEk: a Fully Automated Content-Based Image Query System. In: ACM Multimedia 1996. ACM (1996)
11. Smith, J.R., Chang, S.-F.: Local Color and Texture Extraction and Spatial Query. In: International Conference on Image Processing, Lausanne, Switzerland, pp. 1011–1014. IEEE Press (1996)
12. Deng, Y., Manjunath, B.S.: Unsupervised Segmentation of Color-texture Regions in Images and Video. IEEE Transactions on PAMI 23, 800–810 (2001)

A High Precision Fresco Scanner

Xifan Shi, Xianghua Chen, and Tiefeng Cai

Zhijiang College, Zhejiang University of Technology, Hangzhou 310024, China
zjufan@hotmail.com, {chxh,ctf}@zjc.zjut.edu.cn

Abstract. It is of great significance to digitize ancient paintings and calligraphy. A typical way to acquire them is using a linear CCD based large area table scanner. But it is not suitable for scanning fresco. Our lab has recently developed a new equipment to solve it and hopefully it would shed new light on the documentation of ancient paintings. This paper will discuss the way to improve image sharpness both from theory and practice perspective. In theory, the theoretical optimal aperture determination is discussed. In practice, a test chart is proposed to test the gradual image quality deterioration. From the photo of test chart, the clear part is determined and the percentage of clear part is used to determine the practical optimal aperture. A workflow integrating the above techniques is also proposed. The simulated acquiring experiment shows the method and the scanning hardware can achieve satisfactory results.

Keywords: Digital Acquisition of Cultural Heritage; Computer-aided Cultural Relics Protection; Cultural Heritage Research; Painting High Accuracy Photographing.

1 Introduction

It is of great significance to digitize ancient paintings and calligraphy, especially for a country with five thousand years of history and rich cultural heritages. It shows its advantages in at least three aspects.

First and foremost, for example, the carbon dioxide exhaled by the visitor has caused irreversible diseases to the Dunhuang Fresco such as color changing and fading. Thus, to protect it, the time that the physical Fresco is exposed to visitors must be greatly reduced. Hence, the virtual exhibition is introduced to satisfy the needs of visitors.

Second, for instance, the fresco may be at its original location while the painted sculpture is in Europe. The only way to show its original appearance (before the sculpture was stolen) is on the computer.

Last but not least, the digital replica of high fidelity and precision can be reprinted for commercial usage and earn profit for the preservation of heritage.

In 2003, Franco Bartolinia classified the equipments to acquire an ancient painting and calligraphy into three types: high resolution scanner scanning, film photographing and ensuing scanning and digital photographing (image mosaic is possible) [1]. Since current the resolution of digital photography is exceeding the film photography. Thus,

Z. Pan et al. (Eds.): Transactions on Edutainment VII, LNCS 7145, pp. 214–221, 2012.

currently, they can be classified into two categories: linear CCD based table scanner and photographing based scanner [2]. And their performance can be evaluated in six aspects: i.e., precision, scanning range [3], cost, flexibility, fidelity and maintenance [4]. The latter has great advantages over the former [4]. Among them, the fact that the latter can be erected to scan a fresco is probably the most evident and important advantage. Thus, a fresco scanner is designed in this way and the performance of photographing based scanner should be discussed and if possible, improved.

In 1991 (The research started in 1989.), Martinez [5] and Hamber [6] proposed a photographing based scanner in the VASARI(Visual Arts System for Archiving and Retrieval of Images) Project to digitize paintings. Later the scanner was improved [7] and built in the National Gallery in London, in the Doerner Intitute in Munich and in the Uffizi Gallery in Florence [8][9]. Apart from the Vasari scanner, there are others [10][11][12].

In addition to the hardware, the research focused on multispectral imaging [7][13][14], color accuracy [1][8][10], mosaicking [1][10][15] and geometry accuracy [2][4], but few has considered the clarity of the final digital replica.

Currently, only the minimum resolution is discussed. Sufficient resolution is needed to enable see cracks and brushstrokes. A study of crack sizes showed major cracks to be typically around 0.1mm wide. So the resolution should be 10-20 pixels per mm (254-508 PPI, Pixel Per Inch) of original [16]. Coincidentally, 12 pixels/mm (ca. 300 PPI) is a common document scanning resolution. But few have considered the blur introduced by lens. This is a question that should also be seriously considered. Because if a fresco is scanned at a resolution that is beyond the optical limit, the only consequence is computing and storage overhead and at the same time, no more detail is squeezed out.

In this paper, in addition to the determination of theoretical optimal aperture [4], a procedure to find out the practical optimal aperture and clear part of a photo is presented, which is included in the proposed scanning workflow.

2 Theoretical Optimal Aperture

The confusion of a photo comes from two aspects: depth of field and diffraction. Combining them together, the overall confusion under various apertures (*F* Numbers) is as follows [4]:

$$c_{worst} = \frac{f}{u-f}\left(\frac{f}{uF}|\Delta u| + 2.44\frac{\lambda}{f}Fu\right), \tag{1}$$

where f is the focal length, u the object distance, F the aperture, Δu the ruggedness of the paintings (say 5mm) and λ 0.66 micrometer because the wavelength of more than 90% of visible light is no larger than 0.66 micrometer (similarly hereinafter).

Equation (1) considers the worst case. On average, the overall confusion under various apertures should be:

$$c_{ave} = \frac{f}{u-f}\left(\frac{f}{uF}\frac{|\Delta u|}{2} + 2.44\frac{\lambda}{f}Fu\right). \tag{2}$$

Since recent lenses have no aperture rings, resulting in discrete F numbers such as 3.5, 4.0, 4.5, 5.0 etc, each selectable F number can be substituted into equation (1) or (2) and the theoretical optimal aperture is the F number which makes equation (1) or (2) smallest.

From the minimum value of equation (1) or (2), which makes the photo sharpest (at least in theory), a maximum optical resolution can be computed, as discussed in section 2.2. Also, when equation (1) or (2) has the minimum mathematical value, the F number is determined.

3 Image Processing Based Practical Analysis

3.1 Selection of Clear Part in a Photo

Our customers sometimes complain that some part of the scanned painting is rather blurred. Finally, the blame is put on the lens. As shown in Fig. 1, the image quality at the corner is much poorer than that at the center. If this blurred part participates in the stitching of the final digital replica, some part must be blurred. To eliminate this blurring problem, the blurred part of a photo must be identified and removed before stitching to guarantee the image quality of the final digital replica.

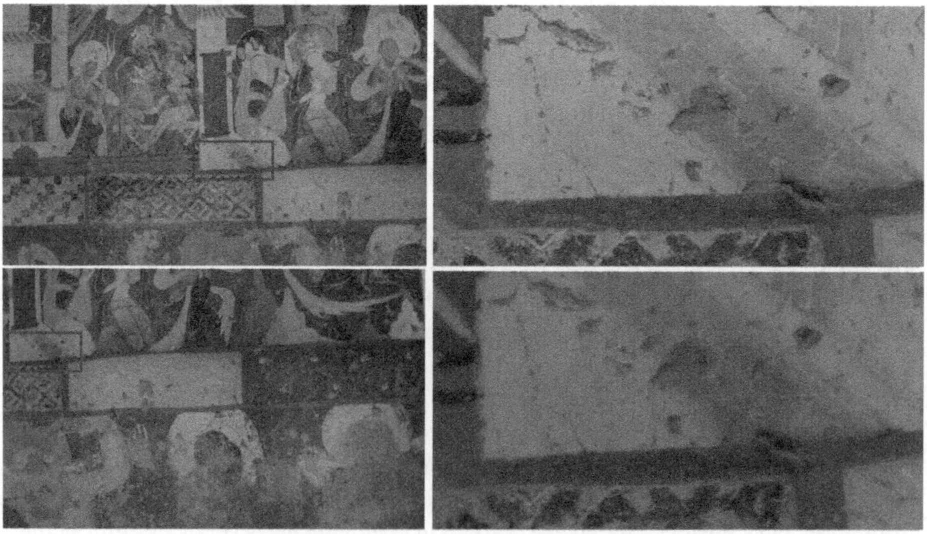

Fig. 1. An example of image quality deterioration from center to corner

Currently, there are two ways to determine the camera quality. One is using an ISO 12233 test chart and this method is employed to test cameras including lenses in the construction of Taibei Imperial Palace painting and calligraphy photographing system [17]. This test can give the accurate resolution both at the center and at the corner, but it cannot reflect the gradual resolution decrease from the center to the corner. Thus, this test cannot answer the question such as when the image quality is under tolerance. Another common camera quality evaluation technique is using MTF (Modulation Transfer Function). The lens manufacturers will give the MTF of their products. The MTF can depict the gradual deterioration from the center to the corner. But this is lens specific and image sensor irrespective. It is a common sense that if a low resolution camera body, say 6 Megapixes, is attached to a lens, the image resolution is almost the same at the center and at the corner (bounded by the relative low resolution of the camera body), while if a high resolution camera body, say 24 Megapixes, is attached to the same lens, the image resolution is dramatically different at the center and at the corner (bounded by the relative low resolution of the lens especially at the corner). But MTF cannot reflect this phenomenon.

So these two methods are almost complementary and a new method that can combine the advantage of both methods should be devised. By photographing the test chart as shown in Fig. 2, the gradual image resolution deterioration can be measured.

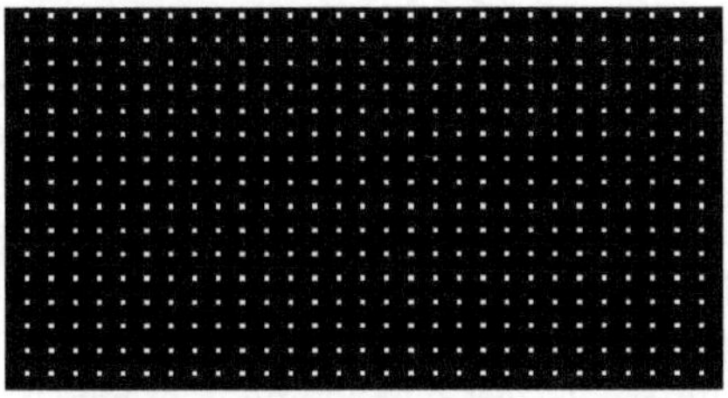

Fig. 2. The proposed test chart

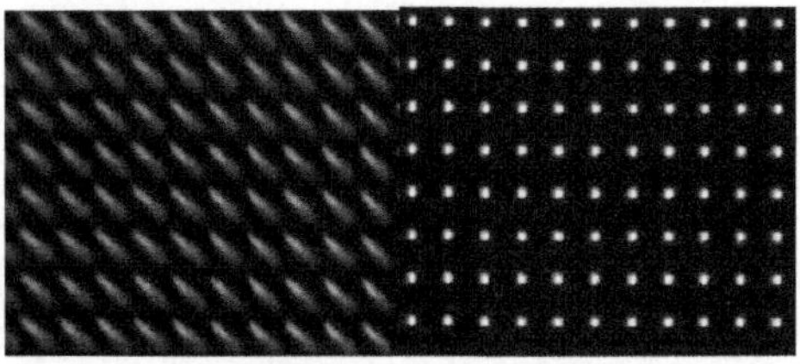

Fig. 3. Tested image quality of the test chart At the top left corner (left) and at the center (right)Using the same lens, camera body and settings of Fig. 2

Since astigmatism is circular symmetric. It means the astigmatism will change according to the distance to the center instead of the angle to the axis. As a result, the photo is divided into (100, for example) rings. For each ring, the test result is averaged.

As illustrated in Fig. 3, a really huge difference in image quality of the test chart is observed. No wonder the corner part is blurred. The astigmatism can be measured by a computer program as follows:

1) Binarize by thresholding
2) Find the foreground pixel groups (Simplified as FPG. All the pixels whose value is greater than the threshold value are merged into one group by connectivity.).
3) Divide the image by a series of (100, for example) concentric circles and compute the average astigmatism image of each ring as follows:
   a) Translate and rotate FPG. Each FPG can uniquely identify one coordinate system (2nd CS). The origin of the 2nd CS is the mass center of

FPG while the positive y axis is the vector from the image center to the mass center of FPG

b) Magnify each FPG (say 2x) to make it more clear

c) For FPGs on the same ring, register each FPG by mass center and x and y axis and average the RGB value of each pixel on the FPG

4) Output the result in a BMP file as illustrated in Fig 4.

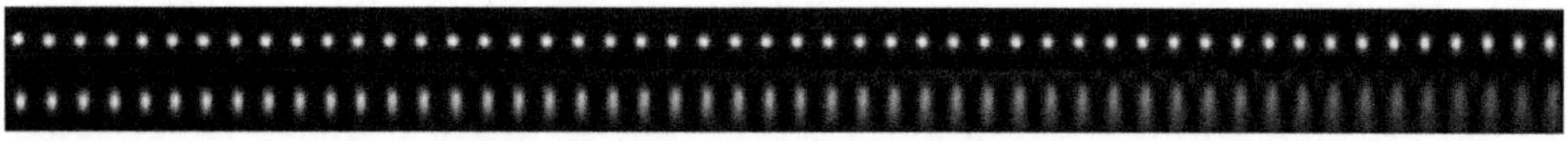

Fig. 4. Measured image quality deterioration of the test chart from the center to the corner. The first line is the dot expansion from 0% to 49% with the step of 1% in radius. The second line is from 50% to 99%. The horizontal is tangential direction while the vertical is radial direction.

From Fig. 4, for the tested lens, it is absolutely usable if radius is within 40%; it is often usable if radius is within 50%; it is sometimes usable if radius is within 67%; it is never usable if radius is larger than 67%.

3.2 Practical Optimal Aperture

In chapter 2, how to find the theoretical optimal aperture is discussed. But this not enough, suppose a certified lens and a defected lens, or a prime lens and a zooming lens with the same focal length. Practice tells us that certified and prime lens should produce sharper image than the defected and zooming one. But according to formula (1) and (2), the sharpness is the same. It means there is a gap between the theory and practice. However, by using the following method, it can be bridged.

First, compute the theoretical optimal aperture as in chapter 2. It can be used as guidance in finding the practical optimal aperture. The test chart is photographed at the vicinity of the theoretical optimal aperture and the result is compared with that of the theoretical optimal aperture. The aperture that makes more part in a photo clear is chosen for the subsequent scanning.

4 System Implementation

4.1 Workflow of Scanning

High precision should at least contain the following five essential parts and if any one is not achieved, a scanner cannot be entitled of high precision and is not suitable for ancient painting and calligraphy digitization. They are line straightness, resolution uniformity [4], luminance uniformity, angle preservation and high definition [2]. Thus, the workflow of scanning should be as follows:

1) Find the theoretical optimal aperture by minimizing formula (1) or (2).

2) According to the theoretical optimal aperture, the practical optimal aperture must be or in the vicinity of the theoretical optimal aperture. The aperture that makes more part (when compared with any other aperture) of the test chart clear is selected as the practical optimal aperture.

Fig. 5. A fresco scanner

Fig. 6. Acquired digital fresco in full (top) and magnified view

3) Calibrate lens distortion by camera calibration toolbox for Matlab [18].

4) Calibrate camera orientation [18][19]

5) Calibrate vignetting function $I_w(r)$ [1][2]

6) Photograph the fresco at the practical optimal aperture block by block to guarantee the last precision criterion, i.e. high definition.

7) Correct vignetting according to the parameters calibrated in step 5 to guarantee the third high precision criterion, i.e. luminance uniformity [2].

8) Cut the clear part identified in step 2 to guarantee the last high precision criterion, i.e. high definition.

9) Correct lens distortion according to the parameters calibrated in step 3 to guarantee the first two high precision criterion, i.e. line straightness and resolution uniformity [4].

10) Correct orientation according to the parameters calibrated in step 4 to guarantee the second and the fourth high precision criterion, i.e. resolution uniformity and angle preservation [2].

11) Stitch the corrected photos by registration and blending

[1] If all of the pertinent settings such as camera body, lens, aperture, camera orientation and object distance are not changed, then these 5 steps can be omitted and the reuse of the previous results is allowed.

4.2 The Hardware and Test Results

As shown in Fig. 5, the fresco scanner is composed of 3 axes. The first direction is moving left and right, parallel to the painting. The second direction is also parallel to the painting, but up and down. The last direction is moving perpendicular to the painting to adjust the resolution. This is because the prime lens has good image quality. But it can not optically change the resolution (Digital zooming is possible, but it is at the expense of deteriorating image sharpness.). So the only possible way to zoom is regulating the distance between the camera and the painting.

All the movements are driven by a computer. Thus after calibrating the motor, if we want to move the camera to a position, say (2300mm, 2400mm, 900mm), first the computer will change the coordinates into the numbers of pulses and then send them to PLC (Programmable Logic Controller), and finally the PLC will output the exact numbers of pulses and the camera will be moved to the desired position. After stop a few seconds for stabilization, a photo is taken and then the camera and lighting system are moved to the next position. In this way, the painting is photographed block by block automatically.

Fig. 6 shows the acquired digital fresco in Fig. 5. The simulated wall painting measures about 0.7 meter tall and 1.4 meters wide. The painting is scanned at 300 PPI, 24 bits color depth and the total resolution is 17075 × 8417, resulting in a TIFF file of 411MB. The detail and the cracks of the painting are successfully acquired.

5 Conclusions and Future Work

In this paper, a high precision fresco scanner is proposed. Also the image quality is improved from optical analysis and image analysis. The scanner is ready to be put into tests at Mogao Cave in Dunhuang and the simulation result shows it can output some important digital replicas of great precision and high fidelity.

The future works are two folds. One is to further research ways to improve image sharpness. The other is to test it in frescoes and find potential drawbacks and ways to improve its performance.

References

1. Bartolini, F., Cappellini, V., Del Mastio, A., Piva, A.: Applications of image processing technologies to fine arts Optical Metrology for Arts and Multimedia. In: Salimbeni, R. (ed.) Proceedings of the SPIE, vol. 5146, pp. 12–23 (2003)
2. Shi, X., Diao, C., Lu, D.: Photo Vignetting and Camera Orientation Correction for High Precision Acquisition. In: Proc. Pacific-Rim Conference on Multimedia, pp. 155–166 (2009)
3. Shi, X., Lu, D., Diao, C.: An Ultra Large Area Scanner for Ancient Painting and Calligraphy. In: Proc. Pacific-Rim Conference on Multimedia, pp. 846–849 (2008)
4. Shi, X., Lu, D., Diao, C.: Blurring and Lens Distortion Free Scanning for Large Area Painting and Calligraphy. Journal of Information and Computational Science, 2121–2128 (October 2009)

5. Martinez, K.: High Resolution Digital Imaging of Paintings: The Vasari Project. Microcomputers for Information Management 8(4), 277–283 (1991)
6. Hamber, A., Hemsley, J.: VASARI, A European Approach to Exploring the Use of Very High Quality Imaging Technology to Painting Conservation and Art History Education. In: Proceedings of an International Conference on Hypermedia & Interactivity In Museums, pp. 276–288 (1991)
7. Martinez, K.: High Quality Digital Imaging of Art in Europe. In: Very High Resolution and Quality Imaging 1996. Proceedings of SPIE, vol. 2663, pp. 69–75 (1996)
8. Martinez, K., Cupitt, J., Saunders, D., Pillay, R.: Ten Years of Art Imaging Research. Proceedings of the IEEE 90(1), 28–41 (2002)
9. Saunders, D., Cupitt, J., White, C., Holt, S.: The MARC II Camera and the Scanning Initiative at the National Gallery. The National Gallery Technical Bulletin 23(1), 76–82 (2002)
10. Fontana, R., Gambino, M.C., Greco, M., Marras, L., Pampaloni, E.M., Pelagotti, A., Pezzati, L., Poggi, P.: 2D imaging and 3D sensing data acquisition and mutual registration for painting conservation. In: Proc. SPIE 2005, vol. 5665, pp. 51–58 (2005)
11. MacDonald, L.W.: A Robotic System for Digital Photography, Digital Photography II. In: Sampat, N., DiCarlo, J.M., Martin, R.A. (eds.) Proceedings of the SPIE 2006, vol. 6069, pp. 160–171 (2006)
12. Voyatzis, G., Angelopoulos, G., Bors, A., Pitas, I.: A system for capturing high resolution images. In: Conference on Technology and Automatics, Thessaloniki, Greece, pp. 238–242, 2–3 (1998)
13. Carcagn, P., Della Patria, A., Fontana, R., Greco, M., Mastroianni, M., Materazzi, M., Pampaloni, E., Pezzati, L.: Multispectral imaging of paintings by optical scanning. Optics and Lasers in Engineering 45(3), 360–367 (2007)
14. Mikyake, Y., Yokoyama, Y., Tsumura, N., Haneishi, H., Miyata, K., Hayashi, J.: Development of multiband color imaging systems for recording of art paintings. In: Part of the IS&T/SPIE Conference on Color Imaning: Device-Indeoendent Color. Color Hardcopy, and Graphic Arts IV, San Jose, California (1999)
15. Cortelazzo, G.M., Lunchese, L.: A New Method of Image Mosaicking and Its application to cultural heritage representation. In: Eurographics 1999 (1999)
16. Martinez, K., Hamber, A.: Towards a colormetric digital image archive for the visual arts. In: Proceedings of the Society of Photo-Optical Instrumentation Engineers, vol. 1073 (1989)
17. The Summary of the Construction of Imperial Palace Painting and Calligraphy Photographing System, Part 2 - Camera Testing (including Lens), `http://tech2.npm.gov.tw/da/ch-htm/pdf%5Ctech%5Ctech-9.pdf`
18. Camera Calibration Toolbox for Matlab, `http://www.vision.caltech.edu/bouguetj/calib_doc/`
19. Shi, X., Diao, C., Lu, D.: An Efficient and Robust Camera Extrinsic Parameters Calibration Algorithm. Journal of Computational Information Systems 3(1), 285–293 (2007)

Multiwavelet Video Coding Based on DCT Time Domain Filtering

Zhijun Fang, Guihua Luo, Jucheng Yang, and Shouyuan Yang

Institute of Digital Media, School of Information Technology, Jiangxi University of Finance & Economics, Nanchang, Jiangxi, 330013
zjfang@gmail.com

Abstract. To improve the video encoding efficiency and deal with the real-time demerits of the multiwavelet time-domain filtering in the 3D multiwavelet, a multiwavelet video coding scheme based on DCT(Digital Cosine Transform) time-domain filtering is proposed in this paper. Firstly, the multiwavelet transformation is applied to get the spatial domain of the frame in video. Then, 3D transformation coefficients are obtained by the DCT time-domain filtering on the multiwavelet coefficients. Finally the 3D transformation coefficients are coded to be embed bitstream by using the symmetric 3-D SPIHT(Set partitioning in hierarchical trees). The experimental results indicate that the new method outperforms those based on 3D DMWT(discrete multiwavelet transform) in terms of PSNR(peak signal to noise ration) with better video quality at the same compression ratio, and it shows lower complexity.

Keywords: Multiwavelet, DCT, Time-domain Filtering, Video Coding.

1 Introduction

As the basic algorithm of the JPEG, DCT is one of the most mature compression techniques. To improve the quality of compression, at first, the original image is divided into 8×8 or 16×16 blocks and each block is manipulated by DCT. It has a good compressing performance on the middle and high compressing rate. But there exists a serious block effect at the low compressing rate. Wavelet transform solves the problem, and becomes one of the hot fields in the world in recent years. JPEG2000 [1]is a symbol of ripeness of wavelet. Multiwavelet transform [2][3] provides a new method for scalability video coding. It expands single scaling function into multi-scaling function and gains greater choice. It not only has the good characteristic of simultaneous localization in both time and frequency domains, but also overcomes the limitation of wavelet transform. Meanwhile□it gives a seamless combination with smoothness, symmetric, orthogonality and so on.

The traditional hybrid video coding architecture, as exhibited in the MPEG standards, involves a two stage approach: a video signal is firstly temporally decorrelated via block-based motion compensation, then it is spatially de-correlated by a 2D spatial transform. Although this approach is effective, it has several drawbacks:

Z. Pan et al. (Eds.): Transactions on Edutainment VII, LNCS 7145, pp. 222–229, 2012.

(1) The feedback loop creates drift, allowing noise in the reconstructed frames to propagate.

(2) A motion estimation based on block often causes blocking effect, and high complexity[4].

(3) This architecture requires a feedback loop in which the reconstructed frames from motion estimation are used as reference frames in the motion prediction of subsequent frames. So any damages of the dates affect all of the consecutive sequence of frames.

To solve the above problems, three-dimensional video image coding appears. In 1987, Karlsson used Haar wavelet for time-domain filtering [5], the results were ideal and had been widely used in video coding[6][7]. In the three-dimensional video image coding, there are mainly three-dimensional DCT[8], three-dimensional wavelet and lifting scheme [9], three-dimensional multi-wavelet video coding[10]. Although the three-dimensional DCT transform video coding is simple and easy to be implemented, in order to reduce the computational complexity, usually the preprocessing of the video image is need before the video image processing block. So the apparent blocking phenomenon will appear in the low rate case of the DCT block-based practice application. The three-dimensional wavelet video coding solves this problem, at the same time, the scaling functions and multiwavelets with high compression ratio of coefficient quantization on the wavelet provides greater flexibility than the single wavelet, it shows great attraction in the three-dimensional video image compression fields, and shows better performances than the other two compression methods [11]. However, the current multi-dimensional wavelet video image coding is mainly used in the case of low bit compression, and the real-time requirements can not be achieved. So the motivation of this paper is to propose a more sparse representation of the video encoding method more than the three-dimensional wavelet to improve the coding efficiency and to meet the demands for the real-time encoding.

According to the visual characteristics of the human eye, it can be known that the human eye has a visual inertia, that is, a particular video frame in the formation of the eyes, the scene changes or sudden disappearance of the video does not cause the loss of image information in the visual nerve center, in the same time, the human eyes has the characteristics of the nature of critical flicker frequency, that is, when the pulse repetition rate is high enough, the feeling of the flashes will disappear, it makes a continuous sense of movement and stability of the image. Thus, the human eyes require a higher spatial resolution on the part of the still image, while a lower temporal resolution requirements. At the low bit rates, because of the visual characteristics, it greatly reduces the impact of subjective quality in the time-domain DCT of one-dimensional compression. Based on the human visual system having a variety of features to cover for the blocking effect with the brightness and frequency activity, in the handling of DCT, we can take full advantage of the visual characteristics of the human eye to determine the application. Thus, although the DCT has poor effects in image processing, DCT has played a very important role in the video coding on time domain processing. According to the characteristics of the video space, combining the human vision features and the nature of a variety of transform, we propose a multi-wavelet video coding technology based on the DCT time-domain filtering, it combines fine properties of multi-wavelet and DCT. Based on the experimental results, the DCT domain filtering technology has the merits that not only the algorithm is simple, but also it has a better PSNR values and time efficiency comparing with the three-dimensional wavelet transform, Haar wavelet filtering techniques.

2 Multiwavelet Video Coding Based on DCT Time-Domain Filtering

Current frame and adjacent frames are highly correlated, one solution method is applying 2D DCT or DWT or DMWT to each frame, and by using motion estimation and compensation to remove temporal redundancies. Though this method achieves the higher compression ratio, it often causes blocking effect and has high complexity, and any damage of the data affects all of the consecutive sequence of frames because the quality of coded frames depends on the reference frames.

The second scheme is directly 3D transformed. A group of pictures consists of several successive frames is decomposed by 3D transformed. The redundancy is calculated from spatial-temporal domain to scaling spatial and transform domain. Compression is easier based on the corresponding weights of dates. Three video transformation methods have been proposed: 3D DCT, 3D DWT and 3D DMWT. Experiment results show that the 3D DMWT is the best solution way, in terms of both visual and PSNR. The transforming technology of 3D signal appears at the high compression ratios, and has poor real-time property.

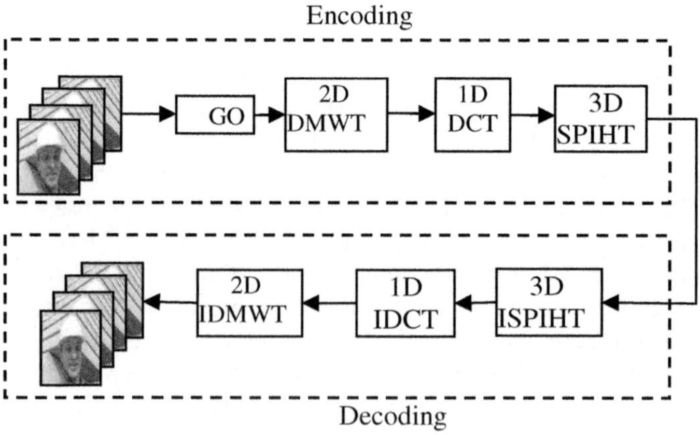

Fig. 1. Experimental framework of 2D DMWT+1D DCT based Video Compression

In certain situation, wavelet and multiwavelet are better than DCT in image compression because of zero-tree encoding arithmetic. Actually, zero-tree encoding arithmetic can also be applied to DCT, and brings better effects. And DCT is superiority to the wavelet and multiwavelet when it is used to one dimensional array with a little sample data. In the real-time case, data quantity of a GOP is generally 8 or 16. DCT is more convenient for time-domain transform. Based on the human vision property, the detailed views of moving object provide less sensitive to our eyes than still image. It will be difficult to feel the so-called block-effect even if the videos be bracketed into groups. For solving the problems mentioned, this paper puts forward the solving scheme that combines DMWT and DCT. Figure 1 illustrates the entire process.

Step 1: The original video is divided into a group of eight frames;
Step 2: DMWT is used to each of these frames individually;
Step 3: Adopting the DCT to time-domain transform;
Step 4: Being coded by 3D SPIH to transform domain data.

3 Multiwavelet Transform of Video Space-Domain

DMWT is used to each of these frames individually, after the original video is divided into a group of eight frames. GHM, Cl and SA4 are often used for compression, which are introduced briefly as below.

3.1 GHM

The filter coefficient {Hn, Gn} of Geronimo-Hardin-Massopust (GHM) multiwavelet are:

$$\begin{aligned}
H_0 &= \begin{bmatrix} 3/10 & 2\sqrt{2}/5 \\ -\sqrt{2}/40 & -3/20 \end{bmatrix} & G_0 &= \begin{bmatrix} -\sqrt{2}/40 & -3/20 \\ -1/20 & -3\sqrt{2}/20 \end{bmatrix} \\
H_1 &= \begin{bmatrix} 3/10 & 0 \\ 9\sqrt{2}/40 & 1/2 \end{bmatrix} & G_1 &= \begin{bmatrix} 9\sqrt{2}/40 & -1/2 \\ 9/20 & 0 \end{bmatrix} \\
H_2 &= \begin{bmatrix} 0 & 0 \\ 9\sqrt{2}/40 & -3/20 \end{bmatrix} & G_2 &= \begin{bmatrix} 9\sqrt{2}/40 & -3/20 \\ -9/20 & 3\sqrt{2}/20 \end{bmatrix} \\
H_3 &= \begin{bmatrix} 0 & 0 \\ -\sqrt{2}/40 & 0 \end{bmatrix} & G_3 &= \begin{bmatrix} -\sqrt{2}/40 & 0 \\ 1/20 & 0 \end{bmatrix}
\end{aligned} \tag{1}$$

3.2 CL

The filter coefficients {Hn, Gn} of the Chu-Lian (CL) multiwavelet are:

$$H_0 = \begin{bmatrix} \frac{1}{4} & \frac{1}{4} \\ -\frac{\sqrt{7}}{8} & \frac{1}{4} \end{bmatrix} \quad G_0 = \begin{bmatrix} -\frac{1}{4} & -\frac{1}{4} \\ \frac{1}{8} & \frac{1}{8} \end{bmatrix}$$

$$H_1 = \begin{bmatrix} \frac{1}{2} & 0 \\ 0 & \frac{1}{4} \end{bmatrix} \quad G_1 = \begin{bmatrix} \frac{1}{2} & 0 \\ 0 & \frac{\sqrt{7}}{4} \end{bmatrix} \tag{2}$$

$$H_2 = \begin{bmatrix} \frac{1}{4} & -\frac{1}{4} \\ -\frac{\sqrt{7}}{8} & -\frac{\sqrt{7}}{8} \end{bmatrix} \quad G_2 = \begin{bmatrix} -\frac{1}{4} & \frac{1}{4} \\ -\frac{1}{8} & \frac{1}{8} \end{bmatrix}$$

3.3 SA4

The filter coefficients {Hn, Gn} of Symmetric-Antisymmetric (SA4) multiwavelet are:

$$H_0 = \begin{bmatrix} \frac{1}{32+8\sqrt{15}} & \frac{1}{8} \\ \frac{1}{32+8\sqrt{15}} & -\frac{1}{8} \end{bmatrix} \Big/ \sqrt{2} \quad G_0 = \begin{bmatrix} -\frac{1}{8} & \frac{1}{32+8\sqrt{15}} \\ -\frac{1}{8} & -\frac{1}{8(4+\sqrt{15})} \end{bmatrix} \Big/ \sqrt{2}$$

$$H_1 = \begin{bmatrix} \frac{31+8\sqrt{15}}{8(4+\sqrt{15})} & \frac{1}{8} \\ -\frac{31+8\sqrt{15}}{8(4+\sqrt{15})} & \frac{1}{8} \end{bmatrix} \Big/ \sqrt{2} \quad G_1 = \begin{bmatrix} \frac{1}{8} & -\frac{31+8\sqrt{15}}{8(4+\sqrt{15})} \\ -\frac{1}{8} & -\frac{31+8\sqrt{15}}{8(4+\sqrt{15})} \end{bmatrix} \Big/ \sqrt{2}$$

$$H_2 = \begin{bmatrix} \frac{31+8\sqrt{15}}{8(4+\sqrt{15})} & -\frac{1}{8} \\ \frac{31+8\sqrt{15}}{8(4+\sqrt{15})} & \frac{1}{8} \end{bmatrix} \Big/ \sqrt{2} \quad G_2 = \begin{bmatrix} \frac{1}{8} & \frac{31+8\sqrt{15}}{8(4+\sqrt{15})} \\ \frac{1}{8} & -\frac{31+8\sqrt{15}}{8(4+\sqrt{15})} \end{bmatrix} \Big/ \sqrt{2} \tag{3}$$

$$H_3 = \begin{bmatrix} \frac{1}{32+8\sqrt{15}} & -\frac{1}{8} \\ -\frac{1}{8(4+\sqrt{15})} & -\frac{1}{8} \end{bmatrix} \Big/ \sqrt{2} \quad G_3 = \begin{bmatrix} -\frac{1}{8} & -\frac{1}{8(4+\sqrt{15})} \\ \frac{1}{8} & -\frac{1}{8(4+\sqrt{15})} \end{bmatrix} \Big/ \sqrt{2}$$

4 DCT of Video Time-Domain

For eliminating redundant of time-domain, DCT is used to one-dimensional transforming of video time-domain. The formulas of the forward and inverse DCT of one-dimensional signal $f(x), x = 0,1,2\cdots n-1$ are:

$$F(u) = \frac{c(u)}{4}\sum_{x=0}^{n-1} f(x)\cos\left[\frac{\pi(2x+1)u}{2n}\right], u = 0,1,2,\cdots,n-1$$
$$f(x) = \sum_{x=0}^{n-1} c(u)F(u)\cos\left[\frac{\pi(2x+1)u}{2n}\right], x = 0,1,2,\cdots,n-1 \quad (4)$$

5 Experimental Analysis

To make sure that the performance evaluation is valid across a wide spectrum of different video types, 32 video frames are extracted from each of nine different QCIF-sized (144×176 pixels) color video sequences in 4:2:0 YUV format: “foreman”, “hall”, “Claire”, “highway”, “carphone”, “coastguard”, “grandma”, “news” and “silent”. These video sequences, with different contents and motions, represent a wide spectrum of possible video sources. The performance comparison is done by using a symmetric three-dimensional SPIHT as the encoder. Low bitrates are tested of the initial experiments: 0.4bit-per-pixel, in order to examine how high levels of quantization affect the performance of new compression.

Given the color video sequences listed above, each frame within a sequence is decomposed into its Y, U, and V color components initially. Thirty-two frames of data from Y color component are grouped together into a 3-D data block and then decomposed using multiwavelet decomposition (3D SA3, 3D GHM and 3D CL) to level 3. Multiwavelet space-domain is decomposed to level 3 and then Haar time-domain is decomposed to level 5 (2D CL +1D Haar, 2D SA4 +1D Haar) , and Multiwavelet space-domain is decomposed to level 3 and then DCT time-domain transform (2D CL +1D DCT, 2D SA4 +1D DCT). Figure 2 illustrates the entire process. The 3D transformation coefficients are coded to an embedded bitstreams using the 3D DPIHT at the 0.4bit-per-pixel.

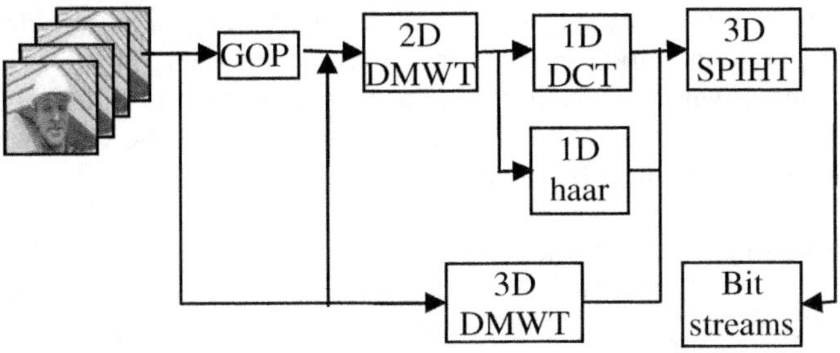

Fig. 2. Experimental framework of the Video Compression

Experimental results as shown in Table 1 and Table 2 show the average PSNR of each kind of method with 3D SPIHT in groups (the original video was divided into a group of eight frames). The results show that 2D SA4+1D DCT has the best PSNR. The experimental results show that the proposed algorithm is effective, and it reduces the algorithm's complexity and increase the accuracy.

Table 1. Average PSNR of different Method with 3D SPIHT

Video	*3D Cl*	*3D GHM*	*3D SA4*	*2D CL+1D Haar*	*2D SA4+1D Haar*	*2D CL +1D DCT*	*2D SA4+1D DCT*
Foreman	23.83	22.573	24.519	25.136	25.488	25.745	26.096
Hall	28.878	23.019	28.887	29.838	30.149	30.272	30.557
Claire	32.798	27.203	32.513	34.656	34.69	35.117	35.104
Highway	30.466	26.836	31.397	31.721	31.809	32.064	32.355
Carphone	27.308	23.499	27.538	28	28.033	28.276	28.380
Coastguard	25.725	23.512	25.988	26.422	26.539	26.923	27.036
Grandma	32.355	27.729	32.931	33.898	34.172	34.237	34.502
News	27.33	22.814	27.616	28.459	28.778	28.78	29.160
Silent	28.178	24.029	29.301	29.422	30.11	29.956	30.419

Table 2. Average PSNR of different Method with 3D SPIHT in Groups

video	*3D Cl*	*3D SA4*	*2D CL+1D Hhaar*	*2D SA4+ 1D Haar*	*2D CL + 1D DCT*	*2D SA4+ 1D DCT*
foreman	22.969	23.435	24.074	24.378	24.23	24.588
hall	23.619	23.767	24.713	24.873	24.744	24.907
claire	27.736	28.488	28.626	29.952	28.676	30
highway	28.975	28.932	29.497	30.096	29.506	30.113

6 Conclusion

This paper tends to applying multiwavelet transform in video frame in spatial domain and then the transform domain data are obtained by DCT time-domain filtering. The 3D transformation coefficients are coded to the embed bitstream using the symmetric 3-D DPIHT. The low frequency epitomizes approximate message after multiwavelet transform, and high-frequency epitomizes detail of image. The high-frequency epitomizes dynamic information after the one-domination time-domain wavelet transform. It plays an important role in the video decoder, but it is easy to lose in encoder and unrecoverable. So, in this paper, time-domain is transformed by DCT in order to reduce the algorithm's complexity and increase the accuracy. The results show that the proposed algorithm is effective.

Acknowledgments. This work is supported by the National Natural Science Foundation of China (60862002,10701040,61063035), and it is also supported by the Science & Technology Project of Education Bureau of Jiangxi Province, China (GJJ11414).

References

1. Taubman, D.S., Marcellin, M.W., Rabbani, M.: JPEG2000: Image compression fundamentals, standards and practice. Journal of Electronic Imaging (2002)
2. Geronimo, J.S., Hardin, D.P., Massopust, P.R.: Fractal functions and wavelet expansions based on several scaling functions. J. Approx. Theory 78(3), 373–401 (1994)
3. Strela, V.: Multiwavelets: Theory and applications, Ph.D. dissertation, Mass. Inst. Technol., Cambridge (1996)
4. Chuang, H.Y.H., Birch, D.P., Liu, L.C., et al.: A High Speed Shift-Invariant Wavelet Transform Chip for Video Compression. In: Proceedings of IEEE Computer Society Annual Symposium on VLSI, pp. 125–131 (2002)
5. Karlsson, G., Vetterli, M.: Subband coding of video signals for packet switched networks. In: Procedings of SPIE Conference on Visual Communications and Image Processing, vol. 845, pp. 446–456 (1987)
6. Schaefer, R., Schwarz, H., Marpe, D., Schierl, T., Wiegand, T.: MCTF and scalability extension of H.264/AVC and its application to video transmission, storage, and surveillance. In: Visual Communications and Image Processing, vol. 5960 (2005)
7. Zhao, G.L., Yu, H.P., Yang, Y.: An adaptive GOP structure selection for haar-like MCTF encoding based on mutual information. Multimedia Tools and Applications 43(1), 25–43 (2009)
8. Chan, K.W., Lee, M.C.: 3D-DCT quantization as a compression technique for video sequences. In: 1997 International Conference on Virtual Systems and Multimedia, p. 188 (1997)
9. Otoniel, L., Miguel, M.R., Pablo, P., et al.: Low bit-rate video coding with 3D lower trees. Computer Science 6077, 256–263 (2010)
10. Sankaralingam, E., Thangaraj, V., Vijayamani, S., et al.: Video compression using multiwavelet and multistage vector quantization. The International Arab Journal of Information Technology 6(4), 385–393 (2009)
11. Chien, J.C.: Low bit-rate color video compression using multiwavelets in three dimensions. [doctoral dissertation]: University of Pittsburgh (2005)

Rendering Realistic Ocean Scenes on GPU

Xingquan Cai*, Baoxin Qian, Haiyan Sun, and Jinhong Li

College of Information Engineering, North China University of Technology,
100144 Beijing, China
xingquancai@126.com

Abstract. In this paper, we present an efficient simulation method for realistic ocean scenes on GPU. Firstly, we generate the planar grid of ocean surface, and divide ocean surface to static area and dynamic area. Then we generate the height field using improved noise, and add the height field to dynamic ocean surface grid. To make the surface animate, we have two transform matrices, translation matrix and rotation matrix. After that, we implement the Snell's law to render light-water interaction effects. Finally, we implement our method on GPU, and we simulate the complex ocean scene. The experiments prove that our method is feasible and high performance. Our method could be used in 3D games, computer generated films, and virtual battlefield environment based ocean scenes.

Keywords: Ocean scenes, Dynamic area, Light-water interaction, Fresnel effect.

1 Introduction

Real-time modeling and rendering of realistic natural sceneries has been one of the most difficult tasks in Compute Graphics, such as the simulation of terrain, trees, flows, cloud, smoke, fog, fire, etc. These natural sceneries effects are routinely created in today's video games. Rendering realistic ocean scenes is one of the hot topics of the simulation of realistic natural sceneries.

Compared with other natural phenomena, the simulation of ocean scenes is more complex. The region of ocean is so large, and the shapes of ocean waves are so irregular and random. The mechanism of ocean wave movement is so complex, and its generation is determined by so many kinds of forces. Therefore, it's difficult to represent the ocean surfaces using the traditional method.

In this paper, we present an efficient simulation method on GPU for realistic ocean scenes. Firstly, we generate the planar grid of ocean surface, and divide our ocean surface to static area and dynamic area. Then we generate the height field using improved noise, and add the height field to dynamic ocean surface grid. To make the

* Supported by National Natural Science Foundation of China(No. 51075423), PHR(IHLB) Grant (PHR20100509, PHR201008202), Funding Project of Beijing Outstanding Academic Human Resource Program (No. 20081D0500200114), and Funding Project of Beijing Municipal Education Committee (No. KM201010009002).

Z. Pan et al. (Eds.): Transactions on Edutainment VII, LNCS 7145, pp. 230–238, 2012.

surface move, we have two transform matrices, translation matrix and rotation matrix. After that, we implement the Snell's law to render light-water interaction effects. Finally, we implement our method on GPU, and we simulate the complex ocean scene. The experiments prove that our method is feasible and high performance. Our method could be used in 3D games, computer animations, computer generated films, virtual battlefield environment based ocean scenes, etc.

In this paper, after exploring the related work of ocean scenes rendering, we present our rendering realistic ocean scenes method on GPU. Finally, we provide the results using our method and draw the conclusion.

2 Related Work

Just as Iglesias [1] shows, modeling and rendering realistic ocean scenes has been investigated by many researchers in the past few years. In this paper, we mainly focus on the ocean surface models dealing with ocean scenes far from the shore, where breaking waves do not appear. We also focus on the light-water interactions and complex phenomena.

Up to now, many models have been proposed, which can be classified into three types, including empirical model, physical model, and spectrum model.

Usually, empirical model explicitly described ocean wave appearance using parametric functions. Simon [2] adopted the linear combination of sine function and quadratic function to simulate the geometrical shape of ocean waves. Foster [3] used a special parametric surface to simulate the ocean waves with curly wave crest. The empirical model methods are simple and intuitionistic, but the generated scenes are less realistic.

Physical model methods usually presented ocean wave motion based on fluid dynamics. Chen [4] adopted the two dimensional Navier-Stokes equation set. Jason [5] used the FFT (Fast Fourier Transformation) method to simulate the ocean surface. Foster [6] proposed a modified semi-Lagrangian method to simulate viscous liquids around objects. But due to the huge amount of calculation of these methods, it is impossible to generate dynamic ocean waves in real time.

Spectrum model methods can simulate some special cases of ocean wave. Among them, Yang [7] modeled ocean waves based on their spectrums and Yan [8] adopted Stokes and Airy model to simulate the motion of ocean waves near real time. Hu [9], Darles [10] and Chiu [11] also used the spectrum model methods to simulate the ocean surface. Wang [12] provided the simulation method of ocean wave based on cellular automata. This type of approaches generally relies on complex mathematical models and the amount of calculation is also large. Similar to the physical model methods, they are more suitable to simulate the motion of ocean waves in animation rather than real-time generation.

In addition to models describing the surface geometry of oceans, a suitable model to present the interaction between water and light is needed to show the surface a realistic appearance. However, the interaction between water and light is so complex, especially the Fresnel effect.

Other Complex ocean phenomena, such as foam, spray or splashes are usually modeled and rendered using particle systems [13]. Thürey et al [14] presented the animation of drops and small scale interactions, such as ripples or splashes.

Unfortunately, there is no efficient method for the simulation of realistic ocean scenes. So we present one method with an efficient surface model and physically based complex Light-water interactions.

3 Rendering Realistic Ocean Scenes on GPU

When we render the ocean scenes, the most important is that we really need to know the shape of the ocean surface, the boundary between the water body and the surrounding air. This surface can often be simplified further to a height field (f_{HF}). A height field is a function of two variables that return the height for a given point in two-dimensional space. Equation (1) shows how a height field can be used to displace a plane in three-dimensional space. $p_{plane}(x,y)$ is the coordinate of the point on the plane, and N_{plane} is the normal vector of the plane.

$$p_{heightfield}(x,y) = p_{plane}(x,y) + f_{HF}(x,y) \cdot N_{plane} \quad . \tag{1}$$

So in this way, we can divide the ocean surface rendering task into four steps: 1) Initialize the planar grid of ocean surface, 2) Generate the height field using noise; 3) Add the height field to ocean surface grid; 4) Render and shade the resulting geometry of ocean surface. Step 1) and 2) are implementing on CPU, and Step 3) and 4) are running on GPU. The following subsections describe our algorithm in detail.

3.1 Generating Ocean Surface Grid

In order to quicken the rendering speed of our method, we initialize and divide our ocean surface to static area and dynamic area. Just as Fig.1a shows, the gray area is the dynamic area. Usually, we never pay close attention to most far-away distance area. So the static area is very simple, and we just select the planar texture mapping. As to the dynamic area, we divide it into several patches. These small patches are full of regular squares, and one square is divided into two regular triangles. Then we will add the height field to these regular squares.

3.2 Generating Height Field

Perlin noise [15] was designed to have some properties, including apparent randomness, reproducible, smooth transition between values. In this paper, we select improved 2D Perlin Noise to generate the height field. To get the height field, we have six steps.

Step 1: Initialize one gradient field. In our gradient field, we have $n \times n$ control points, $C(x,y)$. Every control point has one gradient, $G(x,y)$. $G(x,y)$ is a vector and its direction and magnitude are random value.

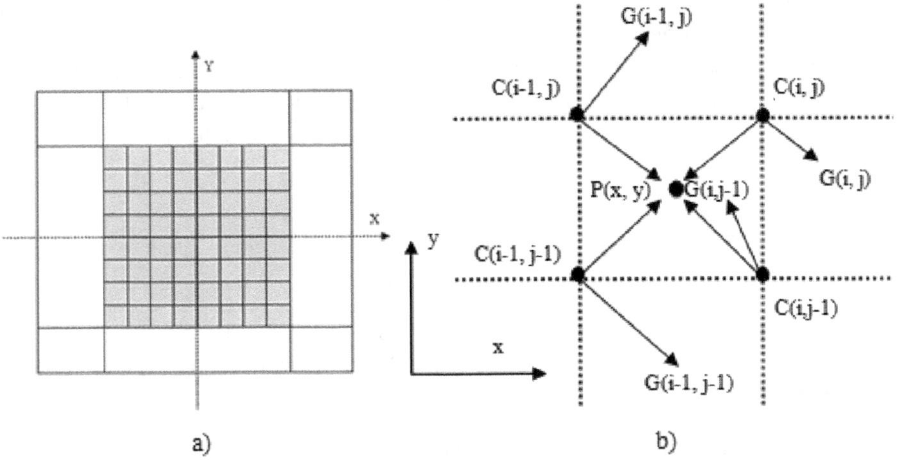

Fig. 1. Dividing into static area and dynamic area, and initializing gradient field

Step 2: Compute the contribution value of every control point. We need to compute the noise function, $Noise(x,y)$. The input parameters of $Noise(x,y)$ is the coordinate of input point, $P(x,y)$. Just as Fig. 1b shows, the point $P(x,y)$ is in the area of four control points, $C(i-1,j-1)$, $C(i,j-1)$, $C(i-1,j)$ and $C(i,j)$ (i and j is in the range 1,2,…,n). We need to compute four values, v_1, v_2, v_3 and v_4, as Equation (2) shows.

$$\begin{cases} v_1 = (I(x,y) - C(i-1,j-1)) \cdot G(i-1,j-1) \\ v_2 = (I(x,y) - C(i,j-1)) \cdot G(i,j-1) \\ v_3 = (I(x,y) - C(i-1,j)) \cdot G(i-1,j) \\ v_4 = (I(x,y) - C(i,j)) \cdot G(i,j) \end{cases} . \tag{2}$$

$$\begin{cases} u = x - (i-1) \\ v = y - (j-1) \end{cases} . \tag{3}$$

$$\begin{cases} f_1 = v_1 - (6u^5 - 15u^4 + 10u^3) \cdot (v_1 - v_2) \\ f_2 = v_3 - (6u^5 - 15u^4 + 10u^3) \cdot (v_3 - v_4) \end{cases} . \tag{4}$$

$$Noise(x,y) = f_1 - (6v^5 - 15v^4 + 10v^3) \cdot (f_1 - f_2) \ . \tag{5}$$

Step 3: Compute the interpolation value of the contribution value. Ken Perlin used the Hermite cubic blending function $3t^3 - 2t^2$ to compute the interpolation value of contribution value. Because Hermite cubic blending method easily causes artifacts to show up when Noise is used in bump mapping, so we select the fifth-degree interpolator, $6t^5 - 15t^4 + 10t^3$, to compute the interpolation value of contribution value. Just as Equation (4) shows, we compute the interpolation value of X direction. Then we make an interpolation of Y direction using Equation (5). In this way, we get the function of noise, $Noise(x, y)$.

Step 4: Create some new noise function. By changing the amplitude and frequency of the noise function, we get a lot of new noise function. Equation (6) shows the amplitude ($ampl$), frequency ($freq$) and persistence ($pers$). Equation (7) gives the new noise.

$$\begin{cases} freq = 2^i \\ ampl = pers^i \end{cases} . \tag{6}$$

$$Noise_i(x, y) = Noise(x \cdot freq, y \cdot freq) \cdot ampl . \tag{7}$$

Step 5: Compound all the noise. We add all the noise function together. Just as Equation (8) shows, we get the smooth noise.

$$OurNoise(x, y) = \sum_{i=1}^{N} Noise_i(x, y) . \tag{8}$$

Step 6: Get the height field of ocean surface according to the compound noise.

3.3 Adding Height Field to Ocean Surface

Since we have gotten the height field, we can use Equation (1) to render the ocean surface. But the surface is static. We should make the ocean surface animate.

$$T_t = \begin{bmatrix} 1 & 0 & 0 \\ 0 & 1 & 0 \\ i \times \Delta x & i \times \Delta y & 1 \end{bmatrix} . \tag{9}$$

To make the surface animate, we need to transform the point of the surface. We have two transform matrices, translation matrix and rotation matrix. Equation (9) is the translation matrix, and Equation (10) is the rotation matrix. The translation matrix and rotation matrix are dependence on the time t_i (i is in the range 0, 1, 2, …, n, …). In Equation (9) Δx and Δy are the increment along the X direction and Y direction. And in Equation (10), $\Delta \alpha$ is the increment of degree and (x_r, y_r) is the rotation center.

We use the translation matrix and rotation matrix to compute the coordinate of animation point. Equation (12) is the compound matrix. In this compound matrix, we get the animation point. Then we use Equation (13) to get the height of the point $p(x, y)$. The height is $H(x, y)$.

$$\theta = \alpha + i \times \Delta \alpha . \tag{10}$$

$$T_r = \begin{bmatrix} \cos(\theta) & \sin(\theta) & 0 \\ -\sin(\theta) & \cos(\theta) & 0 \\ (1-\cos(\theta)) \times x_r + y_r \times \sin(\theta) & (1-\cos(\theta)) \times y_r - x_r \times \sin(\theta) & 1 \end{bmatrix} . \tag{11}$$

$$T_{animation} = I(x, y) \times T_t \times T_r \quad . \tag{12}$$

$$H(x, y) = OurNoise(x_{animation}, y_{animation}) \quad . \tag{13}$$

3.4 Rendering Light-water Interaction Effects

To render the ocean surface in a convincing manner, it is important to understand how light behaves when we look at ocean water in reality. Water is rather transparent, but it has a different index-of-refraction (IOR) than air which causes the photons that pass the boundaries between the mediums to get either reflected or transmitted. The angle of incoming light is θ_i, and the angel of transmitted and refraction light is θ_t. We can obtain the angles θ_i and θ_t from Snell's law (assuming $\theta_i = \theta_1, \theta_t = \theta_2$).

$$OurNoise(x, y) = \sum_{i=1}^{N} Noise_i(x, y) \quad . \tag{14}$$

$$Color_{Water} = F \cdot Color_{reflect} + (1 - F) \cdot Color_{refract} \quad . \tag{15}$$

$$\begin{cases} \theta = \alpha_r \\ k = \cos\theta = V_{reflect} \cdot V_{normal} \\ m = \dfrac{n_1}{n_2} + k^2 - 1 \\ F = \dfrac{(m-k)^2}{2(m+k)^2}\left(1 + \dfrac{(k(m+k)-1)^2}{(k(m-k)+1)^2}\right) \end{cases} \quad . \tag{16}$$

We use Equation (15) to compute the color of ocean water. $Color_{reflect}$ is the color of reflected texture, and $Color_{refract}$ is the color of refracted texture. Equation (16) gives the Fresnel Reflection Coefficient. Because n_1 and n_2 are the refractive indices of the two media, the Fresnel Reflection Coefficient only is related to $\cos\theta$. And $\cos\theta$ is connected with the Normal Vector of the point. Due to the changing Normal Vector, the color of ocean water is changing. In this way, we can render the light-water interaction effects.

4 Results

We have implemented our method to simulate the ocean scenes. Our implementations are running on a Intel Core2 Duo 3.0GHz computer with 2GB RAM, and NVIDIA GeForce8400 SE graphics card with 256M RAM, under Windows 7 system, Visual C++ 8.0, DirectX9.0c SDK and HLSL environment. The rendering system has a real viewport size of 1024×768.

4.1 Comparison with CPU Method

We first propose an experiment on a big planar grid. Our dynamic area size is 2049×2049 and the patch size is 16×16. In order to test and verify our method, we implement one system on GPU based our method and one system on CPU based our method. We divide the patch into a lot of small grid which size is 64×64, 64×128, 64×128, 128×128, 128×256, 256×256, 256×512, 512×512. In order to ensure the objectivity of the experiment data, we sample continuous 2000 frames, note all the FPS (Frame Per Second) and compute the average FPS. We use the Liquid Crystal Display and the highest FPS of our Display is 60 fps.

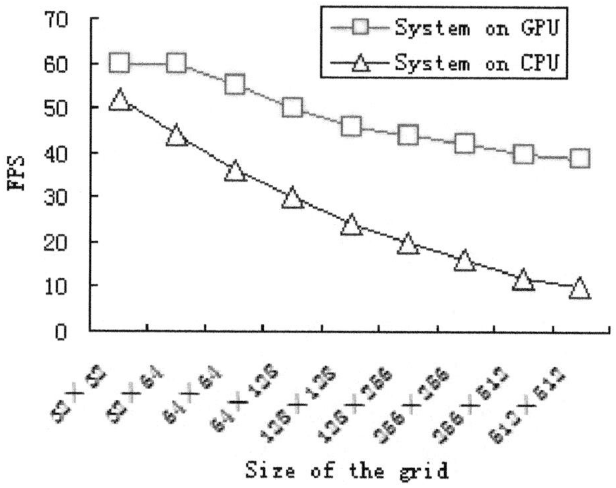

Fig. 2. Comparison GPU system with CPU system

Just as Fig.2 shows, in our experiment, when the size of the small grid is 256×256, the FPS of ocean system on GPU is above 40 fps. But at the similar condition, the FPS of ocean system on CPU is below 18 fps. When the size of the small grid is 512×512, the FPS of ocean system on GPU is above 30 fps, but the FPS of ocean system on CPU is below 10 fps. All these prove that the ocean system on GPU is higher performance than the ocean system on CPU.

4.2 Rendering Complex Ocean Scene

We also implement ocean system on GPU to simulate complex ocean scene, such as calm smoothing ocean, billowy ocean, etc. In order to increase the sense of reality, we simulate the ocean scene with sunset, clouds, sunshine, etc. Fig.3a presents the billowy ocean scene with clouds. We also add some objects like warships and lifeboats to the ocean scene. Fig.3b shows one lifeboat and two warships with shadows on the ocean surface under sunny day. Our system is running smoothly above 25 fps.

a) b)

Fig. 3. Billowy ocean scene with clouds and calm ocean scene with lifeboat and warships

5 Conclusion and Future Work

In this paper, we present an efficient simulation method for realistic ocean scenes on GPU. Firstly, we generate the planar grid of ocean surface, and divide our ocean surface to static area and dynamic area. We select the planar texture mapping to render the static area and add the height field to dynamic area. Then we generate the height field using improved noise, and add the height field to dynamic ocean surface grid. To make the surface animate, we have two transform matrices, translation matrix and rotation matrix. After that, we implement the Snell's law to render light-water interaction effects. Finally, we implement our method on GPU, and we simulate the complex ocean scene, such as calm smoothing ocean, billowy ocean. We also add warships and lifeboats to the ocean scene. The experiments prove that our method is feasible and high performance. Our method could be used in 3D games, computer animations, computer generated films, virtual battlefield environment based ocean scenes, etc. And our method has also been used in the practical projects.

As a future possibility, we are working on adding other effects to our ocean scene and using our method to implement other complex natural phenomenon.

References

1. Iglesias, A.: Computer graphics for water modeling and rendering: a survey. Future Generation Computer Systems 20(8) (2004)
2. Simon, P., Michael, A.: Rendering natural waters. In: Proceedings of Pacific Graphics 2000, pp. 23–30 (2000)
3. Foster, N., Metaxas, D.: Realistic animation of liquids. Graphical Models and Image Processing 58(5), 471–483 (1996)
4. Chen, J.: Toward interactive-rate simulation of fluids with moving obstacles using Navies-Stokes equations. Graphical Models and Image Processing 57(2), 107–116 (1995)
5. Jason, L.M.: Real-Time Synthesis and Rendering of Ocean Water, ATI Research Technical Report (2005)
6. Foster, N.: Practical animation of liquids. In: Proceedings of SIGGRAPH, pp. 15–22 (2001)

7. Yang, H., Hu, S., Sun, J.: A new algorithm for water wave animation. Journal of Computer 25(6), 613–617 (2002) (in Chinese)
8. Yan, L., Li, S.: Real-time Generation of Ocean Wave Surface. Journal of Computer Aided Design and Computer Graphics 38(5), 568–573 (2001) (in Chinese)
9. Hu, Y., Velho, L.: Realistic, real-time rendering of ocean waves. Computer Animation and Virtual Worlds 17(1), 59–67 (2006)
10. Darles, E., Crespin, B., et al.: Accelerating and enhancing rendering of realistic ocean scenes. In: Proceedings of WSCG 2007, pp. 287–294 (2007)
11. Chiu, Y., Chang, C.: GPU-based Ocean Rendering. In: Proceedings of IEEE International Conference on Multimedia and Expo., pp. 2125–2128 (2006)
12. Wang, C., Wang, Z., et al.: Real-time simulation of ocean wave based on cellular automata. In: Proceedings of CAD/CG 2003, pp. 26–32 (2003)
13. Takahashi, T., Fujji, H., et al.: Realistic animation of fluid with splash and foam. Computer Graphics Forum 22(3), 391–400 (2003)
14. Thürey, N., Rüde, U., et al.: Animation of open water phenomena with coupled shallow water and free surface simulations. In: Proceedings of Eurographics Symposium on Computer Animation 2006, pp. 157–164 (2006)
15. Perlin, K.: Implementing Improved Perlin Noise. In: GPU Gems: Programming Techniques, Tips, and Tricks for Real-Time Graphics, 2004, pp. 73–85 (2004)
16. Li, Y., Cheng, T.: Simulation Method for Lake Surface Wave. Journal of System Simulation 21(23), 7507–7510 (2009)

Effect of Body Image Presentation Format to Female Physical Attractiveness

Lili Zhai[1], Xiaoming Qian[1], Rui Wang[1], Jintu Fan[2], and Heyue Wei[1]

[1] School of Textile, Tianjin Polytechnic University, Tianjin, 300160, China
[2] Institute of Textile and Clothing, Hong Kong Polytechnic University, Hung Hom, Hong Kong
qianxiaoming@tjpu.edu.cn

Abstract. In the past studies, female body images in different formats (line drawings, 2D photographs and 3D wire-framed movie clips) have been used as visual stimuli. How the presentation of the body images influence the perception of physical attractiveness is not clear. In this investigation, we compared the use of 2D wire-framed images and 3D wire-framed animations as stimuli for the judgment of female physical attractiveness and estimation of body weight and waist-to-hip ratio (WHR). It was found that 3D wire-framed animations are advantageous in differentiating the attractiveness of female images and providing a more accurate estimation of body weight and WHR. Furthermore, it showed that female images displayed on the computer screen smaller than life size are perceived more attractive than images projected on the wall in life size scale.

Keywords: image format, projected scale, Physical attractiveness, Waist-to-hip ratio, Body mass index, Volume height index.

1 Introduction

In the past decades, female physical attractiveness has gained considerable attention and much work has been directed to investigate the cues to the physical attractiveness. In 1990s, a lot of researchers [1,2,3] used line drawings of female bodies as visual stimuli and showed that, waist-to-hip ratio (WHR) was an important cue to female physical attractiveness with an optimal WHR for attractiveness being 0.7 and the effect of breast size on the female attractiveness was dependent on the overall body fat and WHR.

Female physical attractiveness was further investigated by Tovee and his colleagues using 2D photographs in front and side views of real women as stimuli [4]. They showed that, body mass index (BMI) is a far more important factor than WHR in determining the attractiveness of the female body. They suggested that, Singh's experiments were problematic as the changes of WHR in the line drawings by altering the torso width around the waist not only altered the WHR, but also the apparent BMI [5]. As the value of the WHR rises, so does that of the apparent BMI, and so it cannot be sure from Singh's experiments whether changes in attractiveness rating were made on the basis of WHR or BMI, or both.

Z. Pan et al. (Eds.): Transactions on Edutainment VII, LNCS 7145, pp. 239–247, 2012.

Fan et al [6] used a $[TC]^2$ body scanner to obtain 3D body measurements, which were then used to create short movie clips by Maya software for viewing and rating the attractiveness. The female images in the movie clips were in wire-frame display format, so the effect of skin appearance was eliminated. From their investigations, Fan showed that volume height index (VHI) is a more direct and important determinant of female body attractiveness than BMI and WHR. Smith [7] used 3D color video clips of female subjects standing on a rotating turntable as stimuli, which may show more visual cues to attractiveness, but the effect of skin color and texture cannot be differentiated in the study.

In the past investigations, different types of body images in different scales were used as visual stimuli and different findings were obtained. How the presentation of the body images influence the perception of physical attractiveness is not clear. In order to elucidate the effects of the types and scales of body images on the perception of body attractiveness, in this investigation, we asked eighty participants to rate the attractiveness of 50 female images which had different formats (2D wire-framed images and 3D wire-framed animations) and projected in different scales (on the computer screen and stimulus' real height: projected height=1:1) and forty of those participants to estimate the weight and WHR of each figure knowing the stimulus' height on the computer screen. And then, we compared the attractiveness ratings in different image format and scale and the estimated weights and WHR of females presented using different format.

2 Methods

2.1 Participants

Eighty participants with a mean age of 22.86 years were asked to view and rate the attractiveness of different types of body images in different scales. Additionally, forty of those participants consisting of 20 males and 20 females with a mean age of 22.31 were asked to view the body images and estimate the weight and WHR of the stimulus given the body height.

2.2 Materials

Fifty Chinese females were scanned using a Lectra body scanner to obtain 3D body measurements, which were then used to create 3D wire-framed animations (shown in Fig.1 (a, b)) by Maya software for viewing, rating the attractiveness and estimating weight and WHR. Each movie clip was standardized in the same ways as Fan's previously reported [6]. The pictures were intercepted from computer screen when the female rotated at 0 and 90 degree , respectively. And then, two intercepted pictures of the same female were stitched into a 2D front and side view image using Photoshop software (shown in Fig.1 (c,d)).

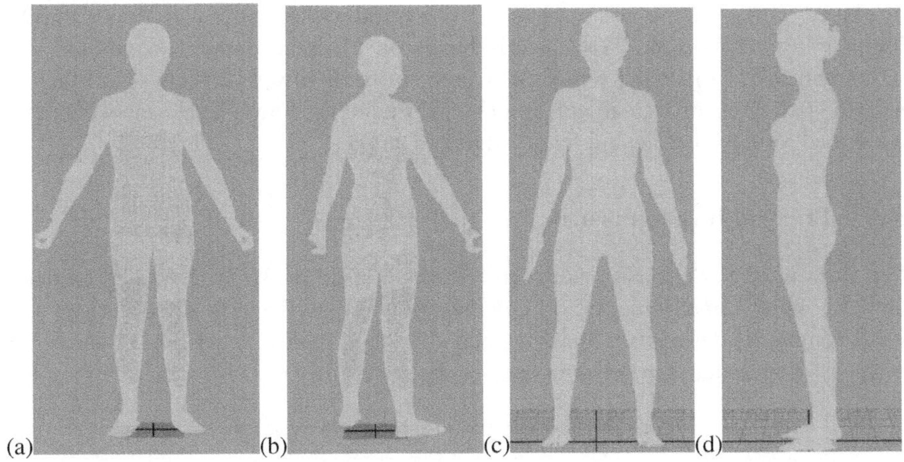

Fig. 1. (a) An example of a 3D animation in the stage of starting. (b) An example of a 3D animation in the stage of rotating 135 degree. (c) and (d) Examples of a 2D image in the front view and in side view.

2.3 Procedure

Since this experiment involved different image formats and projection modes, participants performed their tasks at two locations. One is a computer lab, where participants viewed and rated the images displaying on the computer screen; the other is a meeting room, where participants viewed and rated the images projecting on a wall in 1:1 scale. Participants had ten minutes to relax themselves, before they started rating in another location. Before the first rating, the images were quickly presented to the participants in a random order so that the participants were aware of the range of variability of body features represented in the images. Only on the second run through were they asked to rate the images and were encouraged to use the full set of attractiveness ratings from 1 (least attractive) to 9 (most attractive). The displaying time for each image was 12 seconds.

For estimating the weight and WHR of the females, each image was displayed for 36 seconds on the computer screen. Since the estimation of WHR and weight is complex and difficult, this procedure started three days later.

3 Results and Discussion

3.1 Reliability

The Cronbach's α was used to provide a measure of the reliability of the attractiveness ratings (AR). The Cronbach's α of AR based on the 3D wire-framed animations displayed on the computer screen is 0.946 for both male and female raters and 0.957 for all raters combined; those of AR based on 2D wire-framed images are 0.938, 0.943 and 0.947 for male, female and both, respectively. This shows that there is a very high degree of agreement among the raters. In future analysis, we therefore combined ratings of male and female raters.

3.2 Effect of Images Formats

Fig. 2 shows the relationship between AR rated based on 3D wire-framed animations and 2D wire-framed images. It can be shown that the AR rated based on 3D wire-framed animations are linearly related to those rated based on 2D wire-framed images. The relationship between them is shown as Eq.1.

$$y=0.8687x+0.5454 \qquad (R^2=0.85) \tag{1}$$

Where, y is AR rated based on 2D wire-framed images, and x is AR rated based on 3D wire-framed animations. This means the change of 1.0 grade in AR rated based on 3D wire-framed animations is equivalent to the change of 0.8687 grade of AR rated based on 2D wire-framed images, indicating a better resolution of AR rated based on 3D wire-framed animations.

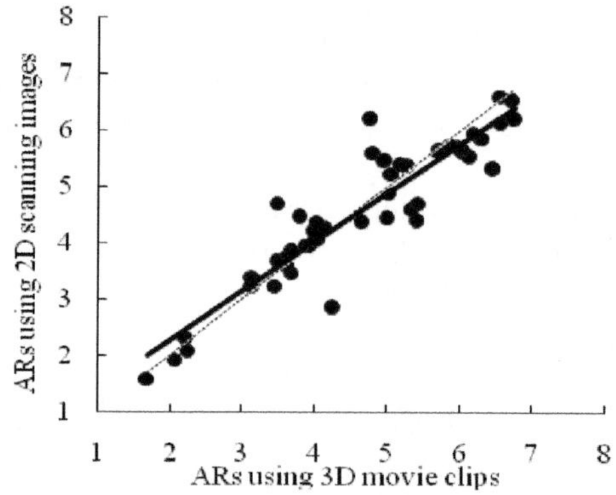

Fig. 2. Plot of the relationship between AR based on 2D images and 3D animations

Since BMI and WHR are important visual cues to female physical attractiveness, in order to further examine the comparative advantage of 2D images and 3D animations as stimuli in the assessment of body image, we asked 40 participants to estimate the weight (relating to BMI strongly)and WHR of females with given heights displaying on the screen. Better estimation of these two parameters should give better judgement of the physical attractiveness.

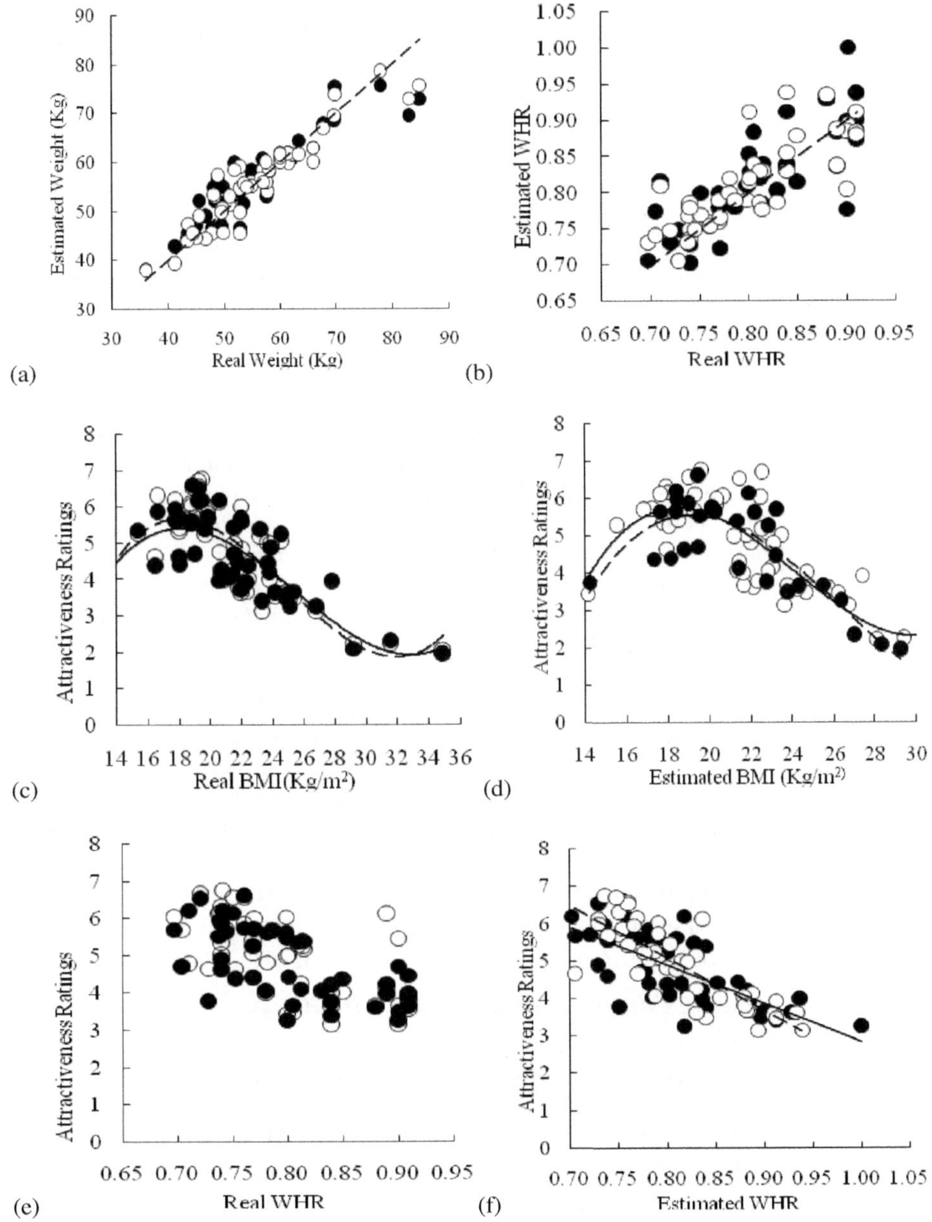

Fig. 3. (a,b) Plot of the relationship between real weight, real WHR and estimated weight ,estimated WHR. (c, d, e, f) Plots of the AR as a function of real BMI, estimated BMI, real WHR and estimated WHR, respectively. Solid dots represent values using 2D wire-framed images and hollow dots represent values using 3D wire-framed animations.

Fig. 3(a) and (b) plot the estimated body weight or WHR against the real body weight or WHR, respectively. It can be seen that the relationships between estimated values and real values are linear for both parameters. The estimate values based on both image formats are arrayed around the equality line, except for larger size females, whose estimated values are relatively lower than the real ones. This is line with the findings of Tovee \cite{Ash}, who suggested that the estimated BMI seem to show a slight 'dip' at the extremes of the BMI range (i.e. very thin or very obese persons), regardless of the observers' BMI. With regard to body weight, the Pearson correlation between the real and estimated values based on 2D wire-framed images is $r = .88$ and that based on 3D wire-framed animations is $r = .93$. Both coefficients are high, which suggests that body weights can be quite accurately estimated from viewing 2D wire-framed images or 3D wire-framed animations, and the latter is slightly advantageous as indicated by the even high correlation coefficient.

For WHR, the Pearson correlation coefficient between the real values and the estimated ones based on 2D wire-framed images is $r =.74$ and that based on 3D wire-framed animations is $r =.82$ indicating that 3D wire-framed animations are better stimuli for the estimation of WHR. In addition, the relatively lower Pearson correlation coefficients of the real and the estimated WHR in comparison with those of the real and the estimated body weight indicates the estimation of body weight is more accurate than the estimation of WHR.

Since 3D wire-framed animations are shown to be the better stimuli for the estimation of body weight and WHR, it is reasonable to believe that 3D wire-framed animations are better in the assessment female physical attractiveness. The relative advantage of 3D wire-framed animations over 2D wire-framed images in the judgment of female attractiveness may be understood by the fact that, when female enter puberty, fat stimulated by estrogen is deposited on the busts, hips, buttocks and thighs, it is difficult for the observers to fully appreciate the fat deposition in the front and side view. 2D images cannot fully capture the visual cues to physical attractiveness.

Fig. 3(c) and (d) plot the AR against real BMI and estimated BMI. Using SPSS, the polynomial multiple regression equations for the real BMI are:

$$y_{2D}=0.002x^3-0.164x^2+3.829x-22.87 \quad (R^2=0.60) \tag{2}$$

$$y_{3D}=0.003x^3-0.208x^2+4.796x-29.41 \quad (R^2=0.64) \tag{3}$$

respectively; those for the estimated BMI are:

$$y_{2D}=0.0031x^3-0.25x^2+6.113x-41.96 \quad (R^2=0.73) \tag{4}$$

$$y_{3D}=0.005x^3-0.342x^2+7.791x-51.35 \quad (R^2=0.81) \tag{5}$$

Respectively, where y2D is the AR based on 2D wire-framed images and y3D the AR based on 3D wire-framed animations. Comparing the percentages of fit of these two pairs of regression equation, it can be shown that AR based on 3D wire-framed animations can be better predicted from the real BMI or estimated BMI.

Fig. 3 (e) and (f) plot the AR against real WHR and estimated WHR, respectively. Using SPSS, the linear regression equations for estimated WHR are:

$$y_{2D}=-10.248x+13.091 \quad (R^2=0.49) \tag{6}$$

$$y_{3D}=-14.228x+16.463 \quad (R^2=0.66) \tag{7}$$

Respectively, where y2D is the AR based on 2D wire-framed images and y3D the AR based on 3D wire-framed animations. Only exists weak negative correlation between AR and real WHR, which is consistent with the findings reported previously [1,2,5]. However, stronger negative correlation exists between AR and estimated WHR. We can see that the AR can be better predicted from the estimated WHR based on 3D wire-framed animations.

3.3 Effect of Images Scale

The attractiveness ratings rated by displaying the images on the 17' computer screen and by projecting them on the wall in 1:1 scale were compared using the Wilcoxon signed-ranks method. The results (z = -5.711; Asymp.Sig. = 1.12E-08) showed significant statistical differences between the AR rated in different projected scale.

Fig. 4(a) plots the relationship between the AR rated by displaying the images on the computer screen and by projecting the images on the wall. As can be seen, the ARs rated on the screen were greater than those rated by projecting the images on the wall in life size (1:1 scale). There is significant linear correlation between them and the regression equation is shown as follow:

$$y=1.058x+0.623 \quad (R^2=0.97) \tag{8}$$

Where, y is the AR rated on the screen, x is the AR rated in 1:1 scale. The linear coefficient was near to unity indicating that the linear regression lines are almost parallel with the equality line. The higher attractiveness ratings for the images displayed on the screen than those projected on the wall may be associated with our visual perception to volume and mass. Generally, stereo objects with small volume and mass are perceived as fine, beautiful, and lovely, whereas stereo objects with big volume and mass are perceived as strong, heavy and huge.

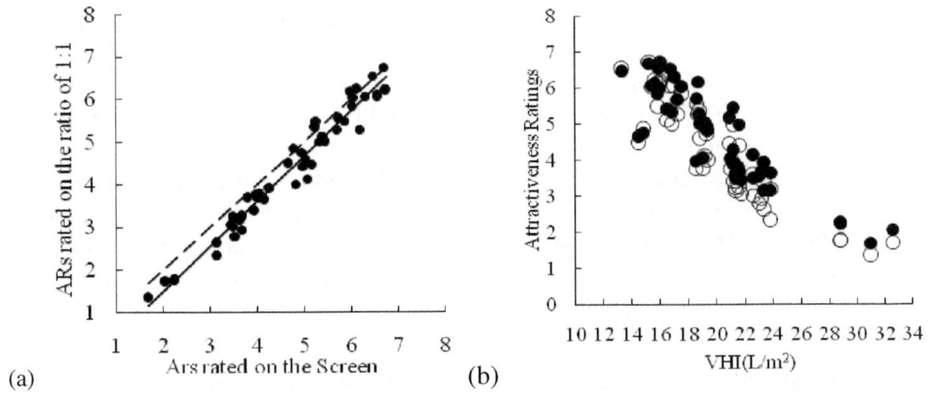

Fig. 4. (a) Plot of the relationship between AR rated in different scale. Equality line of x-value (broken line) and regression line (solid line)are superimposed. (b) Polt of VHI versus AR rated in different scale. Solid dots and hollow dots represent the AR rated on the screen and in 1:1 scale, respectively.

Fig. 4 (b) plots the relationship between VHI and AR rated on the screen or on the wall in life size. Using SPSS, the regression equations for VHI and AR rated on different scale are:

$$y_c=0.003x^3-0.204x^2+4.177x-21.66 \quad (R^2=0.77) \tag{9}$$

$$y_{1:1}=0.003x^3-0.199x^2+3.955x-18.99 \quad (R^2=0.80) \tag{10}$$

Where, yc and y1: 1 are the AR rated on the computer screen and on the wall in 1:1 scale, respectively. It can be seen from Eq.(9) and (10) that except for the coefficient of the constant term, the coefficients of the three degree term, quadratic term and one degree term are very similar which indicate that fitting curves have the similar trend. It suggests that although the attractiveness ratings rated using different image scale are significant difference, the difference can not affect analyze the relationship between AR and the predictors of female attractiveness.

4 Conclusions

The study on the effect of image format and scale on female physical attractiveness is important to a better understanding of how visual perception of body beauty relates to the presentation format of images. In the present investigation, we obtain three main results. The first one is that 3D wire-framed animations are advantageous in differentiating the attractiveness of female images and providing a more accurate estimation of body weight and WHR, by comparing the 2D wire-framed images and 3D wire-framed rotating movie clips as stimuli for the judgment of female physical attractiveness and estimation of body weight and WHR. This is believed due to the fact that observers cannot fully appreciate the fat deposition through viewing the 2D wire-framed images; more visual cues can be captured in viewing 3D wire-framed animations.

The second main result is that female physical attractiveness is more strongly related to the estimated or perceived WHR, although it is very weakly related to the actual or real WHR. This might explain why earlier work by Singh[1,2]showed more importance of WHR, whereas the work by Tovee[4,5] and Fan [6] showed that the effect of WHR to female physical attractiveness was very small.

The third main result is that female images displayed on the computer screen in a smaller than life size scale are more attractive than female images projecting on the wall in life size. This may be due to the fact that small objects are more associated with delicacy and attractiveness, whereas large objects are more associated with strength, heaviness and dominance.

Acknowledgments. This work was supported by research fund of Tianjin Polytechnic University and the research grants (Inter-faculty project: G-YG13 and Niche Area Project: J-BB6T) of Hong Kong polytechnic University to Prof. JT Fan.

References

1. Singh, D.: Adaptive Significance of Female Physical Attractiveness: Role of the Waist-To-Hip Ratio. Journal of Personality Social Psychology 65(2), 293–307 (1993)
2. Singh, D.: Ideal Female Body Shape: the Role of Body Weight and Waist-to-Hip Ratio. International Journal Eating Disorder 16(3), 283–288 (1994)
3. Furnham, A., Dias, M., Mclelland, A.: The Role of Body Weight, Waist-to-Hip Ratio, and Breast Size In Judgments of Female Attractiveness. Sex Roles 39(3), 311–326 (1998)
4. Tovee, M.J., Maisey, D.S., Emery, J.L.: Visual Cues to Female Physical Attractiveness. Proc. R. Soc. Lond. B 266(1415), 211–218 (1999)
5. Tovee, M.J., Cornelissen, P.L.: Female and Male Perceptions of Female Physical Attractiveness in Front-View and Profile. British Journal of Psychology 92(2), 391–402 (2001)
6. Fan, J.T., Liu, F., Dai, W., Wu, J.: Visual Perception of Female Physical Attractiveness. Proc. R. Soc. Lond. B 271(1537), 347–352 (2004)
7. Smith, S.L., Cornelissen, P.L., Tovee, M.J.: Color 3D Bodies and Judgments of Human Female Attractiveness. Evolution and Human Behavior 28(1), 48–54 (2007)
8. Tovee, M.J., Emery, J.L., Cohe-Tovee, E.M.: The estimate of body mass index and physical attractiveness is dependent on the observer's own body mass index. Proc. R. Soc. Lond. B 267(1456), 1987–1997 (2000)

Medical Image Registration Based on Wavelet Transform Using Hausdorff Distance

Jianxun Zhang[1] and Yu Liu[2]

[1] Graduate Division, Chongqing University of Technology, Chongqing 400050, China
[2] School of Computer Science & Engineering, Chongqing University of Technology, Chongqing 400050, China
zjx@cqut.edu.cn

Abstract. Image registration is the process of overlaying two or more images of the same scene taken at different time, from different viewpoints, and/or by different sensors. We propose a new method of medical image registration based on wavelet transform using Hausdorff Distance. Firstly, the image was decomposed by wavelet transform. Secondly, using gradient vector flow detects feature points. Finally, using Hausdorff Distance matching sets of feature points. Theories and experiments indicated that this method has some advantages such as high precision and good robust.

Keywords: Medical image registration, Wavelet Transform, Hausdorff distance.

1 Introduction

Image registration is a fundamental task in image processing used to match two or more pictures taken, for example, at different times, from different sensors or from different viewpoints [1] . It geometrically aligns two images—the reference and sensed images. Typically, it is widely used in remote sensing image, medical imaging, 3D reconstruction, computer vision, etc.

Within the current clinical setting, image registration in the medical plays a very key role. Such applications occur throughout the clinical track of events; not only within clinical diagnostic settings, but prominently so in the area of planning, consummation, and evaluation of surgical and radiotherapeutical procedures. Medical image registration is about determining a spatial transformation or mapping that relates positions in one image, to corresponding positions in one or more other images. Registration aims to fuse data about patients from more than one medical image so that doctors can acquire more comprehensive information related to pathogenesis.

Existing medical image registration techniques can be broadly classified into two categories [2]: feature-based and intensity-based methods. Intensity-based image registration techniques directly depended on the statistical properties of intensity information. Since this method does not need complex preprocess, it has the advantages of high precision and strong robustness. However, object function of the method suffers from the local extreme induced the interpolation. Moreover, the

Z. Pan et al. (Eds.): Transactions on Edutainment VII, LNCS 7145, pp. 248–254, 2012.

computation cost problem should also be considered. A feature-based method requires the exaction of features common in both images. As the principle of this method is simple, it is widely applied in image registration. The method has two key steps: feature extraction and feature matching.

Recently, medical image registration has been developing, and the technology of signal processing-wavelet transform is introduced. Due to wavelet transform has strong space-frequency ability and time-frequency ability, uses wavelet transform in medical image registration is one of development directions. Hausdorff distance is one of the methods for matching features. It does not need to build corresponding relation among the points, and just calculates the similar degree (the max distance) between the two point sets, so it can deal with the situation of many features points.

In this paper, we propose a new method for medical image based on wavelet transform using Hausdorff distance. Firstly, the image is decomposed by wavelet transform. Secondly, gradient vector flow is used to detect feature points. Finally, Hausdorff Distance is used for matching sets of feature points. At last, the image registration is realized.

2 Model of Image Registration

Image registration is a process of finding a transformation that maps one image onto another same or similar object by optimizing certain criterion. It requires define a similarity measure and space transformation. The similarity measure of the two images achieves maximum after the transformation. Let us define the digital image as a two-dimensional matrix by f(x,y). After affine transformations such as zooming, rotating and translation, the image changes to be f(x',y') on the following formula[3]:

$$\begin{aligned} x' &= ax\cos\theta + ay\sin\theta + \Delta x \\ y' &= -ax\sin\theta + ay\cos\theta + \Delta y \end{aligned} \tag{1}$$

Where,θ is the rotation angle, a is the zoom parameters,Δx andΔy are respectively vertical and horizontal translation parameters. If the affine transformation denoted by T, then T(x,y)=(x',y'), here Tx=x', Ty=y'. We define reference image as g(x,y), unregistration image as f(x,y), the registration of g and f can be expressed as T[f(x,y)]=g(x,y)=f(x',y'). The optimizing transformation T was found in a image registration, so the problem comes down to resolving the following optimal problem:

$$\max I(a) = \min(-I(a)) \tag{2}$$

Namely find a to satisfy:

$$a = \arg\max I(a) = \arg\min(-I(a)) \tag{3}$$

Where, a=(Δx, Δy,θ),Δx is vertical translation parameters,Δy is horizontal translation parameters,θ is rotation angle.

3 The Hausdorff Distance

The Hausdorff distance is a non-linear operator, which measures the mismatch of the two sets. Given two finite point sets $A=\{a_1,a_2,\ldots,a_p\}$ and $B=\{b_1,b_2,\ldots,b_q\}$, the Hausdorff distance is defined as[4]:

$$H(A,B)=\max(h(A,B),h(B,A)) \tag{4}$$

where

$$h(A,B)=\max_{a_i\in A}\min_{b_j\in B}\left\|a_i-b_j\right\| \tag{5}$$

$$h(B,A)=\max_{b_j\in B}\min_{a_i\in A}\left\|b_j-a_i\right\| \tag{6}$$

and $\|\bullet\|$ is some underlying norm on the point of A and B(e.g., the L2 or Euclidean norm).

The function h(A,B) is called the directed Hausdorff distance from A to B. The function h(B,A) is called the backward Hausdorff distance from A to B. Intuitively, if h(A,B)=d, then each point of A must be within distance d of some point of B, and there also is some point of A that as exactly distance d from the nearest point of B (the most mismatched point).

The classics Hausdorff distance is simple, but it is sensitive to degradation such as noise and occlusions. Thus, to deal with this problem, some modified Hausdorff distances have been proposed, such as the partial Hausdorff distance. The partial Hausdorff distance is present as follows[5]:

$$H_{K,L}(A,B)=\max(h_k(B,A),h_l(A,B)) \tag{7}$$

where, $h_k(B,A)$ is distances of each point $b_j\in B$ to its nearest point of A, then we rank those distances, and k is q-th quantile. Similarly, $h_l(A,B)$ is distances of each point $a_i\in A$ to its nearest point of B, then we rank those distances, and l is q-th quantile. The partial Hausdorff distance method yields good results for an impulse noise case.

4 Wavelet-Based Decomposed and feature extraction

4.1 Image Pyramids Wavelet-Based Decomposed

In clinical medicine, time-consuming and registration precision are key problems. If less time-consuming and higher accuracy, image registration is applied more widely in clinical. Due to the use of all pixels points will consume more time and memory space; therefore, in order to improve the speed of registration, we adopt wavelet transform as the representation for two main reasons. Firstly, wavelet transform can keep more significant anatomies in medical images. Secondly, wavelet does not blur the images through the hierarchical pyramid.

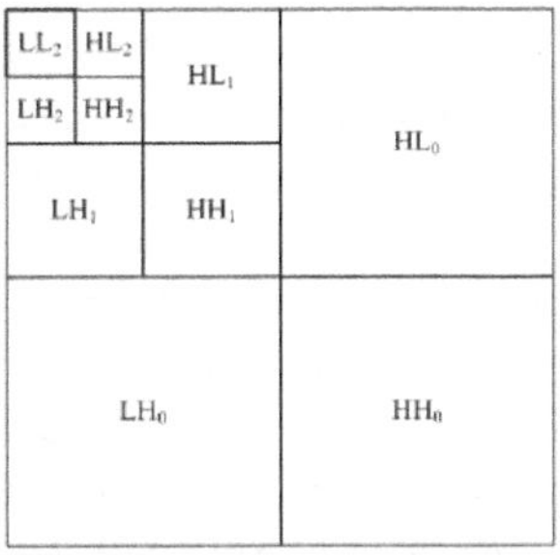

(a) three-level wavelet decomposition

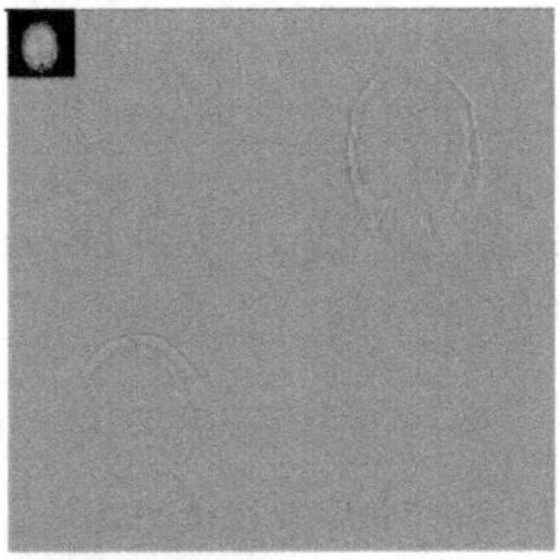

(b) MRI Image Three-Level wavelet Decomposition

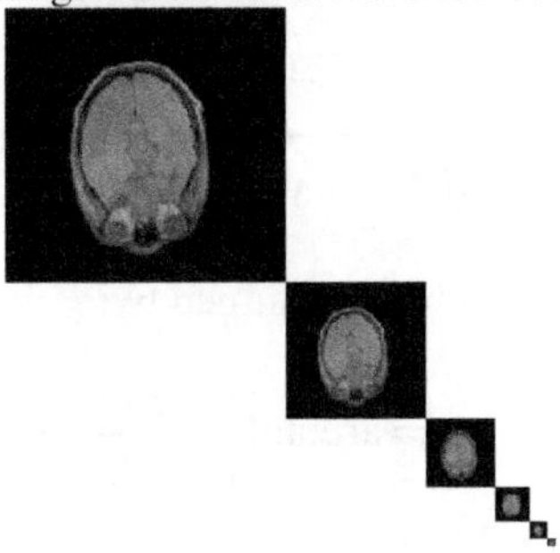

(c) Pyramid images

Fig. 1. Multiresolution Decomposes of Image

Wavelet theory has emerged as an effective means of representing signal in terms of a multi-resolution structure. The Wavelet transform provides not only frequency domain information but also spatial domain information. It does not change the information content present in the signal. It was developed to overcome the short coming of the Short Time Fourier Transform (STFT), which can also be used to analyze non-stationary signals. While STFT gives a constant resolution at all frequencies, the Wavelet Transform uses multi-resolution technique by which different frequencies are analyzed with different resolutions. Based on multi-resolution representation, a signal is divided into a number of components, each corresponding to different frequency bands. Since each component has a better frequency and time localization, the multi-resolution decomposed signal can be processed much more easily than its original representation. The multi-resolution successive approximation not only enhances the resolution of an image, but also reveals the resolution of local features. Wavelet transforms extract local features from images in scale space, then image registration on the basis of the similarity of local features.

We use the standard discrete wavelet transform (with Harr basis function which is easy to implement) algorithm to get wavelet decompositions of images which include four subband images, LL, LH, HL and HH. In our method, we make use of LL subband coeffcients to perform registration (See Fig. 1). Rather than the other three subbands which contain details like edges, LL subband preserves most of the significant information one image has, e.g., anatomical structures, intensity values, etc.

4.2 Feature Extraction

Let us define the original image as f(x,y), and approximation image at a scale 2^j as $W_{2^j} f(x,y)$. Then $W_{2^j} f(x,y)$ is decompose into an approximation image $W_{2^{j+1}} f(x,y)$ at a scale 2^{j+1} and two wavelet coefficient image, $W^1_{2^{j+1}} f(x,y)$ and $W^2_{2^{j+1}} f(x,y)$ which pick up the detail information that is lost between the image $W_{2^j} f(x,y)$ and $W_{2^{j+1}} f(x,y)$.

The modulus maximum of the original image at a scale 2^j can be calculated[6]:

$$M_{2^j} f(x,y) = \sqrt{\left|W^1_{2^j} f(x,y)\right|^2 + \left|W^2_{2^j} f(x,y)\right|^2} \tag{8}$$

The angle of the edges can be determined by:

$$A_{2^j} f(x,y) = \arctan\left(\frac{W^2_{2^j} f(x,y)}{W^1_{2^j} f(x,y)}\right) \tag{9}$$

We now can compute the edge image at scale 2^j by threshold the magnitude function as:

$$E_{2^j}(x,y) = \begin{cases} 0 & M_{2^j} f(x,y) < T \\ 1 & M_{2^j} f(x,y) \geq T \end{cases} \tag{10}$$

Where T is the threshold is value that separates the image into two classes, the edges and the background. Then, $T = \frac{k}{n} \sum_{x=0}^{W-1} \sum_{y=0}^{H-1} W_{2^j} f(x,y)$, where W and H is width and high of the image, n is the whole numbers of the pixels, k is constant. The phase function $A_{2^j} f(x, y)$ indicates the direction of the change of the image intensity which is perpendicular to the edge detection.

4.3 Step of Image Registration

Let us define reference image as g(x,y), floating image as f(x,y), According to the principle of appeal, the g(x,y) and f(x,y) registration step as follow:

Step 1. Let g(x,y) and f(x,y) by image pyramids wavelet-based decomposed. $W_{2^j} g(x, y)$ and $W_{2^j} f(x, y)$ is respectively an approximation image of g(x,y) and f(x,y).

Step 2. Register $W_{2^j} g(x, y)$ and $W_{2^j} f(x, y)$.

A. Extract feature by gradient vector $M_{2^j} f(x, y)$.

B. The feature point coordinates into an array.

C. Calculated Hausdorff distance by the array values.

Step 3. Estimate the initial position according to the result of layer j, hierarchy search until the lowest layer.

Step 4. Image registration by the final match point coordinates calculation for the transformation parameters using Model of Registration.

5 Experimental Results

In this Section, experiment was performed based on the above mentioned method. In Figure 2, sub-figures (a) is the reference image contains Gauss noise, sub-figure (b) is the rotating image, sub-figure (c) is registered image. Experimental present, the method get higher accuracy results to MRI image using Gauss noise.

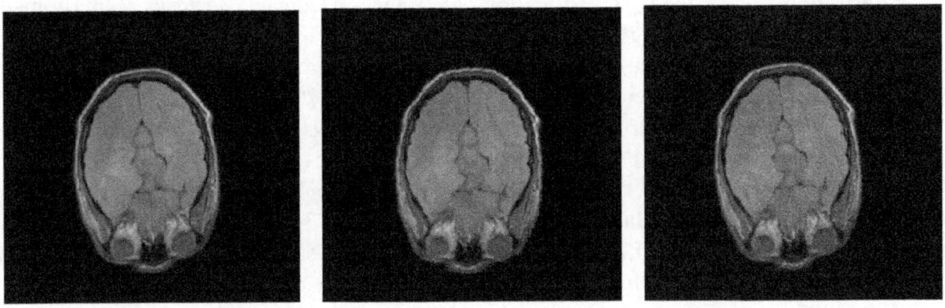

(a) Reference image (b) Floating image (c) Registered image

Fig. 2. Registration example with MRI image

In Figure 3, sub-figures (a) is the reference image, sub-figure (b) is the floating image, sub-figure (c) is registered image. Experimental show, the method get higher accuracy results to large artifact PET image. Results demonstrated that this method was a very robust and fast registration method with high accuracy.

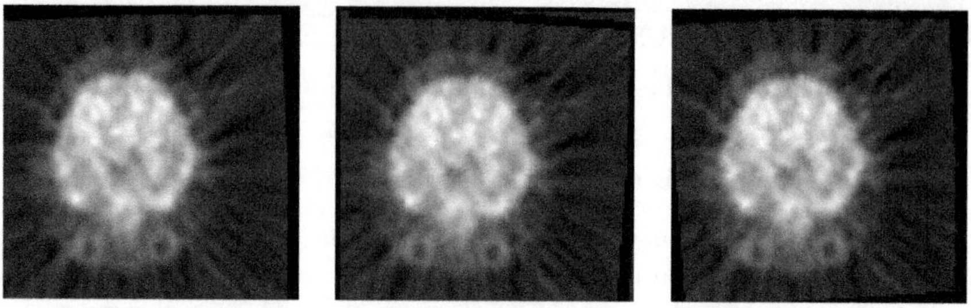

(a) Reference image (b) Floating image (c) Registered image

Fig. 3. Registration example with PET image

6 Conclusions

In this paper, we present a new medical image registration method based on wavelet transform using Hausdorff distance. As compared to traditional registration calculation, this method depends on multi-resolution, feature extraction and Hausdorff distance; therefore, this method was a very robust and fast registration method with high accuracy. As compared to mutual information of image gray scale and entropy of information, this method was characterized by saving operation time, and promoting registration velocity. Therefore, this method is beneficial for medical image registration.

References

1. Zitova, B., Flusser, J.: Image registration methods a survey. Image and Vision Computing 12, 977–1000 (2003)
2. Gao, Z.Y., Qian, Y.X., Lin, J.R., et al.: Current methods of multi-modality image registration and their classification. Foreign Medical Sciences - Biomedical Engineering 23(4), 1206 (2000)
3. Liu, B., Peng, J.: Wavelet Decomposition Based Image registration. Journal of Computer-Aided Design & Computer Graphics 15(9), 1070–1073 (2003)
4. Felzenszwalb, P.F.: Learning Models for Object Recognition. Computer Vision and Pattern Recognition (2001)
5. Niu, L.-P., Mao, S.-Y., Chen, W.: Image Registration Based on Hausdorff Distance. Journal of Electronics & Information Technology 1(29), 35–38 (2007)
6. Niya, J.N., Aghagolzadeh, A., Tinati, M.A., Feizi, S.: 2-step wavelet-based edge detection using gabor and cauchy directional wavelets. Advanced Communication Technology, 115–120 (2005)

Study on Key Technology of HPSIN-Based Vector Geo-data Online Service

Jiali Feng[1], Nan Jiang[1,2], Bin Hu[2], Jiagao Wu[3], and Zhiqiang Zou[3]

[1] School of Geographic and Oceanographic Science, Nanjing University, 210093, China
[2] Key Laboratories of Virtual Geographical Environment, Nanjing Normal University, Ministry of Education, Nanjing, 210046, China
[3] Institute of Computer Technology, College of Computer, Nanjing University of Posts and Telecommunications, Nanjing, 210003, China
njiang@njnu.edu.cn

Abstract. P2P technology can avoid "single point of failure" and "hot spots bottleneck" problems, which exist in traditional centralized system of spatial information. Hybrid P2P Spatial Indexing Network combines distributed Quad-Tree with DHT-based Chord network to maintain both query efficiency and system load balance. In this paper, key technology of HPSIN based distributed vector geo-data online service is studied, the pattern of vector geo-data organization based on Linking Mechanism, segmentation and lossless reconstruction are proposed. This novel organization pattern can be used to form a loosely and globally distributed topology. Segmentation and lossless reconstruction method takes advantage of linking information, to reconstruct the damaged Geometries lossless. Comparative experiment shows that the organization and the associated algorithms are lossless and reliable[1].

Keywords: vector geo-data, HPSIN, Linking Mechanism, lossless reconstruction algorithm.

1 Introduction

Geographic Information Systems (GIS) has entered a pop stage, but "single point of failure" and "hot spots bottleneck" problems exist in traditional centralized system of spatial information. P2P technology offers a novel solution to spatial information online service and a good platform for sharing mass spatial data. Each peer plays roles as both client and server in P2P network, which eliminates the bottleneck and shares resources and services among peers fully[1,2].

---

[1] Project supported by National High Technology Research and Development Program 863 (Project Number 2009AA12Z219, 2007AA12Z207); National Natural Science Funds (Project Number 40801149).

Z. Pan et al. (Eds.): Transactions on Edutainment VII, LNCS 7145, pp. 255–262, 2012.

P2P oriented raster geo-data online service is widely applied, improves the efficiency using "multicast" and "multi-point calculation" of P2P [3,4]; whereas vector geo-data online service still has many issues cannot be handled, such as vector geo-data organization pattern, segmentation, lossless reconstruction, etc.

At present, P2P based geographic data online service model mainly adopts the Chord network layer, the network structure maps control points of space within the scope completely to the Chord nets, to achieve load balance [5]. But problems exist in this kind of pure Chord net, just like the "more network hops" problem, which leads to inefficiency and maintenance difficulties. Currently, Distributed vector geographic data are mainly formed as two organizations: one bases on discrete objects, ensures the integrity of the object without data segmentation, but brings the index redundancy and management difficulties [6, 7]; another bases on "tile", segment vector data into tiles according to spatial reference. This method improves data transmission efficiency and query efficiency, but destroys the integrity of vector objects topology [8, 9, 10], so that some topological algorithm cannot be performed.

Therefore, HPSIN, a vector-oriented hybrid P2P indexing network model, which bases on Chord and Quad-Tree, is studied. And then a pattern of vector geo-data organization based on Linking Mechanism is designed, which forms a loosely distributed topology in HPSIN. On the basis of this design, segmentation and lossless reconstruction algorithm is implemented.

2 Hybrid P2P Spatial Indexing Network (HPSIN)

As shown in Fig. 1, HPSIN adopts mixing index network, which segments the initial data according to MX-CIF quad-tree, and then maps tile index of l_s level to Chord, stores tile index of *level* ($l_s \leq level \leq l_m$) under l_s node, to form a hierarchical cache. We use control point as the cluster formation decision of peers, that is, peers having the same control point will fall into the same cluster. In each cluster, a header peer is

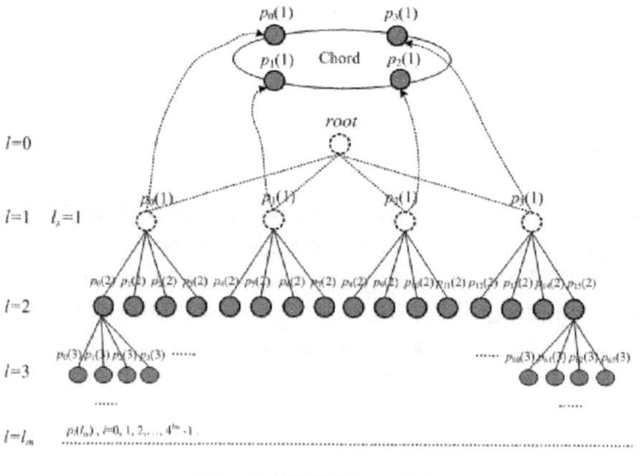

Fig. 1. HPSIN model

selected to be a representation as the cluster. The header becomes an index node of Quad-Tree, who will be assigned to join the upper layer cluster of corresponding control point and participate in the header election in this cluster.

HPSIN model combines structured P2P network and hierarchical P2P network. It can not only make good use of Chord network with the merit of load balancing and hierarchical P2P network with high efficient querying, but also adapt to high dynamic network environment. So that we can take full advantage of P2P, to improve the query efficiency, reduce network transmission. The organization of distributed vector data based on HPSIN and the study on reconstruction algorithm is the most important key technology, which is also the key point of this paper.

3 Distributed Vector Geo-Data Organization

3.1 Linking Mechanism

Linking Mechanism records link relationship between corresponding entities in order to form a loosely distributed topology, which realizes the representation model, and supports lossless reconstruction. Linking information is organized by three levels.

(1) Linking between Tiles

Tile is coded according to MX-CIF encoding rules to explain the adjacency relation and hierarchical relation.

(2) Linking between geometries

In the process of vector data segmentation, the vector object form a number of derivative sub-objects in different tiles. We deliver the logo ID of parent geometry to its sub-geometries, to form the geometry hierarchy. Data reconstruction would be called in merge progress only if geometries have the same ID.

(3) Linking between arcs

The Geometry is actually divided into several end to end arc segments in process; we call the segment point to be "LinkingNode", which records relevant information, like the matching relation between nodes, the connection of arcs, and the relationship to the parent Geometry.

3.2 Tile Representation Model Based on Linking Mechanism

Tile is the minimum unit for network transmission. It is formed by "Tile-Geometry-LinkingNode" hierarchical model (Fig. 2). During recursive segmentation, we should deliver linking information in current level to the corresponding sub-objects in the next level, and update the existing information, to make sure the objects on leaf nodes always have enough information for reconstruction.

<**Tile** Tagged Text>
<TileNum Tagged Text>:= int number;
<Envelope Tagged Text>:= Envelope (xMin, yMin, xMax, yMax);
<**Geometry** Tagged Text>
<GeometryType Tagged Text>:=String GeometryType;
<Coordinates Tagged Text>:= (Coordinate0, Coordinate1, Coordinate2……);
<GeometryID Tagged Text>:=String ID;
< **LinkingNodeList** Tagged Text>:= (LinkingNode0, LinkingNode1… …);
< **LinkingNode** Tagged Text>
<LinkingNode ID Tagged Text>:=int LinkingID;
<LinkingNode INDEX Tagged Text>:=int LinkingNodeIndex;
<LinkingNode ISVERTEX Tagged Text>:=int isVertex;
<LinkingNode NEARESTNODE Tagged Text>:=Coordinate nearestNode;
<**Geometry** Tagged Text>
……

Fig. 2. Representation Model of Tile

3.3 Efficient Lossless Reconstruction Algorithm Based on Linking Mechanism

The efficient lossless reconstruction algorithm based on Linking Mechanism is proposed in this paper, the main idea is described as follows.

```
ReadTile (String fileDirectory)
GetTilePair ( )
For (traverse Geometry1 in Tile1 )
{
  For (traverse Geometry2 in Tile2 )
  {
    If (match the Linking information in Geometry level)
    {
      Match the Linking information in Arc level
      Geometry    resultGeom    =    Geometry1.    union
(Geometry2 )
      Add resultGeom into resultTile
    }
  }
If (There is no corresponding geometry)
Add Geometry1 into resultTile
}
```

Here we take two tiles merging for example (Fig. 3), to specific the steps of Lossless reconstruction algorithm based on Linking Mechanism.

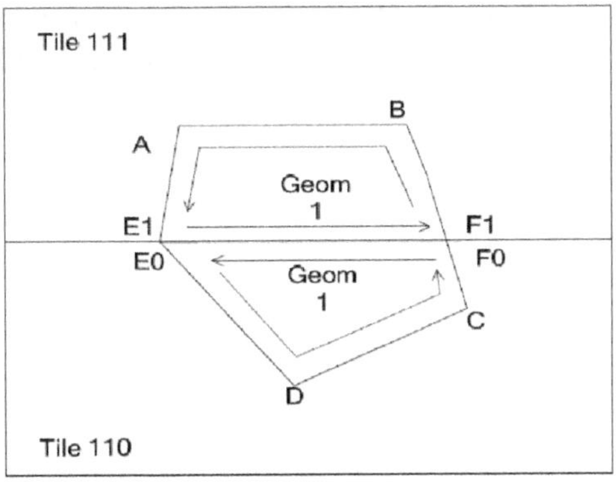

Fig. 3. Lossless reconstruction based on Linking Mechanism

Step 1: Read tiles, recognize the adjacent tile-pair. We get Tile 111 and Tile 110.
Step 2: Traverse geometries in the tile-pair; recognize the corresponding geometry by GeometryID. We get two sons for "Geom1" with the same GeometryID.
Step 3: Geometry reconstruction:
a. Match the Linking information in corresponding geometries, we get two pairs of linkingnodes by comparing LinkingID (Table 1).

Table 1. Matching of LinkingNode

LinkingNode	LinkingID	IsVertex	NearestNode
E0, E1	0	True	Null
F0, F1	1	False	B, C

b. Segment the corresponding geometries at the above linkingnodes, and delete the reverse equal arcs, we get F1-B-A-E1 and E0-D-C-F0.
c. According to the properties of linkingnodes in Table 1, we get that node E is a segmentation point and a vertex of parent geometry as well. So it should be reserved. By contrast, node F is a pure segmentation point which should be replaced by its nearest node. Then we get C-B-A-E and E-D-C (or B-A-E and E-D-C-B). Turn to Step 4.
Step 4: Construct geometry from these arcs, to form a lossless Geom1 (E-D-C-B-A-E). Then delete the matched LinkingNode information, in order to avoid the information redundancy.
Step 5: Add the result geometry into the result tile. At last, output the tile as a file.

4 Distributed Vector Geo-Data Organization

4.1 Introduction to Experiment

JTS (Java Topology Suite) is used as a basic tool for two-dimensional vector calculation in this study. A prototype system for vector geo-data segmentation and reconstruction based on Linking Mechanism is implemented. And we give the analysis about the comparison between our novel method and existing JTS method.

4.2 Analysis of Experiment

As shown in Table 2. The segmentation method based on Linking Mechanism records geometric information and linking information that cause more increase amplitude in data quantity than that in JTS, which however does not affect the network transmission.

Table 2. Comparison of increase of data segmentation

Tile Total / Increased Amplitude (%)	4	16	64	256
JTS Segmentation	0.433	0.821	2.025	3.943
Segmentation based on Linking Mechanism	0.652	1.179	2.703	5.508

The comparison of reconstruction time is shown in Table 3. And the comparison of increased amplitude occurred in data reconstruction is shown in Table 4. Obviously, the method proposed in this paper is much more efficient. More than that, it uses linking information to reconstruct the damaged geometries and then deletes them, so that it achieves lossless reconstruction.

Table 3. Comparison of reconstruction time

Tile Total / Reconstruction Time (s)	4	16	64	256
JTS Segmentation	15.102	38.750	99.929	289.098
Segmentation based on Linking Mechanism	0.610	1.593	4.024	8.105

Table 4. Comparison of data increase in reconstruction

Tile Total / Increased Amplitude (%)	4	16	64	256
JTS Segmentation	3.218	6.932	22.386	60.129
Segmentation based on Linking Mechanism	0	0	0	0

As the above tables show, the efficiency can be improved by our method that leverages additional linking information. The method is proved to be reliable and lossless.

4.3 Prototype System

The prototype system for vector geo-data reconstruction is developed under Eclipse platform. Fig. 4 shows the origin vector data of JiangSu, while Fig. 5 shows the merge result of 64 sub-tiles which derive from the origin tile. As shown in comparison, origin tile and merge result are identical in respect of their shapes and files.

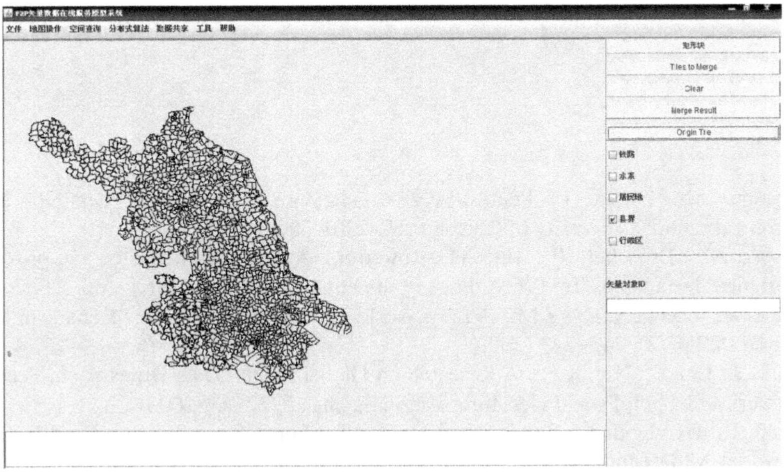

Fig. 4. Origin tile

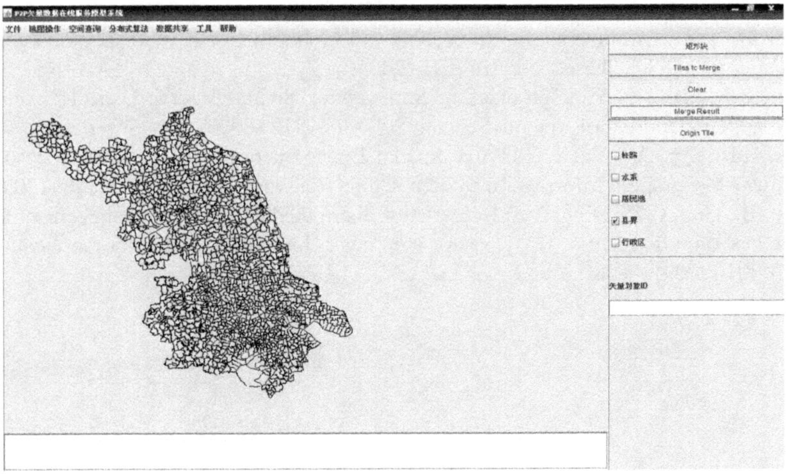

Fig. 5. Sub-tiles merge result

5 Conclusions

Motivated by the difficulties in distributed vector geo-data online service, this paper designs a HPSIN oriented pattern of vector geo-data organization based on Linking Mechanism, as well as a segmentation and lossless reconstruction algorithm. The robustness, efficiency and reliability of the organization and algorithm is shown in experiments. It can be used as a solution to the distributed vector geographic data network management that provides the key technical support to geo-data online service.

References

1. Ripeanu, M., Foster, I.: Peer-to-Peer Architecture Case Study: Gnutella Network. Technical report. University of Chicago. TR-2001-26 (July 2001)
2. Castro, M., Druschel, P., Hu, Y., Rowstron, A.: Exploiting network proximity in distributed hash tables. In: Proceedings of the FuDiCo, Bertinoro, Italy, pp. 52–55 (2002)
3. Yu, Z.W., Zheng, S., Li, Z.M.: A Large-scale Terrain Transmission Mechanism Based on Hybrid P2P 37(2), 243–249 (2008)
4. Ma, X.J., Liu, C., Xie, K.Q.: A Research on Global Spatial Data Directory in Peer-to-Peer Networks. Geography and Geo-Information Science 5, 22–25 (2006)
5. Tanin, E., Harwood, A., Samet, H.: Using a distributed Quad-Tree index in Peer-to-Peer networks. VLDB Journal 16(2), 165–178 (2007)
6. Liu, R.G., Zhuang, D.F., Liu, J.Y.: Distributed Geographical Vector Data Sharing. Journal of Image and Graphic 6(9), 267–276 (2001)
7. Mondal, A., Yi, L.F., Kitsuregawa, M.: P2PR-Tree: an R-Tree Based Spatial Index for Peer-to-Peer Environments. In: Proceedings of the International Workshop on Peer-to-Peer Computing and Databases, pp. 516–525 (2004)
8. Wei, Z.K., Bae, H.Y.: Optimization Strategy for Spatial Vector Data Transmission in Internet GIS. Journal of Remote Sensing 5(4), 865–872 (2000)
9. Dai, H.B., Qin, Y., Yu, J.: Massive Spatial Data Structure and Distributed Resolution to Railway Geographic Information System. China Railway Science 25(5), 118–120 (2004)
10. Gao, B., Guo, C.Z., Ding, S.J.: Research of distributed coordinated management of spatial date based on division of GML vector map layer. Journal of Computer Application 29(1), 297–301 (2009)

Defection Recognition of Cold Rolling Strip Steel Based on ACO Algorithm with Quantum Action

Jinrong Zhang and Yue Wang

School of Computer Science and Engineering, Chongqing University of Technology, 400050 Chongqing, China
zhjr2000@163.com

Abstract. To enhance plate quality of cold rolling strip steel, a method based on Ant Colony Optimization with Quantum Action (ACO-QA) is developed. In this method, each ant position is represented by a group of quantum bits, and a new quantum rotation gates are designed to update the position of the ant. In order to makes full efficiency, a pretreatment using fuzzy method is firstly adapted before resolving the mathematical model with ACO-QA. This method overcomes the shortcoming of ACO, which is easy to fall into local optimums and has a slow convergence rate in continuous space. At last, a field cognition system is designed to test the efficiency of this method. The results show that it can validly identify almost all defection patterns, compared to traditional identification system. The recognition precision of this method is higher and can meet the shape recognition requirements of cold rolling strip steel.

Keywords: defection recognition, cold rolling, ACO, quantum calculation.

1 Introduction

In recent years, the production technology of cold rolled strip steel has progressed greatly at home and abroad. Surface flatness degree is an important quality indicator of cold rolled strip steel. And the shape control has become a hot topic of cold rolling process [1, 2]. Therefore, the strip shape recognition is an important part in control of strip steel rolling process, while only strip shape checked online is identified as controllable defect mode, can we effectively determine precise adjustment of the shape control implementing agencies, thereby producing high-quality steel strip products.

With the development of the strip shape control, there appears some shape cognition methods [3, 4]. Polynomial Regressive Solution (PRS) and Orthogonal PRS are the conventional two. However, the PRS and O-PRS have so bad noise immunity that they only can deal with simple shape deformation and cannot meet the requirement of high precision. Moreover, fuzzy classification and manual neural network (ANN) is used recently [5, 6]. The former is simple and practical while its ability of cognition and precision are inferior to the latter. ANN method allows the measured signal rather large errors and it can magnify the key ingredients and

Z. Pan et al. (Eds.): Transactions on Edutainment VII, LNCS 7145, pp. 263–271, 2012.

depresses the secondary ones. However, the single use of ANN needs to operate on original target image and makes classification directly so that it hinders the accuracy and decrease the velocity of the cognition procedure [7, 8].

In this paper, Legendre polynomial expression is used for description the basic mode of strip shape defections, and its linear combination presents any shape signal model. Based on fuzzy pattern recognition, an improved ant colony optimization methods with quantum solution[9-12] is adapted, reducing the dimension of the solution and the search space, thereby increasing the accuracy and speed of recognition, meeting the high precision shape control requirements.

2 Signal Mathematical Model of the Shape

2.1 Normalization

Due to the factors of mechanical or the heat roller deformation, the metal extends non-uniformly down the width direction when the strip steel being cold rolled, thereby causing different patterns of plate defects. Usually we take the horizontal tension distribution of the strip as the flatness signal σ_i, which is measured by the sensor and needs to be normalized:

$$\Delta\sigma_i = \frac{\sigma_i'}{\max|\sigma_i'|} \qquad (i = 1, 2, \ldots, n) \tag{1}$$

Where, $\sigma_i' = \sigma_i^R - \sigma_i^T$, $\sigma_i^R = \sigma_i - \overline{\sigma_i}$, σ_i' represents the flatness deviation, σ_i^T represents the stress of the flatness, σ_i^R represents the actual residual stress, and $\overline{\sigma_i}$ represents the average flatness stress by measurement or calculation.

2.2 Signal Description

According to the technique of manipulated rolling mill, the process facts and control requirements, the 6 adjustable simple plate defects (Fig.1)

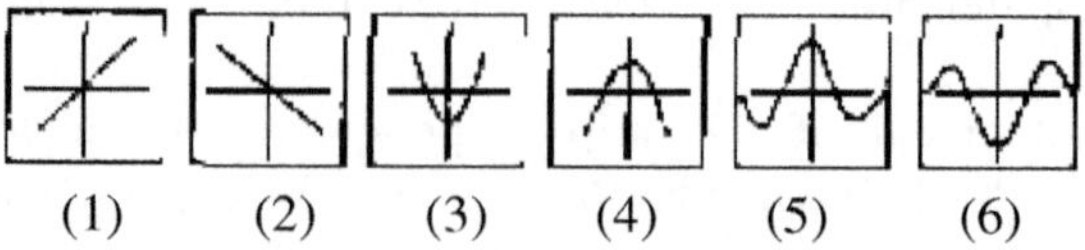

Fig. 1. Six basic shapes: (1) left plat-profile, (2) right plat-profile, (3) middle plat-profile, (4) bilateral plat-profile, (5) quarter plat-profile and (6) side-middle plat-profile

Legendre polynomials are usually used to describe the corresponding residual stress distribution of the above 6 basic standard models. If $\sigma^{(k)}$ represents the sample of normalized standard defects of flatness (k=1, 2… 6), then the standards-based equations of the above six version are as follows:

$$\sigma^{(1)} = p_1(x) = x \quad (2)$$

$$\sigma^{(2)} = -p_1(x) = -x \quad (3)$$

$$\sigma^{(3)} = p_2(x) = 3x^2/2 - 0.5 \quad (4)$$

$$\sigma^{(4)} = -p_2(x) = -(3x^2/2 - 0.5) \quad (5)$$

$$\sigma^{(5)} = p_4(x) = (35x^4 - 30x^2 + 3)/8 \quad (6)$$

$$\sigma^{(6)} = -p_4(x) = -(35x^4 - 30x^2 + 3)/8 \quad (7)$$

Usually the flatness of the strip steel can be expressed by a linear combination of the basic mode flatness signal:

$$\Delta\sigma(x) = \alpha p_1(x) + \beta p_2(x) + \gamma p_4(x) \quad (8)$$

2.3 Mathematical Model

Given signal samples $\sigma(x_i)$, $i = 1, 2, \ldots, n$, we get the target function:

$$\min f = \sum_{i=1}^{n} \left| \Delta\sigma_i - \alpha p_{1i} - \beta p_{2i} - \gamma p_{4i} \right| \quad (9)$$

The processes of the flatness signal pattern recognition is to evaluate the flatness characteristics of α, β and γ to make f minimum.

3 ACO-QA Algorithm

3.1 Fuzzy Pretreatment of the Objective Function

The mathematical model of flatness signal recognition is a non-convex nonlinear equation, which is difficult to get solution directly. To reduce the solving difficulties and improve recognition efficiency, fuzzy pretreatment is first used.

Suppose that $\omega(x_i)$ satisfies the normalization qualification, $\sum_{i=1}^{n} \omega(x_i) = 1$, $X = \{x_1, x_2, \ldots, x_n\}$, some definitions are given as follows:

i) The weighted Hamming distance between the standard signal $\sigma^{(k)}$ and the flatness signal to be solved:

$$H_{\omega}(\Delta\sigma,\sigma^{(k)})=\sum_{i=1}^{n}\omega(x_i)(\Delta\sigma(x_i)-\sigma^{(k)}(x_i)) \tag{10}$$

ii) The closeness of the weighted Hamming distance between the standard sample and the sample to be solved:

$$D(\Delta\sigma,\sigma^{(k)})=\sum_{i=1}^{n}\omega(x_i)(1-\left|\Delta\sigma(x_i)-\sigma^{(k)}(x_i)\right|) \tag{11}$$

iii) The $P_E(K)$ represents the fuzzy degree of samples belongs to K class, that is, the similarity of samples for K class:

$$P_E(K)=E(K)/\sum_{K=1}^{N}E(K). \tag{12}$$

Where,

$$E(K)=\begin{cases} D(i)-D(i+1) & D(i)>D(i+1) \\ 0 & D(i)<D(i+1) \end{cases}. \tag{13}$$

Then, we take the minimum error between the fuzzy identification result and measured results as the objective optimizing function:

$$\min f(x)=\min f(x_1,x_2,\ldots,x_n)=\sum_{i=1}^{n}\left|\sum_{k=1}^{3}P_E(K)\sigma_i^{(k)}-\Delta\sigma_i\right| \tag{14}$$

3.2 Quantum Optimization Algorithm Based on ACO

Generate Initial Population. In the ACO-QA, the probability amplitude of quantum bits is directly taken as the ants' current location encoding:

$$q_i=\begin{bmatrix}\begin{vmatrix}\cos(\theta_{i1})\\ \sin(\theta_{i1})\end{vmatrix}\begin{vmatrix}\cos(\theta_{i2})\\ \sin(\theta_{i2})\end{vmatrix}\cdots\begin{vmatrix}\cos(\theta_{in})\\ \sin(\theta_{in})\end{vmatrix}\end{bmatrix} \tag{15}$$

Where, $\theta_{ij}=2\pi\times rnd$, the *rnd* is a random number between 0 and 1, *i*=1,2,…,m, *j*=1,2,…n. And *m* is the population size, *n* is the space dimension.

The definition domain of variable X_i is $[a_i,b_i]$. Note quantum bits *j* of ant q_i as $[\cos\theta_{ij},\sin\theta_{ij}]^T$,then the corresponding solution space variables are:

$$\begin{bmatrix}p_{i0}^{j}\\ p_{i1}^{j}\end{bmatrix}=\begin{bmatrix}\frac{b_i-a_i}{2} & 0\\ 0 & \frac{b_i-a_i}{2}\end{bmatrix}\begin{bmatrix}\cos\theta_{ij}\\ \sin\theta_{ij}\end{bmatrix}+\begin{bmatrix}\frac{b_i+a_i}{2}\\ \frac{b_i+a_i}{2}\end{bmatrix}$$

Simplify the above formula:

$$\begin{bmatrix} p_{i0}^{j} \\ p_{i1}^{j} \end{bmatrix} = \frac{1}{2}\begin{bmatrix} 1+\cos\theta_{ij} & 1-\cos\theta_{ij} \\ 1+\sin\theta_{ij} & 1-\sin\theta_{ij} \end{bmatrix}\begin{bmatrix} b_i \\ a_i \end{bmatrix} \tag{16}$$

Update Ants' Location. In the ACO-QA, firstly transform the increment of pheromone strength in the path of the ants in general ACO into rotation angle updates of quantum rotation gate; then update qubits carried by ants through the quantum rotation gate; therefore, the update of the ants location is converted to the update of probability amplitude of the ant qubit.

Adjust the Angle Size and Direction of Quantum Rotation Gate. Usually update the qubit with the rotation gate $U(\Delta\theta) = \begin{bmatrix} \cos(\Delta\theta) & -\sin(\Delta\theta) \\ \sin(\Delta\theta) & \cos(\Delta\theta) \end{bmatrix}$.

The following angle step function is put forward to ascertain the size of angle:

$$\Delta\theta_{ij}(t+1) = -\mathrm{sgn}(A)(\Delta\theta_{ij}(t) + c_1\Delta\tau_{Lij}(t) + c_2\Delta\tau_{Gij}(t)), \tag{17}$$

$$\Delta\tau_{Lij}(t) = \sum_{k=1}^{m}\frac{Q}{d_{ij}}, \tag{18}$$

$$\Delta\tau_{Gij}(t) = \sum_{k=1}^{m}\frac{Q}{L_k}. \tag{19}$$

Where, c_1 and c_2 represent the local adjustment factor and the global adjustment factor of the pheromone strength respectively, Q is the pheromone strength, L_k represents the total length of the path that the ant K goes through in this cycle, d_{ij} represents the distance of the path ij that the ant K passes by, and $\Delta\tau_{Lij}(t)$ represents the variation of the global pheromone, $\Delta\tau_{Gij}(t)$ represents the variation of the local pheromone.

Mutation of the Ant Position. Given the mutation rate p_m, assign each ant a random number $rand_i$ between 0 and 1. If $rand_i < p_m$, randomly select $n/2$ quantum bits of the ant, then exchange two probability amplitude with two quantum non-gate, and the optimal position remains :

$$\begin{bmatrix} 0 & 1 \\ 1 & 0 \end{bmatrix}\begin{bmatrix} \cos(\theta_{ij}) \\ \sin(\theta_{ij}) \end{bmatrix} = \begin{bmatrix} \sin(\theta_{ij}) \\ \cos(\theta_{ij}) \end{bmatrix} = \begin{bmatrix} \cos(\theta_{ij}+\pi/2) \\ \sin(\theta_{ij}+\pi/2) \end{bmatrix}. \tag{20}$$

Where, $i \in \{1,2,\cdots,m\}$ and $j \in \{1,2,\cdots,n\}$.

3.3 Algorithm Steps

Suppose that there are *m* ants in three-dimensional space, and the coordinate of each ant is $x_{id} = (x_{i1}, x_{i2}, x_{i3})(d = 1,2,3)$. The corresponding characteristic parameters of flatness to be recognized is (α, β, γ), and note x_{pi} as the best position that ant *i* goes by and x_g as the best position that the ant colony. Algorithm steps are as follows:

Step1. Ant population initialization. Generates ants locations according to Eq (15) to compose the initial population. The initial value of three positions for each ant corresponds to the three non-zero value $P_E(K)$ of fuzzy pretreatment.

Step2. Get solution *P* (*t*) according to Eq(16) and calculate the fitness of each ant according to the specific optimized objective function:

$$\min f(x) = \min f(x_1, x_2, \ldots, x_n) = \sum_{i=1}^{n} \left| \sum_{k=1}^{3} P_E(K)\sigma_i^{(k)} - \Delta\sigma_i \right| .$$

If the ant's the current location is better than their own optimal position in memories, then replace with the current location; if the current global best position is better than that before, then replaced with the current global best position.

Step3. Complete the update of the ant location according to Eq(17), (18), and (19).

Step4. With mutation probability, do mutation operation for each ant according to Eq(20).

Step5. Back to Step2 until meeting with the convergence criteria or reaching the upper bound of generation. Output current location coordinates of the ant.

Step6. End. Return to the current global optimum value x_{id}, and the corresponding three locations (x_{i1}, x_{i2}, x_{i3}), that is, the flatness characteristic parameters (α, β, γ).

4 Experiment and Results Analysis

4.1 System Structure

A typical system designed in Chongqing University Automation Lab is shown in Fig.2. Bus adopts standard VME structure and image collection uses standard linear array scanner with 2048-4096 pixels and more than 10 kHz frame rate. Considering system transacting ability and present ADC's rate, ADS851(40MSPS/14bit) is an appropriate option. Light source we use is high strength strobotron lamp.

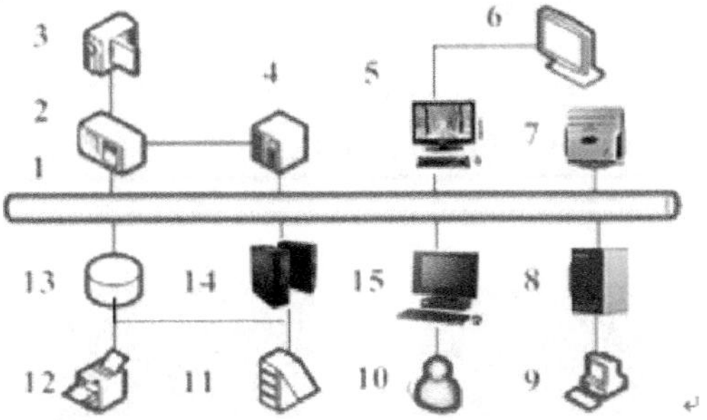

Fig. 2. Structure of cold rolling steel strip visualization detecting system: 1 VME Bus, 2 DSP, 3 CCD, 4 automatic classifier (optional), 5 image showing system, 6 operator monitor, 7 system main controller, 8 net interface, 9 quality control computer, 10 keyboard, 11 data storage system, 12 printer, 13 data analysis module, 14 file and figure management system, and 15 man-machine interface

4.2 Optic Setting

As Fig.3 shows, the light path of CCD adopts telecentric type which can improve measure sensitivity because it enables the CCD focal plane and the steel strip plane superposed.

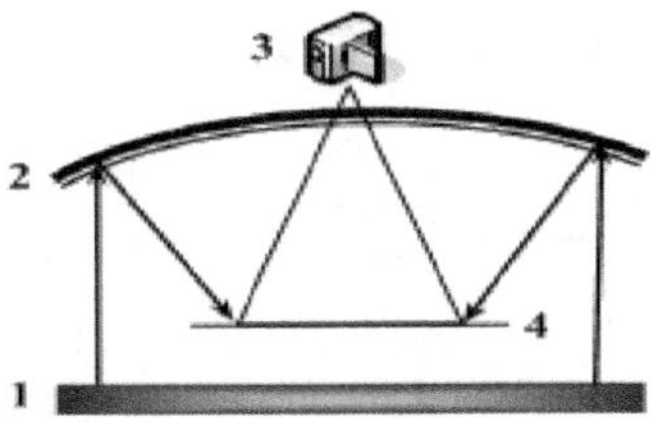

Fig. 3. Telecentric optical system. In this system, 1 is the cold rolling steel strip, 2 is the concave mirror, 3 is CCD and 4 is the plane mirror.

4.3 Field Conditions

Some important parameters used in field experiments are listed in Table 1 and Fig.4 is an instantaneous photograph from CCD video.

Table 1. Some important field parameters

Item	Value
Height of CCD positioned	3.8m
Width of steel strip	1039.8mm
Velocity of steel strip	0.740m/s
Size of image collected(pixel*pixel)	340*768
Frequency of strobotron lamp	12HZ

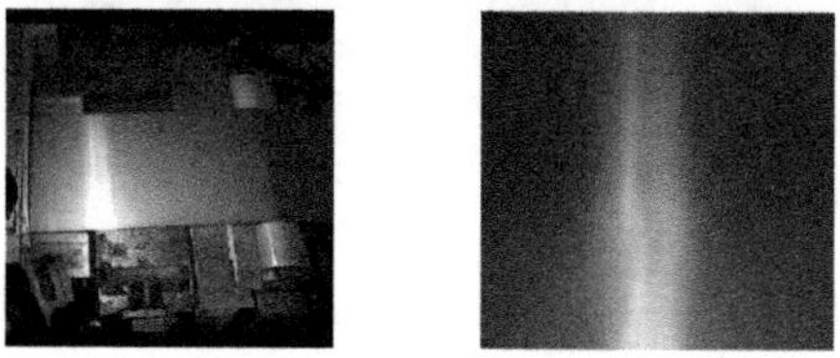

(a) (b)

Fig. 4. Images of work field. It gives site screenshot from video collected by CCD. (a) is the snapshot image from CCD and (b) is the focus part of this image.

4.4 Experimental Results

In pattern recognition field, fuzzy technology and neural network are two important methods, which are used popularly and effectively in many fields. Therefore, experiment uses them to compare with the proposed method ACO-QA in this paper. Experimental results (Table 2) show that the recognition accuracy using ACO-QA is higher than fuzzy method and neural network method.

Table 2. Result comparisons between several different algorithms

Defect Type	Fuzzy Method	NN Method	ACO-QA
(1)	82%	87%	90%
(2)	80%	85%	88%
(3)	81%	86%	91%
(4)	79%	83%	86%
(5)	84%	88%	91%
(6)	83%	86%	89%
Average Accuracy	82%	85%	89%

In Table.2, (1) represents the case of left plat-profile, (2) the right plat-profile, (3) the middle plat-profile, (4) the bilateral plat-profile, (5) the quarter plat-profile, and (6) the side-middle plat-profile.

5 Conclusions

Legendre function is firstly used to describe six kinds of basic shape defects of cold rolled strip steel, which has only three dimensions. Then a method based on novel ant colony optimization algorithm with quantum evolutionary action (ACO-QA) is developed for shape recognition of cold rolled strip steel. Because ACO-QA has an optimal effect almost in low-dimensional and low-interval case, this recognition method loads a pretreatment of fuzzy pattern recognition to the initial shape identification, thereby improves identification accuracy and efficiency of the cold rolled steel strip shape.

Acknowledgments. This work is supported by a Grant for Research Projects of Science and Technology Division from Chongqing Scientific and Technological committee (CSTC2009AC2068) and another Grant for Science Research Starting Projects from Chongqing University of Technology (2008ZD24).

References

1. Anders, G., Carlstad, T.: Modern Approach to Flatness Measurement and Control in Cold Rolling. Iron and Steel Engineer 68(1), 34–39 (1991)
2. Hoshino, I., Kawai, M., Kekubo, M., et al.: Observer-based Multivariable Flatness Control of the Cold Rolling Mill. World International Federation of Automatic Control 6, 149–156 (1993)
3. Shi, Y., Zhang, X.D.: Gabor Atom Networks for Signal Classification with Application in radar Target Recognition. IEEE Trans. Signal Processing 49, 2994–3004 (2007)
4. Wang, X.C., Paliwal, K.K.: Feature Extraction and Dimensionality Reduction Algorithms and their Applications in Vowel Recognition. Pattern Recognition 36, 2429–2439 (2003)
5. Saintey, M.B., Almond, D.P.: An Artificial Neural Network Interpreter for Transient Themography Image Data. NDT&E International 30(5), 291–295 (1997)
6. Zjavka, L.: Differential Polynomial Neural Network. Journal of Artificial Intelligence 4(1), 89–99 (2011)
7. Peng, Y., Liu, H.M.: A Neural Network Recognition Method of Shape Pattern. Journal of Iron and Steel Research 8, 16–20 (2007)
8. Zhang, W.J., Mao, L., Xu, W.B.: Automatic Image Classification Using the Classification Ant-Colony Algorithm. In: International Conference on Environmental Science and Information Application Technology, vol. 3, pp. 325–329. IEEE Press, Wuhan (2009)
9. Han, K.H.K.J.: Quantum-inspired Evolutionary Algorithms with a New Termination Criterion Gate, and Two-phase Scheme. IEEE Transaction on Evolutionary Computation 3(2), 1108–1112 (2004)
10. Zhou, S., Pan, W., Luo, B., et al.: A Novel Quantum Genetic Algorithm Based on Particle Swarm Optimization Method and Its Application. Acta Electronica Sinica 34(5), 897–901 (2006)
11. Socha, K., Dorigo, M.: Ant Colony Optimization for Continuous Domains. European Journal of Operational 185(3), 1155–1173 (2008)
12. Li, P.C., Li, S.Y.: Quantum-inspired evolutionary algorithm for continuous space optimization based on Bloch coordinates of qubits. Neurocomputing 72(1-3), 581–591 (2008)

Line Feature Enhancement Using a New Shift-Invariant Non-aliasing Ridgelet Transform

He Yan[1,2], Youjia Fu[2], and Guangzhi Yin[1]

[1] Key Lab. for the Exploitation of Southwestern Resources & the Environmental Disaster Control Engineering, Ministry of Education, Chongqing 400044, China
[2] College of Computer Science, Chongqing University of Technology, Chongqing 400054, China
cqyanhe@163.com

Abstract. A new shift-invariant non-aliasing Ridgelet transform was presented to avoid aliasing and shift-variant in old Ridgelet transform. Firstly, image size was expanded twice via interpolating zero values,so that the sampling rate in Radon transform domain was improved and the aliasing was reduced; Secondly, the one-dimensional discrete wavelet transform in the old Ridgelet transform was replaced by one-dimensional dual-tree Complex wavelet transform(DCWT) which had both shift-invariant and double directional analysis ability. On this basis, a new image enhancement method for linear features was proposed by using zero-mean Gaussian mode in the shift-invariant non-aliasing Ridgelet transform domain. Experimental result shows that the presented Ridgelet transform can avoid effectively the 'scratch around'phenomenon in reconstructed image and the visual effects of the image enhancement is improved obviously.

Keywords: Ridgelet Transform, Non-aliasing, Shift-invariant, Dual-tree Complex Wavelet Transform, Image Enhancement.

1 Introduction

The discrete Ridgelet transform has broken through the wavelet transform point-like singularity constraint and been widely used in image line detection [1,2]. It consists of a discrete Radon transform and a one-dimensional discrete wavelet transform following. However, the discrete Ridgelet transform proposed by Candes has following two major flaws. The First one is that there is frequency aliasing caused by inverse one-dimensional Fourier transform in the Radon transform. [3, 4]. It leads to a 'surround' phenomenon resulting in the reconstructed image. The second one is that the one-dimensional wavelet transform adopted in the Ridgelet transform lacks of shift-invariant, it leads the aliasing generating in the Radon transform to be amplified in the following one-dimensional wavelet transform. At the same time, because discrete wavelet transform basis function with limited direction is isotropic, the ability of the Ridgelet transform capturing straight line in any direction can be reduced.

In this paper, a new shift-invariant non-aliasing Ridgelet transform was presented to avoid aliasing and shift-variant in old Ridgelet transform. Its realization idea contains

Z. Pan et al. (Eds.): Transactions on Edutainment VII, LNCS 7145, pp. 272–281, 2012.

the following two steps: Firstly, the image size was expanded twice via interpolating zero values, so that the sampling rate in Radon transform domain was improved and the aliasing was reduced. Secondly, the one-dimensional discrete wavelet transform in the old Ridgelet transform was replaced by one-dimensional dual-tree Complex wavelet transform(DCWT)[5] which had both shift-invariant ability and double directional analysis ability. On this basis, a new image enhancement method for linear features was proposed by using zero-mean Gaussian mode in the shift-invariant non-aliasing Ridgelet transform domain.

2 Ridgelet Transform and Its Problems

The discrete Ridgelet transform proposed by Candes contains following algorithm:

1)Radon transform
2)One-dimensional wavelet transform for the results of the Radon transform

As mentioned above, the discrete Ridgelet transform of image $f[x, y]$ is equivalent to do a Radon transform firstly and then following do a one-dimensional discrete wavelet transform. In order to calculate the Radon transform of the function $f[x, y]$, we must do its two-dimensional Fourier transform at firstly, then we do one-dimensional Fourier inverse transform separately correspondence with each two-dimensional Fourier transform value in a straight line through the origin. The discrete Radon transform proposed by Starck in[1] is simple, but there is some aliasing in the frequency domain. The literature [3] first pointed out the problem of the Starck discrete Radon transform. Depending on the define of the Radon transform, the result of a $n \times n$ image Radon transform along the $\theta = 45^0$ line is the projections of the image on the 45^0 line, so there are total $2n-1$ discrete points. If calculating in accordance with the discrete Radon transform proposed by Starck in[1], the image should be discrete Fourier transformed (we can get $n \times n$ points in frequency domain) at firstly, then we should choose these points(total n) in a straight line through the origin and do them inverse Fourier transform. This is clearly that these n discrete points cannot be reconstructed to the $2n-1$ projections in 45^0 straight line of the original image, so a certain degree of aliasing has happened. Such frequency domain points of the Radon transform are back-projected to time domain, the results are two cycle around straight lines, not a single straight line. The discrete Ridgelet transform proposed by Candes has such a "surround" phenomenon also, which reduce the feature of analysis image according to the straight line unit.

Another flaw of the digital Ridgelet transform is that the discrete wavelet transform(DWT) is used after the discrete Radon transform. DWT lacks shift-invariant ,it lead to the aliasing producing in the Radon transform can be amplified in following one-dimensional discrete wavelet transform. At the same time, the basis function of the discrete wavelet transform only have horizontal, vertical and diagonal three fixed directions, it is not conducive to the capture any orientational straight line in a image.

3 The Shift-Invariant Non-aliasing Ridgelet Transform

For avoiding the 'around' phenomena in the reconstruction image, the Radon transform has been improved in some literature, such as [3,4].They pointed out that 'surround' phenomena is due to insufficient sampling in frequency domain during one-dimensional inverse Fourier transform, and for improveing the sampling rate,it needs to improve the spectral density of image in order to get more points for discrete sampling. For example, a $n \times n$ size image can be inserted zero to $2n \times 2n$ size and then be done discrete Fourier transform. Thus there are $2n$ discrete points in each straight line through the origin in frequency domain under no change its image spectrum. It can avoids the aliasing phenomenon in one-dimensional Fourier inverse transform.

The above Radon transform can overcome the aliasing effectively, but also the lack of shift-variant of Ridgelet transform need to be solved further. As dual-tree Complex wavelet transform (DCWT)[5] has better shift-invariant and double orientation selectivity than DCT, so we use one-dimensional DCWT instead of one-dimensional discrete wavelet transform to ensure that our improved Ridgelet transform has both shift-invariant and double direction analysis ability. The algorithm of the new shift-invariant non-aliasing Ridgelet transform can summarized as follows:

Step 1 For a $n \times n$ size image, inserting zero to $2n \times 2n$ size.

Step 2 2D-FFT for $2n \times 2n$ size image.

Step 3 Conversing the results of above 2D-FFT from Cartesian coordinates into polar coordinates, in order to ensure the coordinate transformation reversible, the conversion must be carried out within the interpolation. The literature [2] use the nearest neighbor method to achieve coordinate transformation. To improve the algorithm approximation accuracy and computation rates, in this paper, we use bilinear interpolation.

Step 4 1D IFFT for all dates in polar coordinates along each direction.

Step 5 ID DCWT for last step results.

4 Image Line Feature Enhancement Using a New Shift-Invariant Non-aliasing Ridgelet Transform

The chiefly aim of image feature enhancement is to reduce noise and further aim is to enhance the weak edge features.

4.1 Noise Suppression Using Zero-mean Gaussian Model in Transform Domain

Supposed a noisy image is decomposed to a low-frequency approximation sub-image and a series of different scale high frequency detail sub-images separately in real and imaginary via shift-invariant non-aliasing Ridgelet transform(SINART). As the same treatment will be used for both the real part and the imaginary part, so the following example to explain the real part only. Supposed a noisy image is decomposed to

$\{a_L[u,v], R_l[u,v]\}$ via SINART, where L is the largest scale, $a_L[u,v]$ means the coefficients of low-frequency approximation sub-image, $R_l[u,v]$ means high frequency detail sub-images at $l\,(l \geq 1)$ scale. The purpose of denoising is to recover signal coefficients $s_l[u,v]$ of the actual image from noise pollutional coefficients $R_l[u,v]$, and then we can get denoising image via inverse SINART. Supposed $\delta_l[u,v]$ is noise coefficients in high frequency detail sub-images at $l\,(l \geq 1)$ scale, then there exists:

$$R_l[u,v] = s_l[u,v] + \delta_l[i,j] \tag{1}$$

Supposed $W(u,v)$ is a local neighborhood window which center is $R_l[u,v]$ and size is 5×5 , N is the number of coefficients in the local neighborhood window, σ_n is the noise standard deviation of noisy coefficients and can be estimated by the classical estimation method as follows[6]:

$$\sigma_n[u,v] = \frac{Median(|R[u,v]|)}{0.6745}, \qquad R[u,v] \in W(u,v) \tag{2}$$

Supposed σ^2 is signal variance in the local neighborhood window,it can be gotten by using following maximum posteriori probability estimator:

$$\hat{\sigma}^2[u,v] = \max\left(0, \frac{M}{4\lambda}\left[-1+\sqrt{1+\frac{8\lambda}{M^2}\sum_{[k,l]\in N[u,v]} R^2[u,v]}\right] - \sigma_n^2\right) \tag{3}$$

Using MAP under Bayes framework, we can estimate the signal coefficient as follow:

$$\hat{s} = \arg\max_s p_{s|R}(s|R) = \arg\max_s [p_{R|s}(R|s)p_s(s)/p_R(R)] \tag{4}$$

Supposed p_n is marginal probability density of n , the we can get $p_{R|s}(R|s) = p_n(R-s)$, Operating logarithm on both sides of formula (4) and sort out, we can get:

$$\hat{s} = \arg\max_s [\log p_n(R-s) + \log p_s(s)] \tag{5}$$

In the local area, it can be considered that s obeys the Gaussian distribution which mean is 0 and variance is σ^2, then the high-frequency detail sub-image coefficients at l scale can be estimated as follow:

$$\widehat{s}_l[u,v] = \frac{\sigma^2}{\sigma^2 + \sigma_n^2} \cdot R_l[u,v] \tag{6}$$

Where signal variance σ^2 can be estimated by formula (3), and noise variance σ_n^2 can be estimated by formula (2).

4.2 Feature Enhancement

In the SINART domain, noise variance in different scale sub-band is not same.So the signal and noise variance respectively according to formal (2) and formal (3) are not unbiased estimates. There must be a certain bias. In some the high frequency sub-image, the noise variance value may be estimated bigger according to forma (2),so the signal coefficient value must become small according to forma (6).It means that the weak edges in reconstructed image is smoothed. Therefore it is necessary to discriminate weak edges and enhance them at the same time denoising for the weak edge protection.

We can simply divide noisy image pixels into following three categories: strong edge pixels, weak edge pixels and noise. In the transform domain, the coefficients in all the high frequency sub-image corresponding strong edge pixels have large value at all scales. The coefficients of weak edge pixels in some high-frequency detail sub-images have large value, but in others high-frequency detail sub-images, their values is small. The values of noise coefficients is small at all scale.

Supposed $\widehat{s}_l(u,v)$ are estimated values of the signal coefficients at l scale and (u,v) location point according to equation (6) .It represents a high frequency set of (u,v) location point at all scale. Supposed a and b is average value and max value respectively in this set. The following formula can be used to judge whether the (u,v) location point is corresponding to weak edge pixels:

$$\begin{cases} strong & if \quad a \ge k\overline{\sigma}_n \\ weak & if \quad a < k\overline{\sigma}_n, b \ge k\overline{\sigma}_n \\ noise & if \quad a < k\overline{\sigma}_n, b < k\overline{\sigma}_n \end{cases} \tag{7}$$

Where k is a positive parameter, its value is chosen among 1.5 and 5 at practicality. $\overline{\sigma}_n$ is a average value of noise standard deviation calculated with formula (2) in all high frequency coefficients. If position point (u,v) has been judged corresponding to weak edge pixels using formula (7), Referring to formula (6),we can enhanced the coefficients as following:

$$\widetilde{s}_l(u,v) = \max\left[\left(\frac{k\overline{\sigma}_n}{|\widehat{s}_l(u,v)|}\right)^p, 1 \right] \widehat{s}_l(u,v) \tag{8}$$

Where p is magnify rate, its value is between 0 and 1.

5 Experimental Analysis

To enable an objective comparison with other methods, we also give the Peak-Signal-to-Noise-Ratio (PSNR) values for the standard test image (Obj and House)corrupted by Gaussian white noise . We add a uniformly distributed random variable with zero mean Gaussian white noise to them(the standard deviation is 15,20,25 and 30 respectively) , and apply the discrete wavelet transform(DWT) domain soft-threshold method ,Rigelet transform domain soft-threshold method ,No-aliasing soft-threshold method and proposed enhancement method to the noisy image respectively.This series of experimental datas are summarized in table 1. From table 1,we can see that the test image whether House or Obj at all levels of noise, the SPNR values of denoising images based on Rigelet transform are lower 0.25 to 1 dB than them of the denoising images based on DWT,it is because of serious aliasing in Ridgelet transform domain. The PSNR value of denoising image based on no-aliasing Ridgelet transform proposed in this paper has significantly increased. It indicates that the alising in Ridgelet transform domain is the main reason who results for lower PSNR values.

Table 1. The PSNR of denoised images with different algorithms

Image	σ	Noisy	DWT	Rigelet	Noaliasing Rigelet	Proposed method
obj	15	24.58	27.55	27.25	28.05	28.62
	20	22.08	26.40	26.15	27.01	27.51
	25	20.14	25.49	25.40	26.27	26.73
	30	15.56	24.77	24.50	25.14	25.58
house	15	24.58	25.53	24.33	26.12	26.77
	20	22.08	24.48	23.37	25.07	25.65
	25	20.14	23.67	22.63	24.31	24.92
	30	18.56	23.05	22.04	23.72	24.25

The Fig.1 and Fig.2 are original image and various denoising results when the noise standard deviation is 25. Because the Starck's ridgelet transform lacks of shift-invariant and presence of aliasing, so some " around scratch " phenomenon appears in the reconstructed image as shown in Fig.1 (c) and Fig.2 (c).The new Ridgelet transform has solved the inadequate sampling defects in the Radon transform and use one-dimensional dual tree complex wavelet transform to replace one-dimensional DWT,so it has no-aliasing and approximative shift-invariant property.Therefore, the "scratch around" phenomenon has can be avoided in the denoised image as showed in Fig 1 (e) and Fig.2 (e).The proposed method uses zero-mean Gaussian model to suppress noise and identifies the weak edge and enhance them subsequently, so we can get more better visual effect as showed in Fig.1 (f) and Fig. 2 (f).

The above three experimental approaches are also tested on real SAR image, We select one aircraft L-Band the horizontal polarization SAR image of Chongqing some area (512×512,3.5m×3.8m spatial resolution)to experiment.Fig.3 is the partial original SAR image and the results of filtering.

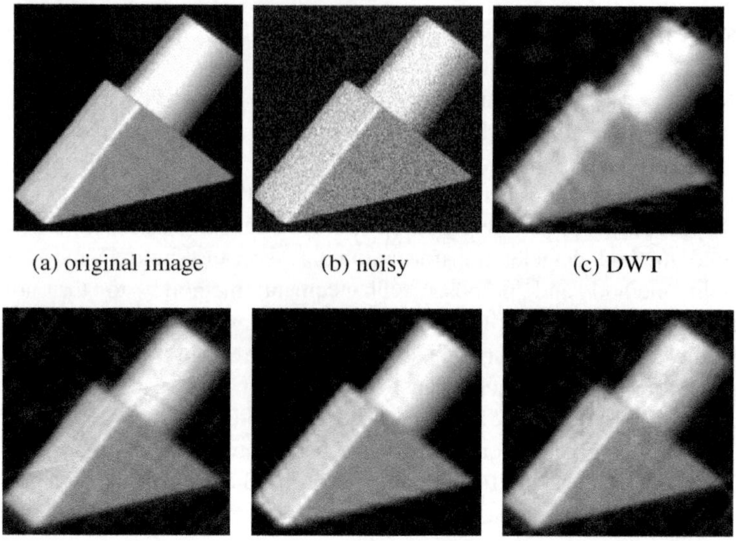

(a) original image (b) noisy (c) DWT

(d) Ridgelet (e) no-aliasing Rigelet (f) Proposed method

Fig. 1. Denoised Obj image with different algorithms(noise standard deviation is 25)

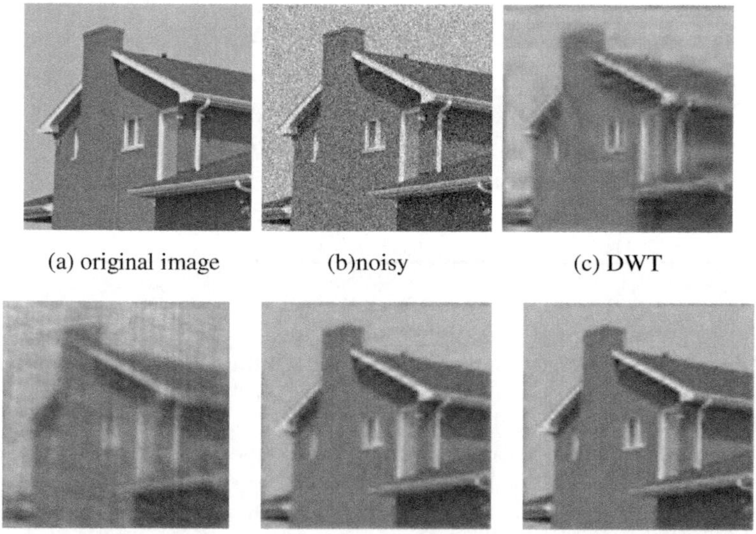

(a) original image (b)noisy (c) DWT

(d)Ridgelet (e) no-aliasing Rigelet (f) Proposed method

Fig. 2. Denoised House image with different algorithms (noise standard deviation is 25)

In the experiments, the algorithm performance is being quantified in terms of smoothing effect and edge preservation. The equivalent number of looks(ENL) is used to measure the smoothing effect of denoising methods. It is defined as ENL= μ^2 / σ^2, where μ and σ^2 are the mean and variance of intensity value over a homogenous region. Another evaluation method is to calculate the smoothness index λ, $\lambda = \sigma / \mu$.

Furthermore,as a measure of edge preservation, the figure of merit(FOM)[7] is adopted, which is defined by following:

$$\text{FOM}=\frac{1}{\max(N_0, N_f)}\sum_{i=1}^{N_0}\frac{1}{1+kD_i^2} \tag{9}$$

Table 2. Comparison of effect of different denoising methods

	μ	σ^2	λ	*ENL*	*FOM*
Noisy	136.11	447.37	0.1555	41.41	0.67
Ridgelet	122.11	397.07	0.1632	37.55	0.54
Noaliaing Ridgelet	130.36	412.78	0.1558	41.17	0.69
Proposed method	157.45	547.21	0.1485	45.30	0.81

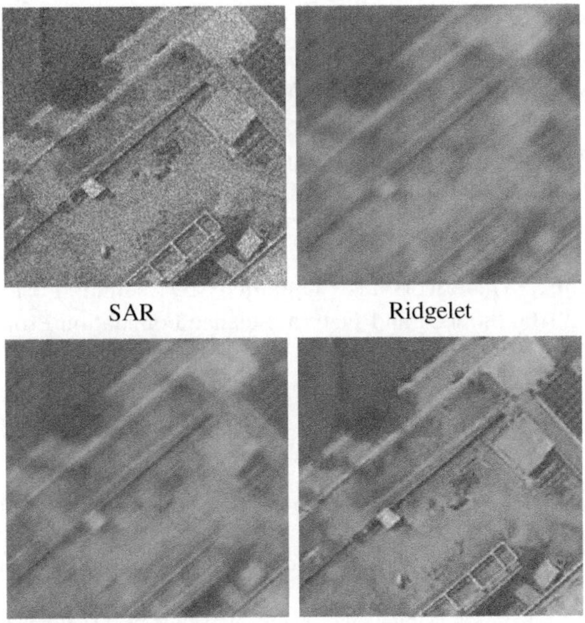

SAR Ridgelet

No-aliaing Ridgele Proposed method

Fig. 3. SAR image enhancement experimental result

Where N_0 and N_f are the number of original and filtered edge pixels,respectively, D_i is the Euclidean distance between the original edge piex and the nearest filtered edge piex,and k is a constant typically set to 1/9. FOM ranges between 0 and 1, with unity for ideal edge detection. A biger values of ENL or FOM means a better denoising effect.

The ENL, λ and FOM values of applying these four denoising algorithms to the original noise SAR images are listed in Table 2.As shown in Fig.3, the proposed algorithm achieves remarkable improvement over the other two methods, It can be found that our proposed method possesses the best standard spatial tradeoff between noise reduction and feature preservation. Experimental results demonstrate that our algorithm has a good denoising performance in SAR image denoising and has particularly highlighted the roads, the car, the terraces and the houses etc.

6 Conclusion

The reason of the obvious "scratch around" phenomenon in the reconstructed image based on Ridgelet transform has been analysed.It has been pointed out that "scratch around" phenomenon is caused by shift- variant and aliasing in Ridgelet transform domain. So a new shift-invariant non-aliasing Ridgelet transform was presented to avoid aliasing and shift-variant in old Ridgelet transform.Firstly, image size was expanded twice via image interpolating zero values,so that the sampling rate in Radon transform domain was improved and the aliasing was reduced; Secondly, the one-dimensional discrete wavelet transform in the old Ridgelet transform was replace by one-dimensional dual-tree Complex wavelet transform(DCWT) which had both shift-invariant ability and double directional analysis ability. Experimental result shows that the presented Ridgelet transform can avoid effectively the "scratch around" phenomenon in reconstructed image.The visual effects of the denoising image is improved and the visual effects of the image enhancement is improved obviously.

Acknowledgments. This work is supported by China Postdoctoral Science Foundation(NO.20100480665) and Natural Science Foundation Project of CQ CSTC, 2008BB2340, China.

References

1. Candes, E.J.: Monoscale ridgelets for the representation of images with edges. Stanford University, report (1999)
2. Hou, B., Liu, F., Jiao, L.: Line character detection based on Ridgelet transform. Science in China(Series E) 33(1), 65–73 (2003)
3. Xiao, X., Li, S.: Edge-preserving image denoising method using Curvelet transform. Journal of China Institute of Communications 25(2), 9–15 (2004)

4. Bai, J., Feng, X.: The digital ridgelet reconstruction based on dual frame. Science in China(Series E) 35(10), 1072–1082 (2005)
5. Kingsbury, N.G.: The dual-tree complex wavelet transform:a new technique for shift invariance and directional filters. In: Proceedings of the 8th IEEE Digital Signal Processing Workshop, Bryce Canyon UT, USA. IEEE Signal Processing Society (1998)
6. Cheng, S.G.: Adaptive wavelet thresholding for image denoising and compression. IEEE Trans. on Image Processing 9(9), 1532–1546 (2000)

Author Index

GPSR Compliance

The European Union's (EU) General Product Safety Regulation (GPSR) is a set of rules that requires consumer products to be safe and our obligations to ensure this.

If you have any concerns about our products, you can contact us on ProductSafety@springernature.com

In case Publisher is established outside the EU, the EU authorized representative is:

Springer Nature Customer Service Center GmbH
Europaplatz 3
69115 Heidelberg, Germany

Batch number: 10844619

Printed by Printforce, the Netherlands